Standard FORTRAN Programming
A Structured Style

The Irwin Series in Information and Decision Sciences

Consulting Editors   Robert B. Fetter   Claude McMillan
                             Yale University   University of Colorado

Standard FORTRAN Programming
A Structured Style

DONALD H. FORD, Ph.D., C.I.S.A.

JOSEPH RUE, Ph.D., C.D.P.

both of
California State University,
Sacramento

1982   Fourth Edition

RICHARD D. IRWIN, INC.
Homewood, Illinois 60430

© RICHARD D. IRWIN, INC., 1971, 1974, 1978, and 1982

All rights reserved. No part of this publication may be reproduced, stored in a retrieval system, or transmitted, in any form or by any means, electronic, mechanical, photocopying, recording, or otherwise, without the prior written permission of the publisher.

1 2 3 4 5 6 7 8 9 0 ML 9 8 7 6 5 4 3 2

ISBN 0-256-02608-4

Library of Congress Catalog Card No. 81-85253

Printed in the United States of America

Dedicated to those who teach and to those who learn
from this book

Preface

This edition focuses on Standard FORTRAN (FORTRAN 77) as specified by the American National Standards Institute (ANSI) Standard X3.9-1978 and by the International Organization for Standardization Standard ISO 1539-1980E. Specialized versions of the language are intentionally ignored. It is not intended to teach a language that must be "unlearned" to process at another installation; the materials are intended to teach a language that can be used on any of many computer systems.

Unlike some other FORTRAN texts, this one avoids frivolous comparisons of the current version to older versions of the language; such comparisons distract readers who are concerned only with *their* version of FORTRAN. However, the text materials which strictly follow the current standard were carefully designed to be compatible with the features of the older ANSI Standard X3.9-1966 as well. This compatibility was accomplished in subtle ways. For example, in all illustrations the optional comma was excluded in the DO statement but included in the computed GO TO.

This fourth edition has been thoroughly revised, updated, expanded, and improved in numerous ways. It has been written specifically as a textbook for a first course in computer programming. The text materials have been tested by thousands of students with diverse backgrounds. It has been used in a variety of environments—colleges, "in-house" training programs, and technical institutes. It has also been used as a self-teaching manual by many learning FORTRAN on their own initiative and as a reference source by those with a basic knowledge of the language.

This edition is designed to permit students to write elementary but meaningful, executable programs by the end of Chapter 2. The approach used has been found effective in helping college-level students begin processing by the end of the second week of an introductory programming course. Beginning programmers must master the logistics of where, when, and how to submit programs and to pick up output before they can begin concentrating on the details of programming. An elementary program or two, processed early in the course, should reinforce this entire cycle from entry to output. Most students are anxious to "get on with it;" so this early experience should be very motivating.

The essential elements of structured programming are emphasized by illustration and example. The importance of program readability, documentation, and segmentation, as well as various concepts of structure and style, are an integral part of appropriate sections throughout the book. The "divide and conquer" approach is illustrated as one technique for solving long, complex problems. Practicality is stressed in appropriate sections. The phrase *defensive programming*, first introduced in an earlier edition of this text, is used to describe the general purpose of programmed controls and an approach used to assure reasonableness of input and output.

There are 404 end-of-chapter review questions, exercises, and programming problems that provide flexibility for choosing the types and quantity of materials to study. A few problems are intentionally minor variations of others. This permits emphasis on alternative techniques without distracting the student by the logic of two completely different problems. Solving such related problems also exposes students to some of the practical difficulties of program modification. It further demonstrates the virtues of writing clear, readable programs.

Our major goals in writing this edition were (1) to make the subject matter even easier to teach and to learn, and (2) to enable users to write better programs with less effort, which is an advantage of a structured programming style.

The first chapter provides a general introduction to computers and computing because no previous knowledge is presumed. The next chapter is an overview of programming in general and FORTRAN in particular. The complete programming cycle is illustrated and explained—problem analysis, planning (with pseudocode and flowchart), coding, compilation/debugging, testing, and execution. Enough detail is provided so that students will be able to begin processing programs at the end of Chapter 2. Those who will be using interactive terminals (rather than punched card equipment) should find Appendix B to be a valuable aid at this point. It is intended to provide a general conceptual understanding of the overall process of communicating to the computer by a terminal; enough detail is provided so the student will need a minimum of instruction about terminal operating requirements for a specific computer installation.

Chapter 3 presents the elements of FORTRAN statements and introduces basic programming concepts. Alphanumeric constants and variables are included in an independent section.

Following a complete coverage of arithmetic assignment statements, Chapter 4 covers implicit specification statements and the DATA statement, then introduces alphanumeric character assignment.

Basic input and output operations are fully consolidated into one chapter. This chapter (Chapter 5) includes alphanumeric input/output operations (in an independent section) in addition to a comprehensive coverage of numeric input and output.

Chapter 6 introduces branching and looping. The chapter is designed so that a major portion can be omitted, without negative impact, by those who wish to place more emphasis on the IF-THEN-ELSE structures covered in the next chapter. Chapter 7 emphasizes program structure and the concept of nesting. It also presents a full coverage of the powerful DO statement.

Chapter 8 is divided into three modules. The first defines arrays. One concise section explains what they are, how they work, and how they can be defined, including optional specification statements. The second module explains how arrays are used and manipulated. Various ways to initialize arrays and several representative activities—e.g., selecting, counting, searching, and sorting—are illustrated and described. The last module covers more powerful techniques, e.g., array input/output using implied DOs and unsubscripted array names. Multiple-dimension arrays are covered in the next chapter.

The last chapter includes four independent modules, one for each type of subprogram. The first, library functions, can be covered effectively at any time after reading Chapter 4. The other three types of subprograms are presented in a sequence that intentionally breaks tradition. SUBROUTINE, the most powerful subprogram of the three, is covered first because it does everything the other subprogram types can do and more. This makes it most useful.

The modular design of this fourth edition allows various pedagogical tracks to learning FORTRAN. Following are illustrative tracks for those who wish to emphasize only selected portions of the language. The time estimates given presumes a lecture/lab type of course with about three hours of lectures per week.

A. Brief coverage (four weeks) for elementary, computational programming concepts. This includes Chapters 1 through 8 with the following section or subsection *exclusions* (designated by chapter number):

   3. Scientific Form Floating Point Constants, and Alphanumeric Constants.
   4. Implicit Specification Statements, and Processing Alphanumeric Data.
   5. Exponential Form, Alphanumeric Format Code, and Additional I/O Techniques.
   6. Computed GO TO, and Arithmetic IF Statement.
   7. IF-THEN-ELSE Statements.
   8. Use of Other Specification Statements to Define Arrays, Illustrative Array Routines, and Other Array Input/Output Techniques.

B. Moderate coverage (seven weeks) for representative report and structured programming concepts. This includes all chapters except 9 with the following section or subsection *exclusions* (designated by chapter number):

   3. Scientific Form Floating Point Constants.
   4. Implicit Specification Statements.
   5. Exponential Form, FORMAT and READ Relationships, Reading Multiple Records, and Writing Multiple Records.

6. Computed GO TO, and Arithmetic IF Statement.
8. Use of Other Specification Statements to Define Arrays, and Other Array Input/Output Techniques.
10. One-Statement Mathematical Function Subprograms, FUNCTION Subprograms, and the COMMON Statement.

C. More extensive coverage (10 weeks) for more complete report and structured programming concepts. This includes all chapters, with the following section or subsection *exclusions* (designated by chapter number):

3. Scientific Form Floating Point Constants.
4. Implicit Specification Statements.
5. Exponential Form.
6. Arithmetic IF Statement.
8. Use of Other Specification Statements to Define Arrays, and Other Array Input/Output Techniques.
9. Three-Dimensional Arrays.

This book is intended to teach FORTRAN as directly and quickly as possible and to whet the student's appetite for more knowledge of the language. Any comments or suggestions for improvement of the text or problems will be most welcome. Please write to Donald H. Ford or Joseph Rue, Information Systems Department, California State University, Sacramento, California 95819.

Grateful acknowledgement is hereby made to the users of previous editions who offered valuable suggestions for improvement. The recommendations of Art Hiltner and Ed Christenson were particularly useful.

We extend our thanks to Kay Ford, who typed the manuscript, and to Glendy Chang, who helped prepare all computer output illustrations. In particular we appreciate the thoughtful comments and useful suggestions of Jeff Roberts with regard to structured flowcharts and programming.

Donald H. Ford
Joseph Rue

Contents

1 **Introduction, 1**
   COMPUTER LANGUAGES, 2
      Machine languages, 2
      Human oriented languages, 3
   FORTRAN, 4
   A COMPUTER SYSTEM, 6
      Hardware, 6
      Internal structure, 9
   COMMUNICATING WITH COMPUTERS, 13
      Time-sharing terminals, 13
      Batched mode processing, 15
      The Hollerith Code, 17
      Fields, 18
      Records and files, 19
   FORTRAN PROGRAMMING, 19

2 **General Approach to FORTRAN Programming, 22**
   PROBLEM ANALYSIS AND DEFINITION, 22
      Pseudocode for program planning, 24
   FLOWCHARTING, 25
   CODING, 29
   COMPILATION AND DEBUGGING, 35
   TESTING AND EXECUTION, 37

3 **Elements of FORTRAN, 40**
   THE CHARACTER SET, 41
      Alphabetic letters, 41
      Numerals, 41
      Special characters, 41
   STATEMENT TYPES, 41
      Input/Output, 42
      Assignment, 42
      Control, 42
      Nonexecutable, 42
   STATEMENT COMPOSITION, 43
      Keywords, 43
      Variable names, 43
      Numbers or constants, 44
      Expressions, 44
      Codes, 44

STATEMENT LINE FORMAT, 44
    Statement label field, 44
    Continuation field, 46
    Statement field, 47
    Identification field, 47
CONSTANTS, 47
    Integer constants, 47
    Floating point constants, 48
    Alphanumeric constants, 51
VARIABLE NAMES, 51
    Integer variable names, 52
    Floating point variable names, 52
    Alphanumeric variable names, 53
ARITHMETIC OPERATORS, 54
DELIMITERS, 54

4 Processing Numeric and Alphanumeric Data, 58

PROCESSING NUMERIC DATA, 58
    Arithmetic statements, 58
    General form, 58
    Arithmetic expressions, 60
    Mixed mode statements, 64
    Truncation of decimal fractions, 65
    Implicit specification statements, 66
    Initialization of variable names, 69
    Helpful coding hints, 71
    Basic numeric output, 72
PROCESSING ALPHANUMERIC DATA, 73
    CHARACTER statement, 73
    Initialization using an alphanumeric assignment statement, 74
    Initialization using a DATA statement, 75
    Basic alphanumeric output, 75
ORDER OF STATEMENTS AND COMMENT LINES, 76

5 Input and Output, 82

INPUT, 82
    Data record input, 82
    The FORMAT statement, 84
    The READ statement, 90
OUTPUT, 93
    Data card output, 93
    Printed output, 98
ADDITIONAL I/O TECHNIQUES, 99
    FORMAT and READ relationships, 99

Reading multiple records, 102
Writing multiple records, 106
Literals, 107
Other line control techniques, 111

6 Control Statements, 117
BRIEF PROGRAMMING REVIEW, 117
STRUCTURED PROGRAMMING, 119
BRANCHING AND LOOPING, 121
GO TO STATEMENTS, 121
   Unconditional GO TO, 122
   Computed GO TO, 122
PERPETUAL LOOPS, 132
ARITHMETIC IF STATEMENT, 133
   General form, 134
   Illustrative examples, 134
   Arithmetic expressions, 141
LOGICAL IF STATEMENT, 141
   General form, 142
LOOP CONTROL, 145
   Uncontrolled loops, 146
   Controlled loops, 147
DEFENSIVE PROGRAMMING, 151
SUMMARY, 152

7 IF-THEN-ELSE and DO Loop Structures, 165
IF-THEN-ELSE STATEMENTS, 165
   IF THEN statement, 165
   END IF statement, 166
   IF-block, 166
   Nested IF THEN statements, 168
   ELSE statement, 168
   ELSE-block, 170
   ELSE IF statement, 171
   ELSE IF-block, 174
   Nesting block IF, ELSE IF, and ELSE statements, 175
   Programming considerations, 177
THE CONTINUE STATEMENT, 180
   General form, 180
THE DO STATEMENT, 180
   General form, 183
   Illustrative examples, 185
   DO loop rules, 191
   Additional programming considerations, 193

8 ONE-DIMENSIONAL ARRAYS, 207

DEFINITION OF ARRAYS, 207
  Use of subscripts to reference array elements, 208
  Use of a DIMENSION statement to define arrays, 209
  Use of other specification statements to define arrays, 211
  Order of statements, 213
USE OF ARRAYS IN PROGRAMMING, 213
  Illustrative problem, 214
  Fundamental array techniques, 215
  Illustrative array routines, 218
  Other array input/output techniques, 226
  Debugging techniques, 233

9 Two-dimensional and three-dimensional arrays, 242

TWO-DIMENSIONAL ARRAYS, 242
  Multiple subscripting, 243
  Multiple dimensioning, 243
  Reading and writing two-dimensional arrays, 244
  Illustrative routines, 247
THREE-DIMENSIONAL ARRAYS, 250
  Multiple subscripting, 250
  Multiple dimensioning, 250
  Reading and writing three-dimensional arrays, 251
  Illustrative routines, 252

10 Subprograms, 259

LIBRARY FUNCTION SUBPROGRAMS, 261
  General description, 261
  Using subprograms, 262
  Illustrative examples, 264
SUBROUTINE SUBPROGRAMS, 266
  General description, 266
  The SUBROUTINE statement, 266
  The CALL statement, 267
  The RETURN statement, 267
  Illustrative examples, 268
ONE-STATEMENT MATHEMATICAL FUNCTION SUBPROGRAMS, 273
  General description, 273
  Dummy arguments, 273
  Illustrative examples, 274
FUNCTION SUBPROGRAMS, 275
  General description, 275
  The FUNCTION statement, 276
  The RETURN statement, 277

Illustrative examples, 278
SUMMARY, 280
THE COMMON STATEMENT, 280
THE POWER OF SUBPROGRAMS, 286

APPENDIX A
Debugging Techniques, 290
THE DEBUGGING PROCESS, 290
ERRORS TERMINATING COMPILATION, 291
   Statement error messages, 291
   Summary messages, 292
   Debugging illustration program—first run, 292
ERRORS TERMINATING EXECUTION, 295
   Error codes, 295
ERRORS IN PROGRAMMING LOGIC, 299
   Detecting logic errors, 299
   Debugging illustration program—second run, 300
   Debugging illustration program—final run, 303

APPENDIX B
Interactive Terminal Operation for FORTRAN Programming, 305
SIGNING ON, 305
CREATING A PROGRAM FILE OR A DATA FILE, 306
MODIFYING A PROGRAM FILE OR A DATA FILE, 307
DELETING A PROGRAM FILE OR A DATA FILE, 307
COMPILING A PROGRAM, 308
EXECUTING A PROGRAM, 308
SIGNING OFF, 308

APPENDIX C
System Control Commands, 309
JOB COMPOSITION, 309

APPENDIX D
Library Functions, 312
INDEX, 315

1

Introduction

Computer programming can be defined as the art of preparing a plan to solve a problem and of reducing this plan to an explicit sequence of machine-sensible instructions. Programming is essential to the use of computers because computers without programs can do nothing.

Learning to program a computer can be compared to learning to ride a motorcycle. A new motorcyclist must learn to balance on the machine, to start, steer, and stop. He must acquire skill in the use of the various switches, pedals, and controls provided by the manufacturer. He must learn to communicate with the machine to use it as an effective means of transportation. But it is possible to become a skilled motorcyclist without understanding the principle of the internal-combustion engine or the technical aspects of the mechanical and electrical systems. Similarly, the beginning programmer need not understand the many technical concepts of computer design and electrical circuits; he must, however, learn to communicate with the machine to obtain the desired results. To communicate machine-sensible instructions, he must use a programming language and an acceptable communication medium. A computer will do only exactly what it is told to do by some human; it does nothing on its own. Programming requires much attention to detail. To emphasize this point by exaggeration, it has been said that if a program includes an upside-down period, results will be unpredictable.

Directing a computer to solve problems is a skill; it can most effectively be learned if knowledge obtained by reading, listening to lectures, and/or observing demonstrations is supplemented by actual practice. After completing Chapter 2 in this book, the reader should begin putting the computer to work and using it as a learning device.

This introduction provides a discussion of computer programming languages, a brief description of computer systems in general, and an introduction to the process of communicating with computers.

COMPUTER LANGUAGES

A computer can perform various arithmetic computations such as addition, subtraction, multiplication, and division. It can perform various logical functions such as comparing two values and determining if the first value is less than, equal to, or greater than the second value, and such as distinguishing plus from minus and zero from nonzero. It can move data from one location in the computer to another. It can also read data and write results. It can do all these things, and more, at fantastic speeds, but it cannot think. It is a robot. It must be told when to start, what data to use, what steps to take, what to do with the results, and when to stop. To perform a specific task, it must be given a detailed series of instructions, called a *program*, in a language it is designed to read and obey.

Machine languages

There are many ways to design a computer or machine to produce an optimum system for specific types of applications. As a result, with few exceptions, each make and model has its own internal coding system, and each is designed to recognize or understand one unique language. Thus, a program written in the language of one machine cannot be processed by another.

The unique language a computer is designed to recognize is called *machine language*. This language consists of machine-sensible instructions which usually take the form of long strings of numbers. These long strings of numbers may be in binary, decimal, or some other representation depending upon the model of machine. For example, 210042800857 is a valid decimal notation "add command" for one model. Some machines are designed to use fixed-length instructions with each instruction requiring the same number of digits; others use instructions of variable length.

The basic characteristics of a machine language are:

1. It is specific in meaning. It is unlike human language in which words and phrases may have different meanings in different contexts. With rare exceptions, if a single character in a machine-language instruction is changed, its entire meaning is changed.
2. It has a relatively small vocabulary. This is understandable when one considers the complex mathematical calculations that can be performed using combinations of only the four instructions for add, subtract, multiply, and divide.
3. It is concise. Lengthy human language verbal instructions can be reduced to a few digits.
4. It is machine oriented rather than human oriented. It has no relationship to the English language.

Programs written in machine language are called *object programs*. Writing object programs is difficult and tedious. Machine-language programmers must have a thorough knowledge of both the language and of the internal operations of the computer to be programmed.

Human-oriented languages

Suppose someone fluent in English only wished to write a letter in Spanish. Perhaps the most impractical approach would be to learn Spanish before attempting to communicate. Obviously, a much faster and easier method would be to write the letter in English and then hire a professional translator to convert the letter into Spanish.

People wishing to write instructions to a computer may face similar communication problems; they may know how to express their instructions in English, but the machine language understood by the computer may be foreign to them. They could, of course, employ a machine-language programmer to perform the translation, thus solving their communication problem. But, consider the advantages if they had a computer program designed to translate English language, accurately and without error, directly into machine language! In a sense, they could then "talk" to a computer.

Unfortunately, no computer programs exist that will translate ordinary English language into machine-language instructions. Attempts have been made to write such programs but not with complete success. These attempts, however, have resulted in translation routines that can make the programmer's job much easier. Human-oriented languages have been developed that are composed of letters, symbols, and numbers, grouped into various combinations to form a limited vocabulary of English and pseudo-English words and expressions. These languages are much easier to learn and to use than the machine language of the computer. The development of human-oriented languages has had a significant influence on the rapid advancement of computer technology.

Translators A program written in a human-oriented language is called a *source program*. The *translator* is a special program, usually supplied by the manufacturer, that converts a human-oriented source program into a unique machine-language object program for the computer model on which it is translated. Source programs, for example, translated on a Control Data Corporation CYBER/170 computer result in /170 object programs; source programs translated on IBM/370 or /1130 computers result in /370 or /1130 object programs respectively. This procedure may appear to involve more work because a program must be written in one language, then translated into another language before it can be processed. It does involve more work, but the extra work is done by the computer at electronic speed. Use of a translation routine results in at least two major advantages. First, the programmer may be required to learn only one language rather than a different language for each computer make and model used. Second, it is faster and easier to write programs in a human-oriented language.

Currently, two broad classes of translators exist—one is called an assembler, the other a compiler.

Assemblers An assembler is used to translate a low-level human-oriented language, called a *symbolic* language, into machine language.

Symbolic languages generally use *mnemonic* (meaning "memory aid") codes, such as A for add, S for subtract, M for multiply, etc. An assembler is usually designed for a specific computer model. It generally converts symbolic-language source programs into machine-language object programs on a one-for-one basis; that is, for each symbolic language instruction, the assembler generates one corresponding machine-language instruction. This one-for-one translation makes it possible for the programmer, if he or she chooses, to match his or her symbolic language instructions to the translated machine-language instructions to see what occurred.

Compilers A *compiler* is used to translate a high-level human-oriented language called a *problem-oriented language*. A compiler is more powerful than an assembler. It may generate, or *compile*, a list of many machine-language instructions for each problem-oriented language instruction. Thus, it is not an easy task to compare a series of high-level language instructions with the translated machine-language instructions, but, fortunately, such a comparison is rarely necessary. The use of high-level language does not require a thorough knowledge of the intricacies of the machine. Problem-oriented languages are not designed for a specific computer; they are designed to be used in solving a special class of problem. They are written in pseudo-English (example: ADD A, B GIVING C) or in common algebraic notation (C = A + B) rather than in mnemonic code.

The beginning programmer might ask at this point why all programs are not written in a high-level language. The answer to this question is that high-level languages have inherent disadvantages that, in some applications, may outweigh the advantages. In general, a program initially written in machine or assembler language will use more efficient code, will make better use of specific machine input/output capabilities, and will tend to use instructions that will execute faster at object time than a compiler-translated program.

FORTRAN, the subject of this book, is a high-level language. Thus, programs written in FORTRAN must go through a "double run" on the computer. The first run is the *compilation* or translation run. This results in a FORTRAN source program's being converted into a machine-language object program. The second run is the *execution* or computation run, in which the machine-language object program processes data and produces the desired results. This can perhaps best be illustrated schematically. (See Figure 1-1.)

Computers can accept both a source program and problem data in one run. The intervening steps are handled automatically, but the logical procedures are the same as illustrated in Figure 1-1.

FORTRAN

Many human-oriented languages are in existence. This book is concerned with the one developed by IBM and originally published in 1957. Called FORTRAN, an acronym for FORmula TRANslation, it is

Figure 1-1
Compiling a FORTRAN source program and executing the object program

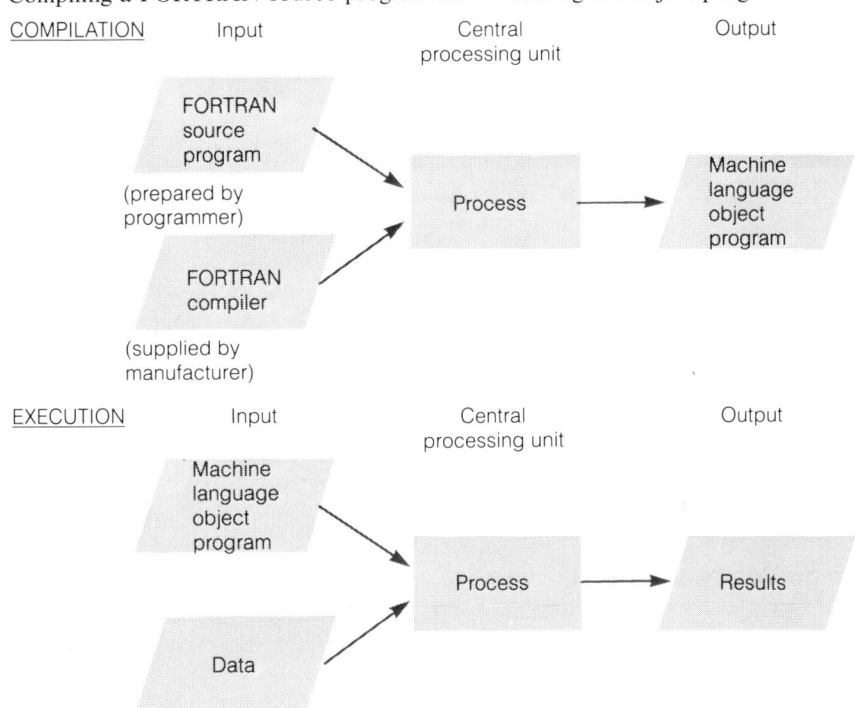

probably the most widely used problem-oriented language. It is often referred to as a "scientific language" and is designed to permit complex mathematical expressions to be stated similarly to regular algebraic notation. It has become an extremely popular language because of the ease with which it can be learned and because of the wide variety of applications for which it has been found suitable.

FORTRAN is not a dead language—it is subject to change. During its brief life span, FORTRAN has been improved by modifications, additions, and deletions. As a result, FORTRAN, like ordinary human languages, suffers from the existence of several versions and dialects; this book uses the current American National Standards Institute (ANSI) Standard version X3.9-1978, commonly called FORTRAN 77.

ANSI introduced this Standard (in 1978) as a guide for manufacturers, consumers, and the general public. Conformance to this Standard is not required; furthermore there are many computer makes and models that differ both in size and in engineering design. Thus, some compilers do not include all ANSI features, while others go beyond the Standard. It should be noted, however, that ANSI has had a major influence on FORTRAN compiler features.

FORTRAN 77 has gained rapid acceptance in the United States and was approved by more than 20 countries before its adoption as an

International Standard (ISO 1539-1980). As a result, anyone who has mastered this Standard version of the language, covered in this book, will find it relatively easy to adapt to the few slight variations that occur in other versions. Thus, in general a FORTRAN programmer can communicate with any modern computer having a FORTRAN compiler. For this reason, FORTRAN is said to be "machine independent" in that it may be written without regard for the specific make or model of machine on which it will be processed.

A COMPUTER SYSTEM

As previously indicated, one of the advantages of FORTRAN, from the beginning programmer's point of view, is that a thorough knowledge of the intricate details of various computer systems and designs is not required; but it is useful to have at least a general understanding of the machine to be programmed. This section illustrates what a computer system looks like and briefly describes how it works. Although a specific machine is used for illustrative purposes, the general concepts apply to all modern computers, regardless of make or model.

Hardware

The physical equipment that makes up a computer system is called *hardware*. A minimum configuration of hardware consists of a central processing unit, one input device, and one output device. Generally speaking, the more input and output devices a computer system has, the more jobs it can do. Figure 1-2 illustrates a large modern computer system.

Figure 1-2
A large modern computer system

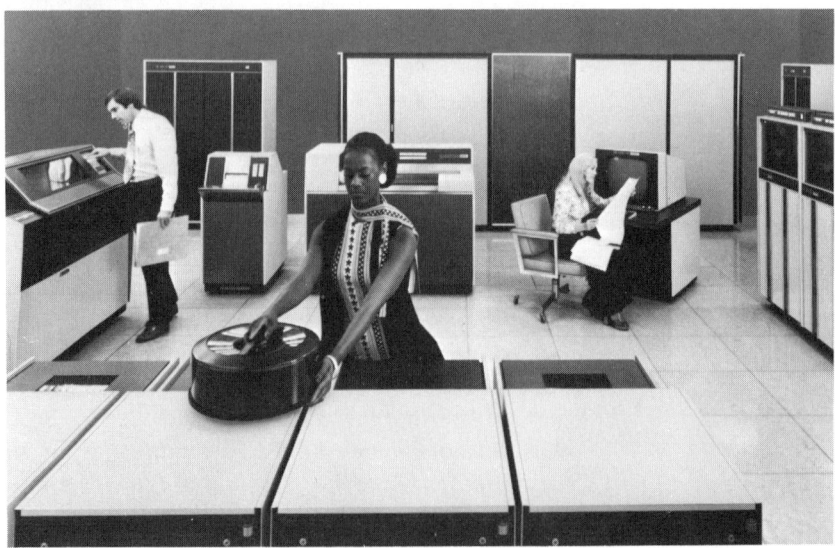

Photo reprinted by courtesy of
Control Data Corporation

Central processing unit (CPU) The CPU is the actual computer. It has three basic internal components. The *"memory" unit* (described in the next section of this chapter) serves as a storage area for both the information being processed and for the program instructions. Mathematical calculations and certain logical operations are performed within the *arithmetic unit*. The *control* or *supervisory unit* directs the overall operations of the computer system and serves as a coordinator between the other internal units and the input and output devices. The CPU has a control panel with various switches and dials used to operate the machine (see Figure 1-3). A light panel instantly indicates to the expert what the computer is doing, or it can be used to indicate the contents of any particular location within the computer.

Printer-keyboard This device, sometimes called the *console*, is also shown in Figure 1-3. It has a standard typewriter keyboard and several special-purpose switches. It can be used as both an input and output device, but, because of its relatively low speed, it is generally used only for communication between the operator and the computer. Although the console is unlikely to be used *directly* by beginning programmers, it is mentioned here because it is an example of a device that might be used *indirectly* by the computer system when processing any and all

Figure 1-3
Printer-keyboard and control panel

Photo reprinted by courtesy of
Control Data Corporation

programs. Installations with a logging routine may use the console to record automatically information regarding each program processed.
Card read-punch This combination input-output device is used to read cards and to punch or "write" cards. Many installations use separate devices for card reading and writing (see Figure 1-4).

Figure 1-4
Card read-punch unit

Photo courtesy of IBM

Printer The printer is a high-speed output device. The model illustrated has a maximum speed of 1,100 lines per minute (see Figure 1-5).
Disk storage drive This high-capacity external storage device may be used for both input and output. The model pictured has removable disk packs; each disk pack has a capacity of approximately 7¼ million

1 / Introduction

Figure 1-5
Printer

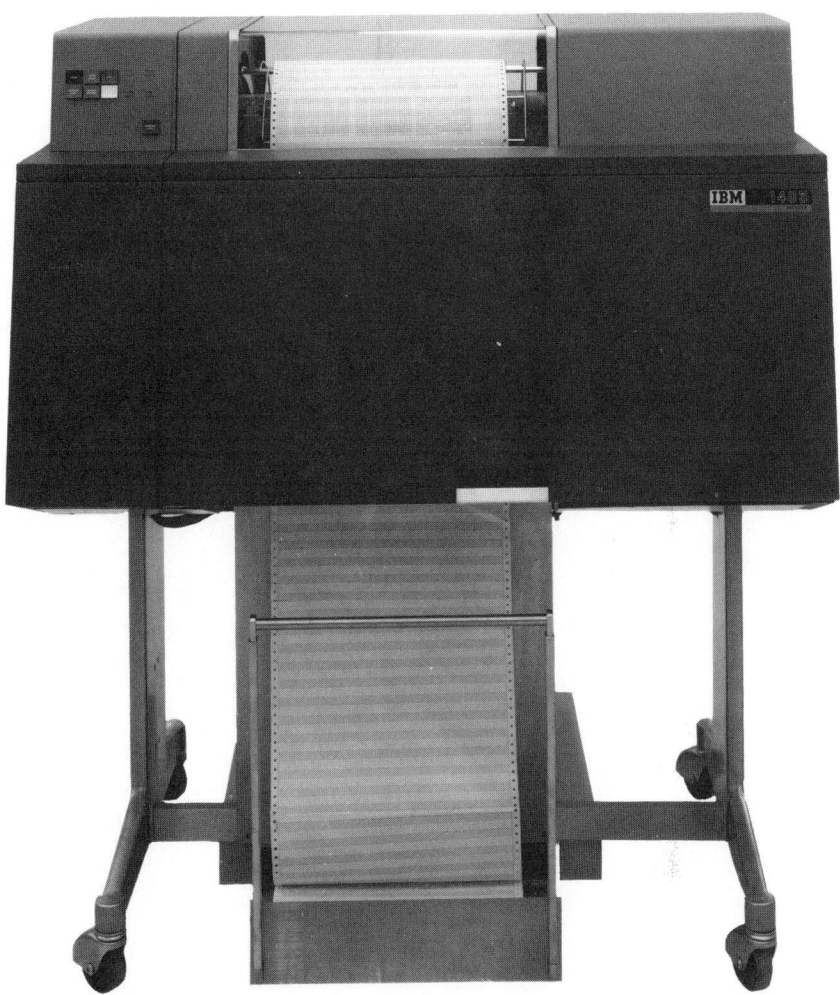

Photo courtesy of IBM

characters (see Figure 1-6). This is another example of an input/output device unlikely to be used *directly* by beginning programmers, but which might be used *indirectly* by the computer system when processing a FORTRAN program. Many installations store their FORTRAN compiler on this general type of high-speed device, where it is instantly available to the computer.

Internal structure

To appreciate the difficulties of programming in machine language and the comparative ease of programming in FORTRAN, it is helpful to have at least a general understanding of the internal storage structure of a computer. *Internal storage* serves as a sort of filing cabinet where

Figure 1-6
Disk storage drive

Removable
Disk Pack

Photo courtesy of IBM

data can be placed, held, and later retrieved in an orderly manner. A popular, glamorous, and somewhat sensational term for internal storage is *memory*.

Prior to the mid-1970s, the most common type of modern internal storage medium was *magnetic core* (see Figure 1-7). A magnetic core is similar in shape to a tiny doughnut or ring. It is slightly smaller in diameter than the letter *o* on this printed page. It is metallic and may be magnetized in either a clockwise or counterclockwise direction. Internal storage contains many thousands of metallic cores which are strung on ultrafine wires arranged in the manner of the matrix. Electrical flow through these wires is used to establish or change the direction of magnetization or polarity and to "read" the direction of polarity. It is unnecessary to understand the many technical aspects of the electronic circuitry to realize that each core has but two possible states. It is often compared to an electric switch or to a light bulb, both of which have but two possible states, *off* and *on*. By convention, when a core has clockwise polarity it is considered to be *on*, representing the binary value one; counterclockwise polarity indicates an *off* condition, representing the binary value zero (see Figure 1-8).

The *binary* numbering system uses only two symbols (usually 0 and

Figure 1-7
Magnetic core storage

Photo Courtesy of IBM

1). To indicate a value greater than nine, using familiar decimal notations, two or more decimal digits are needed. Likewise, to indicate a value greater than one in binary, two or more binary digits are needed. Equivalent decimal and binary notations indicating the values zero through nine are:

Decimal	Binary
0	0
1	1
2	10
3	11
4	100
5	101
6	110
7	111
8	1000
9	1001

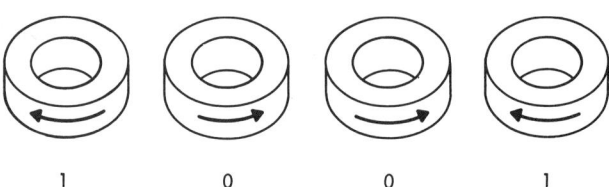

Figure 1-8
Four magnetic cores representing the decimal value nine in binary mode

Data stored in magnetic cores are called *bits*. The word *bit* is a contraction of the two words *binary digit*.

Computer core storage is usually divided into groups of adjacent bits called *bytes*.[1] Byte size depends upon the engineering design, or "architecture," of the particular make and model. These design differences do not change the general concept: a unique combination of zero and one bits within a byte can represent one specific character—numeric, alphabetic, or special. (Advanced techniques for representing more than one character within a byte are ignored in this chapter.) The letter R, for example, might be represented internally in an eight-bit byte as 11011001.

Each byte has an *address* to indicate its specific location. Computer memory is sometimes compared to a post office. Numbers may be used to identify and to indicate locations of mail boxes. The post office box number corresponds to the address of a byte. The contents of a post office box may be cards, letters, packages, etc. These correspond to the contents of a computer storage location, which may be one number, letter, or special character represented by a coded combination of *on* and *off* cores. The difference between the *contents* and *address* of a location is crucial to the understanding of computing. The contents is a character (numeric, alphabetic, or special). The address is an identification of a specific place within storage where a character is located.

```
Address  0 1 2 3 4 5 6 7 8 9
Contents R A 1 7 2 0 7 9 3 5
```

An instruction does not ordinarily *tell* a computer, for example, to add one specific numeric value to another. Instead of specifying numeric values in an instruction, the programmer specifies the addresses where these values are located. Stated another way, the instruction tells the computer to add the contents of one address to the contents of another address.

---

[1] Other terms are sometimes used for these groups, but the ANSI Standard (X3/TR-1-77) term *byte* is by far the most popular.

Figure 1-9
IBM System/370 monolithic chip memory

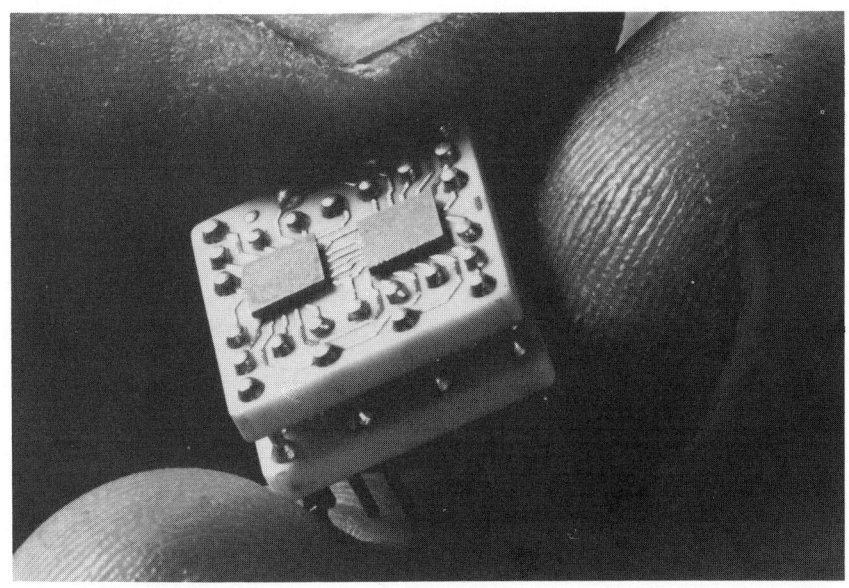

Photo Courtesy of IBM

Byte addresses are numbered consecutively starting with zero and continuing to many thousand or to several million depending on the model. In computer jargon, the term *256K* is used to describe a machine which has approximately 256,000 addressable locations. Likewise, *two megabytes* refers to a machine in the 2-million-byte range.

The newest computers use extremely miniaturized components in place of core storage. Figure 1-9 illustrates the *monolithic chip memory* used in certain models introduced in the early 1970s. This highly dense circuit technology requires only about half the space that conventional core memory needs to achieve an equal amount of storage. The newest memories can store dramatically more information in much less space. But all memories operate in accordance with the general concepts previously described.

COMMUNICATING WITH COMPUTERS

Programmers usually communicate with the computer either directly by using a time-share terminal or indirectly by using punched cards. Both methods are described in following sections.

Time-sharing terminals

Many computers operate in a time-shared processing mode. The main notion is to provide a number of users with simultaneous access to one computer; available computer time is shared by users of multiple terminals. Many types of input/output devices can be used as terminals. One type commonly used by beginning programmers has a keyboard and a cathode ray tube (CRT) display (see Figure 1-10) which may also be connected to a printing device. Terminals are usually placed at locations convenient to users and remote from the computer—perhaps in a nearby room or building or perhaps hundreds of miles away connected to the computer by a telephone line.

Time-sharing terminals are called *on-line* or *conversational mode* devices because they give the user the ability to communicate directly with the computer. The speed of communication may obviously be limited by capabilities of both the user and the device. Although the computer may have the capacity to accept many thousands of characters per second, it is unlikely that the human user can transmit more than a few hundred characters per minute. Likewise, the computer can

Figure 1-10
Time-sharing terminal

Photo Courtesy of IBM

transmit information back to the user at electronic speed, but the terminal printer obviously operates at a much slower pace. A time-shared system reduces the time that the central processing unit (CPU) is not being used when it is available for use. This efficiency is obtained by dividing CPU time among terminal users on some scheduled cyclical basis. A time-shared system may, for example, allocate several thousandths of a second (i.e., several milliseconds) to each terminal user in turn from the first through the last and then repeat the cycle. Response time is such that individual users are scarcely aware they are sharing time with others. In effect, the computer is solving more than one problem at a time. Interactive terminal operations are described in Appendix B.

A printer-keyboard device is only one of many types of terminals. Computer-to-user communication speed can be dramatically increased by using a different type of terminal—e.g., replacing the relatively slow printing device with an almost instant response CRT display unit that looks like a commercial television set. Comparative advantages, costs, and other considerations are beyond the scope of this book—the important point is that output speed can be dramatically increased by replacing the bottleneck device with something faster. Likewise, user-to-computer response time can be improved by replacing the human bottleneck with a high-speed input device. However, it should be recognized that conversational or interactive mode ceases to exist when the user is removed from direct access to the computer. When the user is allowed only indirect access, the computer can be effectively used by operating in the popular *batched mode* described in the next section.

Batched mode processing   Many systems are designed to allow programmers indirect, rather than direct, access to the computer. The set of instructions, inquiries, or other information to be transmitted to the computer is first prepared in machine-readable form on an *off-line* device (one that is not connected to the computer). Typically, information for transmittal to the computer is punched into a machine-readable card (described later in this section) by using a manual device called a card punch or keypunch. Next, the punched cards are submitted for processing. For various reasons, each time a user happens to appear at the processing center the computer is not interrupted, so it can "listen" to the punched card information and respond accordingly. Instead, user jobs are collected in groups or batches, perhaps sorted according to estimated processing time, types of devices required, languages used, or other criteria. At some later time, deemed best by computer management, all jobs in a batch will be processed as a unit. In summary, the user prepares punched cards, submits these cards to the processing center, then returns later to pick up the computer's response. Response to beginning programmers is usually in printed form.

Turnaround   The delay between the time a job is submitted to the processing center and its eventual completion is called *turnaround*.

Batch processing is, of course, dependent upon a variety of local circumstances. A caveat to beginning programmers seems appropriate here: At times when you need the best turnaround, if anything can go wrong it probably will! Typically the end of the school term is a rush time for a computer center because of more jobs and more-complex jobs. At the same time, although somewhat rare, it is not unheard of that a mechanical or electrical malfunction may increase turnaround by 24 hours.

The punched card As previously stated, a common medium of communication with the computer is the punched card, also commonly called the IBM card.

A standard card (Figure 1-11) contains 80 vertical *columns* numbered 1 through 80 from left to right across the card. These can be compared to an 80-space line of printing. Each space on a printed page can contain only one letter, number, or special character if it is to be readable by humans. Likewise, each column on a card can contain only one number, letter, or special character if it is to be readable by the machine.

Each card contains 12 horizontal *rows* of punching positions. The first three rows from the top down are numbered 12, 11, and 0 respectively. The remaining nine rows are numbered sequentially 1 through 9. The card illustrated in Figure 1-11 has the numbers 0 through 9 printed in the lower 10 horizontal rows. Punches in these rows are called *numeric punches*. The 12 and 11 rows at the top of the card are not indicated by printed numbers. Punches in the 12, 11, and 0 rows are called *zone punches*. Note that the 0 punch is both a numeric and a zone punch. Various punches and combinations of punches within the 12 positions in each column are used to record, in machine-readable code, one number, alphabetic letter, or special character.

The top edge of a punched card is referred to as the *12-edge,* the bottom as the *9-edge,* the left as the *1-edge*, and the right as the *80-*

Figure 1-11
The IBM card

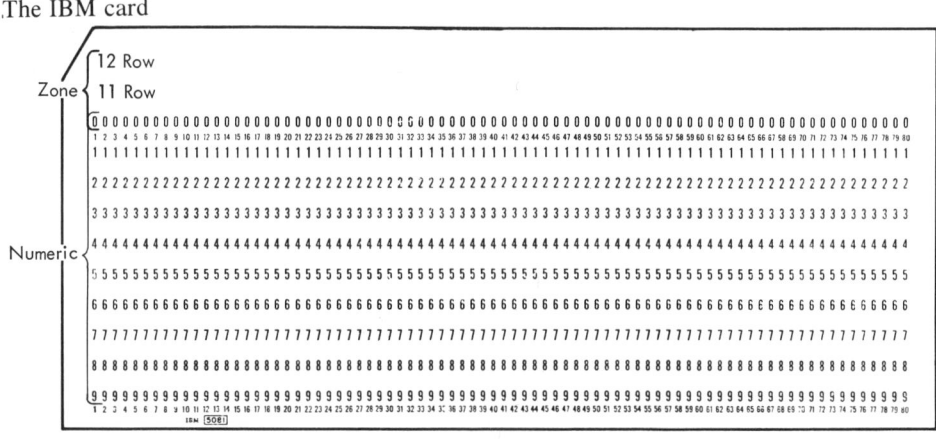

1/Introduction

edge. Ordinarily, a card has printing on only one side, called the *face*. Cards are fed into specific devices in specific ways. Card readers, for example, usually process cards 9-edge first, face down. It should be obvious that if cards are fed into this machine 12-edge first, instead of 9-edge first, the machine will "read" 12s as 9s, 11s as 8s, 0s as 7s, etc. Likewise, if the cards are fed 9-edge first, face-up instead of 9-edge first, face-down, the machine will "read" column 1 as column 80, 2 as 79, etc. Although the programmer may not actually operate the machine, this explanation should indicate the importance of properly arranging all cards before submitting a deck for processing. In referring to what happens when a computer is given invalid, inaccurate, or illogical input, programmers sometimes use the humorous but unofficial description, "garbage in, garbage out."

The Hollerith Code   Dr. Herman Hollerith designed the punched card and its machine-readable code during the 1880s. It may be unnecessary for programmers who use punched cards to memorize the *Hollerith Code*, but it is useful to have sufficient familiarity with it to be able to distinguish between numbers, letters, and special characters. Fortunately, the code for numbers and letters is logical and easy to remember. The machine used to encode or punch cards is commonly called a *keypunch*.

Numeric characters   A numeric character is represented by a single punch in the appropriate numeric punching position (0 through 9) within a column. To represent the digit 2 in any column, for example, a punch is placed in the 2 row only in that column; a 3 is represented by a single 3 punch, etc. Only *one* punch is used within a column to record numeric information. (See Figure 1-12.)

Alphabetic characters   An alphabetic character is represented by *two*

Figure 1-12
Valid FORTRAN characters

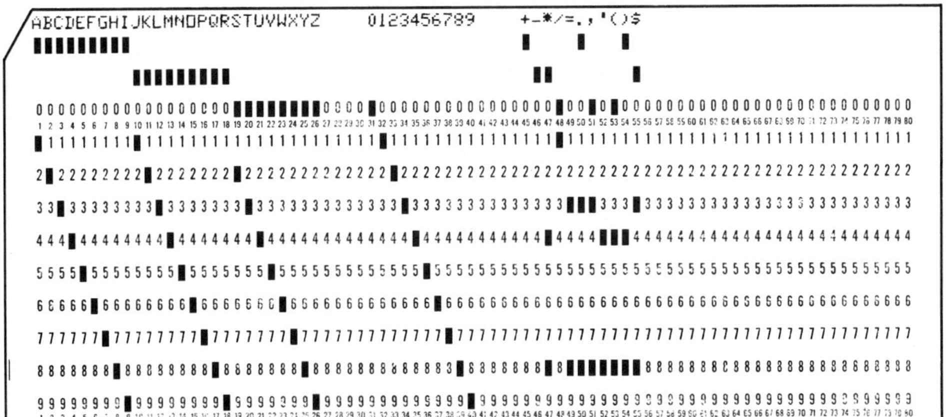

punches within a column; one *zone* punch is combined with one *numeric* punch in the 1 through 9 rows.

Codes for the first nine letters of the alphabet (A through I) use all nine combinations of one punch in the 12 row combined with a punch in one of the numeric rows 1 through 9. The letter A is represented by a 12 punch and a 1 punch, a B by a 12 and 2, C by a 12 and 3, etc.

Codes for the next nine letters (J through R) use all combinations of one 11 punch combined with a punch in one of the numeric rows 1 through 9. The letter J is represented by an 11 and 1, K by an 11 and 2, etc.

By combining one of three zone punches with one of nine numeric punches, there are 27 possible combinations of two punches in a column. But there are only 26 alphabetic letters, so one of these combinations is not used. Hollerith chose to omit the 0 and 1 combination. Thus, the final series of eight letters begins with the letter S, represented by 0 and 2, and ends with the letter Z, represented by 0 and 9.

By remembering that the letter A is represented by a 12 and a 1 and that the combination of 0 and 1 is omitted in alphabetic coding, it is a simple matter to determine the code for any of the 26 letters even though the entire code is not memorized. *It should be especially noted that there is no way to distinguish between lowercase and uppercase (capital) letters in Hollerith Code. As a matter of convention, programmers assume there is no code for lowercase letters, only for uppercase.*

Special characters A special character is represented by no punch, one punch, or by various combinations of two or three punches within a column. The coding for special characters has no particular logic and is unnecessary to memorize (see Figure 1-12). The codes for numbers and letters previously described are standard on all punching machines that use Hollerith Code. It should be noted that codes for special characters may vary with the model of punching machine. The programmer should be aware of this when punching instructions for specific compilers and/or machines.

Fields

A card *field* is a column or group of columns, generally in succession, reserved for a particular item of data or information. The inventory data card illustrated in Figure 1-13, for example, has several fields. These are used to indicate various types of information about one particular inventory item. (A similar card would normally be prepared for each item of inventory.) In the illustration, the first field on the left (columns 1 and 2) is a 2-column numeric field reserved for building number; columns 17 through 55 (a 39-column alphabetic field) are reserved for item description.

Numeric fields Normally, numeric fields are justified to the right. Any unused columns on the left, or high-order, side of a numeric field are filled in with zeros or simply spaced over and not punched. For example, refer to the data card illustrated in Figure 1-13. Building number 4

1 / Introduction

Figure 1-13
Card fields

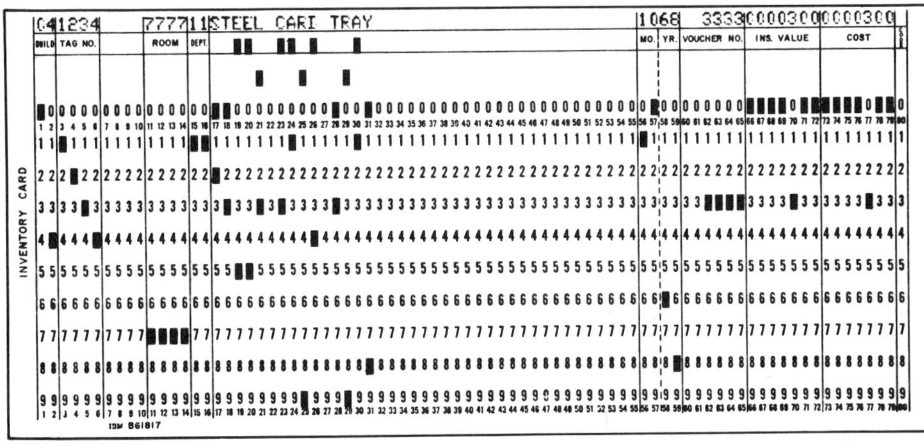

is indicated by a 0-punch in column 1 and a 4-punch in column 2; building number 40 would be indicated by a 4-punch in the first column of the field and a 0 in the second. Note that the voucher number field (columns 60 through 65) is an example in which punching is omitted to indicate zeros in the two high-order (leftmost) positions. Unpunched columns in a card are commonly called blank columns or simply *blanks*.

Alphabetic fields Normally, alphabetic fields are justified to the left. Note the item description field (columns 17 through 55) in Figure 1-13. Punching begins in the first column of the field (column 17) and continues, depending upon the data length, no further than the last column in the field (column 55). In contrast to numeric fields, alphabetic fields always contain blanks, never zeros, in any unused columns.

Field names, lengths, and locations can obviously vary depending upon the data to be recorded. This is a matter of card design. Once fields have been established for a particular record, it is mandatory that these established fields be followed strictly.

Records and files A punched card is commonly called an *external storage record*. The term *external storage* pertains to a medium or device that is not an internal part of the computer and where data can be placed, held, and later retrieved. Data is stored in a card by punching holes into the card in a machine-readable code. A *record* is defined as a collection of one or more fields of related data or information. A group of related records is called a *file*. Thus, a file may contain many records, each record may contain many fields, and each field may contain many columns.

FORTRAN PROGRAMMING A machine-language programmer must have a *detailed* knowledge of the internal structure of a computer, but a FORTRAN programmer does not need such knowledge. This section briefly illustrates why. Subsequent chapters cover the details of FORTRAN programming.

Suppose an input record (card or other) contains two numeric data fields. One field indicates the hours worked by an employee on Sunday, the other the hours worked on Friday. The data are to be read into the computer and stored for later processing. If a programmer decided to write a machine-language program to perform this task, he would be required to indicate the specific addresses or locations chosen for the storage of each input data field. These addresses, in machine language, are in the form of long strings of numbers. Data cannot be located just anywhere—there are certain restrictions. The beginning address of internal data fields for some computers must be evenly divisible by two, four, or eight, depending upon the type of data to be stored. In addition to instructing the computer where each data field begins, the programmer must indicate where each ends. If a machine-language program was written, all of the foregoing indicated information would be contained in instructions consisting of long strings of numbers.

Suppose, however, that the programmer decided to communicate in FORTRAN. To tell the computer to read the data record, instead of a numeric code, he would use the descriptive English word READ. Instead of numeric addresses, he would use descriptive names to indicate *symbolic addresses*. A symbolic address is expressed in symbols convenient to the programmer. For example, the READ instruction could direct the computer to store the data at the symbolic addresses SUNDAY and FRIDAY. Another pseudo-English instruction would describe the type, length, and location of each input record field. The compiler would then perform the task of translating these instructions into machine language. Valid addresses would be assigned automatically, based on the programmer's description of the input record. In most cases the FORTRAN programmer need not be concerned with numeric addresses of internal data fields. To process the data, he simply calls for it by the descriptive symbolic addresses SUNDAY and FRIDAY.

If one character only can be stored at a byte, it is apparent that more than one byte is required to store a multiple-character field such as the number 32,000. The machine language programmer must be concerned with the number of bytes required to store such a field. He must also be concerned with the specific numeric addresses assigned to the various parts of the whole. The FORTRAN programmer, on the other hand, can ignore all these details. Thanks to the compiler, one descriptive name (that acts as a symbolic address) automatically references a group of bytes that is treated as one large internal field where many characters may be stored. Thus, the five-digit number 32,000 may be the contents of *one* FORTRAN address. The maximum value that can be stored at one FORTRAN address is not standard but varies by computer model (e.g., 10^{38} or 10^{308}). Usually the values are large enough to relieve programmers of any worry that they will exceed the

1 / Introduction

capacity of their computer. One easy-to-remember name, such as SUNDAY or FRIDAY, can be used to store almost any value.

It should now be apparent why it is difficult, tedious, and time consuming to communicate with a computer in machine language and why human-oriented languages are so popular. The reader should now begin to appreciate some of the wonders of FORTRAN!

REVIEW QUESTIONS

1. Define the following terms:
   - a. Machine language
   - b. Symbolic language
   - c. Problem-oriented language
   - d. FORTRAN
   - e. Assembler
   - f. Compiler
   - g. Source program
   - h. Object program
   - i. Internal storage
   - j. Turnaround time

2. Distinguish between:
   - a. On-line and off-line
   - b. Core, bit, and byte
   - c. Contents and address
   - d. Compilation and execution

3. The Hollerith Code requires how many punches within a column to represent:
   - a. A number?
   - b. An uppercase letter?
   - c. A lowercase letter?
   - d. A special symbol?

4. Indicate whether the following devices can be used for input, for output, or for both:
   - a. Printer-keyboard or "console"
   - b. Card read-punch
   - c. High-speed printer
   - d. Terminals

5. Who and what determines turnaround time?

6. Why might a beginning programmer prefer to learn FORTRAN rather than a machine language?

7. Convert the current year and your name into Hollerith Code.

8. What is the CPU?

9. Distinguish between conversational mode and batched mode.

10. When processing a FORTRAN program, which must occur first—execution or compilation? Why?

2

General approach to FORTRAN programming

This chapter provides only an overview of programming; it is not intended that the reader comprehend all details of the FORTRAN language illustrations. Its purpose is to present only a general understanding of what programming is. Following chapters cover the detailed rules of writing the language. Stated another way, this chapter covers "the forest," later chapters, "the trees."

Most beginning FORTRAN programmers have had little, if any, experience in organizing their thoughts into a machine-readable, ordered set of instructions. This process demands disciplined thinking, much attention to detail, and an organized problem-solving approach. The several steps generally required in FORTRAN programming may be stated as follows:

1. Problem analysis and definition.
2. Flowcharting.
3. Coding.
4. Compilation and debugging.
5. Testing and execution.

The following five sections explain the above steps. Near the end of the first section, an illustrative problem is presented. This problem is used throughout all sections to supplement discussion and to demonstrate an application of each step. An actual FORTRAN program is thus logically developed, step by step, complete in every detail. The illustrated problem is intentionally very elementary so that the reader can follow the general programming steps and concepts without being distracted by the logic of the problem.

PROBLEM ANALYSIS AND DEFINITION

The first step in solving a problem is to understand it. This may appear evident, but it is not at all uncommon for people to begin writing programs before they fully understand the problem to be solved. A clear and precise definition of the problem is the key to good programming. Lack of advanced planning is an invitation to disaster. Problem definition requires thorough analysis of (1) desired output, (2) required input, and (3) various methods of obtaining the desired result.

The desired output may be known because it is the "answer" to the problem to be solved. However, careful analysis of the probable uses of such output may influence the form, content, medium, number of copies, and other considerations. A programmer rarely enjoys the luxury of making all decisions regarding output because his or her job is usually to solve problems for others. In a commercial setting, careful analysis may indicate no need for a program. For example, suppose an academic administrator requested a program to prepare a list of all seniors eligible to graduate. There may be a program available, previously prepared for use by another administrator, to solve the same problem. There may also be a second program prepared by some other programmer at the request of another administrator to do the same job! It is truly surprising how many times programmers have "reinvented the wheel" because nobody recognized a redundant request.

When a professional programmer begins working on a problem, he or she is usually expected to begin filing various written information that supports the work. When the job is finished, the file should include a copy of the program with numerous notes and documents that, together, form what is sometimes called a *documentation package*. Documentation for printed output should specify content, form layout (printing positions assigned to each output field), number of copies and their distribution, paper weight and color, and other appropriate information. After the program is operational, sample output should be added to the documentation package. The reader, at this point, might wonder, "Do I have to do all that stuff to write FORTRAN programs?" Fortunately, no. Beginning programmers usually solve problems that include a description of the required output, at least in general terms. This paragraph is intended (1) to introduce the important concept of adequate documentation, (2) to indicate that there is much more to programming than just writing instructions for computers, and (3) to present part of the broad overview required for a sound general understanding of programming.

Required input is based on output requirements. Required input is rarely unobtainable; in some cases it must be converted into machine-readable form, and in other cases it may be ready for use and available from one or more sources. Data values required to solve a particular problem may come from a variety of sources including the program itself. A detailed description of all input should be a part of the documentation package; if input is in card form, one or more illustrative cards, as appropriate, should be included.

The third step in problem definition is to determine how to convert input into desired output. A prescribed set of processes designed to solve a problem, in a finite number of steps, is called an *algorithm*. Obviously, there may be many ways to solve a problem. Some of the ways in which algorithms may vary include the number of steps, logical sequences, and the formula(s) (if any) used to solve the problem. Appropriate notes about algorithms used and/or rejected may be included in the documentation package.

Problem analysis and definition involve the preparation of a clear statement of the problem and a determination of the input and output requirements for solution. This step is complete after a useful, convenient summary has been prepared. The basic program may be described in brief but clear informal pseudo-English—sort of an abbreviated outline of the problem-solving steps. To illustrate problem analysis and definition, consider the following introductory problem:

Belmont Sales Corporation has an electrical appliance division that stocks only irons and two brands of television sets. They have recently completed a physical count of each individual product and now want to know the combined sum of all items.

The required output is one printed line that includes the individual counts and the sum of all items:

Print positions	*Contents*
1 through 2	Quantity of Jon Brand TV sets
3 through 5	Blank
6 through 8	Quantity of Kay Brand TV sets
9 through 11	Blank
12 through 15	Quantity of electric irons
16 through 18	Blank
19 through 23	Sum of inventory items

Note that the output description specifies both the size and location of each information field. The term *quantity* implies the required output type (whole numbers). The blank space between the information fields is to aid the reader; the number of blank printing positions may be somewhat arbitrary or may be designed to conform to a preprinted form rather than plain blank paper stock.

The input is one record, with three data fields, in the following format:

Record columns	*Indicates quantity of*
1 through 3	Kay Brand TV sets
4 through 5	Jon Brand TV sets
6 through 9	Irons

Pseudocode for program planning

Brief pseudo-English code summarizing the overall programming logic, or algorithm, for this simple case might appear somewhat as follows:

2/General Approach to FORTRAN Programming

READ units each inventory type: jtvs, ktvs, and irons
calculate sum = jtvs + ktvs + irons
PRINT jtvs, ktvs, irons, and sum
STOP after processing one output record

The illustrative lines above are commonly called *pseudocode*. There are no standard rules for writing pseudocode. It is independent of the FORTRAN language but is written to specify the procedures and the general flow of the planned FORTRAN program.

After developing the program logic and structure by use of pseudocode, the programmer may now prepare a flowchart, described next.

FLOWCHARTING

Now that the desired output and available input have been established and the program logic has been briefly summarized, the next step is preparation of a *flowchart*, which is a graphic representation of the algorithm. A formal flowchart for the illustrative problem is illustrated in Figure 2-1.

The flowchart for the example problem illustrates, in general, how the programmer must organize his thoughts before preparing a machine readable, ordered set of instructions. A computer cannot solve any problem until given an unambiguous, step-by-step procedure to solve it. The importance of flowcharting cannot be overemphasized. Good

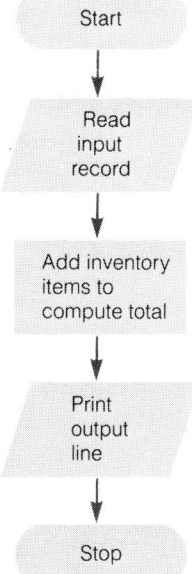

Figure 2-1
Illustrative flowchart

flow chart structure helps assure good program structure. *Before* the actual writing of all but the most elementary programs, it is almost indispensible that a flowchart be prepared. Any documentation package without a flowchart is incomplete.

The illustrative problem, as previously indicated, is very elementary. When faced with a complex application, which may require many pages of symbols, the programmer usually begins with a skeleton flowchart that includes only the major functions. After developing the overall logic, these major functions are broken down into more detail. The amount of detail depends upon the need. There may be a maximum of one symbol for each program step but, in practice, such detail is rare; in fact, it is usually bad practice because it defeats one of the purposes of the flowchart, which is to give a broad overview of the program.

A flowchart may be defined as a graphic representation of the various steps to be taken by the computer, structured to indicate the sequence of these steps. Stated another way, a flowchart is a visual aid and guide for composing FORTRAN statements[1]—a sort of road map to the solution of a problem. Flowcharts, or partial flowcharts, are often used to experiment with different approaches to problem solution. After a program is operational, the supporting flowchart is filed for future reference.

A flowchart is composed of various symbols (usually connected by lines with arrowheads to indicate step sequence) and of brief explanatory remarks. Flowcharting may be defined as an art rather than an exact science because a problem solution may be flowcharted in a variety of ways. The sequence of steps, the detail in which steps are indicated, the extent of explanatory remarks, and the set of symbols used are some ways in which a flowchart of a specific problem can vary. Over the years, various sets of symbols have been used, but the standard set established by the American National Standards Institute, Inc. (X3.5-1970) has become almost universally accepted. Any brief descriptive comment or explanatory note may be written within these standard symbols, which are illustrated and explained in Figure 2-2.

Figure 2-3, on page 28, illustrates a program flowchart of an application designed to calculate and print the overall grade point average (GPA) of a class of 1,000 students. Input for this program is one record for each student; each record contains an *individual* GPA.

Because a flowchart is used as a guide for writing a program, a reasonable amount of thought should precede flowchart preparation. As previously stated, good flowchart structure will help assure good program structure. The following illustrates the type of reasoning one might follow in preparing the flowchart illustrated in Figure 2-3. The program should be designed to read exactly 1,000 numeric values (one value per record), accumulate the sum of all values, divide the sum by

---

[1] Each FORTRAN language instruction, or command, is called a *statement*.

Figure 2-2
Standard flowchart symbols

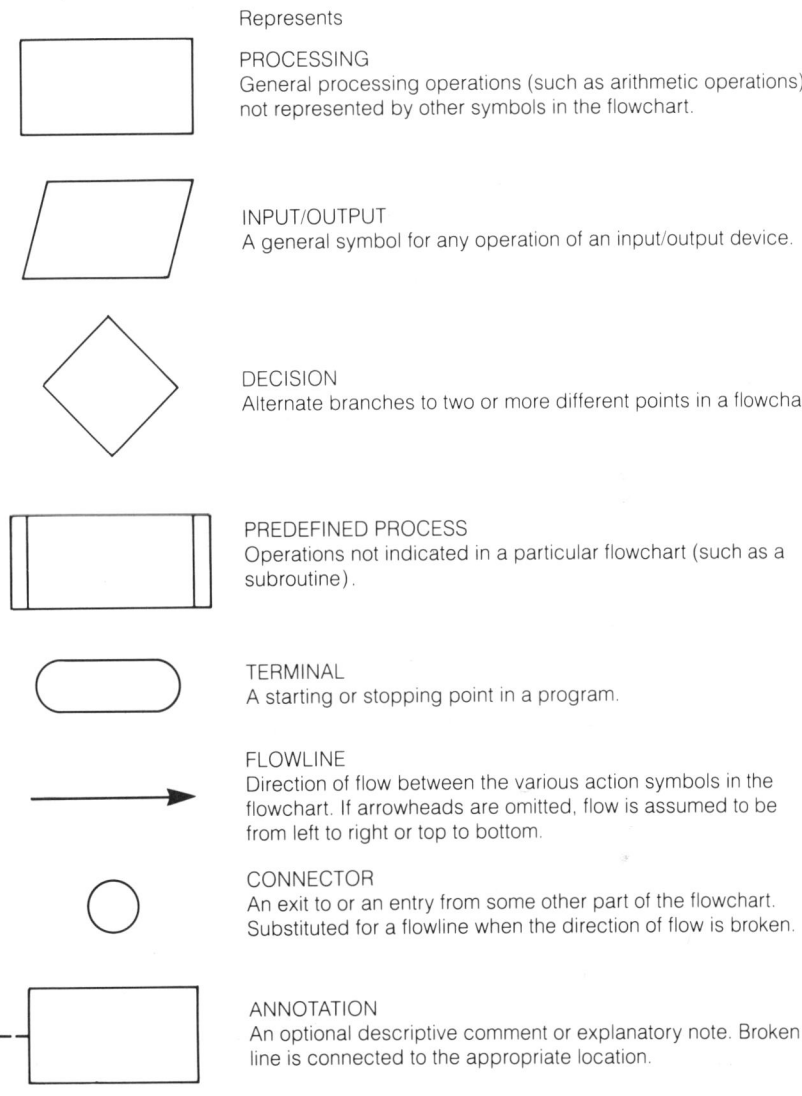

the number of values read, then print (output) the computed average. Rather than give the computer 1,000 READ instructions, it is more efficient to give it one READ instruction and "tell" the computer to repeat the one instruction 1,000 times. Likewise, one add instruction, to accumulate the sum, can be repeated 1,000 times. Before we begin accumulating we must be sure to start with a zero for the same reason that we would clear an ordinary adding machine to zero before accumulating a sum. We must also be sure that the basic read/add operation is repeated exactly 1,000 times. One way is to clear another ac-

Figure 2-3
Illustrative flowchart

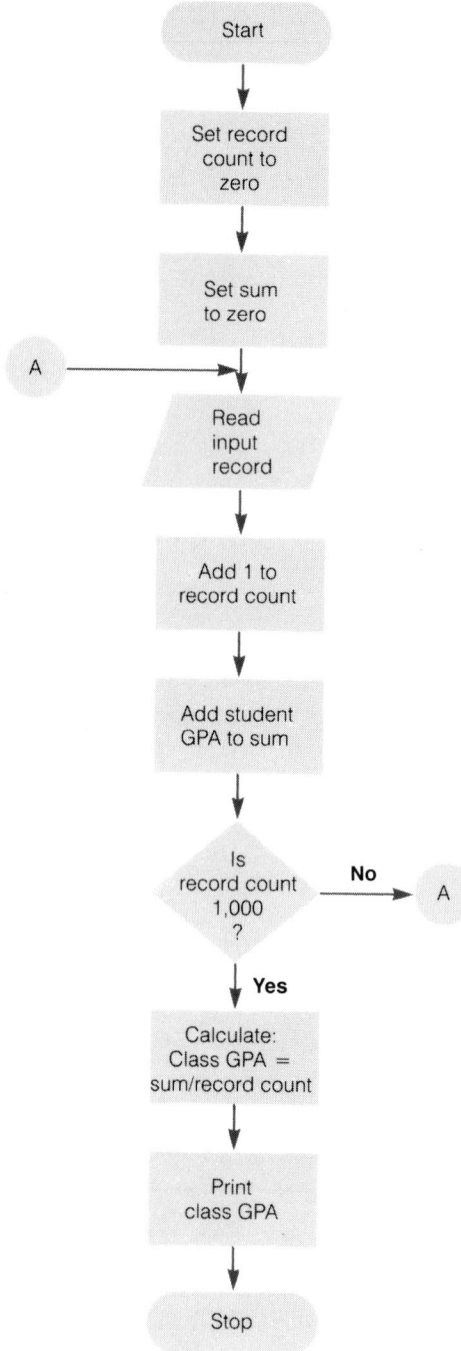

cumulator to zero; then each time the read/add operation is performed, add one to the accumulator and test the sum in the accumulator. The read/add operations should be repeated until 1,000 records have been processed; then the average should be calculated and written.

It is recommended that the general logic of any program, such as described above, be *written* in brief but clear, informal pseudo-English notes before one begins to construct a flowchart. These summary notes may later be included as program comments. It cannot be overemphasized that programs should be written so they communicate to both the computer and to human readers. *Thus, the writing must be clear, concise, complete, and correct. It is not enough to write to be understood—write so that you cannot possibly be misunderstood.*

CODING

Now that the flowchart is completed, the next step is *coding*. Coding is the process of reducing a flowchart to a series of FORTRAN statements (commands). There is no FORTRAN statement that directs the computer to start. (This task is handled by the computer operator and by *system control commands* discussed in Appendix C.) The other symbols in the illustrative flowchart (Figure 2-1) each require one statement. Several other statements, not indicated by flowchart symbols, are also required.

Coding is usually done in pencil on a special FORTRAN coding form. The purpose of a coding form is to indicate the specific number, letter, or special symbol that is to appear in each column of the FORTRAN statements. A detailed explanation of the use of coding forms appears in Chapter 3 of this book, but a few comments are appropriate at this time to get the beginning programmer off to a good start.

Always use block style capital letters; lowercase and script must be avoided because these cannot be punched in Hollerith Code. Use only the best of penmanship—the importance of neatness in coding cannot be overemphasized. The coding sheet serves as a means of communication with the keypunch or computer terminal operator. If coding is misinterpreted, the program will not produce the desired results. The few extra minutes required to do a good job of coding will be more than offset by the savings in debugging time. Extreme care must be taken when coding numbers, letters, and characters which are similar in appearance. A classic example is the letter *O* and the digit zero. To distinguish between them, a slash is used. Unfortunately, some computer centers draw a slash through the letters, whereas others slash the numbers. Most FORTRAN statements contain more zeroes than letter *O*s, but some other high-level languages use more *O*s than zeros. As a matter of convenience, programmers prefer to put the slash on the lesser population. At computer centers where key punch operators must punch program cards written in various languages, confusion can obviously result unless a local shop rule on slashes is adopted. To avoid any misinterpretations, the reader is cautioned to check the requirements of his or her particular computer center.

Beginning programmers are particularly cautioned to distinguish between:

1. The letter *O* and the number 0
2. The letter *I*, the number 1, the slash /, and apostrophe '
3. The letter *Z* and the number 2
4. The letter *G* and the number 6
5. The letter *S* and the number 5
6. The letter *C* and the open parenthesis (
7. The letter *T* and the plus sign +
8. The comma, and the apostrophe '

Coding for the illustrative program, flowcharted in Figure 2-1, could appear as illustrated in Figure 2-4. The coded program is now ready for keying into a computer terminal or keypunching into cards.

Figure 2-4
Coded FORTRAN program

IBM FORTRAN CODING FORM

PROGRAM | PROGRAMMER | DATE | PUNCHING INSTRUCTIONS

```
      PRØGRAM STØCK
      ØPEN(5,FILE='INPUT')
      ØPEN(6,FILE='ØUTPUT')
C         WRITTEN BY O. R. WELL, 8/11/84
C     READ UNITS EACH INVENTØRY TYPE,
C         CALCULATE SUM, PRINT INPUT
C         UNITS AND SUM.  STØP AFTER
C         PRØCESSING ØNE RECØRD.
C     DICTIØNARY ØF VARIABLE NAMES
C         IRONS  - STEAM IRØNS
C         ITEMS  - SUM ØF INVENTØRY ITEMS
C         JTVS   - JØN BRAND TV SETS
C         KTVS   - KAY BRAND TV SETS
C*********************************************
    1 FØRMAT(I3,I2,I4)
      READ(5,1)KTVS,JTVS,IRØNS
C
      ITEMS=KTVS+JTVS+IRØNS
C
    2 FØRMAT(1X,I2,3X,I3,3X,I4,3X,I5)
      WRITE(6,2)JTVS,KTVS,IRØNS,ITEMS
C
      STØP
      END
```

Keypunching from the illustrative coding sheet should result in a machine-readable *source program deck*, as illustrated in Figure 2-5. Note that each line on the coding sheet has one corresponding card in the source program deck. Likewise, if a computer terminal is used, there should be line-by-line correspondence.

FORTRAN programs, by definition, must be composed of *statements* that direct computer operations. *Comments,* although not required, are permitted and should be included to improve readability. Coding sheet lines (and corresponding program cards/lines) that are comments begin with the letter *C*. Most comments provide descriptive information. "Blank comments" may be used to provide blank lines (except for the letter *C*) between various sections as desired by the programmer. There are no hard-and-fast rules covering comments. Their purpose is to supplement statements with descriptive information, thus making it easier for humans to read the program.

Let's briefly examine the first three lines:

```
PROGRAM STOCK
OPEN(5,FILE='INPUT')
OPEN(6,FILE='OUTPUT')
```

It is customary, and good procedure, to start each program by assigning it a name. This is the purpose of the PROGRAM statement. The next two lines are OPEN statements. Each opens one file; device (unit) number 5 is connected to the opened input file and device (unit) number 6 is connected to the opened output file. Don't worry about details at this time—just recognize that the programmer used these statements to assign identification numbers to the devices used for reading input and for writing output.

These first three lines (unlike the rest of this illustrative program)

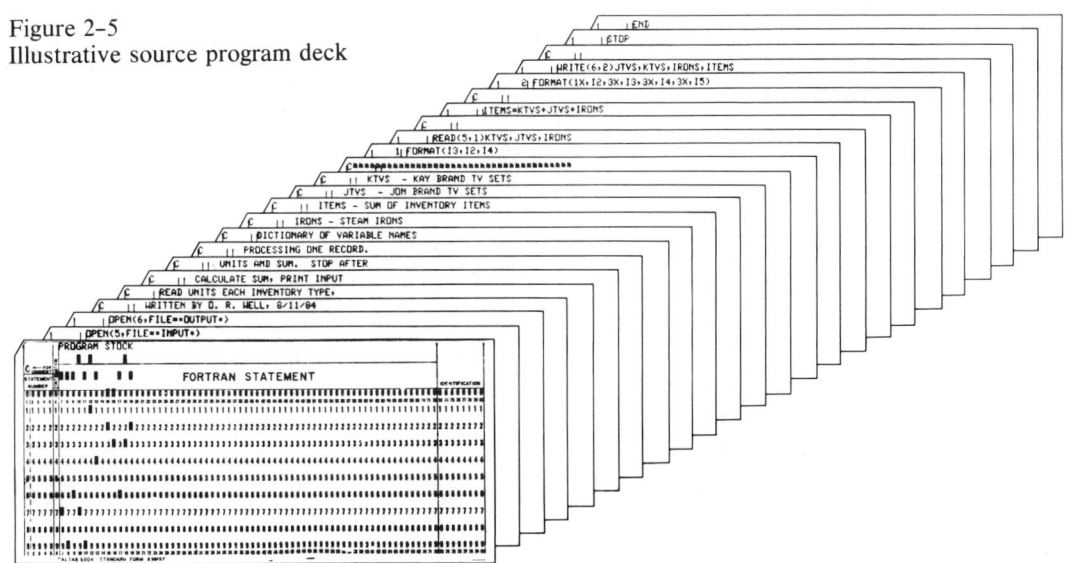

Figure 2-5
Illustrative source program deck

deserve extra discussion because of different requirements at different computer centers. The PROGRAM statement is not required, but we recommend that it be used. An exception must be made when using a compiler that does not meet current FORTRAN standards. In that case, enter the letter *C* in column 1 (i.e., change the statement line to a comment line) to accomplish the same task (naming the program) in a less formal way. Programmers are cautioned to check their local computer center requirements as to the use of OPEN statements. Some installations preassign identification numbers and files to basic input/output devices, so OPEN statements may be redundant and sometimes are prohibited. On the other hand, many installations require OPEN statements for any and all files, but the statement form and contents may differ.

Now, let's briefly examine the introductory comments in the illustrative program (Figure 2-4). The first:

```
C    WRITTEN BY O.R. WELL, 8/11/84
```

identifies the programmer and indicates the completion date. Any and all future program modifications should be supported by additional appropriate comments.

The next group of comments describes the overall program logic and purpose in brief pseudo-English form:

```
C    READ UNITS EACH INVENTORY TYPE,
C       CALCULATE SUM, PRINT INPUT
C       UNITS AND SUM, STOP AFTER
C       PROCESSING ONE RECORD.
```

The above comments are indented so that this comment group is set off to the reader's eye. Indenting all except the first comment in the group is a matter of style, optional with the programmer.

Review and modification of existing programs is a typical and often major part of a programmer's job. Variable names (symbolic addresses) that seem clear and descriptive when composed by the programmer may later appear vague. Of course, more difficulty can be expected if the reviewer is someone other than the original programmer. The final group of comments may ease the reviewer's task:

```
C    DICTIONARY OF VARIABLE NAMES
C       IRONS—STEAM IRONS
C       ITEMS—SUM OF INVENTORY ITEMS
C       JTVS—JON BRAND TV SETS
C       KTVS—KAY BRAND TV SETS
```

A line of asterisks follows the above comments. This is one method to clearly separate the introductory comments from the main body of the program.

It should be noted that the remainder of the program is structured in logical sequence with blank comments dividing it into four basic parts:

input, computation, output, and termination. Some of the words included in the statements are the *variable names* composed by the programmer to serve his special needs as previously discussed. The other words (FORMAT, READ, WRITE, STOP, and END) are called *keywords*. They have a special meaning in FORTRAN (explained later in this section); unlike variable names, they are not symbolic addresses of storage locations.

Now, a cursory examination of each main body statement will be made to give "the feel" of the FORTRAN language.

1 FORMAT(I3,I2,I4)

Statement 1, for which there is no corresponding flowchart symbol, provides the compiler with descriptive information. FORMAT is a keyword. It tells the compiler that this statement describes the size and general composition of an input or output record.

The parenthetical notation describes the record by indicating the number of fields, the length and location of each field, and the type of data contained in each field. It obviously does all this in much less space and with much less effort than would be required to describe it in human language. The three codes within parentheses: I3, I2, and I4, tell the compiler that the record contains three data fields. The first element, I3, indicates that the first field contains *integer* data and is three columns in length. It is the first field specified, so these three columns are necessarily the first three columns in the card. I2 indicates the next two columns constitute another field of integer data. I4 similarly describes the last field.

READ(5,1)KTVS,JTVS,IRONS

The second statement has a corresponding flowchart symbol. Rather than merely providing descriptive information, it directs the computer to perform a specific action. READ is a keyword that tells the computer to read a record. The first number within the parentheses is a code, assigned by the programmer in the first OPEN statement, that indicates which input device the computer is to read the record from; in this case assume code 5 specifies a card reader. The second number is a code that references the nonexecutable statement which describes the record—i.e., the FORMAT statement. The three variable names KTVS, JTVS, and IRONS indicate the symbolic addresses where the input data are to be stored.

Variable names are associated, in order, with their corresponding field descriptor codes. Contents of the first input field (I3) will be stored at an internal location indicated by the first symbolic address (KTVS). Likewise, contents of the second field (I2) will be stored at JTVS, and contents of the third field (I4) at IRONS.

ITEMS=KTVS+JTVS+IRONS

The above command is an arithmetic statement. It indicates that the data contained at the symbolic addresses KTVS, JTVS, and IRONS are to be added and that the sum is to be stored at the symbolic address indicated by the variable name ITEMS

2   FORMAT (1X,I2,3X,I3,3X,I4,3X,I5)

FORMAT statements are used to describe records. If a record is to be *printed*, as in this case, the programmer must start the description with an appropriate line (or *carriage*) control character to control vertical line spacing. This character is never printed. At this point a line control character might be considered "something extra" that must precede the actual output record description. A following chapter covers carriage control in detail. In the meantime, the 1X specification used in this illustration will take care of required control.

Following the carriage control specification is the first field description, I2. As previously discussed, this tells the computer that the record (printed line) begins with a two-position integer field. The letter X is often called the *skip-code*. The field descriptor 3X tells the computer to skip three positions (i.e., leave three blanks). This is similar, in effect, to striking a typewriter space bar three times. Likewise, the last five field descriptor codes (I3, 3X, I4, 3X, I5) describe three-, four-, and five-position integer fields separated from each other by three blanks. Usually good output design requires a reasonable amount of blank space between data fields because readability is a prime concern. An exception is the case when output is designed to fit forms with preprinted vertical lines that visually separate data fields.

To summarize, the statement:

2   FORMAT (1X,I2,3X,I3,3X,I4,3X,I5)

describes a printed record. The first specification (1X) takes care of controlling the movement of the output paper through the printer. Following specifications describe the required output: four integer data fields with three blank spaces (3X) between each.

To complete the discussion of this FORMAT statement, the size of the output fields needs brief further explanation. The size of the input fields (I3,I2,I4) indicates that the largest possible values that could be punched in the input card would be 999, 99, and 9999. The sum of these maximum values is the five-digit number 11097. Thus, to accommodate the largest possible sum, the final output field is specified to be five columns long (I5).

WRITE(6,2)JTVS,KTVS,IRONS,ITEMS

The above statement directs the computer to write the "answer" to the problem. WRITE is a keyword. Assume code 6 indicates output is to be on a high-speed printer. The digit 2 references FORMAT statement number 2 that describes the output record. Stated another way, it tells the computer where to write the answer. The variable name ITEMS indicates the symbolic address where the sum was stored by the arithmetic statement and where it is now available for output. The other variable names indicate locations of numeric values stored by the READ statement.

STOP

The next-to-last statement signals the *logical* end of the program. The compiler will translate this statement into an equilvalent machine-language instruction that, during execution time, will cause the computer to halt rather than to continue executing instructions. More complex programs may have more than one logical end and, thus, more than one STOP statement.

END

The last statement signals the *physical* end of the program. *The END statement must always be the final statement of any FORTRAN program.* The primary purpose of this statement is to indicate to the compiler that this is the terminal point, or end, of the program—there are no more statements to be translated.

Before a source program is submitted for computer processing, it should be *desk checked,* which involves a manual search for any errors that might have occurred up to this point. There are no universal rules as to how detailed this search should be because it depends upon the degree of care previously taken. A desk check might include a reexamination of the flowchart logic, a comparison of the flowchart with the coded program, and a manual manipulation of numeric values precisely as the manipulation is dictated by the program; i.e., the programmer tries to prove that the program will perform as intended. As a minimum, the source program should be checked for obvious keypunching or terminal entry errors.

COMPILATION AND DEBUGGING

If no syntax or logic errors have been made in preparing the FORTRAN statements that constitute the source program, most of the manual work has been completed. Most of the work in the remaining two steps will be done by the computer.

The next step is to compile and debug the program. If the FORTRAN statements contain syntax errors—that is, if any rules of the language have been violated—compilation will terminate because the compiler cannot translate invalid statements. The programmer would then debug his program—that is, search out all errors and make necessary corrections. Debugging techniques which are useful to beginning programmers are described in Appendix A. Because there are no errors in the illustrative program, it will require no debugging.

When the program is compiled, a printed copy of the source program, called a *computer listing*, can be prepared on a high-speed printer as illustrated in Figure 2-6.

To illustrate the types of "bugs" that might inhabit a FORTRAN program (and which must be exterminated before the program can be properly compiled and executed), it will be assumed temporarily that the program *did* contain an error. Suppose that the word STOP, in the program, was misspelled as STIP. The statement, and thus the source program, would not be translated because a programmer-composed word (variable name) is never permitted in a one-word FORTRAN statement and because STIP is not in the compiler's vocabulary of keywords. The compiler would not simply give up at this point; it would do something else, which could be of real benefit to the programmer.

After detecting the error, it would cause both the location of the error and a brief description of the error to be indicated in the program listing. Thus the compiler can not only translate correct programs, it can also point out and describe errors in incorrect programs!

The reader is cautioned not to assume that the compiler will *always* be of such great help in the debugging process. Some errors cannot be detected by the compiler. Suppose, for example, the programmer incorrectly substituted a minus sign for one of the plus signs in the arithmetic statement or that he or she specified the first input field as I2 instead of I3. *Logic errors*, such as these, cannot be detected by the compiler, so the program could be both compiled and executed, but the resulting output would be incorrect.

As previously indicated, there are no errors in the illustrative program, so debugging is not required.

Figure 2-6
Computer listing of illustrative program

```
      PROGRAM STOCK
      OPEN(5,FILE='INPUT')
      OPEN(6,FILE='OUTPUT')
C     WRITTEN BY J. K. WELL, 8/11/84
C     READ UNITS EACH INVENTORY TYPE,
C     CALCULATE SUM, PRINT INPUT
C     UNITS AND SUM.  STOP AFTER
C     PROCESSING ONE RECORD.
C     DICTIONARY OF VARIABLE NAMES
C     IRONS  - STEAM IRONS
C     ITEMS  - SUM OF INVENTORY ITEMS
C     JTVS   - JON BRAND TV SETS
C     KTVS   - KAY BRAND TV SETS
C************************************
    1 FORMAT(I3,I2,I4)
      READ(5,1)KTVS,JTVS,IRONS
C
      ITEMS=KTVS+JTVS+IRONS
C
    2 FORMAT(1X,I2,3X,I3,3X,I4,3X,I5)
      WRITE(6,2)JTVS,KTVS,IRONS,ITEMS
C
      STOP
      END
```

Figure 2-7
Input card for illustrative program

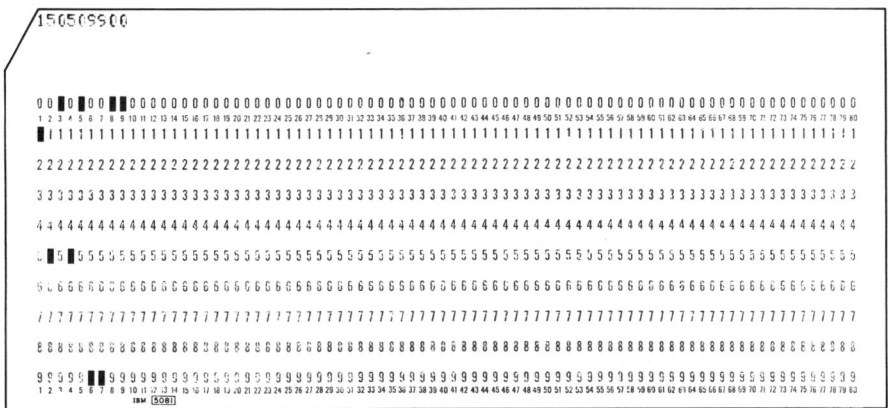

TESTING AND EXECUTION

The final step in arriving at a solution to the problem is to execute the machine-language program generated by the compiler from the FORTRAN statements. To do this, the program is loaded (stored). The data record indicating the number of irons, knives, and mixers is placed in an input device, which in this case is the card reader. The computer is then started, and it executes the program, which consists of reading the input, processing the data, and writing the results. But, before this final step is taken, the programmer normally performs a series of test runs to ensure the effectiveness of the program. To test the illustrative program, several input records that contain known data for which the solutions have been determined in advance could be prepared. These records would be processed by the program and the results compared to the predetermined solutions. If the computer output agrees with the predetermined solutions, the program would be considered free of errors and ready to be used with actual data. If not, it must be debugged and then retested.

The illustrative program is designed to compute the sum of KTVS, JTVS, and IRONS as indicated in the input data record. The output is to be one printed line that contains the input values and the computed total. Assuming the input data are 150, 50, and 9,900 (Figure 2-7), the output will include the computed total 10,100 (Figure 2-8).

It should be observed that the output numeric values were obtained by the computer in two different ways. One value (10,100) was calculated; the other values (150, 50 and 9,900) were obtained from the input

Figure 2-8
Output for illustrative program

50   150   9900   10100

data record. Each time this program is executed it will read one input data record, which might include *any* numeric values. Thus, values obtained from input data records are called *variables*.

When a programmer submits a job for processing it must ordinarily include three types of entries: (1) FORTRAN source program statements, (2) input data, and (3) system-control commands. The first two types of entries have been previously discussed and illustrated. Source program statements are read, then translated into a machine-language program at "compilation time"; input data are read next, then processed (in accordance with program instructions) at "execution time." Source program statements must precede input data in a job because compilation must precede execution.

System-control commands, not previously discussed, are used to direct the computer in this overall process of compiling and executing a job. System-control command requirements vary with the installation, but these commands usually identify the program and the programmer, indicate the type of processing desired and the language being used (e.g. FORTRAN), and specify the sequence of steps to be taken (e.g., compilation before execution). Thus, system-control commands may be interspersed throughout the job. It is the responsibility of programmers to obtain a copy of, and strictly follow, specific requirements of their local computer center. It is not necessary to be concerned with the requirements of *other* computer centers. The curious reader who would feel more comfortable after seeing several typical examples of job composition is invited to examine Appendix C.

REVIEW QUESTIONS

1. Why do *problem definition and analysis* form the first programming step?

2. Flowchart an elementary problem or routine of interest to you. Explain the various steps you have included.

3. What is the purpose of a flowchart or "block diagram"?

4. Give some examples of numerals, letters, and special characters that are similar in appearance. Explain how the programmer distinguishes between look-alike characters.

5. Which FORTRAN statements *must* be numbered?

6. Why must all statement numbers be unique?

7. Distinguish between the STOP and END statements.

8. What is the purpose of a desk check?

9. It has been stated that debugging should be a part of each major programming step. Explain the rationale of this statement.

10. Distinguish between logical errors and syntactical errors and give an example of each. Which type of error is usually more difficult for the programmer to locate?

11. Should every FORTRAN program include comments? Discuss.

12. Name the three types of entries usually included in a job. Describe the purpose of each type.

13. How does the FORTRAN compiler distinguish between comments and statements?

14. Name the major sections of the program illustrated in Figure 2-6.

15. Suppose the input record (Figure 2-7) is changed to include the digit 8 in column 10. How would this affect operation of the program illustrated in Figure 2-6?

PROBLEMS

1. Process the "Stock Program" illustrated in this chapter. Change the program to include your name and the current date. If necessary also change the PROGRAM statement to a comment, and/or modify or omit the OPEN statements to conform to your local computer center requirements.

2. Write a program to solve the equation:

$$NET = N1 - N2$$

Input (N1 and N2) may be any two positive numbers, within the range of 1 to 99. Required output is one line with the computed value of NET followed by your two input values. The following statement may be used to describe the output: FORMAT (1X,I3,2X,I2,2X,I2).

3. If the program described in the preceding problem has been correctly designed, it should work with *any* input values within the range of 1 to 99. Test the program by using it again to process a different set of input values, or, alternatively, your originally selected values in reversed sequence.

3

Elements of FORTRAN

The first section of this chapter describes the basic character set used to compose FORTRAN statements. The next three sections discuss statement types, composition, and form. Later sections explain and illustrate the essential elements that comprise the basic framework for arithmetic statements. The following chapter deals with various methods of combining these elements to form complete arithmetic statements.

Before considering this chapter's main contents, a topic previously mentioned needs further elaboration. The American National Standards Institute, Inc. (ANSI) has established a programming language standard, called FORTRAN 77, that was used as a guide for this book. Thus, some textbook materials must be modified or ignored when programs are written for compilers that do not meet some ANSI standards. When programs are written for one of the many compilers that equal *or exceed* these standards, it is recommended that ANSI standards be followed. There is sound reasoning behind this recommendation. One ANSI standard, covered in detail later in this chapter, permits the programmer to compose variable names that include a maximum of six letters. Programmers who learn to use a maximum of 8 or 10 letters, in compliance with local computer center maximums, are learning nonstandard rules and writing nonstandard programs that will work at relatively few installations. Thus, the emphasis in this book is on general rules rather than rules for a specific compiler. In those instances where no specific standards exist (e.g., the maximum value that can be stored) the programmer must be aware of local limitations, as illustrated later in this chapter. Many installations have more than one FORTRAN compiler, each with unique features and limitations.

Generally, if *standard* rather than device-dependent features are used, the difference between compilers is minor as far as the FORTRAN programmer is concerned. Major differences are not in the FORTRAN language but are related to the design and capacity of the various computer makes and models. The FORTRAN statement to

3/Elements of FORTRAN

multiply two numbers is the same for all computers. However, some computers can work with much larger numbers than other computers. The capacities of a few specific makes and models are included in a few appropriate places in this chapter. Readers should not be concerned with the several exact numbers given for illustrative purposes; it is only important to be aware of the general capacity of the computer they will be using and to recognize that there is a wide range of capacities.

THE CHARACTER SET

FORTRAN is written with a basic set of 49 characters consisting of 26 letters, 10 numerals, and 13 special characters. All FORTRAN elements must be formed from these characters only. Fortunately, the valid FORTRAN characters are all familiar to the reader.

Alphabetic letters

The 26 FORTRAN letters compose the familiar alphabet:

ABCDEFGHIJKLMNOPQRSTUVWXYZ

Numerals

The valid FORTRAN numerals are the familiar decimal digits:

0123456789

Special characters

The 13 valid special characters are:

Blank	
Plus	+
Minus	−
Asterisk	*
Slash (solidus)	/
Equal	=
Decimal point or period	.
Comma	,
Apostrophe	'
Open parenthesis	(
Close parenthesis	)
Dollar sign	$
Colon	:

One special character, the *blank*, deserves special comment. Record columns (or line positions) with no visible characters are called *blanks*. The keyboard operator, like the typist, indicates a blank by striking the space bar. The blank—that is, the absence of a visible character—is considered to be a special character by the FORTRAN compiler.

STATEMENT TYPES

A program consists of a series of instructions that directs the computer to perform a certain task. Each instruction in a FORTRAN program is called a *statement*. It is important to note again that statements cannot be executed; FORTRAN is a high-level language in need of a compiler to translate statements into machine-language instructions that can be executed. Some statements translate directly, or nearly directly, into machine instructions, and others simply provide descriptive information that helps the translation process itself. *Executable statement*, however, is a conventional phrase used to describe a statement that, in effect, directs the computer during execution time. This conventional phrase is used in subsequent discussions.

Statements may be classified into four basic categories: input/output, assignment, control, and nonexecutable.

Input/output

Input/output (I/O) statements direct the computer to READ or WRITE a record, indicate the device to be used (such as card reader, cathode ray tube (CRT), or printer), and reference a nonexecutable statement that describes the record.

Assignment

One major function of an assignment statement is to direct the computer to perform certain arithmetic calculations and to indicate where and how the results are to be stored. Arithmetic assignment statements constitute the "heart" of most FORTRAN programs.

Control

Ordinarily, statements are executed in the order in which they appear in the source program. Control statements can be used to instruct the computer to change this normal order of execution. Control statements, for example, can be used to cause the computer to repeat an instruction or series of instructions a specific number of times, or to execute certain instructions only under specified conditions. Control statements can be used to stop the program.

Nonexecutable

There are several types of nonexecutable statements, but all are used to give the computer information it will need to execute other statements. One type of nonexecutable statement, for example, is called a FORMAT statement. It describes the length and location of each field on a record as well as the type of data contained in each field. The purpose of a FORMAT statement is to provide descriptive information about the record that is to be read or written when an I/O statement is executed.

Input/output, arithmetic, and control statements are called *executable* statements because they indicate a specific action the computer is to take. The FORTRAN compiler translates each executable statement into one or more equivalent machine-language instructions. On the other hand, nonexecutable statements merely provide descriptive information to the FORTRAN compiler. Equivalent machine-language instructions are *not* prepared. This is an important distinction that should be remembered.

3/Elements of FORTRAN

STATEMENT COMPOSITION

FORTRAN statements are composed of various combinations of keywords, variable names, numbers or constants, expressions, and codes.

Keywords

Keywords have a special meaning in FORTRAN. When used in proper context, they identify operations designated by statements or indicate the type of information contained in statements. Most statements, except arithmetic assignment statements, must begin with a keyword. An alphabetized list of these keywords is given in Figure 3-1.

Variable names

A *variable name* is a symbolic address selected by the programmer in accordance with the rules of FORTRAN. Although the address or location remains constant, it is called a variable name because the data contained at the symbolic address may be repeatedly changed during execution of a program.

It is emphasized again that the difference between the *address* and *contents* of an internal storage location is crucial to the understanding of computing. A variable name (symbolic address) is an identification of a storage location. In FORTRAN, the contents of each variable name is not limited to one character but may have many characters.

Figure 3-1
Basic key words used in FORTRAN

ABS	ELSE	OPEN
	ELSE IF	
BACKSPACE	END	PAUSE
	END IF	PROGRAM
CALL	ENDFILE	
CHARACTER	EQUIVALENCE	READ
COMMON	EXIT	REAL
CONTINUE	EXTERNAL	RETURN
		REWIND
DABS	FIND	
DBLE	FLOAT	SIGN
DEFINE	FORMAT	SNGL
DIM	FUNCTION	STOP
DIMENSION		SUBROUTINE
DFLOAT	GO	
DO	GOTO	THEN
DOUBLE PRECISION		
DSIGN	IABS	WRITE
	IDIM	
	IF	
	IFIX	
	INTEGER	
	ISIGN	

Numbers or constants

There are two distinct kinds of numbers everyone uses in daily life, perhaps without realizing they are quite different. These two kinds of numbers are sometimes called measuring numbers and counting numbers.

A measuring number must be capable of expressing fractional precision. In ordinary arithmetical notation, it is called a decimal fraction and is written with a decimal point. The diameter of a circle, for example, may be expressed as 1,357.086 feet, 1,357.09 feet, or as 1,357.1 feet depending upon the precision desired. In FORTRAN, measuring numbers are also written with a decimal point but no embedded commas are allowed. They are called *real numbers, real constants, floating point numbers,* or *floating point constants.* This book generally uses the term *floating point constants.*

Counting numbers are whole numbers that have no fractional part. In FORTRAN, they are always written *without* a decimal point to distinguish such numbers from floating point constants. They are called *integer numbers* or *integer constants.* This book uses the term *integer constants.* As in the case of floating point constants, embedded commas are not allowed.

Expressions

Two types of expressions are covered in this book. The only type covered in this chapter is the *arithmetic expression.* It can consist of a single variable name, a single constant, or a combination of variable names and/or constants separated by arithmetic operators (sometimes called operational signs or operational symbols). Variable names, floating point constants, and integer constants have previously been defined. An example of an arithmetic operator is +. The plus sign in FORTRAN, as in mathematical notation, is used to indicate addition. The use of arithmetic expressions and operational signs is covered in detail in later sections of this chapter and in Chapter 4.

Codes

The FORTRAN language includes various alphabetic and numeric codes. The letters *I* or *F*, for example, are used to specify that a record contains integer or floating point data. Similarly, numeric codes are used to designate specific input/output devices.

STATEMENT LINE FORMAT

A *line* in a program is a sequence of 72 FORTRAN characters. The character positions in a line (numbered consecutively from 1 through 72) are called *columns.* FORTRAN programs must be composed of statements but, if desired, may also include comments. All statements and comments must follow the line format prescribed by the rules of FORTRAN. This required format, described next, is the same regardless of the method of entry—e.g., card reader or computer terminal.

Statement label field

This field is located in the first five columns of the line as illustrated by the card in Figure 3–2. A *label,* also called a *statement number,*

3 / Elements of FORTRAN

Figure 3-2
Card illustrating required format for FORTRAN statements and comments

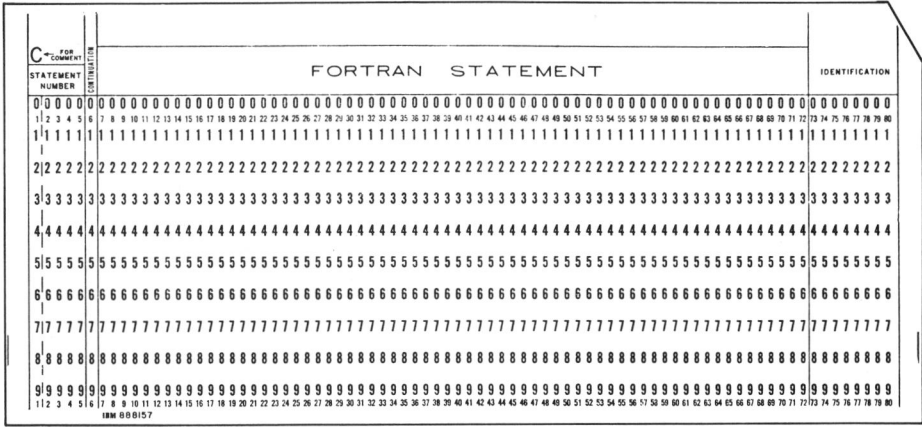

should be right justified in the field. To indicate statement number 72, for example, a 7 should be entered in the fourth column, and a 2 in the fifth. The first three columns may contain zeros or, preferably, blanks. All labels obviously must be unique; that is, two or more statements cannot be identified by the same number.

The only statements that *must* be labeled are those referenced by other statements within the program. Most nonreferenced statements *may* also be labeled, but such practice is not recommended, for two reasons. First, it clutters the program with unnecessary and distracting numbers that take extra effort to code and to key in, thereby increasing the possibility of error. Second, many compilers generate a listing of all labels that are *not* referenced. If such a listing includes only those labels that should have been referenced but were not, it is in effect an error listing and a very useful tool for locating mistakes. The value of such a listing may be greatly reduced if it includes numerous labels that the programmer did not intend to reference.

Statement numbers do not affect the order in which statements are executed; therefore, the programmer may number the statements in any desired sequence. However, it is much easier to find a particular statement if statement numbers are in ascending sequence, so such practice is generally recommended. It is rather common to number statements in increments of 10 (i.e., 10, 20, 30, etc.) to make it easier to insert additional sequentially numbered statements at a later time. Programs may be structured so all statements within a logical group fall within a certain numerical range; for example, in a payroll program, statements used to calculate overtime may be numbered in the 400 series, those for tax calculations in the 600 series, etc. An ordered program, in terms of statement numbers, is a worthy goal but, for practical reasons, it need not be a rigid rule.

Comment lines With one exception only numerals and blank spaces are permitted in the statement number field. The letter *C* in the first column designates that the line is a *comment* rather than a statement. The purpose of a comment is to provide program *documentation*; that is, to make a program easier for humans to read. It is usually desirable to cause a printer to generate a *program listing* that contains one printed line for each statement/comment in the source program deck. It is permissible to enter the letter *C* in column 1 and leave the other columns blank. A "blank comment" may be used to provide a blank line (except for the letter *C*) in a program listing. A comment may precede any statement in the program or may follow any statement except the END statement. The programmer need not be concerned with any rules or restrictions when composing a comment. It may be written in "free form" and may appear anywhere in the comment field, which extends from column 2 through 72. A comment is not a statement, so it is ignored in the translation process. Thus, it does not affect the program execution in any way. There is no limit to the number of comments that may be included in a program except as dictated by the capacity of the computer. Furthermore, comments may be composed of any character compatible to the computer system; special characters that are not included in the FORTRAN character set may be included in a comment. However, it is recommended that comments be restricted to the FORTRAN character set so they will be acceptable to any computer with FORTRAN capabilities.

Most programs that are used over a period of time must be modified (e.g., a new retirement plan may require changes in the payroll program). A wise and liberal use of comments adds considerably to the readability of any program—particularly to one written several months previously. Writing a comment that says "WRITE THE NUMBER OF ITEMS" before the statement WRITE(2,4) ITEMS is of no help. A well-documented program anticipates the questions of a later reader and answers them in advance. Some programmers precede and follow each comment with a blank comment. This sets each comment off to the eye, thus adding to its readability. Likewise, one or more blank comments may be used to separate various sections of a program.

Continuation field Column 6 (Figure 3-2) is a one-column continuation field. Quite often even beginning programmers compose statements too long to be completed on one line. It is permissible to continue a statement on as many as 19 additional successive lines. To indicate to the compiler that a card is a continuation of a statement, rather than the beginning of a new statement, column 6 must contain a *continuation character*. A continuation character may be any valid FORTRAN character except a zero or a blank. This character distinguishes continuation lines from the first line of any statement, which *must* contain a zero or blank in this field. As a matter of convenience, most programmers leave column 6 blank on all lines except continuation lines. It should be noted that

3/Elements of FORTRAN   47

continuation lines should not contain a statement number because it is invalid to reference a partial statement.

Statement field   The statement field, illustrated in Figure 3-2, extends from column 7 through 72. All statements must be confined to this field. If a statement requires more than the 66 columns provided in this field, it must be continued in the same field on successive lines. A common error of some beginning programmers is to write part of a statement outside the boundaries of this field.

Identification field   The rightmost field, illustrated in Figure 3-2, extends from columns 73 through 80 and is called the *identification field*. It is beyond the extent of the 72-column FORTRAN program line. Thus, it is ignored by the compiler during translation. Characters entered in this field may, however, appear in a program listing. The identification field may be used at the programmer's discretion for free-form notations, for numeric sequencing, for program or programmer identification, etc., or it may be left blank.

CONSTANTS   A constant is a known numeric value written in the source program. As the term *constant* implies, the value cannot be changed. It is always composed of one or more decimal digits. It may be positive, zero, or negative. It may be signed or unsigned; if written without a sign, it is assumed to be positive. If signed, the sign must precede the first digit. Embedded commas are not permitted. Two types of numeric constants are recognized in FORTRAN, *integer* and *floating point*.

Integer constants   Integer constants are numbers without decimal points or fractional parts. Such whole numbers are usually used for counting and form a minor part of most FORTRAN programs.

The maximum range of a constant is *not* set by FORTRAN standards. It varies considerably by computer make and model. For example, one computer can handle integers in the range of plus or minus about 30,000, while another has a maximum range of plus or minus about 300 trillion. These examples illustrate that programmers should keep in mind at least the general limitations of the computer they will use to process their programs.

Valid integer constants	*Invalid integer constants*	
000	56+	(Sign must precede digits)
+4	73.	(Decimal point not allowed)
8	7,564	(Embedded comma not allowed)
−7	8123456789	(Exceeds maximum magnitude
27459		on *most* computers)

Floating point constants

Most constants used in FORTRAN programs are in floating point mode (form) rather than integer mode. A floating point constant is a number expressing decimal fractional precision. It is stored internally in two parts. One part is called the *fraction* (or *mantissa*). The size of this fraction is not standard—the number of significant decimal digits (called the *precision*) usually varies from about 7 to 16 depending upon the computer.

The second part of a floating point constant is called the *exponent*. It is used to indicate the location of the decimal point.

As a matter of design, the magnitude of the exponent far exceeds the size of the largest fraction. For example, one computer has the capacity to store a positive or negative fraction of seven significant digits with an exponent in the range of about 10^{-40} through 10^{+40}. Another computer has a precision of 14 decimal digits with a magnitude range of about 10^{-300} through 10^{+300}. Stated in more general terms, these computers can store quite a few significant digits followed by, or preceded by, a very long string of zeros. It is not possible to represent all decimal fractions precisely, but it is possible to approximate many very large or very small intended decimal fractions.

It is not necessary to understand the exact manner in which a constant is actually stored. But it is important to realize that a floating point constant is stored in an entirely different manner than an integer constant. An integer constant, unlike a floating point constant, is stored with no provision for indicating a decimal point location. Thus, integer arithmetic can produce only integer results, but floating point arithmetic can produce results with fractional precision. Integer-mode arithmetic does not present a problem when one whole number is added to, deducted from, or multiplied by another whole number because no fractional part can be expected. When division is performed, however, fractional parts may be expected but cannot be computed. Thus, in integer arithmetic:

$$2/3 \text{ is } 0 \quad -6/4 \text{ is } -1 \quad 500/4 \text{ is } 125$$

But, in floating point arithmetic:

$$2./3. \text{ is } .66 \ldots \quad -6./4. \text{ is } -1.5 \quad 500./4. \text{ is } 125.0$$

If fractional precision is desired, arithmetic calculations must be performed in floating point rather than integer mode.

Decimal form floating point constants There are two types of ordinary decimal form floating point constants. One, per ANSI terminology, is called *real*, and the other *double-precision*. ANSI does not specify magnitude standards except to indicate that both types must be able to assume positive, negative, or zero values and that the designed magnitude of double-precision values must be greater than real values (not double, just greater). Regardless of which type the programmer uses, the computer automatically converts and stores the constant internally as a signed fraction and a signed exponent as previously described.

All decimal form floating point constants must contain one or more decimal digits and a decimal point. The constant may be signed or unsigned; if unsigned it is assumed to be positive. If signed, the sign must precede the first digit. Embedded commas are not allowed. These general rules hold true for all computers. Thus, 1234567.89 is a valid floating point constant in ordinary decimal form. However, whether it is real or double-precision depends upon the number of significant digits and upon the computer used. The difference, as far as the computer is concerned, is that double-precision constants require more internal storage space and slightly reduce calculation speed. The difference, as far as the reader is concerned, will become increasingly important in future chapters where advanced calculation methods are covered; at this point knowledge that there is a difference is sufficient.

Some examples of valid floating point constants in ordinary decimal form are:

$$0.0 \quad +1. \quad -.31416 \quad 587.82$$

Some invalid examples are:

    100   (decimal point omitted)
    37,416.52   (contains embedded comma)
    $51.07   (contains dollar sign)

Scientific form floating point constants Many FORTRAN programmers do not use constants other than the two types previously described: integer and ordinary decimal form floating point. The reason they do not use the third type of constant, described in this section, is perhaps a combination of two major factors: (1) they "grew up" with whole numbers and ordinary decimal fractions so find such constants easy to use, and (2) such constants are well suited for the types of programs they write.

Scientific form floating point constants are particularly useful in programs that include very large or very small numbers. Most readers are familiar with scientific notation even if they rarely use it in their everyday lives. Scientific notation was used previously in this chapter when it was stated that the range of values that can be stored in one particular computer is about 10^{-300} through 10^{+300}.

The two previous examples illustrate scientific (or exponential form) notation as used in ordinary mathematics. Corresponding FORTRAN notation follows the same general concept but must be stated in a somewhat different form. An example is:

$$1.E+17$$

A floating point constant, stated in single-precision exponential form, contains three elements. The first is a *decimal fraction*, which may be signed or unsigned. If unsigned, it is assumed to be positive. If signed, the sign must appear in the first (leftmost) position. The fraction usually includes a decimal point. If the decimal point is omitted, some compilers assume a whole number; that is, a decimal point is assumed to follow the low-order (rightmost) digit.

The second element is the letter E, which indicates to the compiler that the constant is in exponential form.

The third element is called the *exponent*. It must be a whole number; no decimal point is allowed. The exponent may be either signed or unsigned. If unsigned it is assumed to be positive. If signed, the sign must precede the first digit. The decimal equivalent of an exponential form constant is the product of the fraction and 10 raised to the power of the exponent.

Following are some examples of valid single-precision exponential form constants:

FORTRAN notation	*Mathematical notation*	*Decimal equivalent*
.50E4	$.50 \times 10^4$	+5000.
−.00005E+8	$-.00005 \times 10^8$	−5000.
+50.E02	$50. \times 10^2$	+5000.
−50000.E−1	$-50000. \times 10^{-1}$	−5000
1234567.E5	$1234567. \times 10^5$	+123456700000.
.1234567E−5	$.1234567 \times 10^{-5}$	+000001234567

Note that the sign of the fraction indicates whether the value is positive or negative; the sign of the exponent indicates, in effect, which way to move the decimal point from its actual or implied position in the fraction.

Following are some examples of invalid exponential form constants.

Invalid constant	*Reason invalid*
2.2+12	Letter E omitted
50.E	Exponent not indicated; zero is *not* assumed
50.E4.1	Exponent contains decimal point
1,234.75E3	Fraction contains embedded comma
1.2E+127	Exponent exceeds maximum magnitude of *some* compilers

Exponential form is particularly useful to express very large or very small decimal fractions. Not only is it more powerful than ordinary decimal form, but it is also more convenient for both the programmer to write and the keypunch operator to punch 1.E17, for example, rather than 100000000000000000.

Exponential form and ordinary decimal form are the two optional methods for writing FORTRAN decimal fractions. The programmer may select the method more appropriate for the circumstances. The size limitations of the fraction and the exponent vary according to the make and model of the computer as previously stated. With most compilers, programmers must substitute the letter *D* for *E* to specify double-precision. An example of this type of constant is:

$$127.5D+75$$

The compiler does not use the variable name to distinguish between single-precision (sometimes called real) and double-precision floating point data. Either type can be stored at locations indicated by variable names, which begin with a letter *other* than *I* through *N*.

Alphanumeric constants

The two types of numeric constants (integer and floating point), described in previous sections, can be manipulated mathematically; alphanumeric constants cannot.

An alphanumeric constant (sometimes called a *character constant* or a *literal*) is a string of one or more characters. Any character compatible to the computer system is permitted, but it is recommended that composition be restricted to the FORTRAN character set.

The beginning, and the end, of the character string is identified by an apostrophe. Stated another way, an alphanumeric constant must be preceded by *and* followed by an apostrophe. Note that these delimiting apostrophes are not a part of the datum represented by the alphanumeric constant. An apostrophe within the datum may be represented by two consecutive apostrophes with no intervening blanks. Examples of FORTRAN notation for alphanumeric constants follow:

Alphanumeric constant	*FORTRAN notation*
RED	'RED'
BLUE-GREEN	'BLUE-GREEN'
SOPHOMORE	'SOPHOMORE'
JUNIOR	'JUNIOR'
A. B. CEE CO.	'A. B. CEE CO.'
JO'S 888 SUPPLY	'JO''S 888 SUPPLY'

VARIABLE NAMES

A variable name is the symbolic address of an internal storage location. It is called *variable* because the contents of this address may be changed repeatedly during the execution of the program. A variable name is composed by the programmer but must follow the rules of FORTRAN.

1. It must begin with one of the 26 alphabetic letters.
2. If desired, it may contain up to a maximum of five additional letters and/or numbers that may appear in any sequence.
3. The only special character allowed is the blank. Embedded blanks, if any, are ignored by the compiler. In rare cases, an embedded blank may improve readability; but, in most cases, it can cause confusion and should be avoided.

The first letter of a variable name has special significance because it implies whether the particular mode of numeric data stored at this address is integer or floating point. This is a convention of FORTRAN called *implicit definition of mode*. Chapter 4 includes an explanation of how to override this implicit definition of mode by use of a nonexecutable statement called an *implicit specification statement*. For now we will follow the implicit rules described next.

Integer variable names

If integer data are to be stored, locations are indicated by variable names, which must begin with one of the following six letters:

$$I \quad J \quad K \quad L \quad M \quad N$$

An easy way to learn this rule is to remember that one of the letters *I* through *N* is used to begin an INteger variable name.

Numeric data stored at locations indicated by integer variable names are represented internally in the same manner as integer constants. Thus, the same maximum values apply.

The maximum name length (six characters) is an ANSI standard. It is recommended that exceptions be made only if programs must be processed on a machine that permits less than six.

Floating point variable names

The compiler does not use the variable name to distinguish between single-precision (sometimes called real) and double-precision floating point data. Either type can be stored at locations indicated by variable names which begin with a letter *other than I* through *N*.

Numeric data stored at locations indicated by floating point variable names are represented internally in the same manner as floating point constants. Thus, the same restrictions as to maximum values apply.

Following are some selected examples of variable names.

Valid variable names	Mode
X	Floating point
SALES	Floating point
RATE	Floating point
DATA3	Floating point
HOURS	Floating point
PAYNET	Floating point
NET PAY	Integer (equivalent to NETPAY since blanks are ignored)
J23456	Integer
NUMBER	Integer
MIXERS	Integer
JTVS	Integer
KTVS	Integer
Invalid variable names	*Reason invalid*
2ND	First character is not alphabetic
ITEM-2	Hyphen is an invalid character
TOOTHBRUSHES	Exceeds six letters in length

3 / Elements of FORTRAN

The programmer should make a special effort to compose variable names that are as descriptive as possible within the rules. For example, a program to compute payroll might include the variable names HOURS, RATE, and PAY. These names are obviously more descriptive than H, R, and P or (worse yet) X, W, Z. The use of descriptive variable names documents the program; that is, makes it easier to read not only by the programmer but by others.

The programmer will often find it necessary to misspell and/or abbreviate because the first letter of the variable name implies the mode and because the name cannot exceed six letters and/or numbers in length. For example, a program designed to count the input records processed might include the integer variable name KOUNT rather than a floating point variable name such as COUNT. Likewise, a program designed to compute interest on a loan might include the floating point variable name ZINT. In this case, INTEREST could not be used as a variable name for two reasons. First, it exceeds the maximum allowable length (six numbers and/or letters). Second, the implied mode is integer, which is not designed to be used with decimal values.

It is important the the programmer be aware of what the computer does when told to store a decimal value at an integer variable name. It will *truncate* (cut off without rounding) the fractional portion to the right of the decimal point and store only the whole number. Thus, if an attempt is made to store 100.99 at the integer variable name NETPAY, only 100 will be stored. Of course, the fractional portion is retained if a floating point variable name such as PAYNET is used.

Substituting variable names such as KOUNT and KODE for COUNT and CODE is one way to stay within the rules when the most descriptive name begins with a forbidden letter. Another trick of the trade takes advantage of the fact that few descriptive names begin with the letter Z. When composing a floating point variable name, some programmers develop the habit of preceding a forbidden descriptive name with the letter Z. To illustrate, ZMEAN, ZMODE, and ZINT might be used as variable names for mean, mode, and interest.

Alphanumeric variable names

Alphanumeric data include the entire FORTRAN character set. Alphanumeric data (which by definition are *not* numeric although they may include numerals) cannot be manipulated mathematically. Accordingly, the first letter of an alphanumeric variable name has no special significance—any of the 26 letters may be used.

The computer will distinguish between numeric (integer or floating point) and alphanumeric variable names by the context in which they appear in the program. For example, variable names in an arithmetic statement are assumed to be numeric. Likewise, if a variable name such as ITEMS appears in a READ statement, the corresponding FORMAT code, say I4 or A4, will determine whether ITEMS is integer or alphanumeric.

As previously emphasized, variable names should be descriptive.

Thus, COLOR might be used to store alphanumeric data such as RED, BLUE-GREEN, etc., and VENDOR might be used to store a company name such as A. B. CEE CO. Note that a variable name should not exceed six characters but that the *contents* of a variable name has no such restriction.

ARITHMETIC OPERATORS

Arithmetic operators are symbols used to designate arithmetic operations. They are:

Operators	Meaning	"Mathematical notation"	FORTRAN notation
+	Add	$a+b$	A+B
−	Subtract	$a-b$	A−B
/	Divide	$a \div b$ or a/b	A/B
*	Multiply	ab, $a \times b$, or $a \cdot b$	A*B
**	Raise to the power of	a^b	A**B

The add, subtract, and divide operators used in FORTRAN are identical with those used in regular mathematical notation. The asterisk is used to indicate multiplication rather than X because the computer always interprets X as an alphabetic letter. The double asterisk is used to designate exponentiation because input and output devices are not designed to handle the superscripts used in regular mathematical notation.

Only the operators illustrated are valid; no other symbols are allowed.

DELIMITERS

Delimiters are used to separate FORTRAN statements and the various elements within a FORTRAN statement. Stated another way, they are used to tell the computer where one statement or one element ends and the next begins. On this printed page, blank spaces are used to separate the elements (such as words and numbers) in a sentence. In FORTRAN, blanks cannot be used to separate elements because the language not only allows as many blanks to be written between the elements as are necessary to improve the readability of a statement but it also permits embedded blanks within some elements.

The rules of FORTRAN require that in each statement (1) every constant, (2) every variable name, (3) every code, and (4) almost every key word be followed by one or more appropriate delimiters. The delimiters are the following eleven special characters:

$$+ - / * = . , ( ) \, ' :$$

and column 73 in the statement line. If one statement is written on more than one line, column 73 is assumed to be a delimiter only on the last line of the statement. It should be noted that the only FORTRAN special characters that are not delimiters are the dollar sign and the blank.

The uses of these FORTRAN delimiters are illustrated in following chapters in which complete statements are described and illustrated.

REVIEW QUESTIONS

1. The FORTRAN language is composed of how many:
   a. Numerals?
   b. Letters?
   c. Special characters?

2. What numerals, letters, and special characters are permitted in:
   a. Statements?
   b. Variable names?
   c. Constants?
   d. Comments?
   e. The identification field (columns 73-80)?

3. What are the four basic types of FORTRAN statements?

4. What is the difference between a FORTRAN statement that is executable and one that is nonexecutable?

5. Give two examples of a keyword.

6. Name two types of FORTRAN constants, and give an example of each.

7. Give an example of an arithmetic operator.

8. What is the maximum number of statements allowed on one line?

9. What is the maximum number of lines that can be used to contain one statement?

10. Continuation lines cannot be numbered (labeled). Why?

11. Where can comments appear in a program?

12. How many comments may appear in any one program?

13. What distinguishes a continuation line from the first line in a statement?

14. What distinguishes a second continuation line from a first continuation line?

15. Is it permissible for a relatively short statement that could be entered in one line to be entered in two or more lines by use of continuation lines?

16. What happens if a programmer extends a statement beyond column 72?

17. Write the numerical value 7 as:
   a. An integer constant
   b. A floating point constant in
   (1) decimal form; (2) single-precision exponential form; and (3) double-precision exponential form.

18. What is meant by *implicit definition of mode*?

19. Why must the programmer be cautious when using integer mode arithmetic?

20. What is the purpose of a delimiter?

21. The program that follows is the same as an illustration in the previous chapter. Refer to this program to answer the questions that follow.

```
      PROGRAM STOCK
      OPEN(5,FILE='INPUT')
      OPEN(6,FILE='OUTPUT')
C           WRITTEN BY J. K. WELL, 8/11/84
C           READ UNITS EACH INVENTORY TYPE,
C           CALCULATE SUM, PRINT INPUT
C           UNITS AND SUM.  STOP AFTER
C           PROCESSING ONE RECORD.
C           DICTIONARY OF VARIABLE NAMES
C           IRONS  - STEAM IRONS
C           ITEMS  - SUM OF INVENTORY ITEMS
C           JTVS   - JON BRAND TV SETS
C           KTVS   - KAY BRAND TV SETS
C*******************************************
    1 FORMAT(I3,I2,I4)
      READ(5,1)KTVS,JTVS,IRONS
C
      ITEMS=KTVS+JTVS+IRONS
C
    2 FORMAT(1X,I2,3X,I3,3X,I4,3X,I5)
      WRITE(6,2)JTVS,KTVS,IRONS,ITEMS
C
      STOP
      END
```

   a. How many statements are in the program?
   b. How many *different* keywords are used?
   c. How many *different* variable names are used?
   d. If the input statement were changed to:

   READ(5,1)JTVS,KTVS,IRONS

   how would program execution be affected?
   e. Assuming no composition change in any statement, what would happen if the arithmetic assignment statement was *moved* so that it appeared immediately prior to the READ statement?
   f. What would happen if the two FORMAT statements were moved so that they immediately followed the STOP statement? The END statement?

3/Elements of FORTRAN

EXERCISES

On a separate sheet of paper classify the numbered items listed below as one of the following: Integer or Floating point valid constant, Integer or Floating point valid variable name, or Invalid. If invalid, briefly indicate why.

1.	KODE	**10.**	DIAMETER	**19.**	N77A4
2.	-345	**11.**	758	**20.**	INPUT
3.	A$-$1	**12.**	STOP	**21.**	12345678.9
4.	$+3.1416$	**13.**	LENGTH	**22.**	67½
5.	PI	**14.**	1,990.95	**23.**	\$395
6.	2ND	**15.**	METERS	**24.**	27.4E-8
7.	JTVS	**16.**	A	**25.**	73.2$+$E3
8.	$+68$	**17.**	INCHES		
9.	SUBTOTAL	**18.**	R^2		

4

Processing numeric and alphanumeric data

Generally, FORTRAN programs are designed to process data and to produce some output. This chapter covers processing of the two basic types of data previously described: numeric and alphanumeric.

PROCESSING NUMERIC DATA

FORTRAN is a mathematically oriented language, so generally most of the data processed are of the numeric type. Therefore this first and larger of the two main sections of this chapter discusses the processing of numeric data.

Arithmetic statements

Arithmetic assignment statements (more simply called *arithmetic statements* in this book) are the "heart" of most FORTRAN programs. An arithmetic statement can tell the computer where to store a constant or where to store the data contained at a symbolic address. It can also tell the computer to perform certain arithmetic calculations and indicate where and how the results are to be stored. This chapter explains how the previously presented constants, variable names, and arithmetic operators are combined to form arithmetic statements. To assist the reader to visualize statement format, record columns are indicated in this manner:

```
Record columns  |12345|6|7
   Statement         40   N=1
```

General form

The general form of an arithmetic statement is:

4 / Processing Numeric and Alphanumeric Data

```
|12345|6|7
 nnnnn  vn=ae
```

Legend:

nnnnn   A statement *number* (label), which is required only if the statement is referenced elsewhere in the program but which may always be used at the programmer's option.

vn   A *variable name* in either integer or floating point mode.

=   A required separator between the two parts of an arithmetic statement.

ae   An *arithmetic expression*, which may consist of one constant, one variable name, or a combination of constants and/or variable names separated by one or more delimiters.

An arithmetic statement has the same general form but not the same meaning as a regular algebraic equation. The equal sign separating the two basic components of an arithmetic statement does not mean equivalence. The equal sign means "store" or "assign." In effect, the arithmetic statement tells the computer to store the numeric value indicated by the expression on the right of the equal sign at the symbolic address represented by the variable. Stated another way, it says assign, to the variable name on the left, the value of the expression.

For example, the arithmetic statement:

```
|12345|6|7
       N=1
```

directs the computer to store the integer constant 1 at symbolic address N.

Regardless of what was stored at N before this instruction was executed, it will be replaced with the integer constant 1. Furthermore, N will continue to have a "current value" of 1 no matter how many times it is used in the program unless or until it is changed by another statement. This is sometimes referred to as "destructive read in and nondestructive read out." In this respect, a computer can be compared to a tape recorder. If a popular song, for example, is located on a certain area of tape, it can be repeatedly played back or read out. But if a speech is recorded or read in on the same area of the tape, the song is lost and is replaced by the speech.

To illustrate this point, suppose a program contains four arithmetic statements which will be executed in sequence:

```
|12345|6|7
     1  N=7
     2  K=N
     3  J=K
     4  N=8
```

After statement number 1 is executed, N will have a current value of 7. Statement 2 directs the computer to store the current value of N at

K. At this point in the program, both N and K have a current value of 7. After the execution of statement number 3, N, K, and J all have a current value of 7. Statement 4 changes the current value of N to 8 but does not affect the current values of K and J.

Arithmetic expressions

As indicated previously, an arithmetic expression is that portion of an arithmetic statement to the right of the equal sign. It may contain a single constant or a single variable name, as illustrated earlier. It may also contain combinations of constants and/or variable names. This latter type of expression is more complex and requires strict compliance with certain rules.

Rules for writing arithmetic expressions The following rules must be followed when writing arithmetic expressions that contain two or more constants and/or variable names:

Separation of constants and variable names Each constant and/or variable name must be separated by an operational sign to indicate explicitly the desired computation. Arithmetic operations are never implied in FORTRAN. In usual mathematical notation, for example, to indicate "x times y," it is common to write:

$$xy$$

However, xy does not mean "X times Y" in FORTRAN. In fact, XY is not two variable names; but rather it is one variable name containing two valid characters. To indicate "X times Y" in FORTRAN, the programmer must write:

$$X*Y \text{ or } Y*X$$

Likewise, to indicate "12 times k" instead of the regular mathematical notation:

$$12k$$

either of the following notations may be used:

$$12*K \text{ or } K*12$$

Separation of arithmetic operators Two or more arithmetic operators never appear in the sequence in an arithmetic expression. To tell the computer to multiply "A times the negative value -12.5," for example, the expression *cannot* be written as follows:

$$A*-12.5$$

It is valid, however, to write:

$$A*(-12.5)$$

The preceding expression illustrates how parentheses can be used to separate arithmetic operators. Other uses of parentheses are discussed in a later rule.

To review briefly, the valid operators are:

Operator	Operation
+	Addition
−	Subtraction
/	Division
*	Multiplication
**	Exponentiation

Note that the two-symbol combination ** is *one* operator. The operators * and ** are readily distinguished since two operators may not be side by side.

Order of computation The computer evaluates some arithmetic expressions from left to right and others from right to left. The evaluation of more complex expressions may begin in about the middle, then go to the right, back to the left, back to the right again, etc. If the programmer avoids mixed mode *expressions* (discussed in the following section), it is not necessary to comprehend the intricate sequence of steps the computer actually goes through when evaluating a complex expression. It is only necessary to understand the effects of these steps, which are described next.

If an expression contains two or more arithmetic operators, computation is performed from left to right according to the hierarchy:

Hierarchy	Operation
1st	Parenthetical expression
2d	Exponentiation
3d	Multiplication and division
4th	Addition and subtraction

Observe that the hierarchy goes from what might be considered the most difficult to the least difficult.

The following elementary examples illustrate these hierarchical rules:

Example expressions	Evaluated the same as
A+B−C	(A+B)−C
A/B**C	A/(B**C)
(A+B)/C−(D)	((A+B)/C)−D
A−B*C+D	(A−(B*C))+D
−A+B	(−A)+B
−A/B	−(A/B)
−A+B**(C−D)	(−A)+(B**(C−D))

All operations in a given level of hierarchy are performed before going to the next lower level. To illustrate the effects of the steps taken in the evaluation of a longer arithmetic expression, consider the following:

$$A*B-C/D*7.00+G**2.$$

The computer would first scan the expression from left to right looking for parenthetical expressions. Finding none, it would return to the left.

Next, it would scan from left to right again until it gets to the exponential operator. It would then calculate G**2. If the result of this calculation is called "W," the expression will now appear as follows:

$$A*B-C/D*7.00+W$$

On the third scan, it would look for multiplication and division operators. As these are on the same level of hierarchy, it would handle each in order as they appear from left to right. First, A*B would be calculated (call the result "X"). Next, it would calculate C/D (call the result "Y"). Finally, it would calculate Y*7.00 (call the result "Z"). The expression would now look like this:

$$X-Z+W$$

On the final scan, Z would be subtracted from X and then the difference would be added to W. This would complete the evaluation.

The exact sequence of steps that the computer actually goes through, when evaluating an expression, is much more complex than the multiple scanning operation described above, but the net effect is identical. Since the exact order of computation does not take place in the manner indicated, it is important to stress again that to the programmer, only the result—not the internal operation of the computer—is relevant. This is one of the advantages of FORTRAN.

Use of parentheses Parentheses may be used to avoid two sequential operational signs, as already indicated. Parentheses may also be used to specify the order in which calculations are to be performed. In effect, they may be used to alter the lower three levels of hierarchy.

To illustrate the flexibility and convenience the use of parentheses provides, suppose the programmer desires to add A to B to C and then double the sum. Instead of writing the following series of statements:

```
|12345|6|7
    X=A*2.
    Y=B*2.
    Z=C*2.
    ANS=X+Y+Z
```

or one long statement such as:

4/Processing Numeric and Alphanumeric Data

|12345|6|7
ANS=A*2.+B*2.+C*2.

he could write:

|12345|6|7
ANS=(A+B+C)*2.

Because parenthetical expressions are evaluated first, the computer would first compute the sum, then multiply. This expression:

$$(A+B)**(7.5*C)$$

will cause the computer to first add, then multiply, and finally to exponentiate. Note that the use of parentheses, in effect, reversed the lower three levels of hierarchy.

Hierarchy always applies within a parenthetical expression. To illustrate:

$$A/(B+C*D)$$

The computer would first multiply C times D, then add the product to B. Finally, the sum of the latter calculation would be divided into A.

If "nested" parentheses are used, the innermost parenthetical expression is evaluated first. For example:

$$A=B+(C*(G-4.5))$$

The order of calculation would be: G−4.5 (call this "X"), C*X (call this "Y") and finally B+Y.

If beginning programmers have any doubt as to whether parentheses are required in a particular arithmetic expression, it is suggested they be used for clarity. The computer can handle unnecessary parentheses in a fraction of the time required to debug a program in which required parentheses are omitted.

Mixed mode expressions If the constants and the numeric values associated with variable names are not all integer, or all single-precision floating point, or all double-precision floating point, the expression is said to be in *mixed mode*.

Mixed mode expressions are not necessary and are not recommended; A*2.0 rather than A*2 is the preferred form. Most compilers will accept mixed mode expressions but some will not.[1] If the programmer keeps everything on the right side of the equal sign in the same mode, the expression will be acceptable to *any* modern FORTRAN compiler. Integers are stored in an entirely different way than

---
[1] One exception is always permitted and often recommended because it increases computer efficiency: floating point values can be raised to a fixed point power. Note, however, that it is invalid to raise integer values to a floating point power.

are floating point numbers; arithmetic operations cannot be performed unless an expression is consistent in mode. Compilers that allow mode mixing automatically handle the conversion, but this process takes time and can occasionally cause unexpected results.

Mixed mode statements

A mixed mode statement is one in which the variable name to the left of an equal sign and the arithmetic expression to the right are not in the same mode. Mixed mode *expressions* should be avoided, but mixed mode *statements* are not only permissible but are often required.

To illustrate, assume that a routine to compute the dollars and cents VALUE of a particular class of inventory (number of ITEMS times unit price) is to be added to an existing program. Further assume that the existing program has already stored the number of ITEMS in integer mode, but the unit price of $9.25 has not been stored so it must be written into the program as a constant. If a mixed mode expression is to be avoided, the following statement cannot be used because it contains an integer variable name and a floating point constant:

```
|12345|6|7
       VALUE=ITEMS*9.25
```

The programmer can, however, use the following statements:

```
|12345|6|7
       UNITS=ITEMS
       VALUE=UNITS*9.25
```

The first statement will cause the computer to convert the integer value, stored at ITEMS, to floating point mode and then store it at UNITS. The second statement completes the routine and solves the problem without using a mixed mode expression.

Mixed mode statements are sometimes required but are sometimes optional. For example, the integer value 257 could be stored at NUMBER by either of the following two arithmetic statements:

```
|12345|6|7
       NUMBER=257
```

or

```
|12345|6|7
       NUMBER=257.00
```

The latter example above is a mixed mode statement that requires extra machine-language instructions to be generated by the compiler because the floating point constant must be converted to integer mode before it is stored. It therefore requires a larger storage area for the object program as well as more compilation and execution time.

Truncation of decimal fractions

In an arithmetic statement, the mode of the variable names and/or constants to the right of the equal sign determines the mode in which the expression will be evaluated. The mode of the variable name to the left of the equal sign governs the mode in which the results of the expression evaluated will be stored. The idea may be illustrated in this manner:

Answer mode = Arithmetic mode

Caution must be exercised with mixed mode statements or the computer may not furnish the desired results. To illustrate what can happen, assume that the following series of statements are executed sequentially in an attempt to determine the exact amount of interest on a one-year bank loan (interest equals principal times annual rate):

```
|12345|6|7
      PRINC=3500.00
      RATE=.0725
      INT=PRINC*RATE
```

The first two statements establish the current value of PRINC and RATE. The expression in the last statement is evaluated in floating point mode; and the result, in this case, is 253.75. However, when this result is converted to integer mode and stored at INT, the decimal fraction is truncated (dropped without rounding) and only the integer 253 is stored at INT. If the floating point variable name ZINT had been used, instead of the integer variable name INT, the entire amount would have been retained.

To illustrate further, assume that the following arithmetic statements are executed in the order in which they appear:

```
|12345|6|7
    1   I=5
    2   J=4
    3   K=I/J
    4   X=I/J
```

When statement number 3 is evaluated, the result will be the integer value 1 which will be stored at K. (Remember, results of integer arithmetic are always integer; if floating point variable names had been used, the result would have been 1.25.) The result of the evaluation of statement number 4 will also be 1, but it will be converted to the floating point value 1.0 before it is stored at X.

Integer expressions with division operators should always be given special attention. For example, assume J = 5, K = 3, and M = 2. The expression K*J/M will not necessarily yield the same results as K*(J/M). For example, 3*5/2=7 but 3*(5/2)=6.

Now consider the following series of arithmetic statements:

```
|12345|6|7
    1   R=5
    2   S=4
    3   T=R/S
    4   L=R/S
```

When statement number 3 is executed, the expression R/S will be evaluated as 1.25; and this value will then be stored at T. The evaluation of the expression in statement number 4 will be the same, but the fraction .25 will be truncated and only the integer 1 will be stored at L.

Programmers should be aware that fractional portions can be lost in two ways: first, if the computer is told to store a floating point value at a location identified by an integer variable name, and second, if it is told to evaluate an arithmetic expression in integer mode.

As previously indicated, the equal sign does not have the same meaning in FORTRAN as it does in regular algebraic notation. The following two statements emphasize this difference:

```
|12345|6|7
        N=2
        N=N+1
```

The first statement tells the computer to store 2 at N. The second statement is obviously not correct algebraically, but it is a valid FORTRAN statement. It tells the computer to add 1 to the current value of N and then to store the sum at N. Following execution of both statements, N will have a current value of 3.

Implicit specification statements

Numeric data fields are implied to contain integer or floating point data according to the first letter of the assigned variable name, as previously explained. This is a convention of FORTRAN called *implicit definition of mode*.

The purpose of implicit specification statements is to allow the programmer the option to override the implied mode of variable names. Three types of implicit specification statements are described and illustrated in the following sections.

Implicit specification statements should be located near the beginning of the program before any executable statements.

The INTEGER statement This statement allows the programmer the option of starting an integer variable name with a letter other than I through N because it overrides the implicit definition of mode. One INTEGER statement may be used to specify the mode of one or more variable names.

The general form of this statement is:

```
|12345|6|7
 nnnnn   INTEGER vn₁, . . . vnₘ
```

Legend:	
nnnnn	Any unique one- to five-digit integer that specifies the statement number. It is never required because this statement should not be referenced by another statement in the program. It may be used at the programmer's option.
INTEGER	A keyword specifying the type of statement.
$vn_1, \ldots vn_m$	One or more variable names, separated by commas, that are specified by this statement as integer mode. The variable names may appear in any sequence. If only one variable name is included in the statement, it should not be followed by a comma.

To illustrate, the following statement specifies APPLES, GRAPES, PEARS, and PLUMS as integer mode variable names:

```
|12345|6|7
   831   INTEGER   APPLES,GRAPES,PEARS,PLUMS
```

This statement can be convenient to the programmer because it permits the use of more descriptive variable names in some cases. Assume, for example, that the program is designed to compute the number of units in an inventory and that the input data are in integer mode. The variable names in the preceding statement are more descriptive than NUMAPS, NUMGPS, NUMPRS, and NUMPLS.

This technique for changing floating point variable names to integer mode should be used with caution and only when it provides a convenience. It can increase the time required to write and debug a program. It is obviously more convenient to assign an integer code the variable name KODE than to assign the variable name CODE and then write a specification statement to convert it back to integer mode. It can also be confusing, particularly in a program containing many statements, if several floating point variable names are converted and others are not.

The REAL statement This statement can be used to convert one or more integer variable names that begin with one of the letters I through N to single-precision floating point (*real*) mode.

The general form of this statement is:

```
|12345|6|7
   nnnnn   REAL   vn₁,vn₂, . . . vnₘ
```

Legend:	
nnnnn	Any unique unsigned integer that specifies the statement number. It is never required because this statement should not be referenced by another statement in the program. It may be used at the programmer's option.
REAL	A keyword that specifies the type of statement.
$vn_1, \ldots vn_m$	One or more variable names, separated by commas, which this statement specifies as real mode. The variable names may appear in any sequence. If only one variable name is included in the statement, it should not be followed by a comma.

To illustrate, the following statement specifies NETPAY and MONEY as floating point (real) variable names:

```
|12345|6|7
   822   REAL NETPAY,MONEY
```

This statement, like the INTEGER statement, can be convenient to the programmer because it also permits him or her to use more descriptive variable names in some cases. But this technique should also be used with caution and only when it actually provides a convenience. The variable name PAYNET, for example, is probably as descriptive as NETPAY, used in the preceding statement illustration.

This statement, as well as the INTEGER statement, can often be of great convenience at debugging time. Suppose, for example, a programmer had consistently used the variable name NETPAY in several statements in a payroll problem. It can only accommodate whole numbers and will drop the cents in the payroll computations because it is an integer variable name. Rather than change every statement where the variable name NETPAY appears, it may be much more convenient to prepare one specification statement to convert NETPAY to real mode.

The DOUBLE PRECISION statement This statement can be used to convert one or more integer or real variable names to double-precision floating point mode.

The general form is:

```
|12345|6|7
   nnnnn   DOUBLE PRECISION vn₁,vn₂, . . . vnₘ
```

Legend:

nnnnn	Any unique one- to five-digit integer that specifies the statement number. It is never required because this statement should not be referenced by another statement in the program. It may be used at the programmer's option.
DOUBLE PRECISION	A keyword specifying the type of statement.
vn₁, . . . vnₘ	One or more variable names, separated by commas, which this statement specifies as double-precision. If only one variable name is included in the statement, it should not be followed by a comma.

To illustrate, the following statement specifies NUMBER, DOUBLE, and ARRAY to be in double-precision mode:

```
|12345|6|7
   823   DOUBLE PRECISION NUMBER,DOUBLE,ARRAY
```

The specific effect of a DOUBLE PRECISION statement depends upon the make and model of computer. In general, it more than doubles the number of significant digits that can be stored.

4/Processing Numeric and Alphanumeric Data

Initialization of variable names

The computer "knows" the value of each constant because it is told directly by the arithmetic statement in which it appears. But how does the computer know the value of variable names? It doesn't, unless it has been told either by the statement being executed or by some previous statement.

It should be obvious that unless the computer knows the value of J and K it is impossible to solve the following arithmetic statement:

```
|12345|6|7
      I=(J+K)**2
```

There are three ways to set up or *initialize* the values of variable names.

One is by an input statement. For example, a data record may contain the numeral 3 in the first column and the numeral 5 in the second column. Then, by initially reading the record:

```
|12345|6|7
      READ(1,100)J,K
100   FORMAT(I1,I1)
```

3 is set into J and 5 is set into K. This initialization method is fully described in the next chapter.

The other two ways to initialize, described in this section, are by means of an assignment statement or by means of a DATA statement.

Initialization using an arithmetic assignment statement The following series of statements shows how variable names can be initialized by arithmetic statements:

```
|12345|6|7
   1  J=3
   2  K=5
   3  I=(J+K)**2
```

In the above illustration, statement number 1 establishes the initial value of J as 3; statement number 2 initializes K to the value of 5. The numeric value 64, resulting from the evaluation of the arithmetic expression in statement number 3, is stored at the variable name to the left of the equal sign, thus initializing I. Statement number 2 could precede 1, but obviously both must precede 3.

Initialization of variables is a very important concept to comprehend. The term *garbage* is used to describe the contents of an uninitialized variable name. Any variable names in an arithmetic *expression* must have had values stored in them by a previous statement. What will happen if one or more variable names include garbage? There will be a surprise at program execution time!

The position to the left of an equal sign in an arithmetic statement may be the first place that a variable name appears in a program. Programmers should not become so distracted by statement logic that they forget the importance of variable name composition. Names should be as self-documenting as possible. Good descriptors need less supplemental documentation, make the program easier for *people* to read, and reduce the probability of error.

Full names, when possible, are better than abbreviations. If OUNCES is accidentally misspelled, a casual reading of the program will probably detect it. But if it is abbreviated OZ in one place and OZS in two other places in the same program, the error may be difficult to find. Also, there is always the possibility that OZS will be keyed as zero-two-five because of the look-alike characters. Identifiers such as OZS (ounces) and MOD1S5 (module one, subtotal five) should be avoided.

TONS and POUNDS are preferable to T and P, which require extra documentation. One problem with programs that include excessive comments is that readers tend to believe the comments rather than the statements, which may not say what the programmer intended. Comments should be used as a supplement to, but not as a substitute for, well-chosen mnemonic (aid to memory) names. Poor names do not improve with age. Names that are not mnemonic convey no information.

Preferably, names should differ widely; similarities hamper understanding and invite errors. XSQ and XCUBE are preferable to XX and XXX. If long names vary by only one letter, the difference will show up better at the beginning than at the end. Use XVALUE and YVALUE rather than VALUEX and VALUEY; misspellings are less likely to be disguised.

Well-chosen names are of particular importance in long arithmetic statements; they may be complex enough without making it harder for the reader by using obscure code. Good programs communicate to *people* as well as to computers.

Initialization using a DATA statement One method of initializing a variable, using an arithmetic statement, was covered in the preceding section. A second method is by use of a DATA statement.

The general form of a DATA statement is:

|12345|6|7
nnnnn   DATA $vn_1/c_1/,vn_2/c_2/, \ldots vn_m/c_m/$

Legend:

nnnnn	Any unique one- to five-digit integer that specifies the statement *number*. It may be used at the programmer's option but is never required because this statement should not be referenced in the program.
DATA	A keyword specifying the type of statement.
vn	A *variable name* indicating the location where data is to be stored.
/	Required delimiter.
,	Required delimiter.
c	Any constant which may be preceded by $r*$, where r is an integer constant indicating the number of times the constant is to be *repeated*.

4 / Processing Numeric and Alphanumeric Data

To illustrate, the following statement will initialize the variables X and N to 5.2 and 3 respectively:

```
|12345|6|7
      DATA   X/5.2/,N/3/
```

At the programmer's option, a string of variables may precede a string of related constants. The following statement, for example, will have the same effect as the preceding illustration:

```
|12345|6|7
      DATA   X,N/5.2,3/
```

The repeat feature is convenient for initializing a list of variables to the same value. To illustrate, the following two statements each do the same job: they initialize four variables to zero.

```
|12345|6|7
      DATA   A,B,C,D/0.0,0.0,0.0,0.0/
      DATA   A,B,C,D/4*0.0/
```

It is important to realize that DATA statements initialize variables during *compilation,* never during execution. Stated another way, a DATA statement can initialize a variable only once; it may be used to specify beginning values but it cannot change values during execution of a program because a DATA statement is nonexecutable. Either of these statements may be used to initialize KOUNT to zero:

```
|12345|6|7                                     |12345|6|7
      DATA   KOUNT/0/          or                     KOUNT=0
```

However, only the arithmetic statement can be used to *reset* KOUNT back to zero after it has been changed during execution of the program.

Helpful coding hints

The compiler ignores embedded blanks in key words and in variable names because a blank is not a delimiter. Likewise, blanks separating variable names, constants, codes, and delimiters are also ignored by the compiler. Thus, each of the following three statements would be interpreted in the same manner by the compiler (the last two lines are continuations of statement number 44):

```
|12345|6|7
   22  N=KK
   33  N = KK
   44  N
     $ =K
     $K
```

Although one or more blanks separating the various elements of a statement are always permissible, they are never required. The omission of unnecessary blanks obviously permits longer statements to be written in one record and is thus a convenience to both the programmer and the keyboard operator. For this reason, most programmers develop the habit of avoiding unnecessary blanks.

Statement number 44 (above) is our first illustration of a continuation character, so it deserves extra comment. Any standard character, except the zero or blank, is a valid continuation character. The dollar sign was used for two reasons: (1) it attracts the reader's eye and (2) it minimizes the chance of confusion because it is the only ANSI character that has no other syntactic meaning.

The above illustration was designed to illustrate two additional points. Because it was unnecessarily continued, statement number 44 lacks clarity. Statements should not be continued without good reason. Furthermore, if they are continued, they should be divided *between* elements. Coding part of the variable name KK on one line and part on the next is poor practice.

Basic numeric output

This section is intended to provide the minimum information necessary to write output statements for this chapter's programming problems. The next chapter covers output in more depth.

Two statements are required to transmit numeric values from internal storage to a printed output page. The executable statement that tells the computer what to do is called a WRITE statement. It was previously discussed and illustrated in sufficient detail for the reader to solve the elementary applications required for this chapter's programming problems. The statement that describes the written output record is called a FORMAT statement. It needs further explanation at this point.

The nonexecutable statement starts with the keyword FORMAT, which is followed by two or more codes separated by commas and enclosed in parentheses. Because this statement is designed to be referenced, it should always be numbered. An example is:

```
|12345|6|7
    44   FORMAT(1X,I5,12X,F6.2)
```

The computer will interpret the first code (1X) to be a *line control character*; that is, it controls vertical line spacing. The code 1X specifies a blank character which causes single-spacing. It is unnecessary to be concerned with details at this point—there are other valid line control characters, but 1X will do the job.

The code or codes following 1X may vary according to the record being described. In the preceding illustration, I5 specifies that the first field will hold an integer up to five characters in length.

X is called the *skip code* or *blank code*, so 12X specifies there is to be no printing in the 12 positions following the I5 field.

Just as the letter I is a mnemonic or acronym for interger, F indicates floating point. The code F6.2 describes a six-position field that will accept an ordinary decimal form number with two decimal posi-

4/Processing Numeric and Alphanumeric Data

tions. Note that the decimal point takes one of the six field positions, so 999.99 is the largest value that can be printed in an F6.2 field. Likewise, 9.999 or −.123 or .000 could be printed in an F5.3 field.

PROCESSING ALPHANUMERIC DATA

When numeric data are stored, the type may be implied by the first letter of the variable name or it may be declared by a specification statement such as INTEGER or REAL as previously described. On the other hand, when storing alphanumeric data (which may include *any* FORTRAN character) the type cannot be implied by the first letter of the variable name. The type may be specified, however, by a CHARACTER statement.

CHARACTER statement

The CHARACTER statement declares that a variable name is to be used to store alphanumeric data—i.e., *any* valid FORTRAN characters. It also declares the maximum length of the character string.

General form   The general form of a CHARACTER statement is:

```
|12345|6|7
 nnnnn    CHARACTER vn₁*len₁,vn₂*len₂, . . . vnₘ*lenₘ
```

Legend:

nnnnn	Any unique one- to five-digit integer *number* that specifies the statement label. It is never required because this statement should not be referenced by other statements in the program.
CHARACTER	A keyword that specifies the type of statement.
vn	A *variable name* which this statement specifies will be used for storing alphanumeric data.
*	A required delimiter or separator following the integer variable name.
len	An unsigned, nonzero integer constant that specifies the character string *length*—i.e., the number of alphanumeric character positions established for the associated variable name.

Suppose we have a list of names and have determined that the longest is 20 characters. Near the beginning of the program that will process these names, we include the following specification statement:

```
|12345|6|7
         CHARACTER NAME*20
```

If we have several alphanumeric variables of different lengths, we might use several CHARACTER statements or, alternatively, one with several specifications:

```
|12345|6|7
         CHARACTER NAME*20,ADDRES*28,CITY*20,
    $    STATE*2,ZIP*9
```

The CHARACTER statement specifies the length of the character string that can be stored and the variable name where it can be stored. But this statement does not cause any data to be stored—it merely says how much and where it can be stored.

There are three ways to set up, or *initialize,* the contents of variable names. One is by an input statement. For example, a data record may contain a name—e.g., JANE DOE (7 letters and a blank)—in the first 8 positions and an address such as 4212 GUILDFORD COURT in the next 20 positions. Then by initially reading the record:

```
|12345|6|7
          READ(1,100)NAME, ADDRES
    100   FORMAT(A8,A20)
```

JANE DOE is stored at NAME and 4212 GUILDFORD COURT is stored at ADDRES. This initialization method is fully described in the next chapter.

The other two ways to initialize, described in this section, are by using an assignment statement or by using a DATA statement.

Initialization using an alphanumeric assignment statement

An alphanumeric assignment statement differs from an arithmetic assignment statement (previously described) only in the type of expression.

General form The general form of an alphanumeric assignment statement is:

```
|12345|6|7
  nnnnn   vn=e
```
Legend:
nnnnn	Any unique one- to five-digit integer *number* that specifies the statement label. It is required only if this statement is referenced by another statement within the program.
vn	A *variable name* previously specified to be used for storing alphanumeric data.
e	An alphanumeric character *expression*—i.e., an alphanumeric constant (sometimes called a *literal*). It is permissible for vn and e to be of different lengths; if so, e is stored left justified with any excess characters truncated (ignored) or with blanks substituted as necessary to match the length of vn.

Suppose we have declared one alphanumeric variable name to have a capacity to accommodate a four-character string and two others to have a capacity of three and five respectively. Further, suppose we have a series of assignment statements with alphanumeric expressions of different types and lengths. The sequential execution of these assignment statements will have the effects illustrated below:

4/Processing Numeric and Alphanumeric Data

```
|12345|6|7
       CHARACTER DEPT*4,B*3,C*5
       DEPT='ART'
       DEPT='MATH'
       DEPT='HISTORY'
       C=DEPT
       B=C
       C=B
```

e stored at vn as:

A	R	T	

M	A	T	H

H	I	S	T

H	I	S	T	

H	I	S

H	I	S	

Initialization using a DATA statement

The DATA statement may be used to provide, at *compilation* time, an initial value to *any* type of variable name. The DATA statement that follows the CHARACTER specification statement below initializes two alphanumeric variables:

```
|12345|6|7
       CHARACTER STAR*1,CONAME*9
       DATA STAR/'*'/,CONAME/'ABC, INC.'/
```

Basic alphanumeric output

This section is intended to provide the minimum information necessary to write alphanumeric output for this chapter's programming problems. The next chapter covers output in more depth.

Two statements are required to transmit alphanumeric values from internal storage to a printed output page. The executable statement that tells the computer what to do is called the WRITE statement; the nonexecutable statement that describes the written record is called a FORMAT statement. Both statements have previously been described and illustrated using numeric output examples. This section includes the minimum information necessary to solve this chapter's programming problems that include alphanumeric output.

Just as the letters *I* and *F* are acronyms for integer and floating point respectively, *A* indicates alphanumeric. Thus, A12 is the format code to describe a 12-position alphanumeric field.

Assume the following FORMAT statement describes an output record:

```
|12345|6|7
   100 FORMAT(1X,A3,2X,A1,2X,A3)
```

The computer will interpret the first code (1X) to be a *line control character* which, in this case, specifies single-spacing. The remaining codes describe the output record which begins with a 3-position alphanumeric field (A3) followed by a two-position blank field (2X), a one-position alphanumeric field (A1), another two-position blank field (2X), and another three-position alphanumeric field (A3).

The following partial program, which includes the preceding FORMAT statement, provides a more complete illustration from initialization through output:

```
|12345|6|7
      CHARACTER COLOR*3,SIX*1
      DATA COLOR/'RED'/
      SIX='6'
      WRITE(3,100)COLOR,SIX,COLOR
  100 FORMAT(1X,A3,2X,A1,2X,A3)
```

Output from the above partial program will be:

```
| 1 2 3 4 5 | 6 | 7 8 9
  R E D       6     R E D
```

Note that the numeral 6, in the preceding example, is an alphanumeric character. It is available for output but it cannot be mathematically processed.

ORDER OF STATEMENTS AND COMMENT LINES

The PROGRAM and the END should be the first and last statements, respectively, in any program. Between these two statements, comment lines and/or FORMAT statements may appear almost anywhere within the program. However, implicit specification statements should precede DATA statements, and both should precede all executable statements.

An acceptable order for comments, and for all statements shown thus far in this book, is presented below:

PROGRAM statement	
Comment lines and/or FORMAT statements	Implicit statements (INTEGER, REAL, DOUBLE PRECISION, and CHARACTER)
	DATA statements
	OPEN statements
	Executable statements (input/output, assignment, and control) sequenced as per programming logic
END statement	

REVIEW QUESTIONS

1. Arithmetic statements are sometimes called *replacement statements*. Why?

4/Processing Numeric and Alphanumeric Data

2. Name the three main parts of any arithmetic statement.

3. Compare the mathematical meaning of the equal sign to the FORTRAN meaning.

4. Distinguish between an arithmetic statement and an arithmetic expression.

5. "In arithmetic statements, most delimiters serve a dual purpose." Explain.

6. What is the normal order of hierarchy for arithmetic operations?

7. What are the major uses of parentheses?

8. What is a mixed mode expression? Why should it be avoided?

9. The statement K=2*J+3*N includes three variables and two constants. Which of these five elements should have been *initialized* by a previous statement?

10. When the curious expression N−N/2*2 is evaluated, the result may be useful in some advanced programming applications. Do not be concerned with how this result is used but describe, in general terms, what it can indicate.

EXERCISES

1. Are the following valid *arithmetic expressions*? On a separate sheet identify those that are valid as either integer or floating point expressions. Assume that mixed mode expressions are invalid. Rewrite all invalid expressions correctly.

- a. LENGTH*WIDTH*.8
- b. +698
- c. ABLE*BAKER
- d. VALUE*10%
- e. $ALARY
- f. BASE*HEIGHT/2
- g. B+(M−4)*2
- h. A²+B²
- i. A**12.
- j. 12.**A
- k. M(−K)
- l. 3N+8
- m. 2.E+6**X
- n. K+−L
- o. X**Y
- p. R*π*2.
- q. COUNT+1
- r. PRINC*RATE*(DAYS/365)
- s. N+
- t. N+2
- u. 2+N
- v. −2+2
- w. N+N
- x. (X+Y)−(A+B)
- y. [J+(L−2)]*M

2. On a separate sheet indicate whether the following *arithmetic statements* are valid or invalid. All valid variable names represent integer or single-precision values. If the statement is invalid, rewrite it correctly. Assume that mixed mode *expressions* are invalid.

a. ITEMS=KTVS+JTVS+IRONS
b. KOUNT=KOUNT+1
c. 567=569−2
d. PAYNET=GROSS−DED ' NS
e. INTREST=PRT
f. SQROOT=N**.5
g. AREA=PI*RADIUS**2
h. PHD=MA+TWOYRS
i. MEAN=TOTAL/N
j. ASSETS+LIAB=NETWORTH
k. VOLTS=E
l. ANSWER=(A−1)*(A−2)
m. I=J(K*L−M)
n. AMOUNT=$585.50
o. THREE=2.
p. X=A−(B+(C/D)**2.
q. A+B
r. PAY=HOURS*RATE
s. PI=5.141593
t. ANS=X*.12E−5
u. I=3N
v. UNITS=NUNITS
w. XCUBE=X***3.
x. SUMX=X1+X2+X3
y. SUMXSQ=X1**2+X2**2+X3**2

3. On a separate sheet evaluate each arithmetic expression and indicate the numeric value that would be stored at the variable name to the left of the equal sign when the following arithmetic statements are executed:

a. A=2.0*3.0−1.5
b. I=(2.0*3.0)−1.5
c. B=2.0*(3.0−1.5)
d. J=(2.0*(3.0−1.5))
e. C=(2.0+(3.0)*1.5)
f. K=(2.0)+(3.0+1.5)
g. D=(2.0+3.0)*1.5
h. E=5/2*3**2
i. N=2*((2+2*3/2)+4)
j. F=9/2−3+2**2

4. On a separate sheet write the equivalent FORTRAN arithmetic statement for each of the following algebraic equations. Avoid mixed mode expressions. Include parentheses only if required.

a. $CSQ = ASQ + BSQ$
b. $M = 4N + 3K$
c. $A = \dfrac{\pi R^2 H}{3}$
d. $7 + \dfrac{Y}{3} X = T$
e. $X = \dfrac{Y}{B+3}$
f. $Y = \dfrac{5+X}{A-B}$
g. $R = \left(\dfrac{B}{2} + 7\right)^A$
h. $S = \left(\dfrac{3X}{2Y}\right)^{R+2}$
i. $T = \dfrac{1}{3}\left(\dfrac{7X}{B-3}\right)$
j. $A = \sqrt{B^2 + C^2}$

5. What is the current value of ANS following execution of this series of statements?

X=5
Y=4
Z=7.2
ANS=(X+Y)*Y−(Z/Y)

6. Examine the series of statements below. Indicate the specific contents of the variable name, to the left of the equal sign, after each of the assignment statements is executed.

CHARACTER A*2,B*2,C*2,D*3,G*4
A='12'
B='123'
C='AB'
D=A
E=75.00
F=E
G=' THE END '

PROBLEMS

1. Following is the program that has previously been illustrated. Change the illustrative program so that the variables KTVS, JTVS, and IRONS are initialized to 150, 50, and 9900 respectively, by arithmetic statements rather than by the READ statement. That is, delete the READ, the associated FORMAT, and the input data record. Replace these deletions with appropriate arithmetic statements.

```
      PROGRAM STOCK
      OPEN(5,FILE='INPUT')
      OPEN(6,FILE='OUTPUT')
C     WRITTEN BY O. R. WELL, 8/11/84
C     READ UNITS EACH INVENTORY TYPE,
C        CALCULATE SUM, PRINT INPUT
C        UNITS AND SUM.  STOP AFTER
C        PROCESSING ONE RECORD.
C     DICTIONARY OF VARIABLE NAMES
C        IRONS - STEAM IRONS
C        ITEMS - SUM OF INVENTORY ITEMS
C        JTVS  - JON BRAND TV SETS
C        KTVS  - KAY BRAND TV SETS
C***********************************
    1 FORMAT(I3,I2,I4)
      READ(5,1)KTVS,JTVS,IRONS
C
      ITEMS=KTVS+JTVS+IRONS
C
    2 FORMAT(1X,I2,3X,I3,3X,I4,3X,I5)
      WRITE(6,2)JTVS,KTVS,IRONS,ITEMS
C
      STOP
      END
```

2. Write a program to compute the gross pay (in dollars and cents) for one employee. No input data record is to be used. Instead, enter the following values into the program by using arithmetic statements.

$$\text{Time} = 39.25 \text{ hours}$$
$$\text{Rate} = \$12.30 \text{ per hour}$$

Required output is one printed line containing a gross pay, time, and rate. Each output field is to be separated by two or more blank spaces.

3. Write a program to determine the interest and maturity value of a promissory note (in dollars and cents) where:

$$\text{Interest} = \text{PRT}/360$$
$$\text{Maturity Value} = \text{Principal} + \text{Interest}$$

Instead of using an input card, enter all required values into the program as constants.

$$\text{Principal} = \$690.00$$
$$\text{Rate} = 16\tfrac{1}{4}\%$$
$$\text{Time} = 45 \text{ days}$$

Required output is one printed line containing principal, rate, time, interest, and maturity value. Each output field is to be separated by two or more blank spaces.

4. Write a program to compute the capacity in gallons of a cylinder where:

$$\text{Gallons} = \frac{\pi R^2 H}{231}$$

Do not use an input record; enter all required values into the program by using arithmetic statements.

$$\text{Pi} = 3.1416$$
$$\text{Radius} = 2\tfrac{1}{2} \text{ inches}$$
$$\text{Height} = 25 \text{ inches}$$

Required output is one printed line containing pi, radius, height, and gallons. Each output field is to be separated by two or more blank spaces.

5. Write the program described in Problem 4, but change the output so that it is single spaced with the value of: (1) pi printed on the first line, (2) radius and height on the second line, and (3) gallons on the third line.

6. Write a program to compute the ending balance in a savings account where $285.00 is the beginning balance; $1,715.00 is the amount deposited; and $999.95 is the amount withdrawn during the period.

Do not use an input record; enter all required numeric values into the program by using one DATA statement.

Required output is one printed line containing the ending balance amount preceded by this "message":

THE ENDING BALANCE IS $

4 / Processing Numeric and Alphanumeric Data

Enter this "message" into the program by using an alphanumeric assignment statement.

7. Write a program to calculate the number of different seating arrangements that are possible with eight people and eight chairs; that is, solve for eight factorial (8!).

There is no factorial character (!) in FORTRAN. So, based on the materials presented thus far in this book, we must solve the problem by repeated multiplication (use integer arithmetic):

$$8! = 1 \cdot 2 \cdot 3 \cdot 4 \cdot 5 \cdot 6 \cdot 7 \cdot 8$$

Your program is to generate *three* output lines. The first should be your name (initialize a variable using a DATA statement). The second should be the "message":

8 FACTORIAL PROBLEM

(initialize a variable using an assignment statement). The third line should be the computed value of eight factorial.

5

Input and Output

Previous chapters introduced basic procedures for getting data into and out of the computer. The READ, WRITE, and FORMAT statements, as well as the I (integer), F (floating point), and X (skip) codes, have been explained and included in several programming problems. This chapter reviews basic input/output (I/O) procedures and introduces more advanced considerations.

The computer must be supplied not only with the *statements* required to solve the particular problem but also with the specific *data* to be processed when these statements are executed. It is often possible, but not necessarily convenient, to supply all data directly in the program by DATA statements and/or assignment statements. When this method is used, the program might be called self-operational because the program supplies the data as well as the instructions to process them. But many programs require that the data be supplied from one or more records that are not a part of the program. The input section of this chapter explains and illustrates the statements used to describe and read data from input records.

After the data have been processed and the computed results have been internally stored, these results must be returned to the programmer in an acceptable form. The output section of this chapter explains and illustrates the statements required to accomplish this task.

INPUT

Input statements are used to transmit data from an input device into computer storage. Many types of input devices, including magnetic tape drives, magnetic disk drives, punched card readers, and remote terminals, may be used for transmission.

For ease and clarity of presentation, attention in this chapter will center on punched card input and on printed output. The basic concepts apply to other types of input/output devices including remote terminals.

Data record input

Each unit of input, such as a card, is sometimes called a record. Because an input record contains data to be processed, it is often called

5 / Input and Output

a *data record*. A group of related data records is called a file. Each data record is divided into fields containing one or more columns of information. The form of numeric information in a data record is similar to that of constants in a FORTRAN *statement record* (line). If the data are composed of only one or more decimal digits, they are in integer form; if they are composed of only one or more decimal digits and a decimal point, they are in ordinary decimal form; if they are composed of only a fraction, the letter D or E, and an exponent, they are in exponential form. As in the case of constants, high-order signs are optional and embedded commas are prohibited.

It is important to distinguish between *input data records*, which are read at execution time, and *program statement lines*, which are read at compilation time and then translated into instructions that are processed during execution time (See Figure 5-1). The exact format required for all statement lines, as described in Chapter 3, is specified by the rules of FORTRAN and cannot be changed by the programmer. If a statement is not written in prescribed form, it is invalid. The programmer does not describe statement lines to the computer because the format is implied.

Figure 5-1
Statement card and illustrative data card

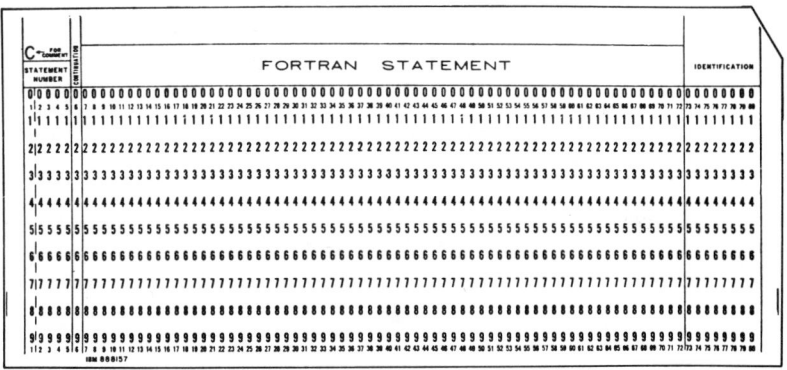

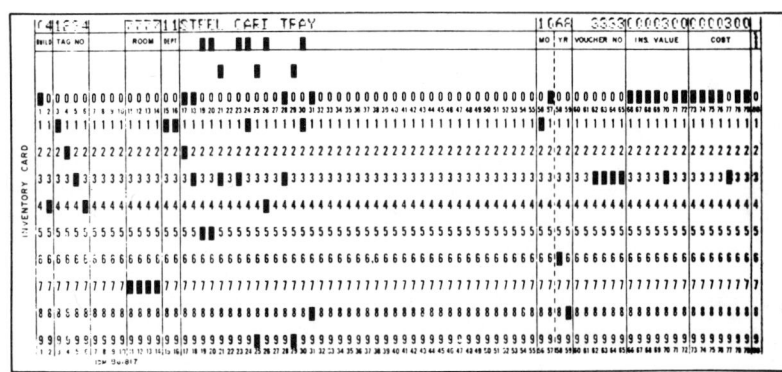

On the other hand, there are no rules restricting the format of *data records*. The number and sequence of fields and the type of data punched in each field are designed to fit the requirements of the problem and the convenience of the programmer and/or keyboard operator. Any or all of the record columns may be used. Because the data record format is optional, it cannot be implied. It must be explicitly described to the computer by means of FORMAT statement.

The FORMAT statement

A FORMAT statement is nonexecutable. Its purpose is to tell the computer where and how data will be found in a data record. It explicitly describes each data field as to type, size, and location. FORMAT statements may appear almost anywhere in the source program, but most programmers develop the habit of placing them all together either at the beginning or end of the program or of placing each immediately preceding or following the I/O statement by which they are referenced.

The general form of a FORMAT statement is:

```
|12345|6|7
 nnnnn    FORMAT(c₁,c₂,c₃, . . . cₘ)
```

Legend:

nnnnn   Any unique one- to five-digit integer that specifies the statement *number*. It is required so that this statement may be referenced by an I/O statement.

FORMAT   A keyword that identifies the type of statement.

$c_1, \ldots c_m$ Indicates one or more format *codes* that must be contained within parentheses and ordinarily separated by commas. These codes serve as field descriptors. The sequence in which they appear must correspond to the sequence of the fields on the data records that they describe. The code specifies the type of data contained in the field, the length of the field in columns, and the position of the decimal point, if any. It may also specify that a field is to be ignored.

Several of the available "edit descriptor" format codes used to describe input data are illustrated and discussed in the following sections.

Integer format code   The code used to describe an integer data field is:

$$rIl$$

Legend:

r   An integer number that specifies the number of times the format code is to be *repeated*. It is optional with the programmer and is omitted if the code is used only once.

I   Specifies that the field contains *integer* data.

l   An integer number that indicates the *length* of the field in record columns.

To illustrate, the following four-field data card:

```
|123|456| 78|9  |
|+12|913| -7| 78|
```

could be described either as:

```
|12345|6|7
```
        FORMAT(I3,I3,I2,I3)

or as:

```
|12345|6|7
```
        FORMAT(2I3,I2,I3)

Note that the preceding data card contains three I3 fields but cannot be described as 3I3 because the format codes must appear in the same sequence as the card fields. Note also that the FORMAT statement specifies the contents of only the first 11 columns. Any data punched in columns 12 through 80 will be ignored. It is permissible to describe a card as containing fewer than 80 columns, but in no case can it be described as containing more than 80.

It is not uncommon for records to contain, in sequence, several identical fields or groups of fields. Of course, the more identical fields that appear in sequence, the more convenient it is to use the repeat specification; it is obviously more convenient to indicate 10I4 than to repeat I4 10 times. Likewise, it is generally convenient to enclose identical *groups* of format codes within parentheses and precede the group by an integer that indicates the number of times the group is to be repeated. The following two statements, for example, are equivalent:

```
|12345|6|7
```
    77   FORMAT(I3,I4,I3,I4,I5)
    88   FORMAT(2(I3,I4),I5)

More than one parenthetical group may be indicated within a FORMAT statement, but parenthetical groups within parenthetical groups are not permitted. Thus, the following statement is *invalid*:

```
|12345|6|7
```
    66   FORMAT(2(I3,4(I2,I5)))

Floating point format codes There are two basic types of floating point data—ordinary decimal form and exponential form. The format codes are different, so each will be discussed separately.

Ordinary decimal form The code to describe floating point (real) fields that contain ordinary decimal form data is:

rFl.d

Legend:

r   An integer that specifies the number of times the format code is to be *repeated*. It is optional with the programmer and is omitted if the code is used only once.

F   Specifies that the field contains *floating point* data in ordinary decimal form.

l   An integer number that indicates the *length* of the data field in record columns.

.d   A decimal point followed by an integer that specifies the number of *decimal point positions*. If the input field contains a decimal point, this specification is ignored by the compiler; but it cannot be omitted by the programmer.

To review integer format codes and also to illustrate floating point format codes, consider the following six-field data card:

```
|12|3456| 78|9   |    |
 27|+2.7|+8|2.12|-.12|257.567
```

The FORMAT statement to describe the above card could be either:

```
|12345|6|7
      FORMAT(I2,F4.1,I2,F4.2,F4.2,F7.3)
```

or the two contiguous F4.2 fields (the fourth and fifth) could be coded as 2F4.2 at the programmer's option.

Chapter 3 called attention to the rule that *constants* written in ordinary decimal form *must* contain a decimal point. This rule for *constants* written in a FORTRAN statement does not apply to decimal *data* entered in a data record; decimal data may be punched in a data card either with or without a decimal point. If a decimal point is not punched in a data field, the compiler automatically assumes a decimal point in the position indicated by the format code. Thus, the data card:

```
|123|4567
 357|
```

could be coded as F3.0 to indicate the decimal datum 357. or coded F3.2, for example, to indicate 3.57 as the decimal datum.

What if the card contained the following datum:

```
|123456|78
 +127.1|
```

and the format code specified F6.3 instead of F6.1? FORTRAN provides that in event of a conflict, a decimal point in an input record overrides the decimal point specified by the format code. In other words, the computer assumes that the data card is correct and ignores the programmer's specification.

This provision of FORTRAN allows some flexibility in placement of data within a field if the data contain a decimal point. For example, assume that a data field is located in the first nine columns in a card. Data are usually entered right-justified in a field as follows:

```
|123456789|
     12.45|
```

It is not necessary to enter zeros in the high-order (leftmost) position in a field because the computer always assumes each blank preceding the first significant digit to be zero. Likewise, each blank following the last significant digit is also always assumed to be a zero. Thus, the decimal value 12.45 could be entered in the field in several ways, including:

```
|123456789|
     12.45|
 00012.450|
 12.45    |
```

The format code must describe this field as floating point with a field length of nine; but because the location of an actual decimal point overrides the format code specification, it could be described several ways, such as:

$$F9.0 \quad F9.2 \quad F9.6$$

Stated simply, floating point data containing a decimal point may be anywhere in the field because leading and trailing zeros do not change the value.

However, if the data field does not contain a decimal point, it must agree with the format code because trailing zeros do change the value. To indicate, for example, 12.45 with an implied rather than an actual decimal point in a field described as F9.2., 12.45 must be right-justified because if it is entered:

```
|123456789|
      1245 |
```

the trailing blank will cause the computer to assume 124.50 as the value. Thus, floating point data with an *implied* decimal point, like integer data, must agree with the corresponding format code.

The ability of the compiler to allow decimal points to be implied and to allow actual decimal points to override format code specifications can be useful to the programmer. To avoid the difficulties inherent in discussion of several methods of representation of floating point data at the same time, *future illustrations in this book will always show a decimal datum with a decimal point. This will readily distinguish it from an integer datum in which a decimal point is never allowed.*

Exponential form Two format codes are provided for programmers who must describe fields containing exponential form data. One specifies single precision, the other, double precision. The general forms are:

> rEl.d and rDl.d
>
> **Legend:**
> r   An integer that specifies the number of times the format code is to be *repeated*. It is optional with the programmer and is omitted if the code is used only once.
> E   Specifies that the field contains single-precision data in *exponential* form.
> D   Specifies that the field contains *double-precision* exponential form data.
> l   An integer number that indicates the *length* of the data field in record columns.
> .d   A decimal point followed by one or more integers that specify the number of *decimal positions* in the fraction preceding the letter E or D. If the number following the decimal point is omitted, the code is invalid (the computer does *not* assume a zero). If the input data field contains a decimal point, this specification is ignored by the compiler, but it cannot be omitted by the programmer.

The following data card for example:

```
|1234 5 6|789    |
 .47E-4|58.E6|+.0374D+22
```

would be described as:

```
|12345|6|7
        FORMAT(E6.2,E5.0,D10.4)
```

Alphanumeric format code   The code used to describe an alphanumeric data field is

$$rAl$$

Legend:
r   An integer that specifies the number of times the format code is to be *repeated*. It is optional with the programmer and omitted if the code is used only once.
A   Specifies that the field contains *alphameric* data.
l   An integer that specifies the *length* of the field.

To illustrate, the following two-field data card:

```
| 1 2 3 4 5 6 7 8 | 9
  M .   B E N     3 80SLSEE
```

could be described either as:

```
|12345|6|7
   100    FORMAT(A8,A8)
```

or as:

```
|12345|6|7
   100    FORMAT(2A8)
```

5/Input and Output

When a variable name in a READ statement is associated with an A format code in the referenced FORMAT statement, it is implied that the variable name will be used to store alphanumeric, rather than numeric data. A CHARACTER statement, to specify the variable name and the maximum length of its contents (as described in Chapter 4), is technically not required.

However, if the CHARACTER statement is omitted, the maximum character string length varies by computer make/model. Usually the length is severely limited to only about four characters. In this case, a 24-column alphanumeric field cannot be described as one A24 field; it must be described as several fields by using multiple-format codes such as 6A4, 8A3, 12A2, 24A1, or some appropriate combination such as 3A4 and 4A3. To match the multiple format codes, the READ statement must have an equal number of variable names.

If, on the other hand, a CHARACTER statement is used, the programmer may specify a character string of any desired length and use one appropriate A code to describe the field. This eliminates the need to handle long alphanumeric fields as several short fields and also relieves the programmer of concern for the design capacity of the specific computer(s) to be used for processing. Thus, a CHARACTER statement is a programming convenience and we recommend its use.

X format code This code, sometimes called the *blank* or *skip code*, specifies that an input field is to be ignored. The general form is:

> 1X
>
> **Legend:**
>
> 1   An integer number greater than zero that specifies the *length* of the field to be skipped when reading an input record. If this number is omitted, the code is invalid (the compiler does not assume a field length of one).
>
> X   Specifies that the field is to be ignored.
>
> To illustrate, the following FORMAT statement:
>
> |12345|6|7
>   100   FORMAT(4X,I2,1X,I3)

will cause the first and third fields on the following data card to be ignored:

|1234|56|7|89 |
+2.4|37| |256|

In effect, the above FORMAT statement indirectly tells the computer that the first data field (I2) begins in column 5 because it specifies that the first four columns are to be ignored. Similarly, it indirectly indicates that the next field (I3) begins in column 8 because column 7 is to be ignored. It should be emphasized that the field length must *precede* the letter X; in all other format codes discussed thus far, the field length must follow the letter which specifies the type of format code.

T format code This code, sometimes called the *tabulator* or *tab code*, specifies directly, rather than indirectly, where reading is to begin. It works in a manner analogous to a typewriter tabulation key. Two or more T format codes are not allowed to appear in sequence. The general form is:

> Tc
>
> **Legend:**
> T   Identifies the type of format code.
> c   An integer number greater than zero that indicates the specific record *column* where the data field described by the following format code begins.

To illustrate, the following FORMAT statement:

```
|12345|6|7
     100    FORMAT(T5,I2,T8,I3)
```

will ignore the first and third fields of the data card illustrated below:

```
|1234|56|7|89 |
+2.4|37| |256|
```

The T5 specification tells the computer that reading is to begin with column 5; likewise, T8 specifies the next field begins in column 8. This illustration should be compared to the one given in the preceding section describing the X format code.

Neither the T nor the X format codes have a provision for indicating the number of times the code is to be repeated. The basic difference between the T and X format codes is that the T code indicates directly where the next field begins, the X code indirectly. Both codes tell the computer to ignore one or more fields, so either may be used to accomplish the same task.

The READ statement

Two statements are required to read data from an input record into internal storage. One is the nonexecutable FORMAT statement previously described; the other is the executable READ statement covered in this section. The READ statement is an executable I/O statement, which can direct the computer to read one or more data cards from a card reader device. The READ statement can also be used with other types of input records, but this chapter, as indicated previously, uses card illustrations to explain the input process.

General form and functions The READ statement tells the computer what to read, specifies the input device where the record is located, and references a FORMAT statement the describes the record. The general form is:

```
|12345|6|7
nnnnn    READ(dc,fn)vn₁,vn₂, . . . vnₘ
```

5 / Input and Output

> **Legend:**
> nnnnn   Any unique one- to five-digit integer that specifies the statement *number*. It is required only if the statement is referenced by another statement in the program.
>
> READ   A keyword specifying the operation to be performed.
>
> dc   An integer number, or an integer variable name, that specifies the *device code*. This should agree with the corresponding code in an OPEN statement (or the appropriate code, preassigned by the local computer center).
>
> fn   An integer *FORMAT statement number* (label) that references the statement that describes the input record. Note that dc and fn must be separated by a comma, enclosed in parentheses, and appear in the order indicated.
>
> $vn_1, \ldots vn_m$ Represents one or more optional *variable names* separated by delimiters. All variable names listed must agree both in mode and sequence with the format codes specified in the referenced FORMAT statement. This string of variable names is often called a *READ list* or *input list*.

Illustrations Regardless of how many fields a record contains, only those specified by a FORMAT statement are available for reading. To illustrate this point, assume that a data card contains two integer fields followed by two floating point fields:

|12|345|6789|
11|222|3.33|.444

If all data on the above card are required for the problem to be solved, each of the four fields must be described by a FORMAT statement. To illustrate:

|12345|6|7
  55   FORMAT(I2,I3,F4.2,F4.3)

Of course, it is not necessary to store data that are not required for the problem to be solved. Data fields that are not described in a FORMAT statement, or that are omitted by use of the X and/or T code(s), are not available for reading. Thus, if only the first field (columns 1 and 2) is to be processed, the data field card could be described as follows:

|12345|6|7
  66   FORMAT(I2)

Likewise, if only the second field (columns 3, 4, and 5) is to be processed, the above-illustrated data card could be described as follows:

|12345|6|7
  100   FORMAT(2X,I3)

When a READ statement is executed, the available data are stored at locations indicated by the list of variable names. To illustrate, assume the following data card:

```
|12|34|56789|    |
 24|75|17.45|.333|.281
```

The following two statements will cause the above data card to be read, and the data in all but the fourth field will be stored:

```
|12345|6|7
     77   FORMAT(I2,I2,F5.2,4X,F4.3)
          READ(1,77)I,N,A,B
```

Four *available* data fields are specified by the format codes (the X field is ignored), and an equal number of variable names appear in the READ list. Note particularly how the implied mode of the variable names listed in the READ statement agrees sequentially with the mode of the data specified by the codes in the FORMAT statement. After the above READ statement is executed, the variable names listed will be initialized to the following values:

I	24
N	75
A	17.45
B	.281

The READ statement, with an associated FORMAT and input data record, is only one way to initialize the values of variable names. There are other ways. As discussed previously, assignment statements and/or DATA statements also can be used. I, N, A, and B could have been initialized to the same values as in the preceding illustration by these four assignment statements:

```
|12345|6|7
         I =24
         N=75
         A=17.45
         B=.281
```

or by this one DATA statement:

```
|12345|6|7
         DATA I,N,A,B/24,75,17.45,.281/
```

It should be noted that constants are *fixed* values, which cannot be changed during execution of a program. Thus, if all data are supplied directly in the program as constants, each time the program is executed it will compute the same results. On the other hand, if data are supplied from input data records that are not a part of the source program, the computed results will vary according to the data values supplied. Thus, a program that includes one or more READ statements can be supplied with *variable* data.

Many programs that include READ statements also include con-

5/Input and Output

stants. A payroll program, for example, may include the social security rate as a constant, but the number of hours and rate of pay would ordinarily be supplied from an outside source such as a data record. This approach would make it possible to use the same program, but different data records, each payroll period. Only a change in the problem, such as the social security rate or I/O requirements, would require a change in the program. Compared to the alternative of supplying all data as constants, this approach would be much more practical. It would save compilation time as well as programming time because the program would not have to be recompiled unless it was changed.

OUTPUT

Output statements are used to transmit data from internal storage to a record in an external output device. Many types of output devices may be used, including magnetic tape drives, magnetic disk drives, cathode ray tubes, audio response units (male or female voice), card punches and printers. The type of output selected by the programmer will depend upon the requirements of the problem to be solved. Generally, as a matter of convenience, the final solution will be printed. If the output will later be required as input to the same or a different program, it will probably be in some form that is machine readable. Programs are often designed to generate more than one kind of output.

No attempt will be made in this book to enter into a full discussion of all the various devices available for output; such a discussion is reserved for a course in computer hardware or systems design. However, the output from two important devices, the card punch and the high-speed printer, will be discussed in detail. Card output will be discussed first, followed by printed output.

Data card output

Output data cards, like input data cards, have no restrictions as to format. The number, sequence, and length of the fields must be designed to fit the requirements of the problem. Because the format is optional with the programmer rather than implied by the rules of FORTRAN, it must be explicitly described to the computer through a nonexecutable FORMAT statement.

The FORMAT statement The general form of a FORMAT statement that is referenced by a WRITE statement is identical to that of a FORMAT statement referenced by a READ statement, which was illustrated previously in this chapter. If desired, one FORMAT statement may be referenced by one or more READ and/or WRITE statements.

Format codes The general form of the format codes used to describe input and output data are also identical, but a few differences in restrictions and uses are discussed next.

It is permissible to omit decimal points in floating point fields on input data cards. But on output data cards, a decimal point is always automatically punched in the position indicated by an F, E, or D format code specification.

The X format code, when used to describe input cards, indicates the field is not to be read. When used to describe output cards, it indicates the field is not to be punched or, stated another way, the field is to be left blank.

On input data cards, the T format code may be used to indicate where to begin reading. On output data cards, it may be used to indicate where to begin writing. Any columns skipped over will, of course, be blank.

The WRITE statement Two statements are required to transmit data from internal storage into an output data card. One is the FORMAT statement previously covered; the other is the WRITE statement, which is discussed in this section. The WRITE statement is an executable I/O statement that can direct the computer to write one or more data cards through the card punch. The WRITE statement can also be used for other types of output records, but this section is concerned with only punched cards as output media.

General form and function The WRITE statement tells the computer what to write, specifies the output device where the record is located, and references a FORMAT statement that describes the record. The general form is similar to the READ statement, but particular attention should be directed to the difference in the device code specification:

```
|12345|6|7
 nnnnn    WRITE(dc,fn)vn₁, vn₂, . . . vnₘ
```

Legend:

nnnnn	Any unique one- to five-digit integer that specifies the statement *number*. It is required only if the statement is referenced by another statement in the program.
WRITE	A keyword specifying the operation to be performed.
dc	An integer number, or an integer variable name, that specifies the *device code*. This should agree with the corresponding code in an OPEN statement (or the appropriate code, preassigned by the local computer center).
fn	An integer *FORMAT statement number* that references the statement that describes the output record. Note that dc and fn must be separated by a comma, enclosed in parentheses, and appear in the order indicated.
vn₁, . . . vnₘ	Represents one or more optional *variable names* separated by delimiters. All variable names listed must agree both in mode and sequence with the format codes specified in the referenced FORMAT statement. This string of variable names is often called a *WRITE list* or *output list*.

To illustrate the WRITE statement, and at the same time to review the FORMAT and READ statements, consider the following *input* data card:

```
|12|34|5678|9
 11 22 7.77 3.33
```

5 / Input and Output

and the following series of statements:

```
|12345|6|7
   77   FORMAT(2I2,4X,F4.2)
        READ(1,77)I,N,A
        WRITE(2,77)I,N,A
   88   WRITE(2,77)N,I,A
```

which will cause the following two *output* data cards to be punched:

```
|12|34|5678|9
 11|22|    |3.33
```
```
|12|34|5678|9
 22|11|    |3.33
```

The first output card is an exact duplicate of the input card except that the third field is blank; but the second output card, resulting from the execution of statement number 88, has the first two data fields reversed because N precedes I in the list of variable names.

All three I/O statements reference the same FORMAT statement in the preceding illustration. This technique is a convenience but it can be used in relatively few applications. It can be used only if the variable names and the corresponding format codes are in the same mode (integer or floating point) and if the field lengths are sufficient to accommodate the data. To illustrate:

```
|123|45|67|89
 111|22|33|.4
```

Assume that the problem requires that the above card be read in and that an output card be punched with the same data but with the fields in a different sequence. The WRITE statement in the following series of statements will cause some problems:

```
|12345|6|7
   99   FORMAT(I3,I2,I2,F2.1)
        READ(1,99)K,L,M,X
        WRITE(2,99)L,K,X,M
```

After the READ statement is executed, the variable names will have the following current values:

Variable name	Current value
K	111
L	22
M	33
X	.4

The WRITE statement will cause the computer to write the two-digit current value of L in the first three-column integer field in the output card because the data fit the field and the modes agree. At this point, the problems begin. The second integer field is only two columns in length, so it cannot accommodate the three-digit current value of K. The transposition of X and M results in a conflict in mode even though the field lengths are compatible. All these problems could be solved by adding the following statement to the partial program:

|12345|6|7
    77   FORMAT(I2,I3,F2.1,I2)

Of course, the format number specified in the WRITE statement must be changed from 99 to 77 so it would reference this additional statement.

Scaling It is the programmer's responsibility to specify an output field of sufficient size to accommodate the output data. The process of determining the required field size is called *scaling*. This process can perhaps best be described by an illustration.

Suppose an input data card has two four-column fields, each containing numeric data in ordinary decimal form. The solution to the problem requires that the data in the first field be multiplied by the data in the second field. The output card is to contain only the product of the multiplication. The programmer has prepared the following statements:

|12345|6|7
    66   FORMAT(F4.1,F4.2)
           READ(1,66)H,R
           ANSWER=H*R
           WRITE(2,44)ANSWER
    44   FORMAT(

Before completing FORMAT statement number 44, the programmer must go through the process of scaling. Assume that both input fields contain unsigned data (if unsigned, data are assumed to be positive). The maximum value of ANSWER requires a format code of F7.3(99.9 times 9.99 equals 998.001).

The programmer must always specify a field of sufficient length to accommodate all whole numbers in the output (that is, the numbers preceding the decimal point), but the length of the fraction (that is, the number of decimal point positions) may be increased or decreased according to the required precision. Thus, if F9.5 is specified, the maximum value of ANSWER will be punched as 998.00100 in the output card field. If this is a commercial application, only two decimal positions (to indicate dollars and cents) might be required. The output field will contain the value 998.00 if the format code F6.2 is specified.

Suppose, however, that the problem is to determine the rental charge in dollars and cents for a certain machine. H represents the hours the machine was used during one day, and R represents the rate per hour, which does not exceed $3.00. Since there are only 24 hours in a day, the maximum value of ANSWER is 72.00, which can be punched in an F5.2 field.

The foregoing illustration indicates that the programmer must be thoroughly familiar with all the facts of the problem to be solved before attempting the scaling process.

It is always the programmer's responsibility to specify a field of sufficient length to accommodate the maximum possible output value. If the value 72.00 is to be punched in an output card, the format code must specify a field length of five or more columns. If a field length of four or less is specified, the computer will usually *not* truncate one or more digits. Instead, it usually will tell the programmer that the field length specification is in error by writing one or more asterisks in the output field. If an attempt is made to punch the value 72.00 using the following FORMAT statement:

```
|12345|6|7
   55   FORMAT(F4.2)
```

the resulting output usually will be:

```
|1234567           |1234567           |1234567
 ****      or       *         or       *.00
```

depending upon the compiler used. Other programming errors can also cause the output to contain one or more asterisks. Even experienced programmers expect to occasionally see "stars" in their output.

There is one more factor to be considered in the scaling process. If there is a possibility that an output field will contain a negative value, one column must be allowed for the minus sign. It will automatically be punched in the column preceding the first significant digit in the field unless no space is allowed, in which case *it will be truncated and the value will appear to be positive*! Many programmers follow the practice of always allowing an extra field position for the minus sign even though the solution to the problem logically calls for a positive answer. The reason for this practice will be explained by use of another illustration.

A program has been written to compute the number of hats on hand at year's end in a clothing store. Essentially, the program is designed to add the units in the beginning inventory to the units purchased and to subtract from this sum the units sold to arrive at the solution. Obviously, the store cannot have a quantity of less than zero hats on hand at year's end, so the program logically appears to call for a positive answer. But there are two basic reasons why the computer may produce a negative result. First, there may be an error in input, such as incorrect, duplicate, or omitted data. Second, the programmer may have committed one or more logic errors when writing the program, such as adding instead of subtracting.

It should be obvious that the scaling process required for complex mathematical problems can be quite complicated and time-consuming, but no complex scaling is required for the solution to any problems in this book. A good rule to follow, if there are no restrictions as to the output format, is always to allow one or more extra columns in the output field.

Printed output Several models of printers are available, which vary as to speed, number of print positions (length of the line in columns), and size of the character set (number of different digits, letters, and special characters). Even though a printer may have 120 or 135 print positions, the record described should obviously never exceed the width of the paper stock used for output. For purposes of illustration, it will be assumed in this book that the printer has 120 character positions and the paper width is of corresponding size. It will also be assumed that the printer character set includes the valid FORTRAN numbers, letters, and special characters.

The output image Before data are transmitted from internal storage to an output device, they go through an *editing* process. This process, among other things, right-justifies the data in the field specified by the format code. It replaces high-order (leftmost) zeros with blanks. It also eliminates plus signs because unsigned data are assumed to be positive. The internal representation of a data record that is to be transferred from internal storage to an output device is sometimes called the *output image*.

If output is to be a punched card, the image is 80 columns long (the computer "knows" that cards are fixed-length records with 80 columns). Thus, if the value of N is +37, and the record is described as FORMAT (I4), the output image will contain blanks in the first two columns, followed by a 3 and a 7 respectively in the next two columns, followed by blanks in the remaining 76 columns. When a WRITE statement is executed, this image will be transmitted to the card output device, which will then punch an output data card that corresponds exactly to this image.

If output is to be a printed line, the image always contains one character more than the number of available printing positions. If the printing device has a maximum capacity of 120 characters per line, the image will contain 121 characters—one character more than can be printed on a line. Thus, unlike punched output, printed output cannot exactly correspond to the output image. This extra character is in the *first* position of the image. When a record is printed, instead of punched, the entire output image is automatically shifted one position to the left. The first character in the image moves into what might be thought of as "zero" printing position and therefore is not printed. The second character in the image becomes the first (leftmost) character in the actual output; the third character in the image is printed in the second position; the fourth character in the third position, etc. The first character in the output image, which is shifted to the zero printing position and therefore does not appear in the output, is called the *carriage* or *line control character*. It is used, by the printer, to control vertical line spacing.

Line spacing control There are two types of spacing on printed output, horizontal and vertical, and both are controlled by the FORMAT statement. *Horizontal* spacing (blank spaces between fields) can be controlled by the T and X format codes as previously described. *Vertical* spacing (between lines) can be controlled by the carriage control characters. Some compilers accept many different carriage control characters, but only four characters are standard. These are:

Line control character	Paper advance before printing
+	No advance
Blank	One line
0 (zero)	Two lines
1	First *printing* line of next page

The most commonly used carriage control character is the blank that causes single-spacing. One way to place a blank in the carriage control character position is to begin the FORMAT statement with an X code that specifies one or more blank positions. For example, 1X, 2X, or 10X can be used to describe a record that begins with a blank field. The *first* blank serves as the carriage control character; extra blanks, if any, appear in the output. Typically, 1X is used to reduce the possibility of confusion. Other ways to specify a blank, as well as ways to specify the other three standard characters, are covered later in this chapter.

ADDITIONAL I/O TECHNIQUES

The purpose of this section is to provide a more comprehensive view of input/output procedures by elaborating on the basic techniques presented in previous sections and by introducing additional techniques that provide flexibility and convenience in programming.

FORMAT and READ relationships

The list of variable names in a READ statement must agree in mode and sequence with the available data fields specified by the format codes, but it is not necessary for the *number* of names to agree with the number of available data fields. The READ list may contain fewer variable names than the number of format codes specified in the FORMAT statement, or it may contain more, as illustrated in the following two sections.

Fewer variable names than available data fields If the list contains fewer variable names than the number of available data fields specified by the format codes, reading stops when the list is satisfied; additional data fields specified by format codes are ignored. In other words, it is the READ statement that determines how many fields will be read, not the FORMAT statement, which only describes the fields and indicates how many are available.

To illustrate, assume the following two input data records, each containing six fields:

|12|345|678|9| | |
27|123|856|12|17.32|867.18

|12|345|678|9| | |
44|555|666|77|88.88|999.99

As a result of the following statements:

|12345|6|7
  22   FORMAT(I2,T6,I3,2X,F5.2,F6.2)
       READ(1,22)M,N,R

only the first of the two input data records will be read; and M, N, and R will be initialized to the current values of 27, 856, and 17.32 respectively. The T6 and 2X format codes specify that two of the six data fields are to be ignored, leaving four data fields (I2,I3,F5.2, and F6.2) available for reading. But the READ list contains only three variable names. Because reading stops when the list is satisfied, the last field available for reading (F6.2) is ignored.

Each time a READ statement is executed, one record is read. To illustrate further, the following series of statements:

|12345|6|7
  1   FORMAT(I2,T6,I3,2X,F5.2,F6.2)
      READ(1,1)M
      READ(1,1)N

will cause the computer to read the first data field in each of the two input data records, and M and N will be initialized to 27 and 44 respectively. To reiterate, the READ statement determines the number of fields to be read, not the FORMAT statement. If the same variable name had been used in both READ statements, it would have a current value of 27 after execution of the first and 44 after execution of the second. Remember, read in is destructive.

More variable names than available data fields The READ list may contain more variable names than the number of available data fields specified by the format codes. If so, what occurs is slightly more complex and requires a more lengthy explanation.

The number of variable names listed in the READ statement determines the number of data fields to be read; reading continues until the list is satisfied. The format codes enclosed in parentheses describe one record; the computer automatically assumes the end of the record has been reached when it gets to the close (rightmost) parenthesis. Thus, if the list contains more variable names than the number of fields specified by the FORMAT statement, two or more records are required to satisfy the list. Exactly how does the computer handle this situation? Whenever it reaches the close (rightmost) parenthesis of the FORMAT statement, it automatically reads another record, transfers back to the open (leftmost) parenthesis, and reuses the same format codes in sequence until the list is satisfied.

To illustrate what happens when there are five variable names in the list but only three format codes specifying data available for reading, assume the following two data records:

```
|12345|67|89|    |
 11.11|66|22|333|77.77
|12345|67|89|    |
 45.67|55|89|012|88.88
```

and the following statements:

```
|12345|6|7
      6  FORMAT(F5.2,2X,I2,I3)
         READ(1,6)B,I,J,A,K
```

After execution of the above statements, the following values will be stored:

Variable name	Value stored
B	11.11
I	22
J	333
A	45.67
K	89

The data records each contain five fields, but the format codes only specify three to be available for reading. The second field is ignored because of the X format code, and the last is ignored because it is not specified. It should be noted that if the last two variable names in the list had not been in floating point and integer mode, respectively, the program would have failed. The variable names and the corresponding format codes *must* be consistent in mode.

One final point: The programmer could have written two READ statements instead of one:

```
|12345|6|7
      6  FORMAT(F5.2,2X,I2,I3)
         READ(1,6)B,I,J
         READ(1,6)A,K
```

and the values stored at B, I, J, A, and K would be the same as previously indicated. This latter series of statements requires more time to write and to execute. It also results in more machine-language instructions, so more storage area is required for the object program.

Reading multiple records

Designing a READ statement that includes more variable names than the number of corresponding format codes or including more than one READ statement in the program are only two of the many techniques that can be used to cause the computer to read more than one input data card. One more technique will be discussed in this section; following chapters will cover more advanced methods.

To understand selective reading, it is necessary to realize the sequence of what happens to an input card when a READ statement is executed. When a card reader is used as the input device, execution of a READ statement always causes one card to be fed from the hopper of the card reader into what is called the *reading station*. (Remember, a referenced FORMAT statement always includes an open parenthesis, which indicates the *beginning* of a record; that is, it signals the computer that a card is to be fed.) The reading station is designed to detect the presence or absence of holes in the various punching positions in the card. Only the card located at the reading station can be read, and a card must always be fed before it can be read. Only one card can be located at this station at any one time. The card located at the reading station is automatically ejected into a stacker, where it is no longer available for reading, whenever another card is fed into this station. Figure 5-2 illustrates this sequence of steps.

It was pointed out earlier in this chapter that the close (rightmost) parenthesis of the FORMAT statement indicates the end of the record. If the READ list contains more variable names than the number of data fields available according to the format codes specified, control automatically returns to the open (leftmost) parenthesis. The computer then reads a new card, reusing the same format codes, until the READ list is satisfied.

A slash (/) within the parenthesis of a FORMAT statement indicates the beginning of a record and causes a new card to be fed. But instead of returning to the open (leftmost) parenthesis and reusing the format codes, the computer continues rightward using any remaining available format codes until the READ list is satisfied or the close (rightmost)

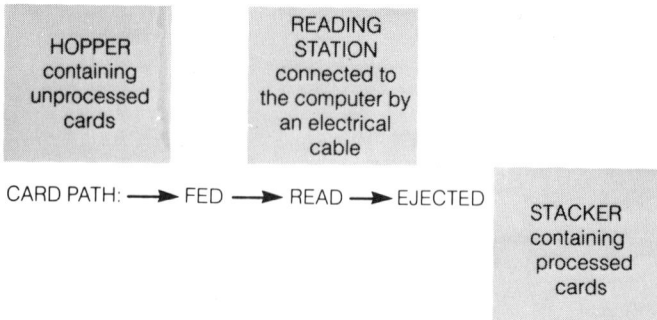

Figure 5-2
Schematic of the card path through a card reader device

parenthesis is encountered. Each slash encountered during the execution of a READ statement causes the card at the reading station to be ejected into the stacker and another card to be fed into position for reading.

To illustrate, assume the following statements:

```
|12345|6|7
     33   FORMAT(I4/I3)
          READ(1,33)M,N
```

Execution of the READ statement will cause the computer to feed one card. (Remember, this statement *always* causes a card to be fed to begin the operation.) Next, the integer data contained in the first four columns (I4) will be read and stored at M. Next, the slash signals the beginning of a second record (and, indirectly, the end of the first record). This will cause another card to be fed into the reading station. Finally, the integer data contained in the *first* three columns (I3) of the second card will be read and stored at N. Because the list is satisfied before the close (rightmost) parenthesis is reached, no more cards will be fed or read. A close examination of the FORMAT statement will reveal that the slash takes the place of the comma, which is usually required as a delimiter to separate the format codes.

Note that the preceding two statements have the same effect as the following four:

```
|12345|6|7
     11   FORMAT(I4)
     22   FORMAT(I3)
          READ(11,11)M
          READ(1,22)N
```

There are usually several ways to read data into internal storage, some of which are more convenient than others. To illustrate, assume a program is to be written that will process the following two data cards:

```
|12345|6789
27.00|
```

```
|12345|6789
11.50|
```

This series of four statements illustrates one way to transfer data from the above cards into internal storage:

```
|12345|6|7
      4   FORMAT(F5.2)
      5   FORMAT(F5.2)
          READ(1,4)DATA1
          READ(1,5)DATA2
```

It is unnecessary to use two FORMAT statements because both data cards, in this case, can be described by the same format code. Instead, both READ statements can reference the same FORMAT statement. The following series of three statements illustrate a second way to read in the two data cards:

```
|12345|6|7
    6   FORMAT(F5.2)
        READ(1,6)DATA1
        READ(1,6)DATA2
```

In this particular problem, it is unnecessary to use two READ statements; the following two statements illustrate a third way to do the same job:

```
|12345|6|7
    7   FORMAT(F5.2)
        READ(1,7)DATA1,DATA2
```

A fourth way, illustrated below, is to use a slash in the FORMAT statement:

```
|12345|6|7
    8   FORMAT(F5.2/F5.2)
        READ(1,8)DATA1,DATA2
```

Of the four illustrated ways to store data, the third is the most convenient because the least coding is required. This method cannot be used, however, unless both data fields can be described by the same format code. To illustrate, assume the data on the following two cards is to be read into internal storage:

```
|12|3456789
27|
```

```
|12345|6789
11.50|
```

In this case, the two cards contain different types of data as well as different field lengths, so the same format code cannot be used to describe both fields.

The following four statements illustrate an inconvenient way to read in the two data cards:

```
|12345|6|7
    9   FORMAT(I2)
   10   FORMAT(F5.2)
        READ(1,9)NDATA1
        READ(1,10)DATA2
```

The following two statements, which can be used instead of the preceding four, illustrate the convenience of a slash:

```
|12345|6|7
   11   FORMAT(I2/F5.2)
        READ(1,11)NDATA1,DATA2
```

For another example, suppose a program is to be written that will compute the total amount of sales for one of the many products sold by a company. There are two data cards for each product, and each contains two fields. The first field on each card indicates the product identification number. The second indicates the amount of sales; one card indicates year-to-date sales prior to the current month, and the other indicates sales for the current month only. Following are the two data cards for product number 6666:

```
|1234|56789
 6666|12345.78
```

```
|1234|56789
 6666|222.22
```

If a slash is used, one FORMAT statement can describe both data cards. The following statements tell the computer to store the data from each of the four fields:

```
|12345|6|7
   38   FORMAT(I4,F8.2/I4,F6.2)
        READ(1,38)IDNUMB,YR2DAT,IDNUMB,CURENT
```

Data are stored at the variable names in the same sequence in which these names appear in the READ list from left to right. Thus, the computer will store 6666 from the first card at IDNUMB, but later it will replace this value with the identification number from the second card, which, in this case, is also 6666. This is not a recommended technique, but it is illustrated to show what happens when a variable name appears more than once in a READ statement.

The following statements tell the computer to store the identification number from only the first card:

```
|12345|6|7
   39   FORMAT(I4,F8.2/4X,F6.2)
        READ(1,39)IDNUMB,YR2DAT,CURENT
```

In this case, only three fields are available for reading; so the READ list includes only three variable names. The same results will be obtained if T5 is substituted for the 4X format code. Note that a T or X format code tells the computer to skip to the next *field,* but a slash tells it to skip to the next *record*. The slash permits the programmer to describe more than one record in one FORMAT statement.

A FORMAT statement may include more than one slash and/or more than one pair of parentheses. The effect of "nested parentheses" is beyond the scope of this section. The important concept to remember is that the first open parenthesis and each slash always indicate the beginning of a record. Thus, one or more records will be read each time a READ statement is executed; one record cannot be read by more than one READ statement, but one READ statement can read one or more records.

Writing multiple records

The movement of *input* records through a card reader device is controlled by beginning-of-record indicators in the referenced FORMAT statement; the first open parenthesis and each slash causes a record (card) to be advanced, as explained in the preceding section. However, the movement of *output* records through a high-speed printer is controlled in a different manner, as explained in this section.

When output is printed, each line is considered to be a record. A beginning-of-record indicator, in a referenced FORMAT statement, does *not* automatically advance one record (one line of printing). Thus it is possible to use two or more different WRITE statements to cause printing on the same line. It is also possible, and not unusual, to use a WRITE statement to cause printing on more than one line. Line spacing (record advancement) is controlled by line control characters, which may be supplemented by slashes.

Slashes can be used to supplement, but not to replace, line control characters as illustrated below:

```
|12345|6|7
   66   FORMAT(1X,I3/1X,I4)
        WRITE(3,66)M,N
```

Examine the above FORMAT statement. The open parenthesis indicates the beginning of a record but does not advance the paper. The first character in the record (a blank specified by the 1X code) is the line control character. It will cause the paper to advance one line before printing, in the first three positions, the value stored at M. The slash indicates the beginning of a second record (and thus the end of the first). Again, this beginning-of-record indicator does not advance the paper. The second line control character (another blank), which appears at the beginning of the second record, causes the paper to advance one line before printing, in the first four positions, the value stored at N. The close parenthesis indicates the end of the second record. Note that two records were described in this one FORMAT statement and that both record descriptions started with a line control character. These characters, not the beginning-of-record indicators, controlled the line spacing.

Any record with one or more output fields must begin with a line control character. However, it is possible to omit output fields in a record; that is, output may include a blank line. This is illustrated in the next example, which includes two adjacent slashes:

```
|12345|6|7
   66   FORMAT(1X,I3/ /1X,I4)
        WRITE(3,66)M,N
```

Again, the value of M will be printed in the first three positions after a one-line advance. The first slash signals the beginning of a second record. The next slash implies the end of the second record by signaling the beginning of the third. Nothing can be printed in the second record because it includes no field descriptors. It is a blank record—i.e., all characters are blank. The *first* of this series of blank characters is the line control character which advances the paper one line. Finally, the line control character for the third record (1X) advances the paper another line, on which the value of N will be printed. The result will be double-spacing; that is, there will be one blank line between the two printed fields. In summary, the FORMAT statement describes three output records (lines). The first line will have the value of M, the second will be blank, and the third will have the value of N.

Slashes are not line control characters; they are beginning-of-record indicators. But when two or more beginning-of-record indicators appear in sequence, the effect is one or more blank records. A blank record always has a blank in the first (line control character) position, so each blank record causes the paper to advance one line.

The following statement could be used to advance three lines before printing and then to advance one more line:

|12345|6|7
55   FORMAT(1X/1X/1X,I3/1X)

The above statement describes four records. Each of the four begins with 1X, which specifies a blank as the line control character. Note that it is redundant to specify a blank line control character for the three blank lines, because it is implied. To illustrate, the next statement is more convenient to write and does the same job as the preceding statement:

Beginning of Record: 123   4
                              ↓↓↓   ↓
55 FORMAT(//1X,I3/)

The above open parenthesis, which does not advance the paper, indicates the beginning of a record. The first slash indicates the beginning of a second record (it also closes the first record, which had no contents). "No contents" is another way of saying that it has blanks in all record positions (including the first, which is always the line control character). The blank line control character causes the paper to advance to the next record (line). Likewise, the second slash indicates the beginning of the third record. Because the second record is also blank, the paper advances another line. Next, the explicit line control character (1X) in the third record causes another advance. Following these three consecutive advances, a number may be printed in the I3 field. The last slash indicates the beginning of the fourth record. This final record has no content (it is closed by the parenthesis), so the paper advances a final time.

Literals

Thus far in this chapter, only numeric output has been considered. Obviously a page full of numbers with no descriptive columnar headings or other identifying information could be confusing to the user. To avoid this problem the programmer may use alphanumeric messages that are commonly called *literals*. A literal is any string of characters, as previously described.

Two methods for storing literals at a variable name (by a DATA statement or by an assignment statement) were covered in Chapter 4. This section illustrates how to include literals in a FORMAT statement. Two types of literals are covered in this section.

"Hollerith messages" The H or "Hollerith" format code allows the programmer to write any message he desires within the FORMAT statement. When the FORMAT statement containing a "Hollerith message" is referenced by a WRITE statement, the message is automatically placed in the output image. The general form of the H format code is:

> lHm
>
> **Legend:**
>
> l   An integer number that specifies the *length* of the message field in columns or print positions.
>
> H   Specifies that the field contains a Hollerith message.
>
> m   Represents the *message* that must contain the exact number of characters specified by the field length. The message may be composed of any valid data characters—it is not restricted to the FORTRAN character set.

Hollerith messages may be more than one character in length and may be used for more than one purpose, as is discussed later, but this section is first concerned with their use as line control characters. The following incomplete statements illustrate the four one-character Hollerith messages that can be used to control line spacing:

```
|12345|6|7
        FORMAT(1H+, . . .)    (no advance before
                                 printing)
        FORMAT(1H  , . . .)   (advance one line before
                                 printing)
        FORMAT(1H0, . . .)    (advance two lines
                                 before printing)
        FORMAT(1H1, . . .)    (advance to top of next
                                 page before printing)
```

To illustrate, assume that the stored values of NN and AA are 33 and 22.44 respectively. The following statements:

```
|12345|6|7
   88   FORMAT(1H0,I2,2X,F5.2)
        WRITE(3,88)NN,AA
```

will cause the paper to advance two lines and then to print the following output:

5/Input and Output   109

```
|12|34|56789

 33|   |22.44
```

An H format code may appear in any sequence in the FORMAT statement. Although it may be used for carriage control, its main purpose is to make the output more easily understood by the reader. For example, assume that the stored values of NUMEMP and PAY are 27 and 16.20 respectively. The following statements:

```
|12345|6|7
   16   FORMAT(12H EMPLOYEE # ,I2,11H WAS PAID $,F5.2)
        WRITE(3,16)NUMEMP,PAY
```

will result in the following printed output:

```
|12345|6|7
EMPLOYEE # 27 WAS PAID $16.20
```

Note that the first Hollerith message contains three blanks. The first blank is used for carriage control, so it does not appear in the printed output. The second blank provides a space between EMPLOYEE and # in the printed output. The last blank results in a space preceding the value of NUMEMP. Contrast this with the second message, which does not provide a space following the dollar sign. All characters, *including blanks,* are counted to determine the message length. Note also that no variable name in the WRITE list corresponds to the data in the Hollerith message.

The programmer can think of the Hollerith message as being stored in the FORMAT statement; each time this statement is referenced by a WRITE statement, the message is written automatically.

A Hollerith message is often called a *literal* because the message is literally written character for character as it appears in the FORMAT statement. The H format code was the only way literals could be written in older standard versions of FORTRAN. Since the introduction of FORTRAN 77, compilers have added a new standard method, which is usually more convenient. This new method, described next, has gained rapid acceptance and is exceedingly popular. This method was previously briefly discussed in the DATA statement and in the alphanumeric assignment statement sections. The next section covers its use in a FORMAT statement.

Literals within apostrophes Literal data may be enclosed within apostrophes, in which case no field length is specified. Either of the following statements will produce the same results when referenced by a WRITE statement:

```
|12345|6|7
   7   FORMAT(5X,I3H MY ANSWER IS,F7.2)
   4   FORMAT(5X,' MY ANSWER IS',F7.2)
```

The following incomplete statements provide all possible carriage control characters in the first position of the output image:

```
|12345|6|7
    3    FORMAT('+',...)    (no advance before
                                  printing)
    4    FORMAT(' ',...)    (advance one line before
                                  printing)
    5    FORMAT('0',...)    (advance two lines
                                  before printing)
    6    FORMAT('1',...)    (advance to top of next
                                  page before printing)
```

This type of literal provides an easy method of writing headings over data columns. For example, these two statements:

```
|12345|6|7
   37    FORMAT(T3,'COL-1',T9,'COL-2')
         WRITE(3,37)
```

will produce the following printed output:

```
|123456789
  COL-1  COL-2
```

The T format code specifies that the first literal begins in column 3; but when the output image is shifted one position to the left, the literal is printed starting in column 2. The apostrophes are *not* printed, only the literal contained within the apostrophes. It is possible to have an apostrophe within a literal if it is indicated by two consecutive apostrophes. For example, the literal 'JOE DOE''S' will be printed as JOE DOE'S. Note that the WRITE statement does not contain a list of variable names because the FORMAT statement does not contain any format codes that specify data fields.

Unlike variable names, literals may be composed of more than six numbers and/or letters and may include any valid data character. The two literals in the preceding illustration can be treated as one literal at the programmer's option. The following two statements, for example,

```
|12345|6|7
   38    FORMAT(T3,'COL-1 COL-2')
         WRITE(3,38)
```

will also produce this output:

```
|12345|6|789
  COL-1  COL-2
```

Another variation, which will produce the same output, would be to include two blanks preceding COL-1 in the literal:

```
|12345|6|7
   39    FORMAT('   COL-1  COL-2')
```

To illustrate further, the following statements can be used to print a multiple-line heading:

```
|12345|6|7
   22   FORMAT(T2,'MARCH')
   66   FORMAT(1X,'TOTAL')
        WRITE(3,22)
        WRITE(3,66)
```

The above statements will produce the following printed output:

```
| 1 2 3 4 5 |6|7
MARCH
TOTAL
```

A more convenient method of producing the same output would be to include a slash in the FORMAT statement to control the vertical line spacing:

```
|12345|6|7
   44   FORMAT(T2,'MARCH'/1X,'TOTAL')
        WRITE(3,44)
```

Finally, a convenient technique for providing "headers" with multiple lines of varying lengths is illustrated next:

```
|12345|6|7
   88   FORMAT(T50,'XYZ CONSTRUCTION, INC.'/
   $           T50,'    EMPLOYEE ROSTER    '/
   $           T50,'    AS OF DECEMBER 31, '/
   $           T50,'          1984         '//)
        WRITE(3,88)
```

Other line control techniques   As previously indicated, both Hollerith messages and literals within apostrophes can be used to provide any of the four valid carriage control characters. A blank (but not a plus, zero, or one) can be provided in several other ways.

X format code   This code causes blanks in output. If used as the *first* code in the FORMAT statement, it causes the output image to contain a blank in the first position. When the output image is shifted left, the blank becomes the line control character. As a result, when a WRITE statement is executed, the paper will advance one line before printing. For example, if A has a value of 12.45, the following statements:

```
|12345|6|7
   17   FORMAT(1X,F5.2)
        WRITE(3,17)A
```

will cause the value of A to be printed in the first five printing positions.
T format code   This code can also be used to cause a blank in the line control position of the output image. The following statements will have the same effect as the preceding two statements:

```
|12345|6|7
   18  FORMAT(T2,F5.2)
       WRITE(3,18)A
```

The T2 format code specifies that the first (and only) available field begins in position 2, so the first position of the output image is blank. But when the output image is shifted left one position, the blank becomes the line control character which causes the paper to advance one line before the record is printed. The F5.2 field starts in the first printing position rather than the second because of the left shift. Note that whenever a printer is used as the I/O device, the first position of any field following a T format code is always *T minus 1*. Thus, the specification T20,I4 would cause the I4 field to start in printing position 19, not 20.

Overformatting   Another technique that can be used to cause the paper to advance one line before printing is to *overformat* the first field; that is, specify the field longer than required for the output data. If the first output field, for example, is determined via the scaling process to contain a positive value with a maximum length of five positions, the programmer might specify the format code at F6.2 instead of F5.2. This will cause the first position in the output image to contain a blank because high-order zeros and plus signs are edited out.

The overformatting technique, as well as the X and T format codes, can also be used to insert blanks between output data fields, thus providing *horizontal* spacing. This is usually desirable on printed output because it facilitates reading. If I, J, and K, for example, have current values of 111, 222, and 333 respectively, the following statements will cause I to be printed in the first three positions and will force three blanks between each data field:

```
|12345|6|7
    3  FORMAT(I4,I6,I6)
       WRITE(3,3)I,J,K
```

The resulting printed output will be:

```
|123|456789|
 111   222   333
```

This completes the presentation of all essential information required to write programs that will solve a wide variety of elementary problems that have a limited amount of input and output. Beginning programmers soon discover that the art of preparing statements is very exacting. If even one comma is omitted or incorrectly positioned, the program will either fail to compile or it will produce invalid output. Even experienced programmers expect a few "bugs" and consider themselves lucky if a program properly compiles and executes the first time it is processed. Fortunately, much can be learned by searching out and

5 / Input and Output

correcting various types of programming errors. Debugging techniques which will be useful to beginning programmers are illustrated and explained in Appendix A.

REVIEW QUESTIONS

1. Variable names may be initialized by assignment statements, DATA statements, or input statements. Discuss the appropriateness of each method.

2. The program should always describe the format of input records but should never describe the format of FORTRAN statements. Why?

3. A valid FORTRAN statement may be in *almost* any location in the program. What locations should be avoided?

4. Are the following two statements equivalent?

>   66   FORMAT(2(I2,I3))
>   66   FORMAT(I2,I2,I3,I3)

5. Name one advantage of using implied, rather than actual, decimal points in input data.

6. Is it valid for two or more X format codes to appear in sequence?

7. What are the device codes for the basic I/O devices used to process your programs, and who assigns them?

8. Consider the following two statements:

>   2 FORMAT(I2,2X,I2)
>   READ(1,2)M,N,K

How many input fields will be read?
How many input records will be read?
How many input records are described?

9. What term is used to describe the process of determining required data field sizes?

10. What output can be expected if an attempt is made to print the number 123 in an I2 field?

11. Describe the various methods by which the programmer may specify the line control character to be (A) a blank and (B) a one.

12. What characters may be included in a literal?

13. What is meant by overformatting?

14. The X format code can be used to control both horizontal and vertical spacing of printed output. Explain.

15. Describe the printed output, assuming this series of three statements:

    N=18
    WRITE(3,6)N,N,N,N
    6 FORMAT('1',3HSAM/1X,I2/ /I3/'0',I2,1X,I2/'SAM')

PROBLEMS

1. Write a program to:
   a. Read two data records with one READ statement. Two data values (100 and 20) should be entered in the first record but only one (an 8) in the second.
   b. Square each of the three data and sum the squares.
   c. Print the three input numbers under the heading DATA VALUES and print the sum under the heading SUM OF SQUARES.

2. Write a program to convert Fahrenheit temperature to Celsius. The conventional formula is:

$$C = \frac{5}{9}(F-32)$$

The Fahrenheit temperature is to be read from a five-column field on an input record. The datum may be any number that includes a decimal point and one decimal position (such as 212.0°).

Output should be printed as follows (Xs represent digits):

```
            TEMPERATURES
        FAHRENHEIT   CELSIUS
          XXX.X       XXX.X
```

One FORMAT statement should describe the two-line header and another the numeric output.

Test the program by running it a second time using an input record with a different value.

3. Write a program to compute the average of four values (10.05, 20.20, 30.25, and 40.00). Use four input data records with one value in each. Print the headings SUM and AVERAGE; below these headings print the numeric sum of the four values (use F4.0 code) and the numeric average (use F5.2 code).

4. Change the program described in Problem 3 above so that the four values are all read from one input card.

5. This problem emphasizes output formatting, including a review of line control characters, literals, slashes, alignment, and continuation characters. Do not use a READ, DATA, CHARACTER, or assignment statement.

Write a program that will print out your first and last initials in the following general form:

5 / Input and Output

```
XXXXXXXX        XXXXXXXX
XX    XX        XX
XX    XX        XX
XXXXXXXX        XXXXXXXX
XX                    XX
XX                    XX
XX              XXXXXXXX
```

Output should begin near the top of a page and should be approximately centered from left to right. If you prefer, other symbols may be substituted for the letter X.

6. Write a program to compute the total charge for one customer where net charge equals units times unit price and total charge equals net charge plus freight charge. Input consists of two records. The first input record is in the following format:

Field name	Record column	Required field contents
Customer name	1–4	X CO
Number of units	5–7	156
Unit price	8–12	01.16

The format of the second input card is as follows:

Field name	Record column	Required field contents
Customer name	1–4	X CO
Freight charges	5–9	07.17

Use only one READ statement to read the two input cards.

Use two WRITE statements to obtain the output that is to consist of two printed lines separated by one blank line. The first output line is to contain the following headings in the position indicated:

Print positions or "columns"	Required field contents
1–8	CUSTOMER
11–15	UNITS
18–27	UNIT-PRICE
30–36	FREIGHT
39–43	TOTAL

The second output line should be blank, and the third should contain output data in the following format:

Field name	Print positions or "columns"
Customer name	3-6
Number of units	12-14
Unit price	20-24
Freight charges	32-35
Total charge	39-44

 Control Statements

The first five chapters of this book were designed to provide the reader with the technical vocabulary as well as the information required to write elementary but complete programs. Many illustrations were used to explain the uses of statements and to impress the reader with the fact that programming is an art rather than an exact science. The rules of FORTRAN are strict, but there are many optional methods of achieving the same results. Various options may be chosen to save programming time as well as compilation and/or execution time.

Before considering the advanced programming techniques covered in this chapter, it may be advisable to review briefly the general FORTRAN programming routine covered thus far.

BRIEF PROGRAMMING REVIEW

The computer is a robot. It must be told when to start, what to do, and when to stop. The computer operator and certain system control commands, described in Appendix C, tell the computer when to start. After the computer is started, the program statements tell the computer what data to use, what steps to take, what to do with the results, and when to stop.

Data are stored internally at symbolic addresses represented by variable names composed by the programmer. The first letter of a variable name implies the mode in which numeric data will be stored as covered in Chapter 3.

All data required for solution of the problem to be solved must be provided to the computer. Such data may be provided directly in the program and/or from an external source. Chapter 4 discussed how assignment statements and DATA statements can be used to provide data directly in the program. Chapter 5 illustrated how the READ statement, referenced to a FORMAT statement, can be used to obtain data from an external source.

Arithmetic statements, covered in Chapter 4, can be used to tell the computer what to do with the data and how and where to store the results. The arithmetic expression to the right of the equal sign may contain various combinations of variable names and/or constants separated by one or more delimiters. The manner in which such an expression is written determines the type and sequence of calculations to be performed as well as the mode of the result. The variable name to the left of the equal sign implies the mode and specifies the symbolic location where the result of the arithmetic expression is to be stored. If the mode of the result of an arithmetic expression is not consistent with the mode in which the result is to be stored, the computer automatically converts the mode of the result before storing it.

The computer automatically executes statements in the order in which they appear in the program. The location of FORMAT statements is optional because they are nonexecutable. But it is the programmer's responsibility to arrange all executable statements in logical order. The computer is told to terminate the program by a STOP statement, described in Chapter 2. The last statement in every FORTRAN program must always be an END statement.

All programs have a *logical* as well as a *physical* end. The logical end is that point in the program where all statements have been executed the desired number of times and the program has completed the task for which it was designed. The physical end is the last statement in the source program.

The *logical*, not the *physical*, end of a program is indicated by a STOP statement. Its purpose is to tell the computer to terminate execution of the program. It may appear at any point in the program provided it will not be executed until the program is finished. Some programs, illustrated later in this book, have several logical ends and so require several STOP statements; but all programs should include at least one. Its general form is:

|12345|6|7
nnnnn   STOP

Legend:

nnnnn   Any unique one- to five-digit integer that specifies the statement *number*. It is required only if the statement is referenced by another statement in the program.

STOP   A keyword that specifies the operation to be performed.

The *physical* end of a program is indicated by an END statement. It tells the computer that any statements, comments, or data records that might follow this statement are not a part of the source program, so that they will be ignored in the translation process. Stated another way, the END statement tells the computer that it now has the entire source program and can begin translating.

The general form of an END statement is:

|12345|6|7
        END

END is a keyword that identifies the statement. It should be noted that this statement is *not* numbered. A number is not required because it is not permissible to reference this statement by another statement in the program. Some compilers permit this statement to be numbered, but others assume an error so this practice is not recommended.

The END statement is a special type of statement in the sense that it has a primary function and also a sort of backup or default function. As previously stated, its main function is to indicate the physical end of the sequence of statements and comment lines that compose the program. Its default function is to serve as an executable control statement if and when—usually because of an omitted STOP—the END statement is encountered during execution of the program. If the END statement is executed in a *main* program (as distinguished from a subprogram covered in Chapter 10), it will terminate execution of the program.

It is important to distinguish between the logical and physical ends of a program. It is possible to have several logical ends but only one physical end. Thus, a program may have no more than one END statement. If it is omitted, the program may not compile.

STRUCTURED PROGRAMMING

The concept of structured programming involves the design of a program into a group of modules. Each module follows sequentially. For example, a program may start with an Initialization Module, then have a Process Module, and finally end with a Termination Module. In turn, each module may be divided into submodules. Thus the Process Module mentioned above can be separated into an Input Submodule, a Computation Submodule, and a Report Submodule. This process of breaking modules into smaller modules is repeated until the program becomes a structure of simple modules.

Any computer program can be designed to follow any one or more of only three logic structures: sequential, selective, and repetitive. (See Figure 6-1.)

Sequential structure is simply one action followed by another. All programs, except one, presented thus far in this book have been sequential only. These programs were designed to start at the "top" and work on "down," processing each executable statement, in turn, only once and then terminating. All computer programs have some sequential structure; most also have selective and repetitive structure. (See Figure 6-2.)

Selective structure begins with a test for a condition—e.g., Is A equal to B? Then the program will branch to follow one of the alternative paths selected by the results of the logical decision.

A repetitive structure is designed to repeat one or more operations until some condition is satisfied (e.g., until 10 lines have been written).

If modular programming concepts are effectively followed, the general design simplicity of each of the three logic structures can be main-

Figure 6-1
The three programming logic structures

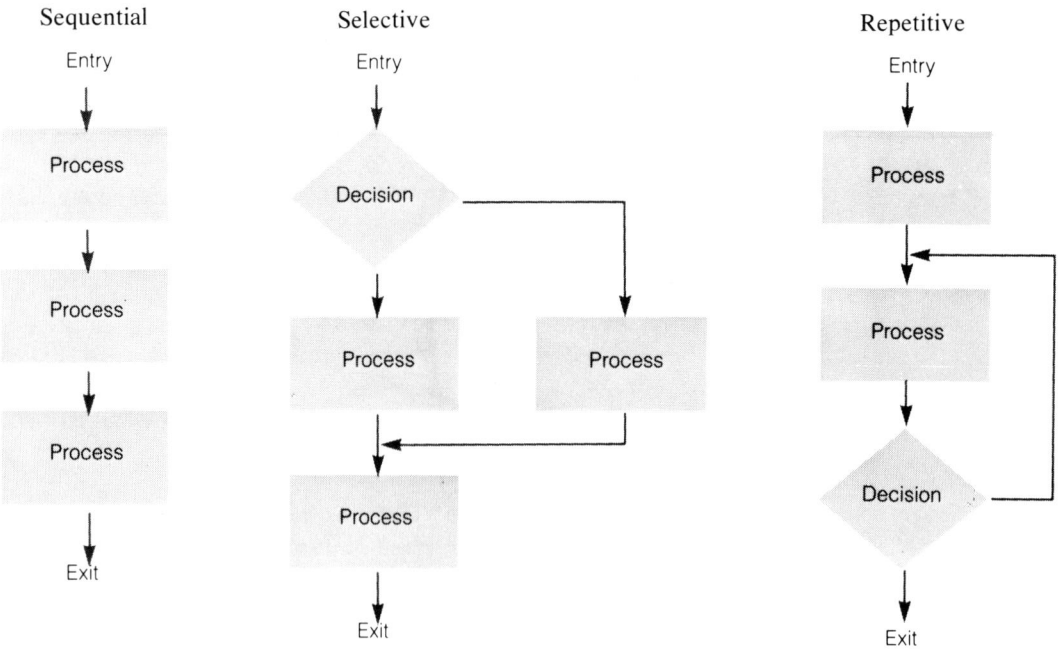

Figure 6-2
A simple combination of the three programming logic structures

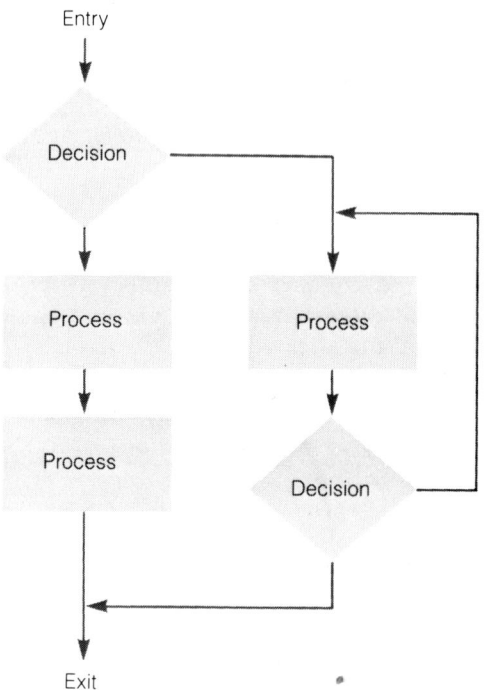

6/Control Statements

tained, even in complex programs. Examples of these will be explained later in the text as they become relevant.

FORTRAN originally was not designed to be a language for structured programming. However, over the years modifications have made it much more compatible to structuring. With a few modifications, FORTRAN is destined to be a fully structured language. In fact, compilers now exist with enhancements that go beyond the language standard and that enable programmers to design and to code fully structured programs.

The general concepts of good programming structure and design are emphasized in appropriate places throughout this book.

BRANCHING AND LOOPING

Normally the computer executes statements in the order in which they appear in the program. Several control statements are available to enable the programmer to change this normal order of execution. If a control statement is to tell the computer to execute a statement that is *not* the next in sequence, there must obviously be some way to reference the specific statement within the program to which control is to pass. This referencing is done by use of statement numbers (alternatively called *labels*).

The preceding chapter illustrated how READ and WRITE statements are referenced to nonexecutable FORMAT statements by use of statement numbers. Control statements, which can change the normal order of execution, also reference statements by number, but there is one important distinction—such control statements must always reference an *executable* statement. It is invalid for control statements to reference a nonexecutable statement or a statement label that does not exist in the program.

It is often desirable to cause the computer to go back and repeat the execution of a segment of the program or even the entire program a number of times using different data each time. Some programs require different statements to be executed under different circumstances. Such "decision making" requires a control statement that allows referencing to two or more alternative statement numbers.

The process of causing the computer to skip to an executable statement either preceding or following a control statement is called *branching*. A series of instructions that are repeated during the execution of the program are referred to as a *loop*. The process of repeating a series of instructions is called *looping*.

GO TO STATEMENTS

This section describes two types of GO TO statements. One type is an *unconditional* control statement. It is called unconditional because it allows only one statement to be referenced; when executed, it always branches to the same statement.

The other type is a *conditional* control statement. It allows two or more statement numbers to be referenced. It is conditional in that it causes branching to one of two or more statements based on a decision made by the computer.

Each type is discussed and illustrated in the following sections.

Unconditional GO TO

This is the less complicated of the two types of GO TO statements. The general form is:

|12345|6|7
 nnnnn   GO TO sn

Legend:

nnnnn   Any unique one- to five-digit integer that specifies the statement *number*. It is required only if the statement is referenced elsewhere in the program.

GO TO   A keyword specifying the operation to be performed. The keyword is GOTO (without an embedded blank), but this is one of those rare cases in which an embedded blank (which is always permitted in keywords) is usually used to improve readability.

sn   An integer label (*statement number*) that references an executable statement appearing elsewhere in the program.

The following statement causes a branch to statement number 18:

|12345|6|7
        GO TO 18

It should be noted that no delimiter is used to separate the keyword from the statement number. Although unnecessary, programmers often provide a blank following the keyword to improve readability.

The unconditional GO TO is an executable statement that directs the computer to branch to the statement referenced. It may reference any preceding or following executable statement but should never reference itself. It should be noted especially that *the first executable statement following an unconditional GO TO must always be labeled* because it can never be executed unless there is a way to reference it.

Computed GO TO

The computed GO TO can also be used to skip ahead or back in the program. It is a conditional control statement because it causes branching to one of two or more statements based on a decision made by the computer. The decision is based on the current value of a specified integer variable name. The general form is:

|12345|6|7
 nnnnn   GO TO($sn_1,sn_2, \ldots sn_m$),ivn

Legend:

nnnnn   Any unique one- to five-digit integer that specifies the statement *number*. It is required only if the statement is referenced elsewhere in the program.

GO TO   A keyword specifying the operation to be performed.

6/Control Statements

$(sn_1, \ldots, sn_m)$	A list of two or more *statement numbers* enclosed in parentheses. Each must be separated by a comma. The statement numbers are used to reference executable statements appearing elsewhere in the program.
,ivn	An optional comma followed by an *integer variable name* (often called an *index*), which must have a positive, non-zero current value.

It should be noted that an open (leftmost) parenthesis is required as a delimiter following the keyword GO TO. The last statement number in the list is followed by two delimiters: a close (rightmost) parenthesis and a comma. The comma, included in all illustrations in this book, may be omitted at the programmer's option.

The computed GO TO tells the computer to branch to the statement whose *position* in the list of statement numbers corresponds to the current value of the integer variable name. Thus, if the current value is 1, it will branch to the statement whose number appears first in the list, if 2 to the second in the list, etc. For example, the statement:

```
|12345|6|7
     GO TO(4,3,3,9),K
```

will cause a branch to statement number 4 if the current value of K is 1, to statement number 3 if the current value is either 2 or 3, and to statement number 9 if the current value is 4. Note that the computer associates the current value of K with the *position* of the statement number in the list, not with the actual number of the statement. For example, if the current value of K is 4, it does not go to statement number 4. Instead, it goes to the fourth statement number in the list, which in this case is statement number 9.

Because the current value of the integer variable name is used as a sort of pointer or indicator to tell the computer which statement in the list is to be executed next, it is often called an *index value*. To facilitate discussion, this term is used throughout the remainder of this book.

The programmer may include as many statement numbers in the list as is desired. The statement numbers may appear in any sequence, and the same number may appear more than once in the list, as illustrated in the example.

But what if the index value in the preceding example had been other than 1, 2, 3, or 4? Then it would be considered an *invalid* index value, which will be covered in later sections of this chapter. Before covering various complexities, the use of the computed GO TO using valid and convenient index values will be explained by an illustrative program.

Valid and convenient index values To illustrate the use of the computed GO TO statement, consider the following problem. (Examine the problem carefully because several illustrations based on this problem will be used throughout this chapter.)

Lucky Company management has decided to pay a special bonus to all employees. The bonus is to be based upon a percentage of the current weekly payroll. The bonus percentage varies according to the number of years the employee has worked for the company. The weekly payroll input records include a code to indicate the type of bonus each employee is to receive. The bonus plan may be summarized as follows:

Years of employment	Percentage of weekly pay	Bonus code
More than 5	200%	01
1 to 5	100	02
Less than 1	50	03

The weekly payroll cards are in the following format:

Field name	Record columns	Illustrative field contents
Employee number	1–4	1234
Department number	5–6	09
Hours worked	7–11	38.50
Rate per hour	8–16	11.25
Date of birth	17–22	120934
Bonus code	23–24	01

A program is to be written that will read only one input card, compute the designated bonus, then write only one output card. The required format of the output card is as follows:

Field name	Record columns
Employee number	1–4
Regular pay	5–11
Bonus	12–19
Total pay	20–27
Bonus code	79–80

Card output is illustrated to avoid the distractions of headings, slashes, carriage control characters, and field separators that are required for printed output. Emphasis is on control statements and related program structure and logic.

The flowchart in Figure 6-3 illustrates one method of solving the Lucky Company problem. The diamond-shaped "decision symbol" in the flowchart indicates a three-way branch. This will be represented by a computed GO TO statement in the illustrative program that follows. After branching to one of the three different bonus computations, the

Figure 6-3
Flowchart for the Lucky Company problem illustrating three terminal points

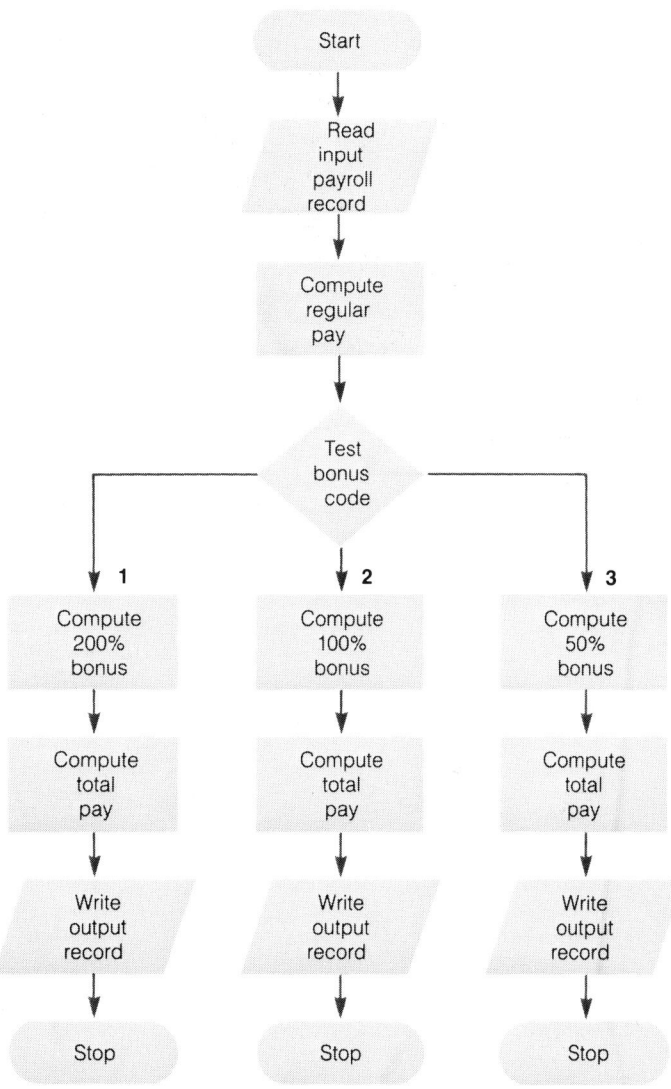

program will flow "straight line" until it is terminated by a STOP statement.

Because the problem does not require the data contained in either the department number or date-of-birth fields, it will be ignored in the FORMAT and READ statements. This will save programming time and will reduce the amount of computer memory required to store the object program. The variable name in the computed GO TO statement will be called KODE instead of CODE because it must be in integer mode. The flowchart in Figure 6-3 calls for three STOP statements, but there can be only one END statement. As always, the END statement must appear last in the program. The program illustrated in Figure 6-4 is one method of solving the Lucky Company problem.

The program (Figure 6-4) has been written using the flowchart in Figure 6-3 as a guide. The index value of the computed GO TO statement causes a branch to one of three statements, which is the beginning of a complete routine. Except for the bonus computation, all three routines are identical.

Introductory comments should be included to document a program. They have been excluded here to place emphasis on the basic program

Figure 6-4
Program for the Lucky Company problem illustrating three terminal points

```
|12345|6|7
         PROGRAM PAYROL
         OPEN(1,FILE='INPUT')
         OPEN(2,FILE='PUNCH')
      77 FORMAT(I4,2X,2F5.2,T23,I2)
      88 FORMAT(I4,F7.2,2F8.2,T79,I2)
C
         READ(1,77)NUMEMP,HOURS,RATE,KODE
C
         REGPAY=HOURS*RATE
C
C
C        ***BONUS IS BASED ON YEARS OF EMPLOYMENT
C             AS INDICATED BY KODE
C             KODE        YEARS
C               1        MORE THAN 5
C               2        1 TO 5
C               3        LESS THAN 1
C
         GO TO(55,65,76),KODE
      55    BONUS=REGPAY*2.00
            TOTPAY=REGPAY+BONUS
            WRITE(2,88)NUMEMP,REGPAY,BONUS,TOTPAY,KODE
       1    STOP
C
      65    BONUS=REGPAY
            TOTPAY=REGPAY+BONUS
            WRITE(2,88)NUMEMP,REGPAY,BONUS,TOTPAY,KODE
       2    STOP
C
      75    BONUS=REGPAY/2.00
            TOTPAY=BONUS+REGPAY
            WRITE(2,88)NUMEMP,REGPAY,BONUS,TOTPAY,KODE
C
       3    STOP
            END
```

logic, structure, contents, and form. Blank comments have been liberally used to separate the various program sections. Note that the explanatory comments describe the purpose and meaning of the codes. On the other hand a comment such as: GO TO STATEMENT 55 IF THE CODE IS 1, TO 65 IF 2, OR 75 IF 3 would do nothing to improve clarity. Comments that merely echo program statements are redundant and dangerous. As previously stated, the trouble with redundant comments is that readers tend to believe the comments rather than statements, which may not say what the programmer meant. Remember, comments should be used as a meaningful supplement to, not a substitute for or a restatement of, clear FORTRAN statements.

Also note the structure of the GO TO section in Figure 6-4. The three GO TO "targets" (statements 55, 65, and 75) and their related statements have been indented a few columns; they are further set off to the reader's eye by the use of blank comments. This illustrates a type of writing style designed to make the program more readable. Separating code into appropriate blocks of related statements is an important contribution to good program structure.

Two prime virtues of programming are clarity and simplicity. Several short comprehensible arithmetic statements (that do the job) are better than one that is long and complex; excessive comments and redundant statements should be avoided. *Good programmers write to express, not to impress.*

A major criticism of the program (Figure 6-4) under discussion is that it unnecessarily repeats several identical statements. Figure 6-5 is a simplified flowchart of the Lucky Company problem. This flowchart has been used as a guide for writing a shorter, more efficient, and easier-to-read program that will produce the same results. This program (Figure 6-6) is designed to demonstrate how the unconditional GO TO, previously described, can be effectively used in combination with a computer GO TO statement. The following discussion relates to this more efficient program.

If the index value of the computed GO TO statement is 1 or 2, the computer will branch to statement numbers 55 or 65 respectively. The unconditional GO TO following these statements causes the computer to jump directly to statement 76. The combinations of the computed GO TO and unconditional GO TO statements thus cause the computer to omit statements that should not be executed. If the index value is 3, the computer will skip ahead to statement number 75. It is unnecessary to follow this statement by a GO TO 76 statement because the computer automatically will go to statement 76 since it is next in sequence.

A comparison of the two programs (Figures 6-4 and 6-6) will illustrate several advantages of the modified version that does the same job with about 20 percent fewer statements. The simpler program is easier to read, saves coding and keypunching time, lessens the chance of error, and can be operational sooner.

A disadvantage of the longer program, besides its sheer size, is the

128   Standard FORTRAN Programming: A Structured Style

Figure 6-5
Flowchart for the Lucky Company problem illustrating one terminal point

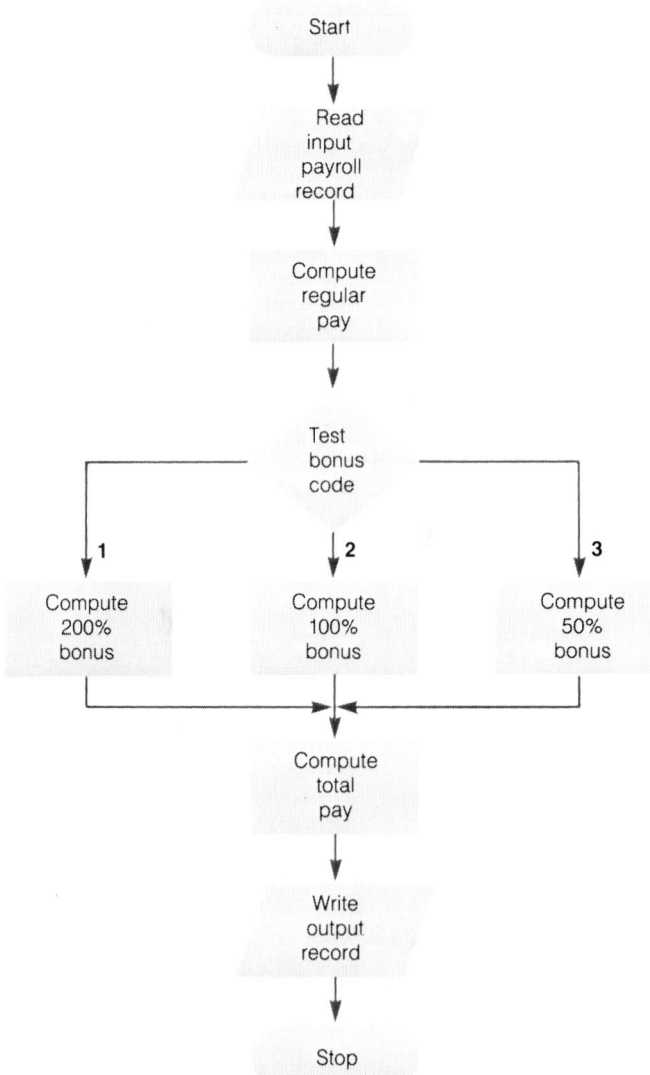

statement-numbering technique. It appears to have no logic. When statement numbers are ordered sequentially, the reader knows whether to look ahead or back to find a referenced statement. Furthermore, only five statements are referenced, but eight are numbered. The numbers (1, 2, and 3) identifying the three STOP statements are unnecessary, and confusng to a human reader. (Consider the difficulty of finding statement number 65 if *all* statements had been given unordered identifiers.) Incidentally, the first two STOP statements could be re-

Figure 6-6
Program for the Lucky Company problem illustrating one terminal point

```
|12345|6|7
      PROGRAM PAYROL
      OPEN(1,FILE='INPUT')
      OPEN(2,FILE='PUNCH')
C
      READ(1,77)NUMEMP,HOURS,RATE,KODE
C
      REGPAY=HOURS*RATE
C
C
C     ***BONUS IS BASED ON YEARS OF EMPLOYMENT
C          AS INDICATED BY KODE
C          KODE      YEARS
C           1        MORE THAN 5
C           2        1 TO 5
C           3        LESS THAN 1
C
      GO TO(55,65,75),KODE
   55 BONUS=REGPAY*2.00
      GO TO 76
C
   65 BONUS=REGPAY
      GO TO 76
C
   75 BONUS=REGPAY/2.00
C
C
   76 TOTPAY=REGPAY+BONUS
C
      WRITE(2,88)NUMEMP,REGPAY,BONUS,TOTPAY,KODE
C
   77 FORMAT(I4,2X,2F5.2,T23,I2)
   88 FORMAT(I4,F7.2,2F8.2,T79,I2)
C
    3 STOP
      END
```

placed by GO TO 3 statements, which would cause a branch to the third STOP. However, branching around branches is not recommended; it does not make the program easier to understand.

The shorter program, with one exception, illustrates good statement numbering technique. The one exception is the STOP statement. It was numbered 3, the same as the last STOP in the longer program, to facilitate discussion in following sections.

Establishing convenient index values The bonus code punched in the input cards of the Lucky Company was either 1, 2, or 3, which was convenient for the programmer. But what if instead of a 1, 2, or 3, the cards have been punched with either a 6, 8, or 12 respectively? Then the programmer has several alternatives.

The programmer could for example, change the computed GO TO statement as follows:

|12345|6|7
     GO TO(3,3,3,3,3,55,3,65,3,3,3,75),KODE

Now, if the index value is 6, the computer would branch to the sixth statement number in the series, which is 55. Likewise, if the index value is 8 or 12, the computer would branch to statement numbers 65 or 75 respectively. Statement number 55 must appear in the sixth position in the list. The programmer is not permitted to pick any number at random as a sort of "filler" for the five positions in the list that precede the 55. The numbers used must reference an executable statement which appears in the program. In this case 3 references a STOP statement in each of the two preceding program illustrations. Thus, the program will terminate if, as the result of an error, the index value is 1, 2, 3, 4, 5, 7, 9, 10, or 11.

It should be apparent that if the bonus code had been 97, 98, or 99 instead of 1, 2, or 3 respectively, the length of the computed GO TO statement would require several continuation cards.

The programmer can often avoid extremely long computed GO TO statements by converting the bonus code punched in the card to a more convenient value. To illustrate this technique without using large values, assume again that the bonus codes are 6, 8, or 12 instead of 1, 2, or 3 respectively. The programmer could replace the one computed GO TO statement in the Lucky Company program illustrations with the following two statements:

|12345|6|7
     KKODE=KODE/2-2
     GO TO(55,65,3,75),KKODE

The above arithmetic statement will cause the following values to be stored at KKODE:

KODE	KKODE
6	1
8	2
12	4

Note that the variable name in the computed GO TO statement must be KKODE instead of KODE in this illustration.

It is not necessary to use a different variable name to change the index value. The programmer, for example, could use the following two statements:

6/Control Statements

```
|12345|6|7
      KODE=KODE/2-2
      GO TO(55,65,3,75),KODE
```

The above arithmetic statement will change the values of KODE from 6, 8, or 12 to 1, 2, or 4. This is not a good technique in the case of the Lucky Company problem because KODE is required in the output; it will be necessary to convert the value of KODE back to 6, 8, or 12 before the WRITE statement is executed.

A "tricky way" to accomplish the desired result would be to use the following two statements:

```
|12345|6|7
      KKODE=KODE/4
      GO TO(55,65,75),KKODE
```

Because the result of integer mode arithmetic is always integer, the above arithmetic statement will store the following values at KKODE:

KODE	KKODE
6	1
8	2
12	3

This technique is illustrated to review the effect of integer arithmetic and to demonstrate that just as there may be several ways to skin a cat, likewise there may be several ways to write a statement. But programmers are cautioned that cute programming such as this may sometimes cause unforeseen problems elsewhere in the program.

Establishing valid index values There are only first, second, third, fourth, etc., positions in the list of statement numbers in a computed GO TO statement. Thus, a zero or a negative index value is invalid. If the Lucky Company had used the bonus codes 0, 1, or 2 instead of 1, 2, or 3, an arithmetic statement could be used to validate the invalid code:

```
|12345|6|7
      KKODE=KODE+1
```

It was emphasized earlier in this chapter that the variable name in a computed GO TO statement must be in integer mode. If, for some reason, a value to be used as an index is in floating point mode, it must be converted to integer mode to make it valid.

Effect of invalid index values A valid index value cannot be less than one or greater than the number of choices provided in the computed GO TO list. The following statement, for example, contains a list of six statement numbers and thereby provides six choices, depending upon the value of N:

```
|12345|6|7
      GO TO(1,2,5,2,7,4),N
```

If, in the above example, the value of N is less than one or more than six, it is invalid. It is invalid because, if the index value is not within the range of one through six, the computer has not been instructed where to go.

If an index value falls outside the allowable range, it may be the result of a keyboard operator error. It could also be caused by the programmer not providing for all possibilities or committing a logic error in the program.

Standard FORTRAN provides that if the index value is outside the allowable range, the computer will automatically "drop through" and execute the next statement. This can be used to advantage; but unless the program is carefully designed, it might still fail or give incorrect results. In the case of the Lucky Company programs, illustrated previously in this chapter, an invalid index value would always result in the employee's receiving a 200 percent bonus.[1]

PERPETUAL LOOPS

When a program includes statements that cause branching and loops, a common programming error is to create a loop from which there is no possible exit. To illustrate, consider the following partial program:

```
|12345|6|7
    22   FORMAT(I4,I5)
    33   FORMAT(I7)
    70   READ(1,22)I,J
   700   K=I+J
         WRITE(2,33)K
         GO TO 70
         STOP
         END
```

The statements in this illustration will be executed in order until the GO TO branch is encountered. Each time this unconditional GO TO statement is executed it causes the computer to branch back to the READ statement and repeat the program. The sequence in which the statements appear makes it impossible for the program to execute the STOP statement. The program contains an uncontrolled or *perpetual loop* from which there is no possible exit.

Does this mean the computer will run forever? No, there are several types of "interruptions" which will cause the computer to terminate execution of the program. It should be emphasized that these "interruptions" are provided by the computer system, not by the FORTRAN compiler. A program, for example, will always terminate during the execution of a READ or WRITE statement that references an I/O

---

[1] At this point Problems 1 through 5 may be done before proceeding with the rest of the text.

device that contains no records. A program will also terminate if an input record is read that contains an invalid character according to the format code specifications. This illustrative program will probably not terminate until either the input or output device runs out of records or until the READ statement causes the computer to read a system control command containing invalid characters according to the input format codes (I4, I5).

This final example is identical to the preceding one except that the unconditional GO TO statement is located in a different sequence and the program contains two errors occasionally encountered by programmers as a result of improper coding.

```
|12345|6|7
    22   FORMAT(I4,I5)
    33   FORMAT(I7)
   7 0   READ(1,22)I,J
  70 0   K=I+J
         GO TO 70
         WRITE(2,33)K
         STOP
         END
```

First, note the two errors. The last digits (zero) of statement numbers 70 and 700 appear in column 6 instead of column 5. A zero in column 6 has the same effect as a blank, so the computer assumes that the READ statement is numbered 7 and the arithmetic statement is numbered 70.

Because the unconditional GO TO precedes the WRITE statement, the computer will read only one card, execute the arithmetic statement, and then get into a perpetual loop. And what a perpetual loop—it will continually compute and store the sum of I and J! This program is unlikely to be terminated by an I/O device's running out of cards or by the reading of invalid input data, because only one card is read and the WRITE statement can never be executed. This program probably will be terminated by the computer operator or possibly by an automatic timing device.

It is the programmer's responsibility to provide an exit from loops. One method of providing an exit is described and illustrated in the following section.

ARITHMETIC IF STATEMENT

This statement is technically called the "Arithmetic IF," but, for ease of discussion, it will be simply called the IF in this book. The IF is similar to the computed GO TO in that both are conditional control statements that cause the computer to skip ahead or back to some other executable statement in the program. However, they differ not only as to the format but also in the number of branches that can be provided and in the way in which they operate.

The computed GO TO references two or more executable statements, but the IF must always reference three. The computed GO TO contains an integer index value, established by a previously executed statement in the program, that is used to determine where to branch. But the IF statement contains an arithmetic expression that may be in either integer or floating point mode. When the IF statement is executed, the result of this expression or "argument" is computed. This result is not stored at a symbolic address, as is caused by an arithmetic statement, but is automatically compared to zero. The computer then branches to one of the three referenced statements, depending upon whether the result is evaluated as less than, equal to, or greater than zero. Stated another way, the branch is dependent upon whether the result of the arithmetic expression is negative, zero, or positive.

General form

The general form of an IF statement is:

```
|12345|6|7
 nnnnn    IF(ae)sn₁,sn₂,sn₃
```

Legend:

nnnnn — Any unique one to five-digit integer that specifies the statement *number*. It is required only if the statement is referenced elsewhere in the program.

IF — A keyword specifying the type of operation to be performed.

(ae) — Any invalid *arithmetic expression* enclosed in parentheses that is evaluated to determine whether the current value of the result is less than, equal to, or greater than zero.

sn_1 — An integer that references the statement that will be executed next when the evaluation of (ae) is negative.

sn_2 — An integer that references the statement that will be executed next when the evaluation of (ae) is equal to zero.

sn_3 — An integer that references the statement that will be executed next when the evaluation of (ae) is positive.

Illustrative examples

The following example of an IF statement will be used to illustrate its form and function:

```
|12345|6|7
         IF(KODE-2)55,65,75
```

In this illustration if KODE has a current value of 1, the evaluation will be less than zero, which will cause a branch to statement number 55; if KODE is 2, the zero evaluation will cause control to pass to statement number 65; if KODE is 3, the next statement executed will be number 75. This IF statement could be substituted for the computed GO TO statement in the Lucky Company programs presented earlier in this chapter because if the KODE is always 1, 2, or 3, it has the same effect as:

6/Control Statements

```
|12345|6|7
      GO TO(55,65,75),KODE
```

If the bonus codes in the Lucky Company problem were always 97, 98, or 99 instead of 1, 2, or 3 respectively, the following statement:

```
|12345|6|7
      IF(KODE-98)55,65,75
```

could be substituted for the following two statements:

```
|12345|6|7
      KKODE=KODE-96
      GO TO(55,65,75),KKODE
```

The evaluation of the arithmetic expression in an IF statement is always less than, equal to, or greater than zero, so it is impossible to "drop through" to the next statement; therefore, *the first executable statement immediately following an IF statement must always be numbered* because unless it can be referenced, it can never be executed. When one of the statement numbers in the IF statement references the immediately following statement, a more efficient object program is compiled.

IF statements are sometimes used in combination with a computed GO TO to eliminate invalid index values that may result from keypunching errors. To illustrate, assume that the Lucky Company problem used 6, 7, or 8 instead of 1, 2, or 3 for the bonus codes. The following series of statements will cause the computer to branch to statement number 3 (a STOP statement) if the bonus code is any integer other than 6, 7, or 8:

```
|12345|6|7
      IF(KODE-6)3,98,98
   98 IF(KODE-8)99,99,3
   99 KKODE=KODE-5
      GO TO(55,65,75),KKODE
```

The first IF statement above will cause the computer to branch to statement number 3 (STOP) if KODE is less than 6. If KODE is equal to or greater than 6, control will pass to the next IF statement, which will cause a branch to the STOP statement if KODE exceeds 8. Thus, control will pass to statement 99 and on to the computed GO TO only if the current value of KODE is 6, 7, or 8.

The preceding examples illustrated the form and general function of IF statements. The following problem will demonstrate a more complex application.

Joe's Store example Joe's store is open for business seven days a week. At the end of each day a data card is prepared that indicates the amount of sales for each department. The problem is to prepare a program to compute the total sales for each day, and also the total sales for the month. The input data file contains 31 cards (already sequenced by date) in the following format.

Field name	Record columns	Illustrative field contents
Department 1	1-6	100.00
Department 2	7-12	200.00
Department 3	13-18	300.00
Department 4	19-24	400.25

Output for each day is to be single-spaced on a printer in the following format:

Field name	Print positions or "columns"
Department 1	1-6
Department 2	9-14
Department 3	17-22
Department 4	25-30
Daily total	51-57

The *monthly* total is to be printed in "columns" 50-57. It is to be separated from the last daily total by one blank line and preceded by this literal message:

MONTHLY TOTAL $

A flowchart for this problem is illustrated in Figure 6-7. The solution to the Joe's Store problem requires a program that will:

1. Compute and write the total sales for each day.
2. Accumulate a running sum of the total sales for the month as each card is processed.
3. Write the total sales for the month after exactly 31 input cards have been processed.

The routine for computing and writing the total sales for each day can be repeated 31 times, but it is more efficient to use only one routine and a looping technique. The unconditional GO TO cannot be used to cause looping in this case because it will result in a perpetual loop as illustrated earlier in this chapter. This problem requires an exit from the loop after 31 input cards have been processed, so the monthly total will be printed before the program terminates.

The total sales for the month can be accumulated by beginning the program with an arithmetic statement that initializes the current values

6/Control Statements

Figure 6-7
Flowchart for Joe's Store problem illustrating a controlled loop

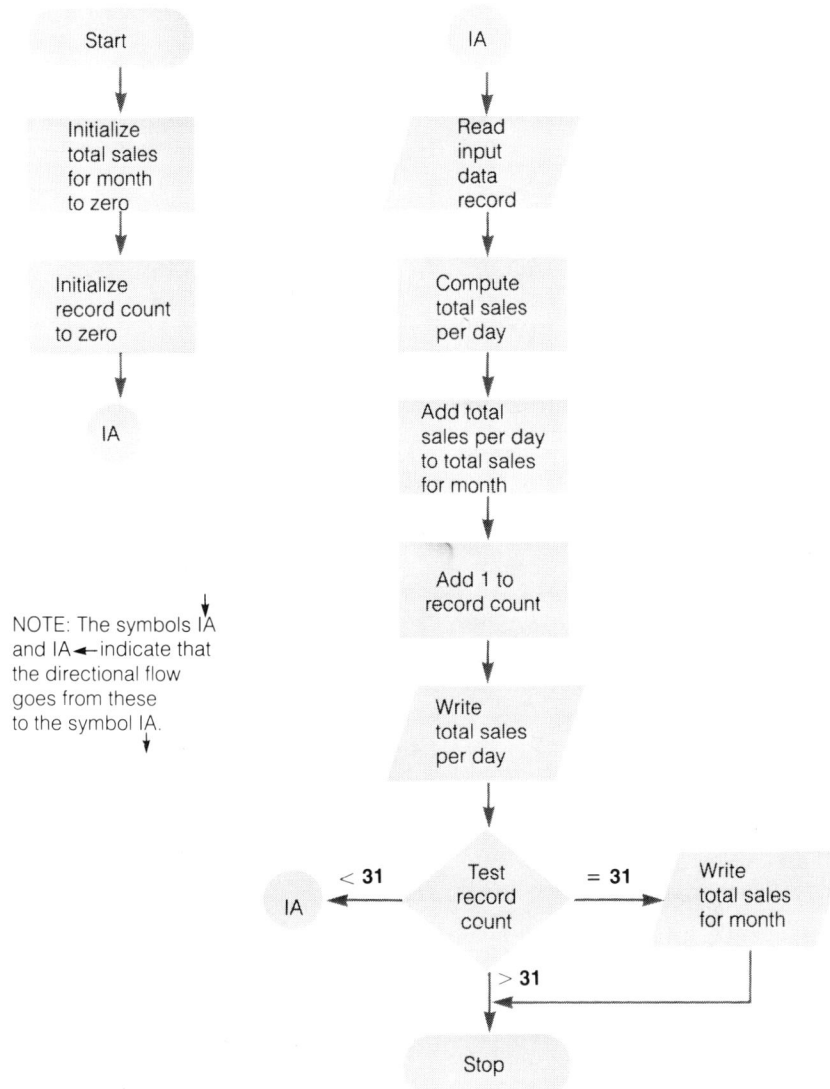

of a floating point variable name such as TOTMTH to zero. After the total sales for each day are computed, the amount can be added to TOTMTH (a process called *incrementing*).

To avoid an uncontrolled or perpetual loop, an integer variable name, such as KOUNT, can be initialized to zero and incremented by 1 on each pass through the loop. An IF statement can be used to provide an exit from the loop after 31 input cards have been processed.

The program in Figure 6-8 was written using the flowchart (Figure

Figure 6-8
Program for Joe's Store problem illustrating a controlled loop

```
|12345|6|7
      PROGRAM PAYROL
      OPEN(1,FILE='INPUT')
      OPEN(3,FILE='OUTPUT')
      TOTMTH=0.00
      KOUNT=0
C
C
   10 READ(1,100)DEPT1,DEPT2,DEPT3,DEPT4
C
      TOTDAY=DEPT1+DEPT2+DEPT3+DEPT4
      TOTMTH=TOTMTH+TOTDAY
      KOUNT=KOUNT+1
C
      WRITE(3,200)DEPT1,DEPT2,DEPT3,DEPT4,TOTDAY
C
      IF(KOUNT-31)10,20,30
C
C
   20 WRITE(3,300)TOTMTH
C
   30 STOP
C
  100 FORMAT(4F6.2)
  200 FORMAT(1X,F6.2,3F8.2,T52,F7.2)
  300 FORMAT(/T36,'MONTHLY TOTAL $',T51,F8.2)
      END
```

6-7) as a guide. Introductory comments were omitted to shorten the illustration, which is designed to emphasize program logic in general and loop control in particular. Note, however, that the program is not fully documented. It is not difficult to determine what the program does: it reads four values, computes and prints the sum, repeats this operation 31 times, then prints the grand total. However, the program gives no clue as to *what* is read except that it appears to have something to do with departments 1, 2, 3, and 4. At least one comment should be included to indicate clearly that the program works with daily sales. The program would then "stand alone."

Now, let's briefly review the basic loop control logic illustrated in Figure 6-8. After each of the first 30 input records is processed, the IF statement will be evaluated as less than zero, causing a branch to the READ statement and a recycle through the loop. After the 31st record is processed, the IF statement will be evaluated as equal to zero so the computer will exit from the loop, branch to the final WRITE statement, then automatically execute the next statement (STOP) in order. The program logic makes it impossible for KOUNT to exceed 31, so the IF statement can never be evaluated as more than zero. Thus, the third

6/Control Statements

statement number in the IF list appears unnecessary in this case. It cannot be omitted, however, because the rules of FORTRAN require that an IF statement must always reference three executable statements.

The following three statements in the Joe's Store program control the number of times (or *iterations*) the computer cycles through the loop:

```
|12345|6|7
        KOUNT=0
        KOUNT=KOUNT+1
        IF(KOUNT-31)10,20,30
```

Many variations of these statements could be used to produce the same results. The IF statement, for example, could be changed to provide an exit from the loop when KOUNT exceeds 30 instead of when it equals 31:

```
|12345|6|7
        IF(KOUNT-30)10,10,20
```

It would also be possible to initialize KOUNT to some value other than zero and/or to increment KOUNT by some value other than one. Of course, any change in the initialization and/or incremental values would also require a change in the IF statement to accomplish the desired results.

The following statement in the Joe's Store problem reviews three methods of obtaining blanks in the output image:

```
|12345|6|7
   200  FORMAT(1X,F6.2,3F8.2,T52,F7.2)
```

Legend:

1X   Causes a blank in the first position of the output image that, when shifted left, causes single-spacing.

3F8.2   Causes two blanks to precede these three six-position data fields as a result of overformatting.

T52   Causes a string of 20 blanks to precede the last data field.

To illustrate a technique often useful in programming, the Joe's Store program is designed so that each line indicating the total sales for the day can be sequentially numbered from 1 through 31. FORMAT statement number 200, for example, could be changed to include one additional format code at the end of the list:

```
|12345|6|7
   200  FORMAT(1X,F6.2,3F8.2,T52,F7.2,I4)
```

and the first WRITE station could be changed to include one more variable name at the end of the list:

```
|12345|6|7
            WRITE(3,200)DEPT1,DEPT2,DEPT3,DEPT4,TOTDAY,KOUNT
```

It should be noted that if KOUNT is incremented immediately *following* instead of preceding the execution of the above WRITE statement, the lines will be numbered sequentially from 0 through 30 instead of 1 through 31.

The Joe's Store program contains only one loop. The statements comprising the loop (called the *loop range*) will be executed 31 times. Each time the computer passes through the loop range it will use different input data because read in is destructive; that is, each time the READ statement is executed, the variable names are initialized to the data values contained in the input record.

Many programs require more than one loop and may also require some or all of the data from each of selected input records to be saved for later use in the program. More complex applications will be covered in later chapters but the following illustration will demonstrate the general principle of multiple loops and of saving data for later use in the program.

Signa Phi Nothing Fraternity example Signa Phi Nothing Fraternity has recently completed a charitable fund drive that extended over a period of several weeks. Some students gave nothing, some contributed once, others two or more times. For each contribution received, an input record was prepared in the following format:

Field name	Record columns	Illustrative field contents
Student number	1–4	1001
Amount received	5–9	12.50

The total number of records prepared is unknown, but it is known that 1,000 students made one or more contributions during the fund drive. The problem is to prepare a program that will compute the total amount received from each student and the total amount collected during the fund drive.

The records have been arranged in ascending sequence by student number. Each student has a unique number. Thus, all records for each student are together rather than randomly scattered throughout the input file. The last record in the input file has the value 9999 in the student number field. It is a *trailer record* (discussed later) to signal the end of the input file.

The required output for each student is one printed line indicating the student number and the total amount contributed in the following format:

Field name	Print positions or "columns"	Illustrative field contents
Student number	1–4	1001
Total donations	8–13	125.50

6/Control Statements

The final output line, indicating the total amount of contributions received during the fund drive, is to be in the following format:

Field name	Print positions or "colunns"
Fund drive total	6–13

All output is to be double-spaced on a printer.

The Signa Phi Nothing Fraternity problem can be solved by a program that will compare each record read in, other than the first, to the preceding record to determine whether the student number has changed. A solution to this problem is illustrated by the flowchart in Figure 6–9 and the complete program in Figure 6–10.

Arithmetic expressions

Any valid arithmetic expression may be placed between the parentheses of an IF statement. It may be in integer or floating point mode. Great care must be taken with floating point expressions or undesired branching may result, because exact values are rare in this mode.

Beginning programmers often find the truncation resulting from integer division to be rather distracting. Using floating point values alleviates this truncation problem but does not entirely eliminate it. Just as some fractional values cannot be represented exactly in decimal notation (such as $\frac{1}{3}$, which is *about* .33333), likewise, some cannot be represented exactly in binary. To complicate the situation further, some fractional values that can be represented exactly in decimal notation (such as $\frac{1}{10}$, which is .1) have no exact binary equivalents. Thus, when an innocent-looking decimal value is converted to binary for internal storage, it may be truncated to the allowable number of binary digits. As a consequence, a floating point expression that should obviously yield an exact decimal result may not do so within the computer. In most computations, this presents no difficulty because the computer maintains far more precision than is required for output. When testing for a zero condition in an IF statement with a floating point expression, however, difficulties usually arise because an exact zero seldom will be found. For this reason, it is recommended that beginning programmers avoid floating point expressions in IF statements whenever possible. The two illustrative programs in the preceding section demonstrated how the IF statement can be used to provide an exit from a loop. A later section covers loops in general and three different methods of loop control.

LOGICAL IF STATEMENT

A logical IF is a two-way decision statement. It is a convenient selection program structure statement that evaluates an expression as either true or false.

Figure 6-9
Sigma Phi Nothing Fraternity problem flowchart illustrating multiple loop and a technique for saving data for later use in program

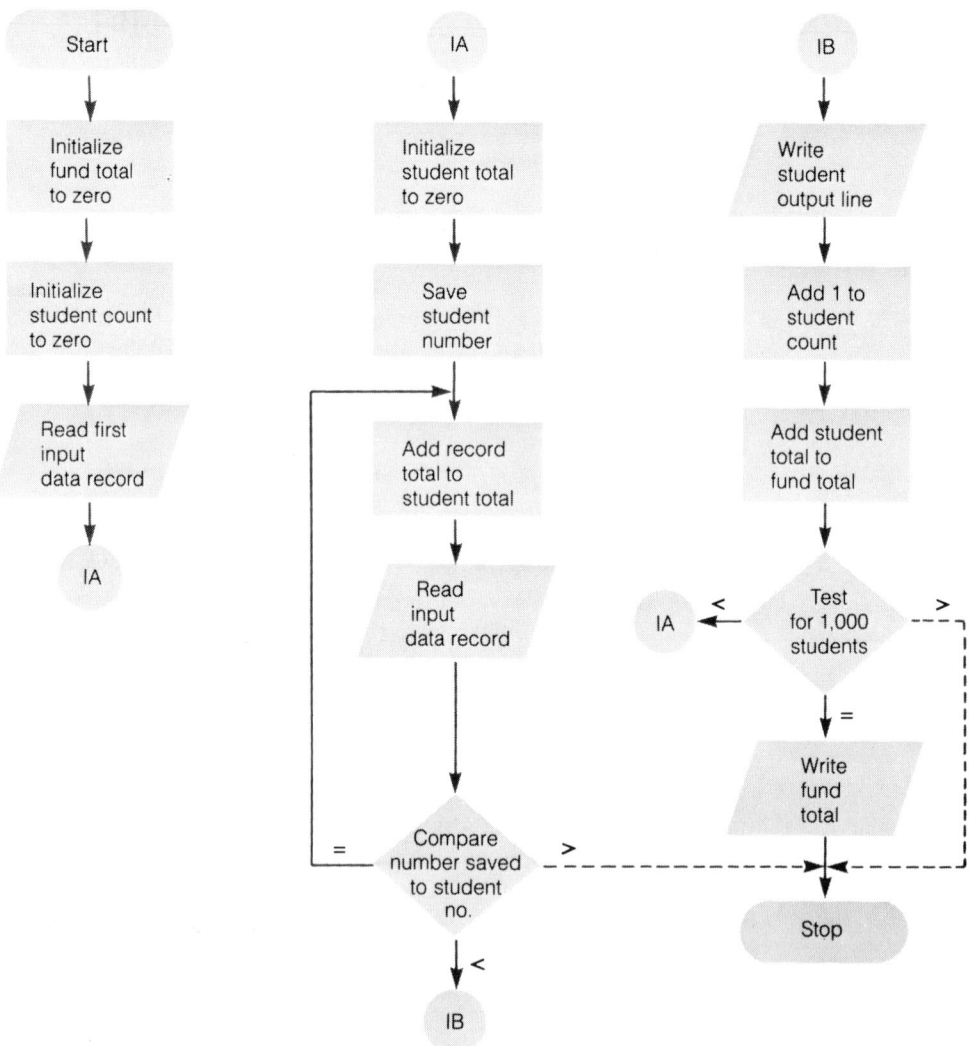

General form

The general form of a logical IF statement is:

```
|12345|6|7
nnnnn    IF(le)s
```

Legend:

nnnnn   Any unique one-to-five digit integer that specifies the statement *number*. It is required only if the statement is referenced elsewhere in the program.

IF   A keyword specifying the type of operation to be performed.

(le)   Any valid *logical expression* enclosed in parentheses that is evaluated to determine whether it is true or false.

Figure 6-10
Program for Signa Phi Nothing Fraternity problem

```
|12345|6|7
              PROGRAM PAYROL
              OPEN(1,FILE='INPUT')
              OPEN(3,FILE='OUTPUT')
              FUNTOT=0.00
              KOUNT=0
              READ(1,100)NUMSTU,CDTOT
      C
      C
          1   STUTOT=0.00
              NUMSAV=NUMSTU
      C
          2   STUTOT=STUTOT+CDTOT
              READ(1,100)NUMSTU,CDTOT
              IF(NUMSAV-NUMSTU)4,2,6
      C
          4   WRITE(3,200)NUMSAV,STUTOT
              KOUNT=KOUNT+1
              FUNTOT=FUNTOT+STUTOT
              IF(KOUNT-1000)1,5,6
      C
      C
          5   WRITE(3,300)FUNTOT
          6   STOP
      C
        100   FORMAT(I4,F5.2)
        200   FORMAT('0',I4,T9,F6.2)
        300   FORMAT('0',T7,F8.2)
              END
```

> s An executable *statement* which is executed if the logical expression is true but is ignored if the logical expression is false. It may be any executable statement except an END, IF-THEN, ELSE, ELSE IF, END IF, DO, or another logical IF statement.

The simplest form of logical expression consists of two similar mode arithmetic expressions separated by one relational operator, which must be preceded and followed by a period. The six relational operators are:

Relational operator	Meaning
.EQ.	Equal to ($=$)
.NE.	Not equal to ($\neq$)
.GT.	Greater than ($>$)
.LT.	Less than ($<$)
.GE.	Greater than or equal to ($\geq$)
.LE.	Less than or equal to ($\leq$)

The following example illustrates the form and function of the logical IF:

|12345|6|7
```
       IF(A.EQ.B)D=D*2.0
```

In this illustration, if A and B are equal (i.e., if the logical expression is true), the arithmetic statement that doubles the stored value of D is executed; if A and B are not equal (i.e., if the logical epression is false), the arithmetic statement is ignored, and control passes on to the next executable statement. This alternative processing is diagrammed below.

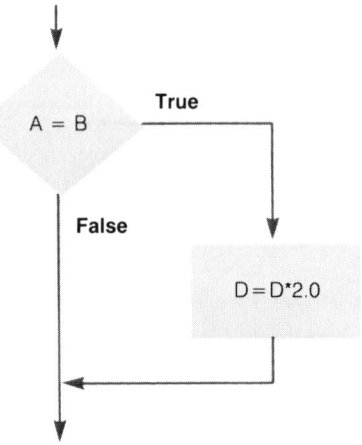

The following logical IF:

|12345|6|7
```
       IF(M*2.LE.N-3)GO TO 18
```

causes a branch to statement number 18 if the logical expression is true but "drops through" to the next executable statement if the logical expression is false.

More powerful logical expressions may be formed by combining logical operators with relational operators. The three logical operators are:

Logical operator	Meaning
.AND.	Conjunction
.OR.	Disjunction
.NOT.	Negation

Like relational operators, logical operators must always be preceded by and followed by a period. AND and OR may be used to connect expressions containing relational operators. It is recommended that parentheses be included for clarity. The following two statements have the same meaning:

|12345|6|7
```
        IF(A.EQ.B.AND.A.NE.C)X=Y*2.
        IF((A.EQ.B).AND.(A.NE.C))X=Y*2.
```

In the above cases, if *both* relationships are true, the "tag along" arithmetic statement will be executed, and then control will pass to the next executable statement. If, on the other hand, either relationship is false, control will drop through to the next executable statement. Note that the next statement will be executed in either case but the arithmetic "tag along" will be executed only if the expression is true.

In contrast, the following statement uses OR instead of AND:

|12345|6|7
```
        IF((A.EQ.B).OR.(A.NE.C))GO TO 20
```

When OR is used, if *either or both* relationship is true, the entire logical expression is true. Again, control passes to the next statement if false but, if true, control goes to statement 20 as directed.

ANDs and ORs may be intermixed in any manner, provided the logical elements can be evaluated as true or false. In the following example, if either the first relationship is true or if both of the second two relationships are true, the entire logical expression is evaluated as true:

|12345|6|7
```
        IF((X.LE.8.5).OR.(A.EQ.B.AND.C.GT.D))STOP
```

A NOT preceding a relational expression negates it; that is, it causes the expression to be true only when it is false. Sometimes it is easier for a programmer to think "if it is not true that A is equal to 7.5, then write the subtotal." The IF statement could then be:

|12345|6|7
```
        IF(.NOT.(A.EQ.7.5))WRITE(3,1)SUBTOT
```

Extremely complex combinations of logical and relational operators are easily understood by the computer. However, the programmer should always keep the reader in mind and avoid any temptation to display virtuosity. Write to express, not to impress!

Figures 6-11 and 6-12 show the use of the logical IF with the Signa Phi Nothing Fraternity example described in the previous section of this chapter. Notice how the logical IF syntax reduces the three-path decision to a two-path decision.

LOOP CONTROL

Loops may be classified into two basic types: uncontrolled and controlled. Each type will be illustrated by partial programs in the following sections.

146   Standard FORTRAN Programming: A Structured Style

Figure 6-11
Signa Phi Nothing Fraternity problem flowchart using two-way decision blocks

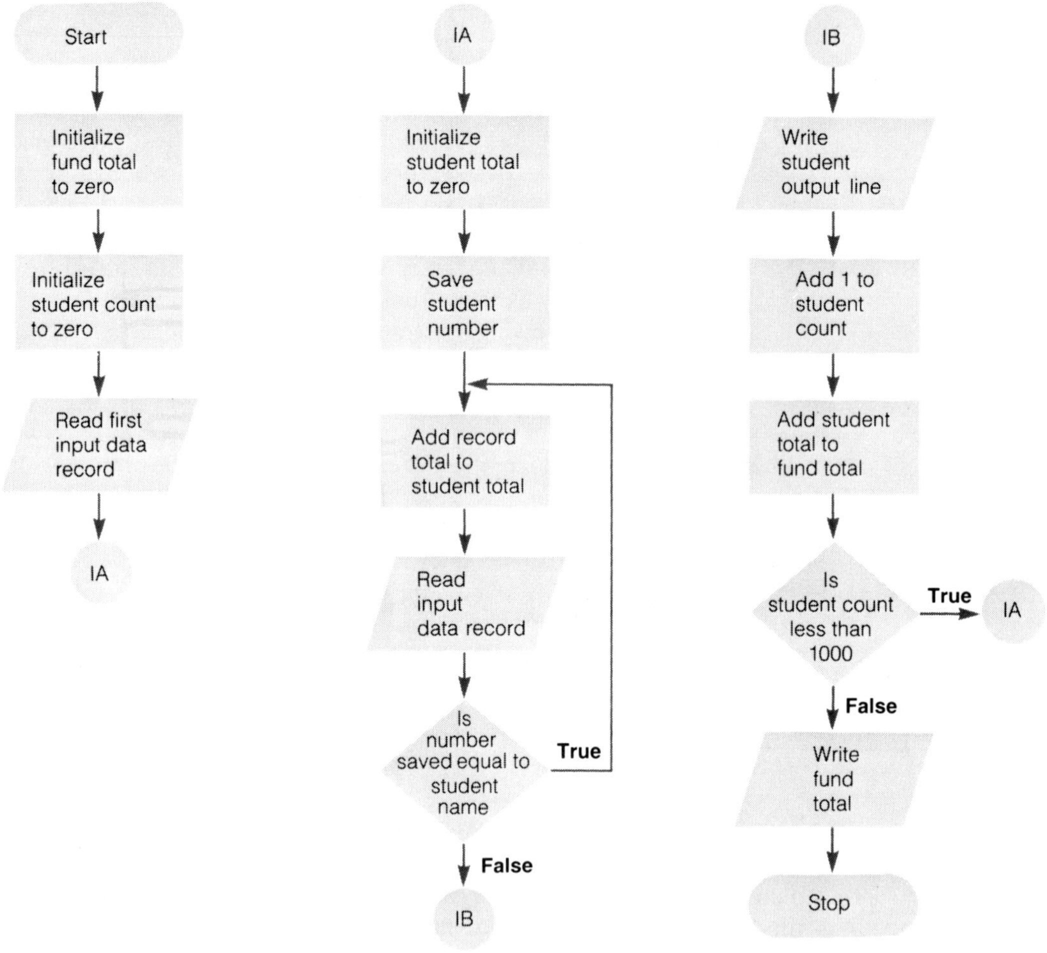

[Flowchart: Three columns showing Start/IA/IB flow paths for the Sigma Phi Nothing Fraternity problem]

Uncontrolled loops   This is the perpetual, or closed, loop discussed previously; for example:

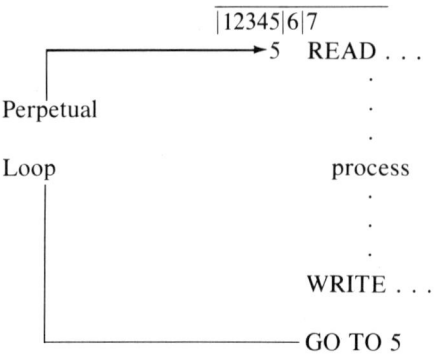

Figure 6-12
Program using logical IF statements for Signa
Phi Nothing Fraternity problem

```
|12345|6|7
         PROGRAM FUNDS
         OPEN(1,FILE='INPUT')
         OPEN(3,FILE='OUTPUT')
         FUNTOT=0.00
         KOUNT=0
         READ(1,100)NUMSTU,RECTOT
C
C
      1  STUTOT=0.00
         NUMSAV=NUMSTU
C
      2  STUTOT=STUTOT+RECTOT
         READ(1,100)NUMSTU,RECTOT
         IF(NUMSAV.EQ.NUMSTU)GO TO 2
C
         WRITE(3,200)NUMSAV,STUTOT
         KOUNT=KOUNT+1
         FUNTOT=FUNTOT+STUTOT
         IF(KOUNT.LT.1000)GO TO 1
C
C
         WRITE(3,300)FUNTOT
         STOP
C
    100  FORMAT(I4,F5.2)
    200  FORMAT('0',I4,T9,F6.2)
    300  FORMAT('0',T7,F8.2)
         END
```

A perpetual loop provides no programmed exit and continues until it is interrupted by the computer system or by the operator. It should be avoided.

Controlled loops

Controlled loops require:

1. A point of entry into the loop.
2. One or more executable statements that are to be repeated.
3. A method of determining the number of iterations (how many times the loop is to be repeated).
4. An exit point from the loop.

Programmers should be particularly cautious to avoid omitting data or cycling through the loop an incorrect number of times. Usually the first and last passes through the loop cause the most problems.

Three methods of loop control will be illustrated, all using a logical IF statement as an exit point.

Loop control by program constant   The number of passes through the loop may be determined by the program rather than from an external source. This type of approach is illustrated below.

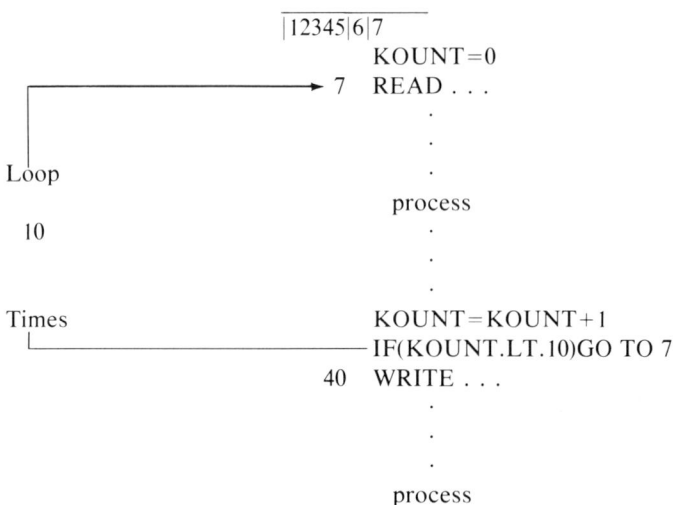

This program is designed to process 10 records only before breaking out of the loop. To process an input file containing more or less than 10 records, the program must be changed and recompiled. This technique can be used only if the number of required passes through the loop is known.

Loop control by header record variable   This method also requires that the number of required passes through the loop be known but will work for any number of input records without changing the program. Instead of entering the number of required passes through the loop directly into the program as a constant, it is read from a data record. This record is called a *header record* because it is the first record processed. Because it controls the number of passes through the loop, it is sometimes called a *control record*. To illustrate:

6/Control Statements

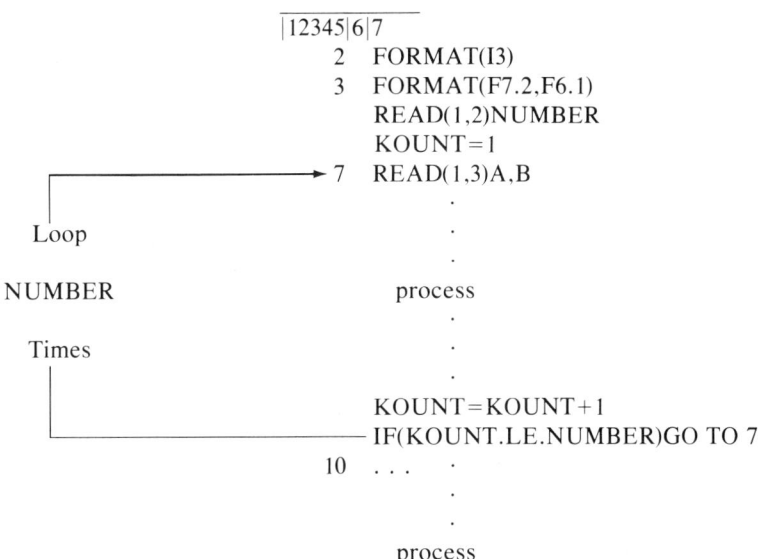

This program will always process the number of records indicated by the header record before it exits from the loop.

Loop control by trailer record variable This method will also process any number of records without changing the program. It has a further advantage in that it is unnecessary to know the number of records in the input file. The program is written to automatically break out of the loop when the last data record (which serves as a *control record*) is read. The *trailer record* is always last in the input data file. It is in the same format as all other input data records but must contain a unique value in one of the fields.

Suppose, for example, each input data record contains the following data fields:

Field name	Record columns	Illustrative field contents
Customer number	1–4	1234
Amount	5–10	526.32

The trailer record is in the same format but contains the unique number 9999 in the customer number field and zeros in the amount field. To illustrate, the below partial program includes an optional procedure that tells the computer to count the passes through the loop. The resulting information can be used for a variety of purposes such as sequentially numbering the output lines and calculating various averages.

Note that the program is structured so that the trailer record is not counted or processed.

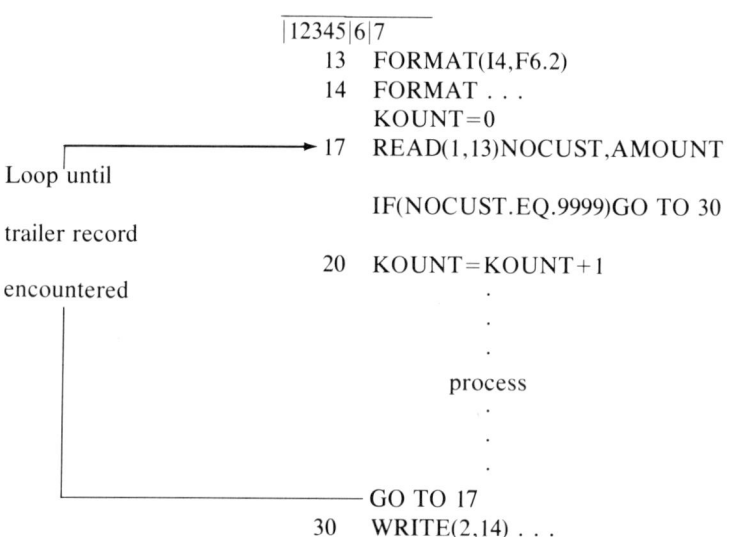

Programmers should be familiar with both fixed loop control and variable loop control; they should also learn to recognize which is more appropriate in the circumstances. To illustrate, a program for analyzing some data for a state government may require one loop iteration for each county. If the state has 52 counties, the program should say so; the user should not be required to provide this information each time the program is run. Likewise, if a program includes some type of monthly analysis, the program, not the user, should indicate that there are 12 months in a year. On the other hand, a weekly payroll program should not be designed to write checks for a constant number of employees when that number continually varies.

A good program is written with the user in mind. The easier it is for him or her, the better. Requiring the user to provide constants and to count input records is an invitation to program failure. Computers count faster and better than people, so let them do it.

Loop control by end-of-file specifier A modification to the READ statement can be used to tell the computer to keep reading until it reaches the end of the input record file and then to transfer control to a specified statement within the program; that is, the computer is told what to do when it runs out of input data. The following partial program illustrates this most useful end-of-file specifer:

6/ Control Statements

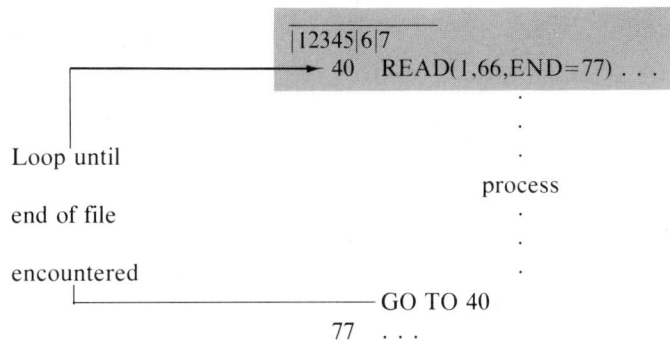

```
                            |12345|6|7
                         ┌→ 40   READ(1,66,END=77) . . .
   ┌────────────────────┘                              ·
   │ Loop until                                        ·
   │                                          process  ·
   │ end of file                                       ·
   │                                                   ·
   │ encountered                                       ·
   └────────────────────────────────── GO TO 40
                                    77  . . .
```

The notation END=77 tells the computer to go to statement number 77 when it runs out of input records. Note how easy it is to use this special feature: simply include the short unique notation within a standard READ statement.

DEFENSIVE PROGRAMMING

Good programmers follow a practice that we call *defensive programming*. They anticipate that sooner or later someone will make a mistake, and their program will be given incorrect input. On the assumption that input cannot be trusted, they incorporate adequate program controls to assure that error conditions will be detected, appropriately handled, and promptly reported to the user. This section does not cover program controls in depth. It merely illustrates some general notions of the basic problems and illustrates some defensive programming techniques.

Nearly everyone has heard of instances where checks have been issued for an amount such as $400,000.00 instead of $400.00 because of "computer error." In this case, if the output field had not been overformatted, the three extra zeros could not have been printed. Likewise, if no check should exceed $800, for example, one logical IF statement could test for this condition. Such tests cannot be used to prevent all errors, but they can limit the size of errors. Tests may be made for minimum as well as maximum amounts. For example, one logical IF statement could be used to prevent writing amounts that are less than or equal to zero. This would eliminate the possibility that a customer might receive a computer-printed statement indicating that a balance of $0.00 is past due. (This has happened!)

Many (but not all) output problems result from bad input. As previously noted, input should not be trusted. All fields considered to be critical to output should be tested for reasonableness. Even fields not directly used in calculations may require testing. For example, it is not reasonable for a numeric date field to include months that are less than one or more than 12; code fields should likewise be tested for validity. Many programs should include complex tests far beyond the scope of this section. A payroll program, for example, should not write checks to nonemployees; all employees should be paid, but none should be paid more than once for the same work.

When an error is detected, the computer should take appropriate action, which usually includes printed notification to the user. For example, if an error is detected in the middle of a weekly payroll run, a message should be written to describe briefly the error and identify the incorrect record; then the program should continue processing other records. In some cases when an error is detected, it may be appropriate to immediately terminate the program.

Most of the tests mentioned in this section can easily be made by using one or more of the control statements previously described. Of course, beginning programmers cannot be expected to include all these tests in practice programs. But, they should be aware of the problems and understand the reasons professionals "launder" their input and output with defensive programming techniques.

SUMMARY

The unconditional GO TO causes a one-way branch that is not based on a computer decision. The other control statements covered in this chapter are designed to cause a computer decision; the logical IF involves a two-way decision, the arithmetic IF a three-way decision, and the computed GO TO a two- or more-way decision as illustrated below:

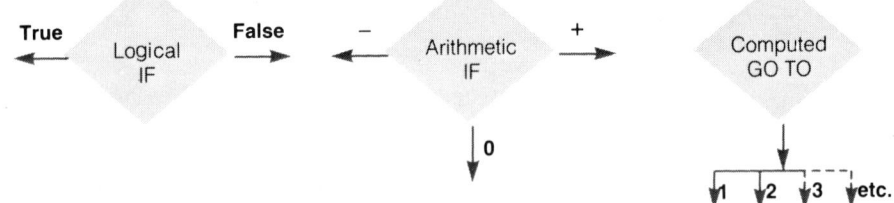

It is impossible to "drop through" an unconditional GO TO or an arithmetic IF. Therefore, the first executable statement following these control statements must be numbered or they cannot be executed. On the other hand, it is possible to "drop through" a computed GO TO and a logical IF, so it is not mandatory to number the first executable statement following these control statements unless other considerations in the program logic require such numbers for referencing purposes.

Generally, the flowchart will indicate the appropriate control statement to be used in the circumstances. Although different control statements can often be used to accomplish the same task, careful selection can simplify the program logic. A major objective should be to minimize multiple and complex branches, thus improving program structure and, in turn, clarity.

6 / Control Statements

REVIEW QUESTIONS

1. Distinguish between branching and looping.

2. Distinguish between a conditional and an unconditional branch.

3. The first executable statement that follows an unconditional GO TO or an arithmetic IF should always be numbered. Why?

4. Should the first executable statement following IF (K.EQ.M) GO TO 3 be numbered? Why or why not?

5. When numbered unconditional GO TOs are included in a program, it is probably poorly structured with "leapfrog branches." Why?

6. What is defensive programming and why is it important to professional programmers?

7. A trailer record in a data file and an END statement in a program serve somewhat similar purposes. Explain.

8. Distinguish between fixed loop control and variable loop control. Indicate, in general, when each is appropriate.

9. A header record is sometimes used to indicate the number of input records; it is often used to provide other information. Give a specific example of such other information.

10. "It doesn't matter how a program is written, if it does the intended job." Discuss.

11.
```
        A=.10
        B=A*20.0
        IF(B-2.0)30,40,50
     30 WRITE(3,35)B
     35 FORMAT(1X,F3.1)
```

When the above statements are executed, the IF will cause a branch to statement number 30 instead of 40 (try it!). Why is the expression evaluated as less than zero?

Statement 30 will cause the computer to write 1.0 instead of a lesser value. Considering your answer to the preceding question, why?

12. Consider the following statements:

```
     20 IF(K.GE.7)N=L
     30 M=J
```

Under what conditions will N=L be executed? Under what conditions will M=J be executed?

13. Consider the following statements:

```
     20 IF(7.LE.K)GO TO 30
        N=N+1
```

Under what conditions will GO TO 30 be executed? Under what conditions will N=N+1 be executed?

14. Consider the following statements:

    20 IF(K.EQ.N)GO TO 30
    30 GO TO 88

Under what conditions will GO TO 88 be executed? Critique the program structure.

15. Consider the following partial program:

            KOUNT=0
     20   READ . . .
              .
              .
              .
            KOUNT=KOUNT+1
            IF(KOUNT.LT.10)GO TO 20
     30   . . .

How many times will the READ statement be executed? Assume the READ statement *should* be executed 10 times; modify the above logical IF or write a different control statement that will do the job.

EXERCISES

Consider the following commands and indicate the errors, if any, in each case.

1. 35 GO TO 1,100

2. 45 GO TO 666001

3. 55 GO TO 55

4. 65 GO TO(1,2)A

5. 75 GO TO(33,44,44,33)K−10

6. 85 GO TO(3,2,1)NUMBERS

7. 95 IF(K=3)22,33,44

8. 105 IF(K+2*N)66,77,88

9. 115 IF(K.NE.J),GO TO N

10. 125 IF((A.EL.B).AND.(C.EQ.D),STOP

6/Control Statements

PROBLEMS

The first five problems are designed to review the unconditional and computed GO TO statements. Each program should be written to provide for all possible branches even though only one specific data record is to be processed.

1. Rise & Son Corporation makes modular panels for solar heating systems. Customers are charged $400 per unit plus shipping costs, which vary according to distance:

Freight zone	Per unit freight charges
1	$ 7.50
2	12.25
3	18.75

Write a program to compute the total charge for one sale. Use a computed GO TO statement to test the freight zone. Input is one record in the following format:

Field name	Record columns	Required field contents
Customer number	1–4	1001
Freight zone	5	2
Units sold	6–7	10

Required output is one printed line in the following format:

Field name	Print positions or "columns"
Customer number	1–4
Freight zone	7
Units sold	10–11
Total charge	14–21

Remember to use good program structure and adequate documentation.

2. Write a program to calculate the amount of interest and the maturity value of a bank loan. Use good program structure and adequate documentation. Calculations should be based on the standard formulas.

$$I = PRT/365 \text{ and } M = P + I$$

Input is one record in the following format:

Field name	Record columns	Required field contents
Note number	1-6	012345
Principal	7-15	007563.24
Time in days	16-19	0270
Rate code	20-21	02
Customer name	22-35	MARIE S. CURIE

Three different rate codes are used to indicate the interest percentage as follows:

Rate code	Interest rate (percent)
01	20.00
02	16.75
04	12.50

Use a computed GO TO statement to test the rate code.

Required output is one printed line containing the same data as the input record as well as interest and maturity value, which should both be carried to two decimal places. The required format is:

Field name	Print positions or "columns"
Note number	1-5
Principal	6-14
Time in days	15-18
Rate code	19-20
Interest	25-31
Maturity value	35-42
Customer name	46-59

3. Itsuptoo University charges each student a registration fee that is the sum of two factors: (1) $22.50 per credit hour and (2) a tuition charge (indicated later below). Write a program to calculate the registration fee for one student. Input is one record in the following format:

Field name	Record columns	Required field contents
None	1	Blank
Student number	2-6	12345
None	7-8	Blanks
Date of birth	9-14	121259
Tuition code	15	2
Credit hours	16-19	12.5
Student name	20-31	PIERRE CURIE

6/Control Statements

Four codes are used to indicate the amount of tuition as follows:

	Tuition code	Tuition amount
Resident undergraduate	1	$228.00
Nonresident undergraduate	2	592.00
Resident graduate	3	268.00
Nonresident graduate	5	632.00

Use a computed GO TO statement to test the tuition code. Required output is one printed line in the following format:

Field name	Print positions or "columns"
Student number	1-5
Student name	8-19
Registration fee	22-28

Remember to use good program structure and adequate documentation.

4. Write a program to compute the net price of a sales invoice where:

   List price = Units times unit price
   Discount = List price times discount percentage
   Net price = List price less discount

Input is one record in the following format:

Field name	Record columns	Required field contents
Customer name	1-5	A. SU
Units	6-7	10
Unit price	8-12	37.95
Discount code	13-14	03

Four codes are used to identify the discount percentage:

Type of customer	Discount code	Discount percentage
Wholesaler	0	60
Retailer	1	40
Cash customer	2	10
Charge customer	3	5

Use a computed GO TO statement to test the discount code.
Required output is one printed line in the following format:

Field name	Print positions or "columns"
Customer name	1–5
Net price	7–13

Remember to use good program structure and adequate documentation.

5. Speedtrap City has a population of only 200 citizens. It is divided into two sections by a major highway that passes through the main business district. The posted speed limit is 55 m.p.h. for the highway but only 30 m.p.h. within the city limits. Electronic timing devices have been installed at each end of the city to detect speeders.

Anyone arrested for exceeding the speed limit has two choices. He may go directly to the police department traffic division and pay a fine of $5 for each mile per hour in excess of the posted speed limit (a speed of 30½ m.p.h. would result in a fine of $2.50). His second choice is to wait and appear in traffic court, which convenes at 7 P.M. each evening. If he is found guilty, he is fined $3 for each mile per hour in excess of the posted limit. If the fine is not paid, he is given a jail sentence.

One input record, in the following format, is prepared for each offender who exceeds the 30 m.p.h. speed limit:

Field name	Record columns	Required data
Culprit number	1–5	12345
Arresting officer number	6–7	02
Actual speed in m.p.h.	8–13	055.50
Disposition code	14–15	22

Four disposition codes are used:

Disposition	Code
Paid fine immediately	22
Found guilty	24
Found not guilty	26
Jailed	28

Write a program to read one input record and compute the fine if the input card is coded 22 or 24 (compute nothing if the record is coded 26 or 28). Use a computed GO TO statement to test for the disposition code. If the record is coded 22 or 24, print one output line in the following format:

Field name	Print positions
Culprit number	1-5
Amount of fine	7-12
Disposition code	14-15

Use good program structure and adequate documentation.

6. Write the program described in Problem 1 in this chapter with the following change only: Do not use a computed GO TO to test the freight zone. Instead, use the logical IF.

7. Write the program described in Problem 2 in this chapter with the following change only: Do not use a computed GO TO to test the rate codes. Instead, use the logical IF.

8. Write the program described in Problem 3 in this chapter with the following change only: Do not use a computed GO TO to test the tuition code. Instead, use the logical IF. Design the program logic so that invalid codes cannot be processed.

9. Write the program described in Problem 4 in this chapter with the following changes only: Do not use a computed GO TO to test the discount code. Instead, use the logical IF. Also, design the program to process an input file containing 10 records. Output is to be printed on 10 single-spaced lines. Required input data:

Customer number (cols. 1-5)	Units (cols. 6-7)	Unit price (cols. 8-12)	Discount code (cols. 13-14)
54321	10	37.95	03
2	10	37.95	02
3	10	37.95	01
4	10	37.95	00
5	10	37.95	01
6	10	37.95	02
7	10	37.95	03
8	10	37.95	03
9	10	37.95	00
10	10	37.95	01

10. Write the program described in Problem 5 in this chapter with the following changes only:

A. Assume that the input file contains 10 data records instead of 1 (use appropriate loop control). Required input data:

Culprit number (cols. 1-5)	Arresting officer number (cols. 6-7)	Actual speed in m.p.h. (cols. 8-13)	Disposition code (cols. 14-15)
12345	01	055.50	22
6	2	31.00	22
7	3	31.00	24
8	4	31.50	24
9	5	32.00	26
50	6	32.00	28
1	7	40.00	24
2	8	40.00	24
3	9	80.00	28
4	10	31.50	26

B. Output (for each record coded 22 or 24) is to be doubled-spaced on a printer.

11. Assume you take a job at a pencil factory for 31 days. The factory has a large inventory but is short of cash, so you agree to be paid in pencils. You are to receive one pencil the first day. Each succeeding day you are to receive twice as many pencils as the day before. Thus, you will receive two the second day, four the third, eight the fourth, etc.

Write a program to compute the number of pencils you will earn each day and a running total of your "earnings." No input record is to be used. Output is to be on a printer, indicating on 31 successive lines the line number, your pay for each day and the accumulated amount of your "earnings" to date. Output is to be in FORMAT (I3,2I14).

Use good program structure and adequate documentation.

12. Study the following program to determine what it does:

```
      PROGRAM TWELVE
      OPEN(1,FILE='INPUT')
      OPEN(3,FILE='OUTPUT')
C
    1 FORMAT(I6,2I7)
    2 FORMAT(I6,2I7//)
C
      READ(1,1)NUMBR1,NUMBR2,NUMBR3
C
         IF(NUMBR1.GT.NUMBR2)NUMBIG=NUMBR1
         IF(NUMBR1.LE.NUMBR2)NUMBIG=NUMBR2
         IF(NUMBIG.LT.NUMBR3)NUMBIG=NUMBR3
C
      WRITE(3,2)NUMBR1,NUMBR2,NUMBR3,NUMBIG
C
      STOP
      END
```

Modify the above program so it will process an input file with appropriate data of your choice. Each record should contain three integers of five or less digits each. Your input file should include at least three records.

6/Control Statements

13. Prepare a program to compute the social security deduction and net pay for each employee and to compute the total social security deduction and total net pay for all employees. Time and a half is paid for all hours in excess of 40. Assume that the social security rate is 6.7 percent and that all employees are subject to this deduction.

The input data file contains one record for each of the 10 employees in the following format:

Employee number (cols. 1-4)	Date of birth (5-10)	Hours worked (11-15)	Rate per hour (16-19)	Dept. number (20)	Employee name (61-80)
1001	100948	39.00	6.50	1	PATRICIA B. ANDERSON
1002	111249	35.00	7.80	2	WASHINGTON H. BROWN
1003	111249	39.25	5.65	3	JANE ANN COOPER
1004	111249	41.75	7.00	4	RAYMOND D. DOOLITTLE
1005	111249	60.00	6.00	5	SAMUEL R. ENGERS
1006	111249	38.50	6.20	6	PATRICIA FITZGERALD
1007	111249	80.00	7.00	7	MARTIN S. GERSZEWSKI
1008	111249	45.00	5.00	8	CARL J. HILL
1009	111249	18.00	6.42	9	RAYMOND P. INOMOTO
1010	111249	50.00	9.00	1	MARK A. JOHNSON

Use appropriate loop control. Read only the input data fields required to solve the problem.

Required output for each employee is one printed line containing the following data fields from left to right:

Field name
Employee name
Employee number
Rate per hour
Hours worked
Social security deduction
Net pay

"Dress up" output with reasonable spacings between fields and with a heading indicating the contents of each field. (The net pay field, for example, may be headed up with the words *NET PAY*.)

Required output for the final line (total social security and net pay for all employees) should be positioned so it appears directly below the fields totaled with the decimal points aligned. Use good program structure and adequate documentation.

14. Write the program to compute the end-of-month balance for each pilot member of a local flying club. The number of records to be processed is unknown. The last record in the data file is a trailer record which contains the unique value 999 in the Pilot Number field. Use appropriate loop control based on this trailer record. Use the following input data records:

Pilot number (cols 1–3)	Amount (6–12)	Code (15–16)
101	−107.50	01
102	−107.50	01
102	6.50	02
102	1.00	02
103	−107.50	01
103	7.50	02
103	10.00	03
103	10.00	03
104	15.50	01
104	25.00	02
104	15.50	03
999	(trailer record)	

Three code numbers are used to identify the type of input record as follows:

a. Code 1 identifies a *Balance forward* record. Each pilot has one such record, which may contain:
    A. A *positive* balance (if he owes the club money from last month).
    B. A *negative* balance (if he has overpaid and has a credit balance).
    C. A *zero* balance.
b. Code 2 identifies a *Flight charge* record. There is one such record for each flight made during the month. All amounts are *positive*.
c. Code 3 identifies a *Payments on account* record. There is one such record for each payment made by the pilot. All amounts are *positive*.

Input data records are in ascending numerical sequence by pilot number. All input records must be processed; none can be omitted. Required output is one or more descriptive header lines followed by one line only for each pilot, which contains his number and end-of-month balance with reasonable spacing between the fields.

Use good program structure and adequate documentation.

15. Write a program to compute the total *hours* of computer time used by each student in computer programming class number 66 and the total *hours* of computer time used by all students in this class.

The input file contains one record for each time a student in *any* computer programming class processes a "job" (program). The records have been sorted by student number; thus all records for each student are together rather than scattered randomly throughout the input file. Each student has a unique number, but the numbers are not related to the class. That is, student number 01 may be in class 66, number 02 in class 33, number 03 in class 66, etc.

The number of records for each student is unknown. The number of students is also unknown, so appropriate control is required to determine the end of the input file.

No student is enrolled in more than one class. All records for classes other than class number 66 are to be ignored.

6/Control Statements

Input data records

Student number (cols. 1-4)	Class number (5-6)	Minutes for job (7-12)	
1111	66	1.25	
1111	66	28.75	
1112	66	120.00	
1113	67	240.00	
1114	66	59.50	
1114	66	15.50	
1115	65	240.00	
1115	65	240.00	
1116	98	360.00	
1117	14	8.00	
1118	66	48.60	
1118	66	11.40	
1118	66	60.23	
1119	66	33.00	
1119	66	33.23	
1120	66	48.23	
1120	66	12.00	
0000	99	000000	(optional trailer record)

All output is to be single-spaced on a printer. The total time on the final output line is to be followed by one blank and the literal message HOURS

Required output for each student in class number 66

Field name	Print positions or "columns"	Illustrative field data
Student number	1-4	1111
Class number	7-8	66
Hours of time	10-16	0.50

Required final output

Field name	Print positions or "columns"	Illustrative field data
Total time	1-8	22.74

Use good program structure and adequate documentation.

16. Write a program to compute the total cost and the average cost of processing programs written by members of your class. Processing cost is $82.50 per hour.

The input file contains one record for each time a student processes a job (program). The records have been sorted *alphabetically* by student name; thus all records for each student are together rather than scattered randomly throughout the input file. The number of records for each student is unknown.

Each student has a unique number, but the numbers have *not* been assigned in alphabetic sequence. All students in your class have been assigned numbers within the range of 1001 through 1050, but the input file contains records for students other than those enrolled in your class. Students enrolled in other courses have been assigned numbers outside this range, but no student is assigned the unique number 9999, which is reserved for a "trailer record." The use of a trailer record is optional.

Input data records

Student number (cols. 7-10)	Student name (21-40)	Hours for job (66-71)
1017	ADAMS, JOHN	1.000
1050	BAKER, JOHN	.384
1050	BAKER, JOHN	.116
1026	CARLSON, JOE	.200
1080	CARLSON, SAM	10.000
1011	DOBBS, JOE	3.000
0999	ELLIS, JOE	1.234
2000	ELLIS, JOHN	5.678
1033	ELLIS, SAM	3.000
1001	FEATHERINGHAM, JAMES	4.000
1049	GATES, JOE	.008
1049	GATES, JOE	.002
1022	HALL, JANE	2.000
1002	IVERS, MARY	5.000
3412	JAMES, ALICE	5.000
5555	JAMES, CARL, JR.	5.333
1044	JAMES, DIANE	60.975
1044	JAMES, DIANE	60.025
9998	KELLY, SAM	12.345
9999	***TRAILER RECORD***	000000

The program output may include or exclude the student names, at your option.

Required output for each student in your class is one line that contains the student's number and the total cost of processing his or her jobs. The final output line is to contain the total cost of processing all jobs in your class and the average processing cost per student. All output is to be doubled-spaced. Each output field should be scaled to determine its proper size. Use good program structure and adequate documentation.

7
IF-THEN-ELSE and DO loop structures

Previous chapters included a description of various procedures that can be used for loop control and for processing a limited amount of alphameric input and output. This chapter expands upon these procedures by introducing more powerful control statements and more convenient programming techniques.

IF-THEN-ELSE STATEMENTS

This section describes statements that allow great flexibility in program control. These statements implement the IF-THEN-ELSE structure, which is useful to avoid programming that contains complex, intertwining branching (sometimes referred to as "spaghetti" programming). Included in the IF-THEN-ELSE statements are the IF THEN, the END IF, the ELSE, and the ELSE IF statements. These four statements together form a powerful extension of the logical IF statement, which was covered in the preceding chapter.

IF THEN statement

The IF THEN statement is technically called the block IF statement in ANSI FORTRAN standards. But to avoid confusion between the term *block IF* and the term *IF-block* (another ANSI standard term covered later in this chapter), the more descriptive term IF THEN is used consistently throughout.

The general form is:

```
|12345|6|7
nnnnn    IF (le) THEN
```

Legend:
nnnnn   Any unique one-to-five digit integer *number* that specifies the statement label. It is required only if the statement is referenced elsewhere in the program.
IF   A keyword specifying the type of operation to be performed.
(le)   Any valid *logical expression,* enclosed in parentheses, that is evaluated to determine whether it is true or false.
THEN   A keyword specifying that the IF (le) operation is to be per-

> formed involving one or more statements that follow on subsequent lines.
>
> *Note:* Do not have any statement following the word THEN on the same line as the IF (le) THEN.

The logical expression is described in the previous chapter in the LOGICAL IF STATEMENT section. If the logical expression of the IF THEN statement is evaluated and found to be *true*, then any statements that follow are executed.

For example, the statement:

```
|12345|6|7
       IF (KOUNT.LT.NUMBER) THEN
```

is executed by determining whether the logical expression KOUNT.EQ.NUMBER is true; if it is true, then any executable statements that appear on the lines *following* this statement are performed. The statements are performed until either an END IF, an ELSE, or an ELSE IF statement is encountered. An explanation of these statements follows immediately.

END IF statement

The END IF is a statement that is used to indicate the end of any statements that are to be executed only after the corresponding IF THEN statement is evaluated as true. The general form is:

> ```
> |12345|6|7
>        END IF
> ```
>
> **Legend:**
> END IF   A keyword specifying the type of operation to be performed. It is written often as one word: *ENDIF*.

IF-block

All the executable statements occurring between the IF THEN statement and the END IF statement are referred to as an *IF-block*. It is useful to indent the IF-block in order to separate the IF-block from the rest of the source code in a clear, visual manner. The following illustrates an IF-block that consists of one statement only: KOUNT=KOUNT+1.

```
|12345|6|7
       IF (KOUNT.LT.NUMBER) THEN
          KOUNT=KOUNT+1
       END IF
```

The previous example is equivalent to the following logical IF:

```
|12345|6|7
       IF (KOUNT.LT.NUMBER) KOUNT=KOUNT+1
```

It may seem, from the previous examples, that the logical IF is a simpler form. However, the power of the IF THEN lies in the fact that *more* than one statement can be performed.

7/IF-THEN-ELSE and DO Loop Structures

In the next example, if it is true that KOUNT is less than NUMBER, then the IF-block, which consists of the three statements following the IF THEN statement, is performed, and the program continues after the END IF statement. If it is false that KOUNT is less than NUMBER, then the three statements of the IF-block are ignored, and the program continues on. The flowchart and coding for this are illustrated in Figure 7-1.

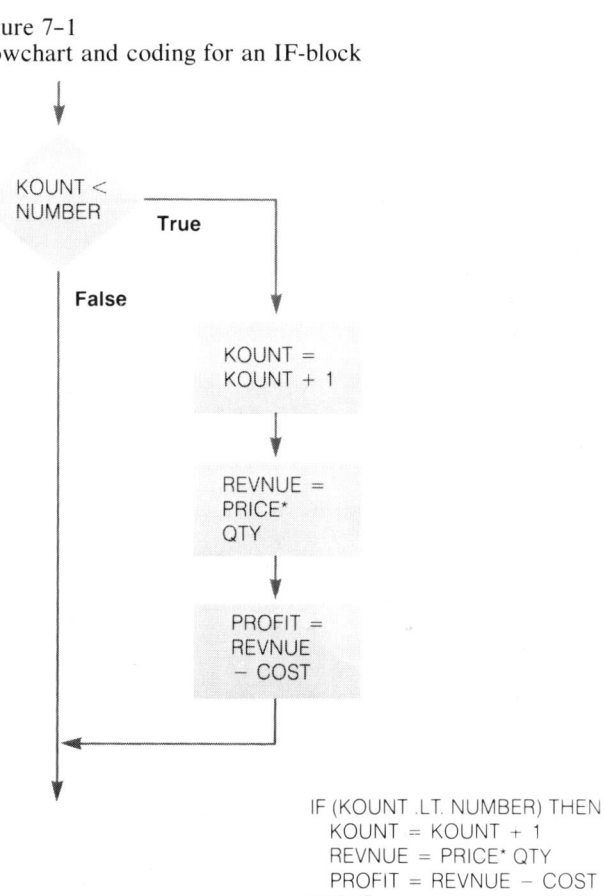

Figure 7-1
Flowchart and coding for an IF-block

```
IF (KOUNT .LT. NUMBER) THEN
   KOUNT = KOUNT + 1
   REVNUE = PRICE* QTY
   PROFIT = REVNUE - COST
END IF
```

A simplified diagram and coding structure for the previous flowchart are illustrated in Figure 7-2. A rectangle is the convention that is used to indicate the presence of one or more statements that are executed as a set. In the diagram of Figure 7-2, the shaded rectangle indicates the execution of the *three* statements of the IF-block as shown in Figure 7-1. The IF THEN statement that precedes the IF-block is shown in the diagram as a decision symbol with the logical expression inside the symbol and the word *IF* beside it. The word *THEN* is placed above the directional arrow that denotes the path taken when the logical expression is true. The END IF that follows the IF-block is shown in the

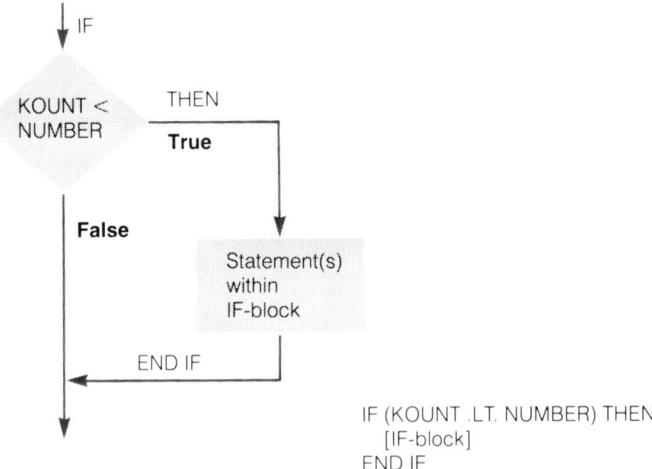

Figure 7-2
Simplified flowchart and coding structure

IF (KOUNT .LT. NUMBER) THEN
  [IF-block]
END IF

diagram with the words *END IF* beside the directional arrow that continues into the rest of the flowchart.

Nested IF THEN statements

When an IF THEN is contained within the IF-block of another IF THEN, the inner IF THEN, with its associated IF-block and END IF, is said to be *nested*. Figure 7-3 illustrates a nested IF-block. The outer IF-block will be identified with the subscript *1*. The inner (nested) IF-block will be identified with the subscript *2*.

In Figure 7-3, note that the use of indentation in the source code helps to set off the nested IF THEN. The indented END IF belongs to the inner, nested IF THEN; the last END IF belongs to the outer IF THEN. An example of complete code for the previous illustration is shown in Figure 7-4.

In the program section given in Figure 7-4, when A = B or A > B, control branches to the outer END IF, and the program continues. But if A < B, one is added to KOUNT1; then the message "A IS LESS THAN B" is printed. Next, B and C are compared. When B = C or B > C, then control branches to the inner END IF, which in turn passes control to the outer END IF, and the program continues on. But if B < C, then one is added to KOUNT2 and the message "A IS LESS THAN C" is printed before the program continues.

Since every IF THEN must have its own END IF, one END IF is not sufficient (nor is it correct) to end a group of nested IF THEN statements. If there are two, three, or more IF THENs, then there must be two, three, or more corresponding END IFs.

ELSE statement

The ELSE statement is used in conjunction with an IF THEN statement. ELSE signifies the start of one or more statements that are

7/IF-THEN-ELSE and DO Loop Structures

Figure 7-3
Nested IF THEN structure

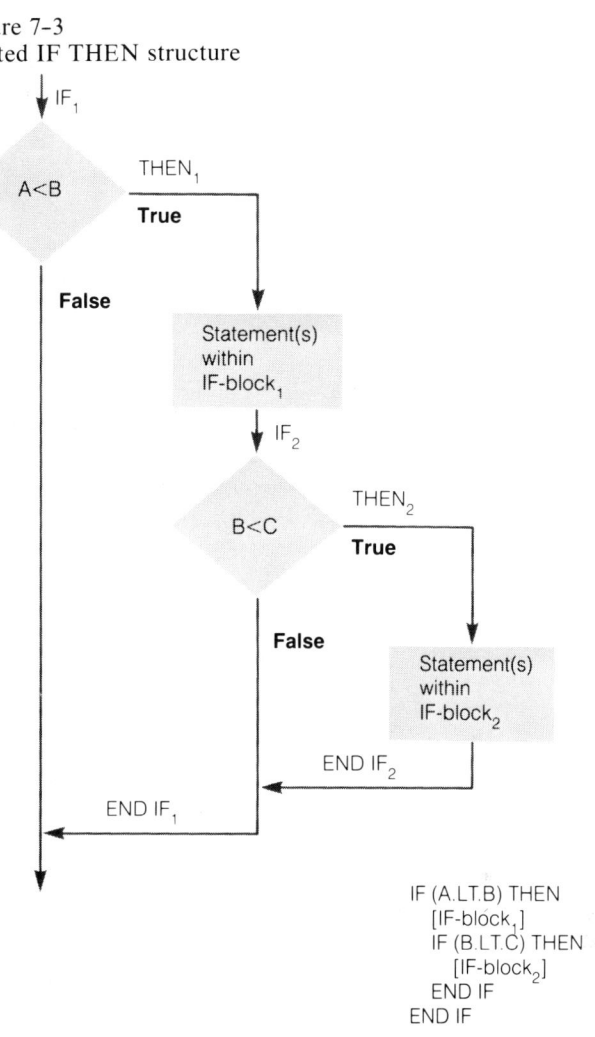

```
IF (A.LT.B) THEN
   [IF-block₁]
   IF (B.LT.C) THEN
      [IF-block₂]
   END IF
END IF
```

Figure 7-4
Illustration of nested IF THEN code

```
|12345|6|7
      IF(A.LT.B) THEN
         KOUNT1=KOUNT1+1           ⎫
         WRITE(3,100)              ⎬  IF-block₁
 100     FORMAT(1X,'A IS LESS THAN B')  ⎭
         IF(B.LT.C) THEN
            KOUNT2=KOUNT2+1        ⎫
            WRITE(3,200)           ⎬  IF-block₂
 200        FORMAT(1X,'A IS LESS THAN C')  ⎭
         END IF
      END IF
```

to be performed when the IF THEN logical expression is *false*. ELSE also indicates the end of the IF-block, since the ELSE occurs between the IF THEN and the END IF. The general form is:

|12345|6|7
    ELSE

Legend:
ELSE   A keyword specifying the type of operation to be performed involving one or more statements that follow on subsequent lines.

ELSE-block

All the executable statements occurring between the ELSE statement and the END IF statement are referred to as an *ELSE-block*. It is analogous to the IF-block. The distinction between the IF-block and the ELSE-block is the performance, given the true or false state of the logical expression in the IF THEN. If the logical expression is true, then the IF-block statements are performed. If the logical expression is false, then the ELSE-block statements are performed. Figure 7-5 illustrates this.

Figure 7-5
Simplified flowchart illustrating the IF-block and associated ELSE-block

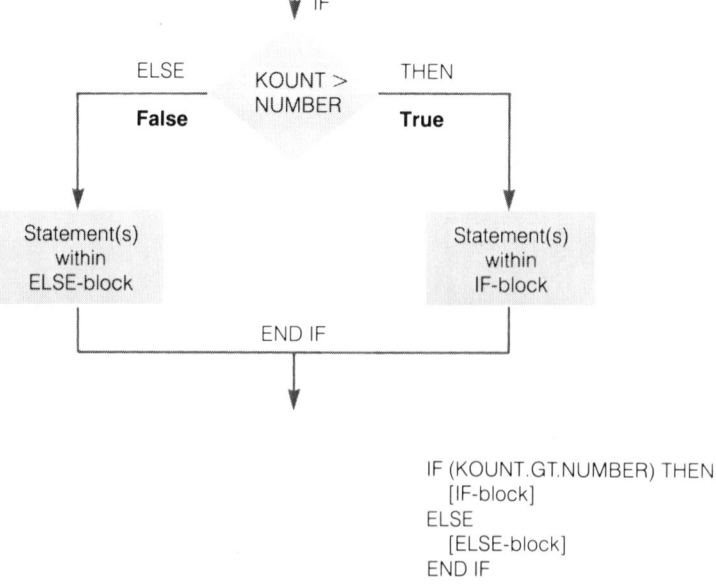

```
IF (KOUNT.GT.NUMBER) THEN
    [IF-block]
ELSE
    [ELSE-block]
END IF
```

It is strongly recommended that, when coding, you indent the ELSE-block just like the IF-block. By indenting the IF-block and its

7/IF-THEN-ELSE and DO Loop Structures

corresponding ELSE-block to the same position in the source coding, you make the decision logic easier to follow. Indentation is particularly helpful when there are a considerable number of nested IF-blocks.

Figure 7-6 illustrates the presence of the ELSE-block.

In the example shown in Figure 7-6, when KOUNT is less than NUMBER, the IF-block statements are performed; control is then passed to the END IF statement, and the program continues on with the statements following the END IF. When KOUNT is *not* less than NUMBER, then the ELSE-block statements are performed; control is then passed to the END IF statement, and the program continues on with the statements following the END IF.

Figure 7-6
Illustration of IF THEN and ELSE code

```
|12345|6|7
      IF(KOUNT.LT.NUMBER) THEN
         KOUNT=KOUNT+1              ⎫
         REVNUE=PRICE*QTY           ⎬  IF-block
         PROFIT=REVNUE-COST         ⎭
      ELSE
         WRITE(3,500)               ⎫
  500    FORMAT('0','END OF FILE')  ⎬  ELSE-block
                                    ⎭
      END IF
```

The use of IF-block and ELSE-block structures can greatly reduce undesirable intertwining control branching. For example, note the relatively more simple control branching when IF-THEN-ELSE structures are used in Figure 7-7 to implement the Signa Phi Nothing Fraternity program that was given in Figure 6-9 of the preceding chapter.

Notice also that the number of source code lines is greater in Figure 7-8 than in Figure 6-10. In this case, there is a trade-off between the number of source code lines and the simplicity of control branching. It pays, however, to have a simpler control branch structure whenever a program has to be modified. The modification can be made more quickly, and the probability of making an error is less.

ELSE IF statement

The ELSE IF statement is used only in conjunction with an IF THEN statement. It signifies a test that is to be performed when the logical expression of the IF THEN is evaluated to be *false*. Its occurrence also indicates the end of the IF-block, since the ELSE IF statement occurs between the IF THEN and the END IF. The general form is:

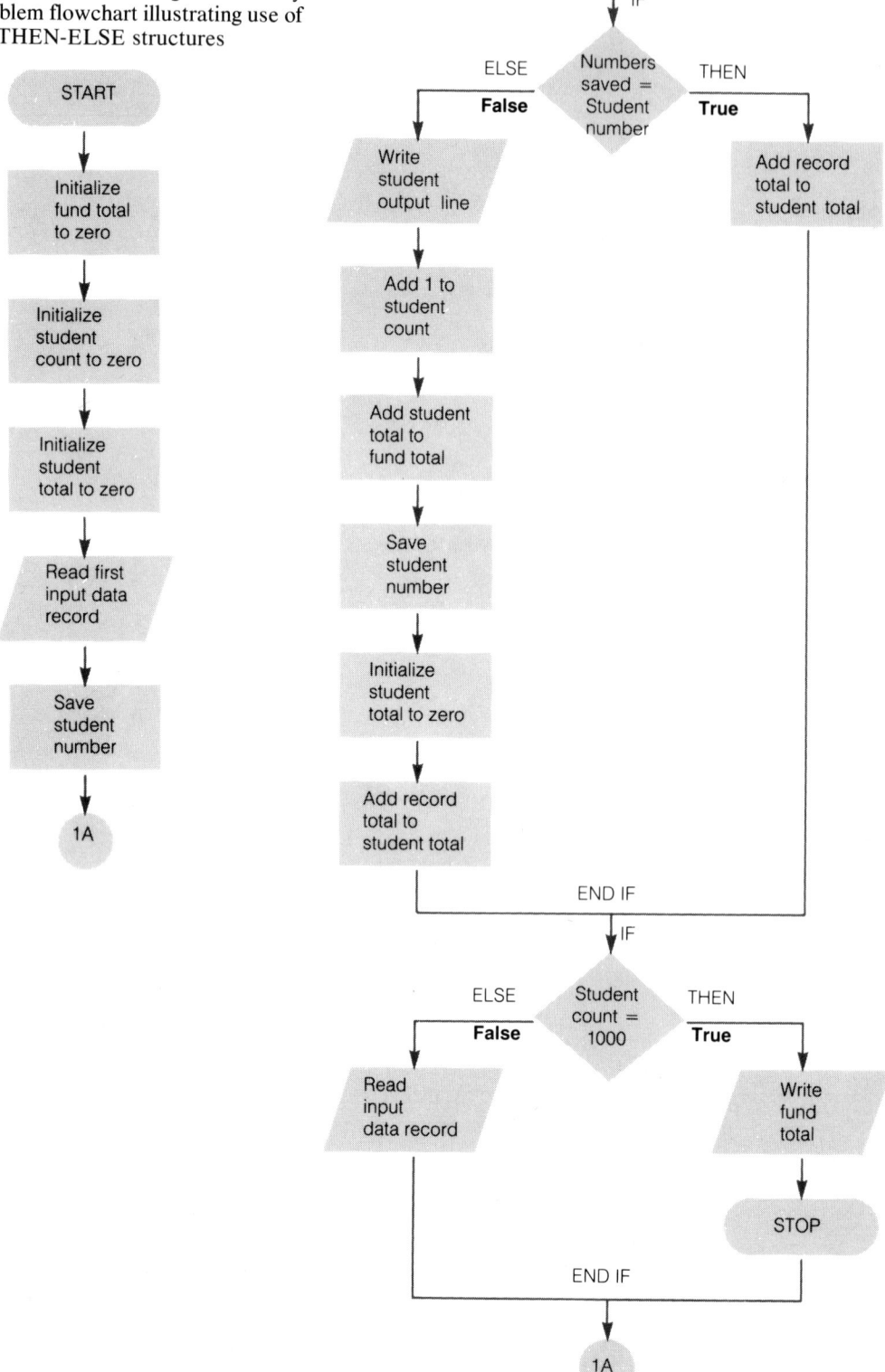

Figure 7-7
Signa Phi Nothing Fraternity problem flowchart illustrating use of IF-THEN-ELSE structures

Figure 7-8
Program using IF-THEN-ELSE structures for
Signa Phi Nothing Fraternity problem

```
|12345|6|7
            PROGRAM FUNDS
            OPEN(1,FILE='INPUT')
            OPEN(3,FILE='OUTPUT')
            FUNTOT=0.00
            KOUNT=0
            STUTOT=0.00
            READ(1,100)NUMSTU,RECTOT
      100   FORMAT(I4,F5.2)
            NUMSAV=NUMSTU
C
C
      400   IF(NUMSAV.EQ.NUMSTU) THEN
               STUTOT=STUTOT+RECTOT
            ELSE
               WRITE(3,200)NUMSAV,STUTOT
      200      FORMAT('0',I4,T9,F6.2)
               KOUNT=KOUNT+1
               FUNTOT=FUNTOT+STUTOT
               NUMSAV=NUMSTU
               STUTOT=0.00
               STUTOT=STUTOT+RECTOT
            END IF
C
C
            IF(KOUNT.EQ.1000) THEN
               WRITE(3,300)FUNTOT
      300      FORMAT('0',T7,F8.2)
               STOP
            ELSE
               READ(1,100)NUMSTU,RECTOT
            END IF
C
C
            GO TO 400
            END
```

|12345|6|7
         ELSE IF (le) THEN

Legend:

ELSE IF   A keyword specifying the type of operation to be performed. It is written often as one word: ELSEIF.

(le)   Any valid *logical expression* enclosed in parentheses that is evaluated to determine whether it is true or false.

THEN   A keyword specifying that the ELSE IF (le) operation is to be performed involving one or more statements that follow on subsequent lines. *Note:* Do not have any statements following the word THEN on the same line as the ELSE IF (le) THEN.

ELSE IF-block

All executable statements occurring between the ELSE IF statement and the next ELSE IF, ELSE, or END IF statement are referred to as an *ELSE IF-block*. The ELSE IF statement is used when there is *more than one* alternative path that follows the associated IF THEN. This is in contrast to the ELSE statement, which is used when *only one* alternative path follows the associated IF THEN. Figure 7-9 illustrates the use of ELSE IF-blocks.

Had the previous example (Figure 7-9) ended with an ELSE, then the ELSE-block would have been performed only if the logical expressions of the IF THEN and *all* ELSE IFs were false. This is shown in Figure 7-10.

Although the previous examples have, at most, two ELSE IFs associated with an IF THEN, the programmer can use as many ELSE IFs as necessary.

The use of the IF-block, ELSE IF-block, and ELSE-block structures can help to simplify the coding of complex decision paths. One

Figure 7-9
Simplified flowchart illustrating the IF-block and associated ELSE IF-block

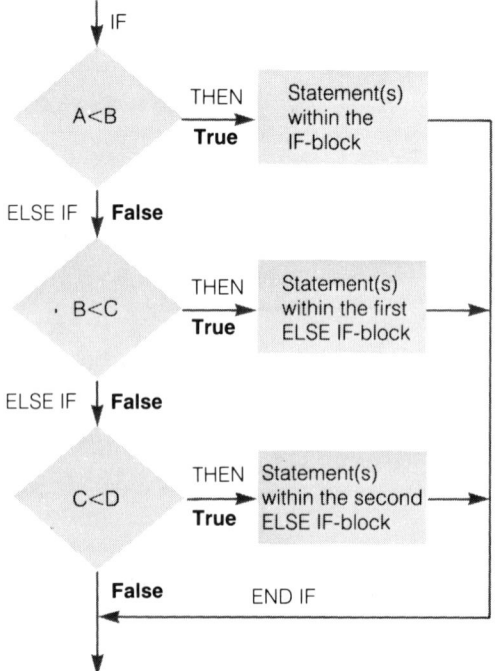

```
IF (A.LT.B) THEN
   [IF-block]
ELSE IF (B.LT.C) THEN
   [first ELSE IF-block]
ELSE IF (C.LT.D)
   [second ELSE IF-block]
END IF
```

7 / IF-THEN-ELSE and DO Loop Structures

Figure 7-10
Simplified flowchart illustrating the use of ELSE with ELSE IF

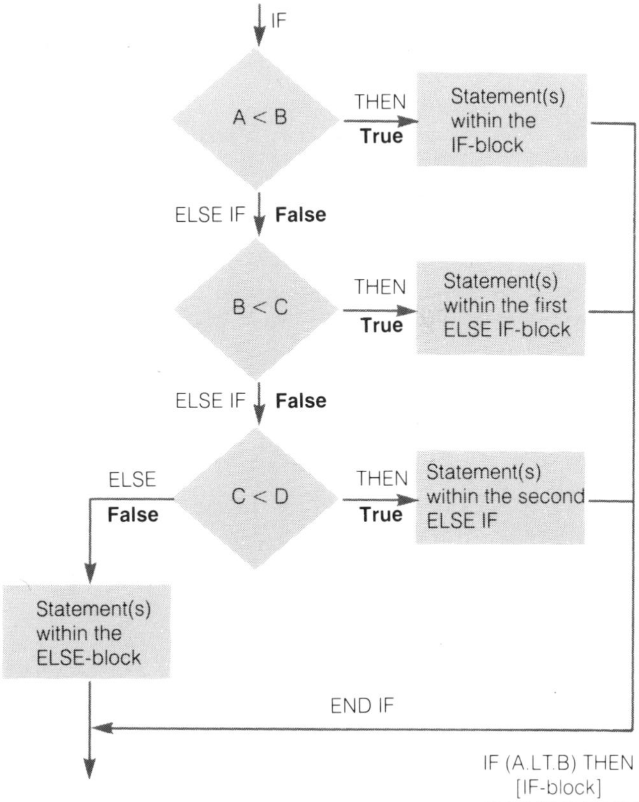

```
IF (A.LT.B) THEN
    [IF-block]
ELSE IF (B.LT.C) THEN
    [first ELSE IF-block]
ELSE IF (C.LT.D) THEN
    [second ELSE IF-block]
ELSE
    [ELSE-block]
END IF
```

such simplification is the avoidance of excessive GO TO statements. For example, note in Figures 7-11 and 7-12 the avoidance of GO TOs when IF-THEN-ELSE structures are used to implement the Lucky Company problem of the previous chapter as illustrated in Figures 6-5 and 6-6. Although this problem does not involve an excessive number of GO TO statements, it is useful to illustrate how ELSE IF statements can be used for alternative paths.

Nesting block IF, ELSE IF, and ELSE statements

Earlier in the chapter it was pointed out that an IF-block can be nested within another IF-block. When nesting involves both ELSE-blocks and ELSE IF-blocks, a much more complex structure can result. Some of these possibilities are shown in Figures 7-13 and 7-14.

Figure 7-11
Lucky Company problem flowchart illustrating use of IF-THEN-ELSE structures

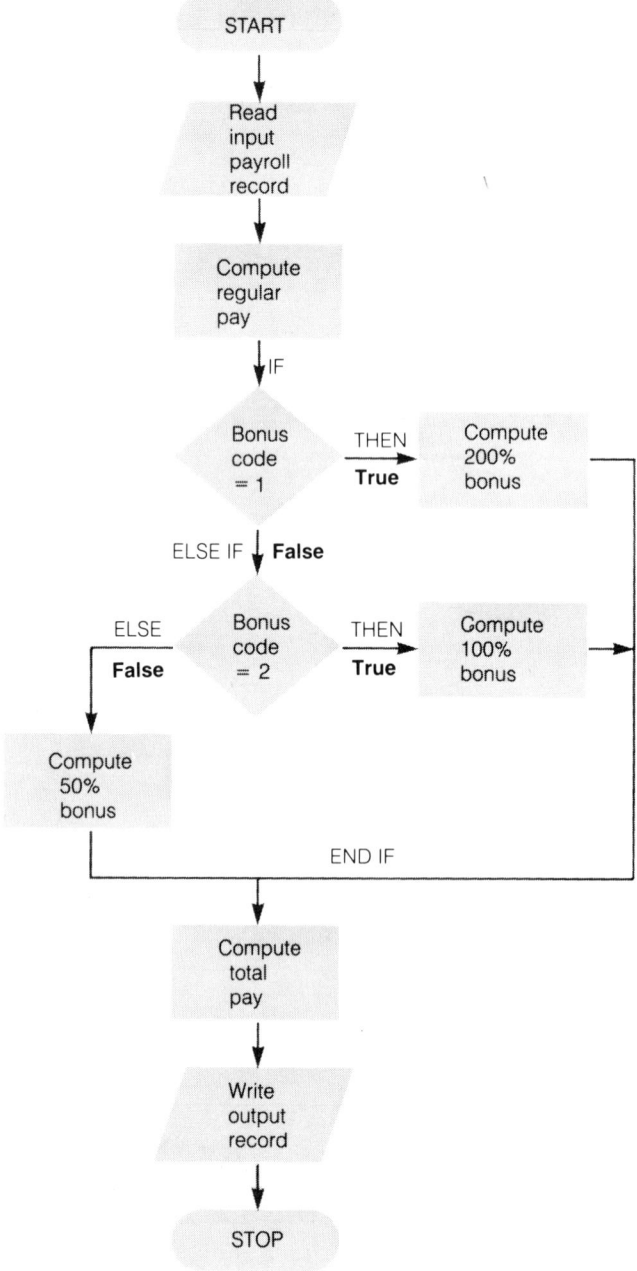

Nested IF THEN statements may also have ELSE or ELSE IF statements at the same level of nesting. This is illustrated in Figure 7-13.

Figure 7-12
Program using IF-THEN-ELSE structures for Lucky Company problem

```
|12345|6|7
         PROGRAM PAYROL
         OPEN(1,FILE='INPUT')
         OPEN(2,FILE='PUNCH')
         READ(1,77)NUMEMP,HOURS,RATE,KODE
      77 FORMAT(I4,2X,2F5.2,T23,I2)
C
         REGPAY=HOURS*RATE
C
C
C        *** BONUS IS BASED ON YEARS OF EMPLOYMENT
C             AS INDICATED BY CODE
C             KODE       YEARS
C               1        MORE THAN 5
C               2        1 to 5
C               3        LESS THAN 1
         IF(KODE.EQ.1) THEN
            BONUS=REGPAY*2.00
         ELSE IF(KODE.EQ.2) THEN
            BONUS=REGPAY
         ELSE
            BONUS=REGPAY/2.00
         END IF
C
         TOTPAY=REGPAY+BONUS
         WRITE(2,88)NUMEMP,REGPAY,BONUS,TOTPAY,KODE
      88 FORMAT(I4,F7.2,2F8.2,T79,I2)
C
         STOP
         END
```

IF THEN statements can be nested within ELSE-blocks or ELSE IF-blocks. This is illustrated in Figure 7-14.

The variety of IF-THEN-ELSE structures is considerable. This variety gives the programmer an opportunity to be creative and to exercise flexibility in program design. But a word of caution is in order. If the levels of nesting are too deep, or should the IF-THEN-ELSE structure be too complex, then errors can slip into the original coding or into the modification of the code. For example, an unintentional nesting or misplacement of an END IF statement can seriously distort the logic of the program. Such errors can easily happen with overly complex structures.

Programming considerations

The IF-THEN-ELSE structures have certain rules that must be observed.

Figure 7-13
Nested ELSE IF-blocks and ELSE-block

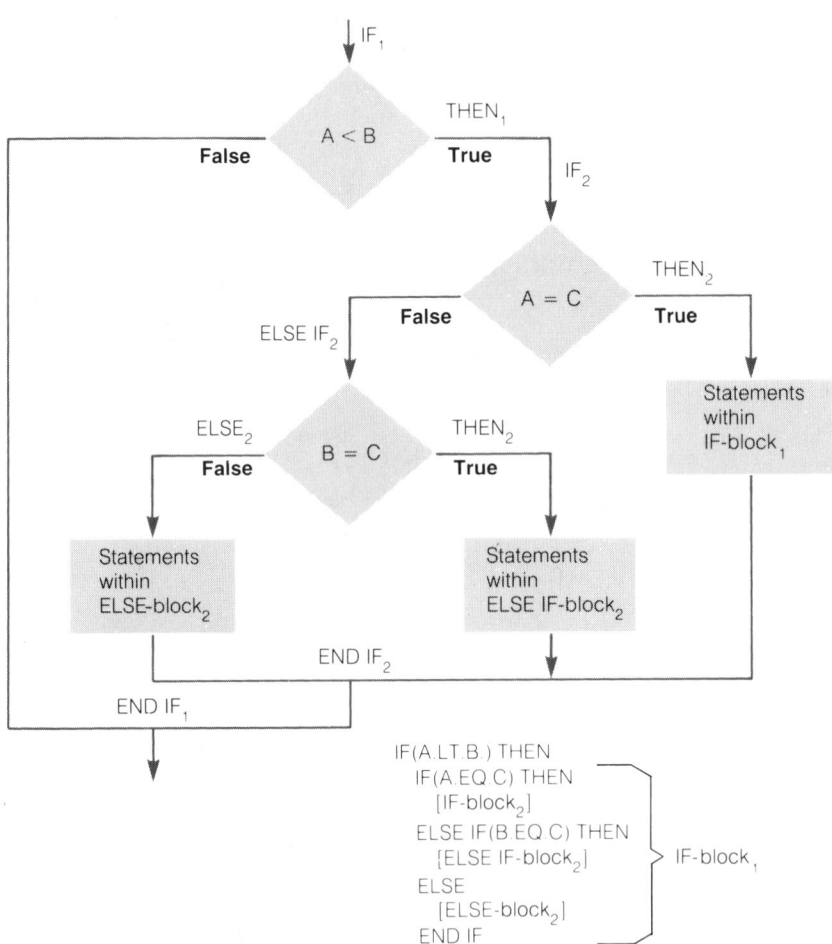

1. Branching *into* a block from outside the block is *not* permitted. This is the case whether the block is an IF-block, an ELSE-block, or an ELSE IF-block.
2. It is permitted to branch to an IF THEN. It is not permitted to branch to an ELSE, ELSE IF, or END IF.
3. Branching *out* of a block is always permitted. This is the case whether the block is an IF-block, an ELSE-block, or an ELSE IF-block.
4. An IF THEN can have only one associated ELSE. However, an IF THEN can have one or more associated ELSE IFs. With these ELSE IFs, an associated ELSE can appear only after the last ELSE IF.
5. Any block (i.e., IF-block, ELSE-block, ELSE IF-block,) may be *empty*. The term *empty* implies that there are no statements in the block to be executed. A word of caution: Some compilers do not

7/IF-THEN-ELSE and DO Loop Structures

Figure 7-14
IF THEN nested with an ELSE-block

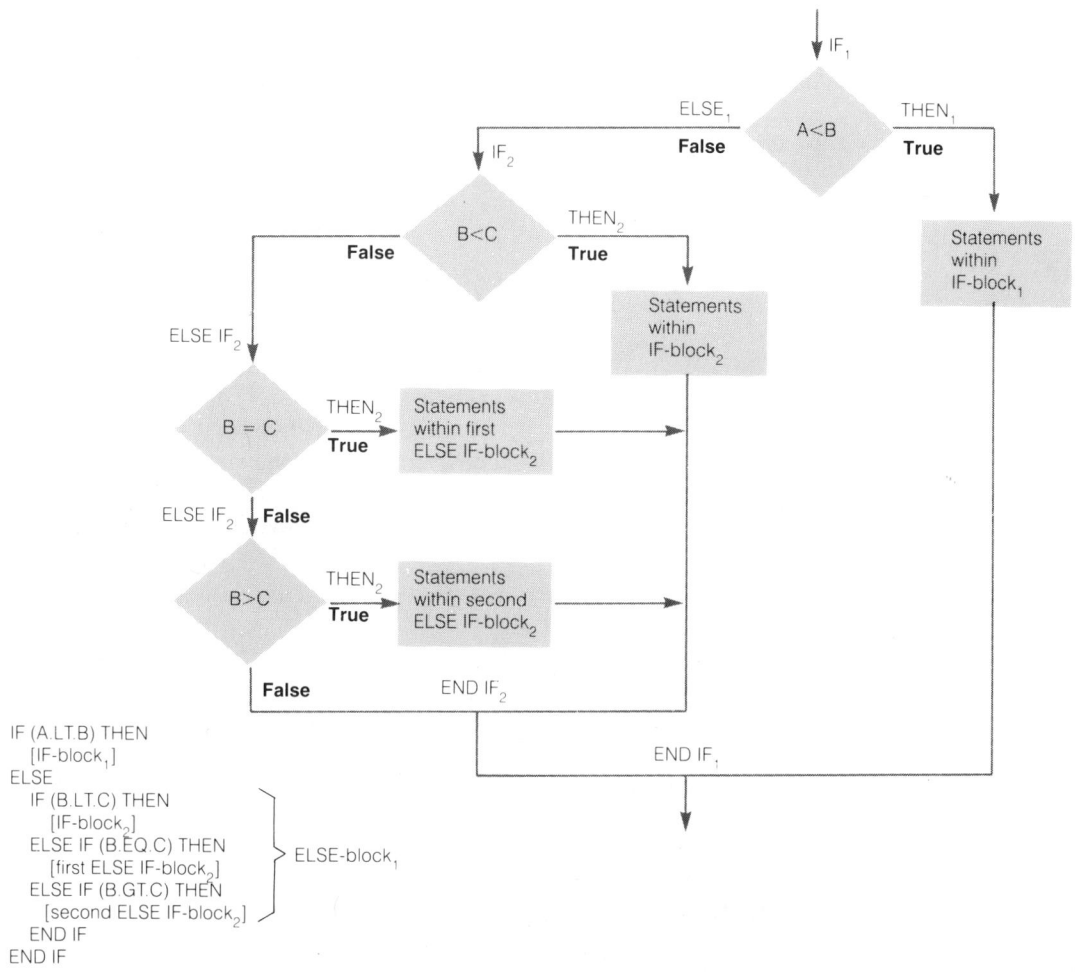

```
IF (A.LT.B) THEN
   [IF-block₁]
ELSE
   IF (B.LT.C) THEN
      [IF-block₂]
   ELSE IF (B.EQ.C) THEN
      [first ELSE IF-block₂]
   ELSE IF (B.GT.C) THEN
      [second ELSE IF-block₂]
   END IF
END IF
```

follow this standard rule—that is, they do not accept an empty block. Of course, empty blocks can be avoided by a careful change of the logical expression. For example, the following empty IF-block

```
|12345|6|7
      IF(A.NE.B) THEN
      ELSE
         KOUNT=KOUNT+1
      END IF
```

can be recoded as follows:

```
|12345|6|7
      IF(A.EQ.B) THEN
         KOUNT=KOUNT+1
      END IF
```

In the above example, by testing whether A is equal to B (rather than not equal to B), the empty block is avoided and an ELSE-block is eliminated.

Another possibility is the inclusion of the CONTINUE statement in the empty block. This makes the block "nonempty." The CONTINUE is a special type of statement that causes no action to be taken. It serves as a filler to avoid an empty block.

```
|12345|6|7
      IF(A.NE.B) THEN
         CONTINUE
      ELSE
         KOUNT=KOUNT+1
      END IF
```

When A is not equal to B, then the CONTINUE statement is encountered. No action is performed; control then goes to the END IF statement, and the program continues on with the statements following the END IF.

The CONTINUE statement is explained more fully in the next section.

THE CONTINUE STATEMENT

The CONTINUE statement is an executable "dummy statement" that is commonly used as a programming convenience. It does not affect the program logic; when the CONTINUE statement is executed, it has no effect—the computer continues on to whatever it would ordinarily do next. It is a particularly convenient statement to use as the last statement in a DO loop.

General form

The general form of a CONTINUE statement is:

```
|12345|6|7
 nnnnn    CONTINUE
```

Legend:
nnnnn   Any unique one- to five-digit integer that specifies the statement number. It is usually required because this statement is usually referenced by a DO statement or by a control statement *within* a DO range.

CONTINUE   A keyword specifying the type of statement.

Use of the CONTINUE statement is illustrated and explained in appropriate places in the following section, which covers DO loop programming structures.

THE DO STATEMENT

The DO statement is one of the most powerful in the FORTRAN language. Its purpose is to provide in one statement the four operations required for loop control:

7 / IF-THEN-ELSE and DO Loop Structures

1. Establish a counter, or *index*, by initializing a variable name to a specific current value.
2. Increment that value by a specific amount on each cycle through the DO loop.
3. Test that value each cycle and provide an exit from the DO loop after the required number of cycles, or iterations.
4. Designate the statements within the DO loop that are to be repeated. Stated another way, indicate or define the extent of the DO loop that is called the *DO range*.

For example, suppose it is necessary to execute this operation 20 times and then exit from the loop and continue further processing:

As illustrated in Chapter 6, loop control can be provided as follows:

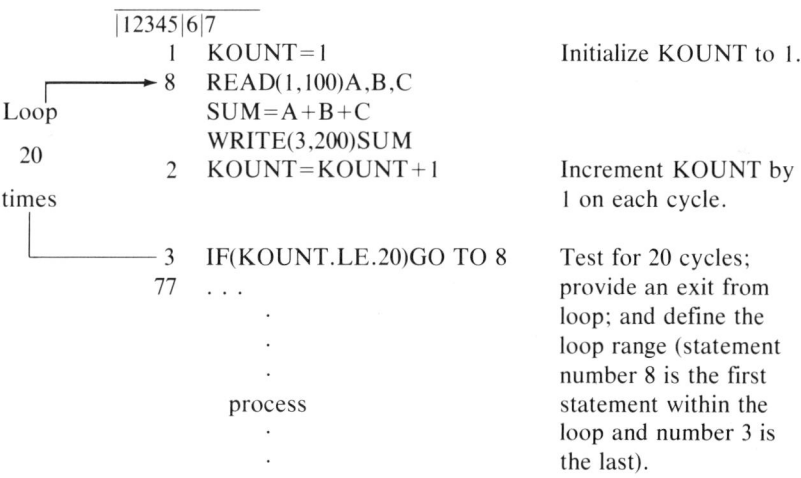

The three statements (numbered 1, 2, and 3) providing loop control in the above illustration can be replaced by one DO and one CONTINUE, thus saving the programmer time and probably requiring less compilation and execution time. The following partial program will provide the same results as the preceding illustration.

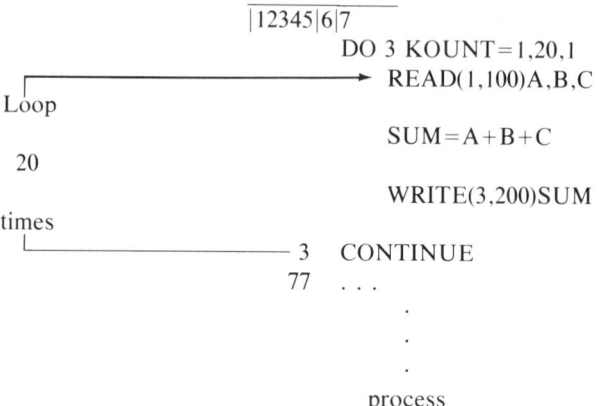

process

The DO statement in the preceding partial program directs the computer to execute the statements through statement number 3 in sequence 20 times; or, stated another way, "DO through 3, 20 times."

Let's briefly examine the DO statement in the preceding program segment:

```
|12345|6|7
      DO 3 KOUNT=1,20,1
```

"DO 3" directs the computer to process all executable statements through number 3. "KOUNT=1,20,1" tells the computer: Initialize KOUNT (a variable) to 1; test KOUNT to see if it is within the limits for continued looping—if it is, the statements to be executed are processed, KOUNT is incremented by one, and then it is retested; after 20 iterations (passes through the loop), exit and then start processing the statements that follow the DO loop.

The operation of DO loops is fully explained and illustrated in following sections. But before examining the details, a few general introductory definitions and comments seem appropriate.

A DO statement specifies a loop. A DO loop starts with a DO statement and ends with the terminal statement that is identified by label (statement number) within the DO statement.

The *DO loop range* consists of all the executable statements in a DO loop, except for the DO statement. That is, it is the set of statements that may be repeatedly processed in accordance with the control parameters of the DO.

As a matter of style, we use a CONTINUE statement as the last statement in every DO loop. This adds clarity to the program structure—every DO loop starts with a DO and ends with a CONTINUE. As a matter of clear style, we also indent (three spaces) all statements between the DO and CONTINUE; this sets off visually the block of statements controlled by the DO. The objective is to make programs more readable to the person writing them as well as to others who may be responsible for review and maintenance.

7 / IF-THEN-ELSE and DO Loop Structures

General form

The general form of a DO statement is as follows:

|12345|6|7
nnnnn   DO sn i=e_1,e_2,e_3

Legend:

nnnnn   Any unique one- to five-digit integer that specifies the statement *number*. It is required only if the statement is referenced elsewhere in the program.

DO   A keyword that specifies the type of statement.

sn   A *statement number* that specifies the last statement in the DO loop range. This referenced statement is sometimes called the *target*.

i   An *integer variable name*, called the DO variable, whose current value is initialized and incremented as controlled by the DO statement. It serves as a counter of the number of iterations through the loop. It is sometimes called an *index*.

=   A required delimiter or separator following the integer variable name.

e_1 An *expression* which may be an unsigned integer constant or an integer variable name whose current value is used to initialize or establish the original value of the index (i) when the DO loop is first entered. This original value should be one or more.

,e_2 An *expression* which may be an unsigned integer constant or integer variable name, preceded by a comma, whose current value is used as a *test value*. After executing the last statement (sn) in the DO range, control returns to the beginning of the DO range. If the current value of the index or counter (i) exceeds this test value, the computer exits from the loop by automatically "dropping through" to the first executable statement following the last statement (sn) in the DO range; otherwise it automatically cycles through the loop again.

,e_3 An optional *expression* which may be an unsigned integer constant or integer variable name, preceded by a comma, whose current value should be one or more. It is used as an *increment* value. Each time control returns to the first statement from the last statement (sn) in the DO range, this increment value is automatically added to the contents of the DO variable—i.e., the counter or index (i). It should be noted that (e_3) is the only optional element of the DO statement. If this increment value is omitted, the computer automatically assumes an increment value of 1. If it is omitted, the preceding comma must also be omitted.

The general form of the DO statement may be summarized as follows:

	Statement label of last statement in the DO range	Integer variable named used as an iteration counter or index		Initial value of iteration counter or index	Test value	Increment value
DO	sn	i	=	e_1	,e_2	,e_3

DO loop processing has the effect of the steps illustrated in Figure 7-15.

The sequence of the effective steps is:

1. Initialize the index.
2. Determine if the index value exceeds the test value. If so, exit; if not, go to Step 3.
3. Execute the statements within the DO range.
4. Increment the index, then return to Step 2.

It has been repeatedly emphasized throughout this text that the programmer should attempt to select variable names that are as descriptive as possible within the rules of composition. In the case of DO loop variables, programmers commonly use single-character names (e.g., N) or double-character names (e.g., KK). This convention improves program readability because it readily identifies the variable as a DO loop index. It also reduces the amount of coding (and, consequently, the number of coding errors). The savings in coding will be a major factor in the following two chapters in which the DO loop variable is repeatedly used as a subscript index to identify positions of elements in an array.

With a few exceptions, intended to emphasize that the DO loop

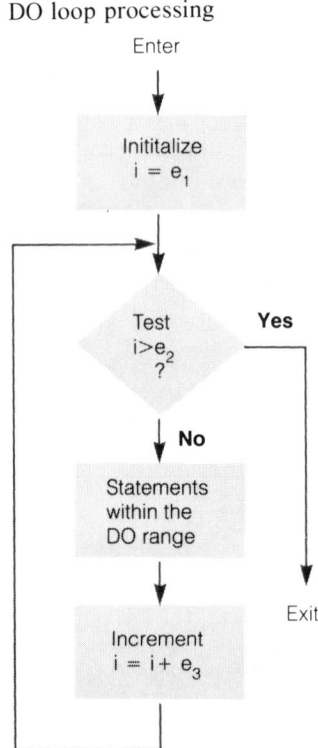

Figure 7-15
DO loop processing

7/IF-THEN-ELSE and DO Loop Structures

variable is an index for loop control, we consistently follow this convention. Any convention that improves readability, saves coding time, and reduces the probability of an error is worth following. We highly recommend it.

Illustrative examples

Any integer number greater than zero may be used as the initial, incremental, or test value. If the incremental value is omitted, it is assumed to be one. To illustrate, each of the following DO statements is designed to cause the statements within the DO range to be executed *five* times:

	Index values prior to loop exit
DO 6 INDEX=1,5,1	1, 2, 3, 4, 5, 6
DO 6 INDEX=1,5	1, 2, 3, 4, 5, 6
DO 6 INDEX=2,6,1	2, 3, 4, 5, 6, 7
DO 6 INDEX=3,7	3, 4, 5, 6, 7, 8
DO 6 INDEX=25,30	25, 26, 27, 28, 29, 30, 31
DO 6 INDEX=1,9,2	1, 3, 5, 7, 9, 11
DO 6 INDEX=1,10,2	1, 3, 5, 7, 9, 11

The last *two* DO statements above will operate as follows: INDEX will be initialized to one when the DO loop is entered. On each successive pass through the loop, INDEX will be incremented by 2 changing its current value to 3, 5, 7, 9, and 11. After five passes through the loop, the current value of INDEX will be 11. This *exceeds* the test values of 9 or 10, so it will cause an exit from the loop. If the test value had been 8, an exit would have occurred after only 4 iterations, whereas an 11 test value would have caused 6 iterations.

It should be noted that, if both the initialization *and* the expressed or implied incremental values are one, the test value will always indicate the exact number of passes that will be made through the loop. This "one-one combination" is easy for the programmer to use and is quite popular. It should be noted, however, that in many cases the program logic may make it desirable or mandatory to initialize and/or increment by some value other than one.

Some brief illustrations may be helpful at this point. The following series of statements will sum the first 10 integers:

```
|12345|6|7
      INTSUM=0
      DO 4 K=1,10,1
      INTSUM=INTSUM+K
    4 CONTINUE
```

An increment value of 2 is used in the next illustration of a routine that sums all *odd* integers through 10:

```
|12345|6|7
      INTSUM=0
      DO 4 KK=1,10,2
         INTSUM=INTSUM+KK
    4 CONTINUE
```

Two is used as both the initialization and incremental value in the following illustration of a routine that sums all *even* integers through 10:

```
|12345|6|7
      INTSUM=0
      DO 40 N=2,10,2
         INTSUM=INTSUM+N
   40 CONTINUE
```

The following series of statements is designed to sum every fifth integer from 25 through 50:

```
|12345|6|7
      INTSUM=0
      DO 4 K=25,50,5
         INTSUM=INTSUM+K
    4 CONTINUE
```

The next routine is identical to the preceding one except that it includes a provision for output within the loop and immediately following the exit. The generated output is shown to the right of the program segment below:

```
|12345|6|7                            Output
         INTSUM=0                      25
         DO 4 K=25,50,5                30
            INTSUM=INTSUM+K            35
            WRITE(3,100)K              40
  100    FORMAT(1X,I3)                 45
      4  CONTINUE                      50
C                                     225
         WRITE(3,100)INTSUM
```

There are many cases where it is desirable or required that an integer variable name, instead of an integer constant, be used for the initialization, incremental, or test values. To control, for example, a loop using "header record" technique, covered in the previous chapter, would require a variable name (e.g., NUMBER) as the test value:

7/IF-THEN-ELSE and DO Loop Structures

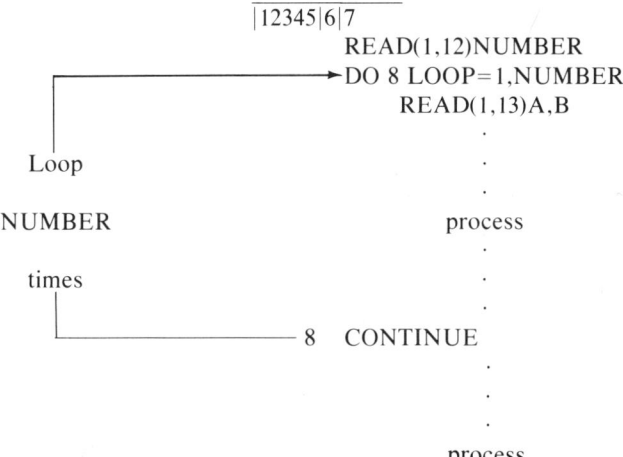

If integer variable names are used for the initialization, test, and incremental values, the DO statement can be extremely powerful, because the current values of any or all of these variable names can be changed according to a multitude of conditions. Thus, one DO may replace hundreds of statements, depending upon the complexity of the problem to be solved.

The following straightforward program, which uses header record control, computes an arithmetic mean. Note that input variables are printed on lines that are numbered by using the DO index.

```
|12345|6|7
        READ(1,100)KOUNT
        SUMX=0.0
C
        DO 66 JJ=1,KOUNT
          READ(1,200)X
          SUMX=SUMX+X
          WRITE(3,300)JJ,X
     66 CONTINUE
C
        COUNT=KOUNT
        AMEAN=SUMX/COUNT
        WRITE(3,400)SUMX,AMEAN
        STOP
C
    100 FORMAT(I2)
    200 FORMAT(F6.2)
    300 FORMAT(1X,I2,3X,F6.2)
    400 FORMAT(/1X,'SUM',F8.2/ /2X,'MEAN',F6.2)
        END
```

Multiple DO statements As many DO statements as the problem requires and the computer system capacity permits may be used in a program. It may contain more than one independent DO loop, and/or it may contain nested DO loops. Examples of each type are illustrated next.

Independent DO statements The following partial program illustrates two independent DO loops:

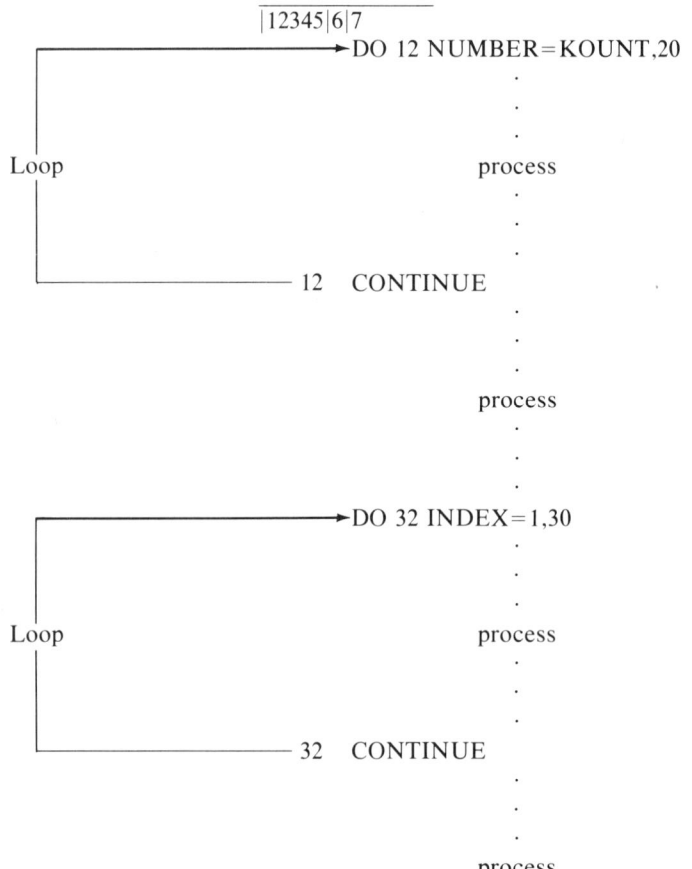

Nested DO statements When one DO loop is contained within the range of another DO loop, the inner loop is said to be *nested*. The following partial program illustrates a nested DO loop:

7/IF-THEN-ELSE and DO Loop Structures

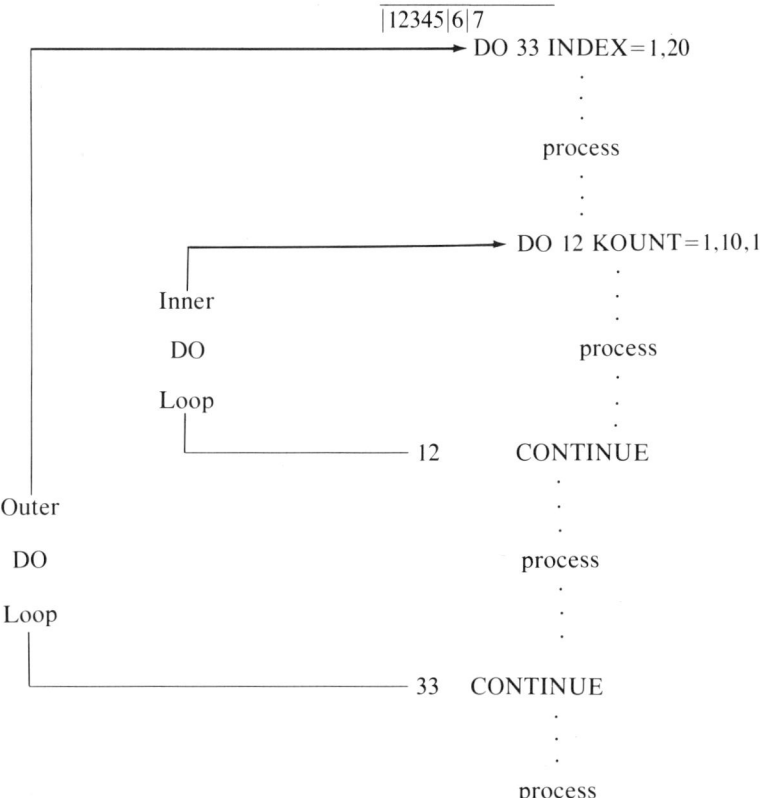

The preceding illustration will cause the computer to cycle through the outer loop 20 times and inner loop 200 times (the nested loop will be cycled 10 times on each cycle through the outer loop).

To illustrate more explicitly, the following program:

```
|12345|6|7
         DO 77 K=1,2
     50  FORMAT(1X,'1ST OUTER')
         WRITE(3,50)
C
         DO 66 M=1,3
     60      FORMAT(1X,'INNER')
             WRITE(3,60)
     66  CONTINUE
C
     70  FORMAT(1X,'2ND OUTER')
         WRITE(3,70)
     77  CONTINUE
C
     80  FORMAT(1X,'FINAL')
         WRITE(3,80)
         STOP
         END
```

will produce the following output:

```
1ST OUTER
INNER
INNER
INNER
2ND OUTER
1ST OUTER
INNER
INNER
INNER
2ND OUTER
FINAL
```

The programmer may nest as many DO loops as are required. One or more additional DO loops, for example, could have been nested within the inner loop in the preceding illustration. The following series of statements further illustrates the effects of nested DOs:

```
|12345|6|7
        NUMBER=0
        KOUNT=0
        DO 40 J=1,20,1
           DO 30 K=1,10,1
              KOUNT=KOUNT+1
     30    CONTINUE
           NUMBER=NUMBER+1
     40 CONTINUE
```

The preceding illustration will cause the computer to cycle through the outer loop 20 times and the inner loop 200 times (the nested loop will be cycled 10 times for each cycle through the outer loop). Thus, after both loops have been "exhausted," KOUNT will have a value of 200 and NUMBER a value of 20.

To illustrate further:

```
|12345|6|7
        KOUNT=0
        DO 30 J=1,10,1
           DO 20 K=1,5,1
              KOUNT=KOUNT+1
     20    CONTINUE
     30 CONTINUE
```

In the above case, KOUNT will contain 50 after the smoke has cleared.

Now, consider the following series of statements:

7 / IF-THEN-ELSE and DO Loop Structures

```
|12345|6|7
        N=0
        DO 200 J=1,2
          K=J
          DO 100 L=1,4
            M=L
            N=N+1
100     CONTINUE
200     CONTINUE
```

Immediately after execution of the above statements, the variables have these values: J=3, K=2, L=5, M=4, and N=8.

The programmer may nest as many DO loops as required. Inner and outer loops may have the same "target," but in this book separate targets are used for the sake of clarity. The programmer must be cautious that the range of inner loops does not extend beyond the range of outer loops. Following are examples of proper and improper uses of nested DO loops.

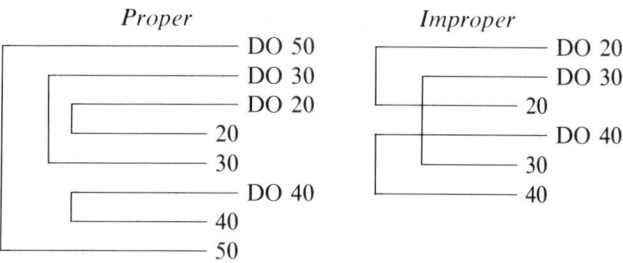

DO loop rules

Two definitions, given earlier, are repeated in this paragraph for ease of reference while you read the rules covered in this section. A *DO loop* starts with a DO statement and ends with the terminal statement that is identified by label (statement number) within the DO statement. The *DO range* consists of all the executable statements in a DO loop, except for the DO statement. That is, it is the set of statements that may be repeatedly processed in accordance with the control parameters of the DO.

The DO statement is very powerful, but it has numerous restrictions. The most general restriction is that the executable statements within the DO range must not conflict with the general operations of the DO statement. More specific restrictions are included in the DO loop rules that follow.

1. The last statement in the DO range must be an executable statement. But it must not be an executable statement that conflicts with the normal looping action. For example, the last statement cannot be a GO TO, IF, STOP, DO, etc. Again, it is strongly recommended that DO loops be terminated with a CONTINUE

statement. This relieves the programmer of concern with the numerous restrictions regarding the last statement in the DO range, thus reducing the probability of an error.

2. The DO variable, as well as any variables used for the initialization, test, and incremental values, may be *used* within the DO range but must not be *changed* without the DO range. In programmer jargon, these variables may be used but not abused.

   For example, within the range of the DO loop below, the WRITE, IF, and arithmetic statements are valid because they *use* but do not change the DO variable:

   ```
   |12345|6|7
         DO 88 K=1,10,1
             WRITE(3,100)K
             IF(J.GE.K)N=N+1
             M=K*2
      88   CONTINUE
   ```

   On the other hand, the following statement is not allowed within the DO range above because it attempts to *change* the DO variable and thus interferes with normal looping:

   ```
   |12345|6|7
             K=K+2
   ```

3. A DO loop may be entered only through a DO statement. Transfer from a statement outside a DO loop to a statement within the DO range is prohibited. Stated simply, DO loops must be entered through the "top."

4. When a DO loop is entered, the DO variable is initialized. An initialization value must not be changed by a statement within the DO range. Thus, transfers to a DO statement from anywhere within the range controlled by that statement are forbidden. Stated another way, a DO statement should not be referenced by any statement within the loop and DO statement controls.

5. There are two ways to exit from a DO loop.
   a. "From the bottom." The normal method of exit is automatic; control drops through to the first executable statement following the DO range when the current value of the index exceeds the test value.
   b. "From the side." The programmer may provide a special exit; it is always permissible to transfer control out of any DO loop (independent or nested) by a statement (e.g., a logical IF) within the DO range.

6. When nested DO loops are used, the following rules apply:
   a. A different DO variable must be used for each DO loop in a nest.
   b. All statements in the range of the inner (nested) DO loop must be included within the range of the outer DO loop.

7/IF-THEN-ELSE and DO Loop Structures

   c. As previously indicated, all DO loops must be entered by the DO statement that defines the loop. Thus, in the case of nested DO loops, the outermost loop must be entered first and the innermost last.
7. When a DO statement appears in an IF-block, the entire DO loop must be within that IF-block. The same rule applies when a DO statement appears in an ELSE-block or an ELSE IF-block.
8. When a block IF statement appears in a DO loop, the corresponding END IF must also appear within that DO loop.

Additional programming considerations

The main purpose of a CONTINUE statement is for programmer convenience. It may be used to end a DO loop that would otherwise end with a forbidden statement. It may also be used to end a DO loop that would otherwise end with a valid statement that must not be executed under certain conditions. Examples are discussed and illustrated in this section.

Assume that a problem requires that 100 records be read and processed. The input file contains three data fields: A, B, and KODE. All input records containing the value 7 in the KODE field are to be ignored; the data in the A and B fields of all other records are to be added and the resulting SUM written; the SUM of each record processed is to be accumulated for further processing.

The following partial program illustrates an example of a situation where a CONTINUE statement is required because of a control statement *within* the DO range.

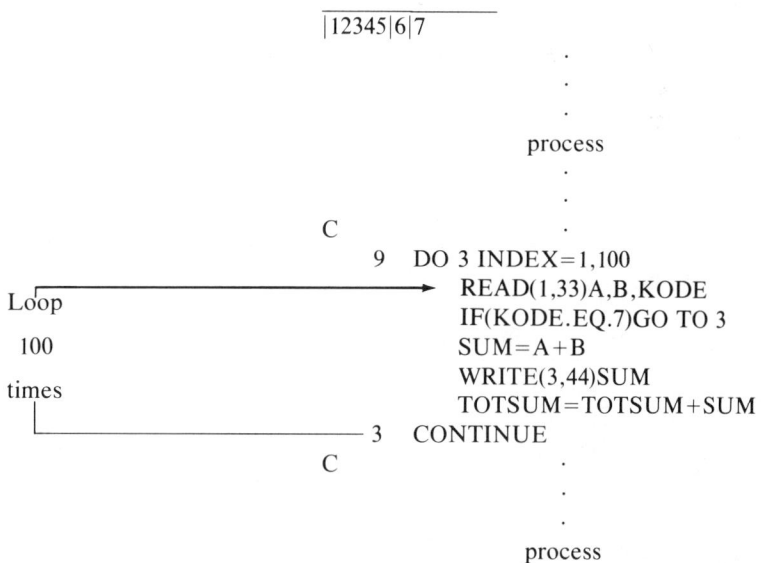

It should be noted that the DO variable (INDEX) is incremented only when there is an automatic return from the last statement in the DO range. Thus, in the above illustration the only statement that the IF statement can reference (within the program logic) is the CONTINUE statement.

The next partial program includes CONTINUE statements and nested DOs. The inner loop calculates the ending balance for 10 consecutive years by compounding interest annually at a specified rate on an original $500 investment. The outer loop controls the interest rates and causes each table (produced by the inner loop) to be printed on a different page. Note that the outer DO provides the inner DO with three different rates (5 percent, 7 percent, and 9 percent); the index is initialized at 5 and incremented by 2 in this example.

```
|12345|6|7
C
        DO 130 K=5,9,2
            ZK=K
            RATE=ZK/100.
            PRINC=500.00
            WRITE(3,60)
   60       FORMAT('1')
C
            DO 120 N=1,10
                PRINC=PRINC+(PRINC*RATE)
                WRITE(3,100)N,PRINC
  100           FORMAT(1X,I2,2X,F8.2)
  120       CONTINUE
C
  130   CONTINUE
C
```

The illustrated programming style sets off each DO loop to the reader's eye. DO loops are preceded by and followed by blank comments; they begin with a DO and end with a CONTINUE, and the other statements are indented a few columns.

DO statements may include integer variables, instead of integer constants, for the initialization, test, and incremental values. For example, the following statement is designed to loop N times:

```
|12345|6|7
        DO 88 K=1,N
```

N, of course, must be properly initialized prior to execution of the DO. One way to do this is to read a header record that sets the value of N. In this case, defensive programming could be used to assure that N is valid (a positive nonzero integer).

```
|12345|6|7
      IF(N.GE.1)GO TO 66
         WRITE(3,55)
55       FORMAT(1X,10('*'),' MISSING OR INVALID'/
$        '+',30X,'HEADER RECORD'/)
         STOP
C
66    DO 88 K=1,N
```

The above program segment tells the user the probable cause of the error, then stops the program instead of trying to go through the DO loop zero (or less) times. The error message, of course, should be appropriate for the circumstances; in many cases it would be useful to also write the invalid N value. The format code 10('*') flags the error message by a string of ten leading asterisks; 10 ('*') is a programming shortcut that is the equivalent of '**********' or 10H**********. The main point of the preceding illustration is that the programmer should anticipate potential loop control problems and provide for appropriate action.

Some DO loops are intentionally designed to be terminated by a special exit ("from the side") rather than a normal exit ("from the bottom"). This is illustrated by the statements below and the discussion that follows.

```
|12345|6|7
      DO 55 K=1,13
         READ ... ID ...
         IF(ID.EQ.9999)GO TO 95
         .
         .
         .
55    CONTINUE
C
      WRITE(3,75)
75    FORMAT(1X,'** TOO MANY INPUT RECORDS')
      STOP
C
95    ...
```

Assume the above routine is designed to read a maximum of 13 input records, 12 data records (perhaps one for each month of the year), and one trailer record. Each includes an identification number (ID). When the IF detects the trailer record, control exits "from the side." Note that, logically, input should not exceed 13 records (12 data and one trailer), so control should never exit "from the bottom." However, it will if the user provides more than 12 input data records. Defensive programming anticipates this possibility and provides statements to handle it.

REVIEW QUESTIONS

1. Contrast and compare the logical IF and the IF-THEN-ELSE structures.

2. What is the purpose of the END IF?

3. When is it appropriate to use ELSE IFs?

4. What are nested IF-THEN-ELSE structures? Can one END IF be used to complete one or more nested IF THEN's?

5. Discuss the rules pertaining to branching into and out of IF-THEN-ELSE structures.

6. As a general rule, anything that interferes with the normal operation of the DO is prohibited. Describe how the following rule violations interfere with the normal operation of the DO:
    a. The last statement in the DO range is a DO statement.
    b. A DO loop is initially entered at a numbered statement in about the middle of the loop by a transfer from an IF statement outside the loop.
    c. A DO loop is reentered by a transfer to the DO statement from a statement within the DO loop.
    d. The DO loop index is a floating point, rather than an integer, variable name.
    e. The number stored at the variable name representing the initialization value (m_1) is changed by an arithmetic statement within the DO loop.

7. What type of statement is the DO (I/O, assignment, control, or nonexecutable)?

8. What type of statement is the CONTINUE?

9. Why do most programmers always terminate a DO loop with a CONTINUE statement?

10. CONTINUE statements are always allowed as the last statement in a DO range. Are they ever allowed anywhere else in a program?

11. What happens if the DO statement does not include an incremental value (e_3)? a test value (e_2)?

12. What types of statements are permitted to *follow* immediately the DO?

13. What are nested DOs, and how many DOs are allowed in a nest?

14. May the DO index be used in an arithmetic statement to the right of the equal sign? To the left?

7/IF-THEN-ELSE and DO Loop Structures

15. Distinguish between a normal and a special exit from a DO loop.

16. Under what conditions may a DO loop be entered at a point other than at the beginning of the loop?

17. Some programmers always precede and follow each DO loop by one or more "blank comments." What is the purpose of this convention?

18. Give an example of an application where a DO loop might be intentionally designed so that control exits "from the side" rather than "from the bottom."

19. Sometimes two different DO loops within a program may use the same variable name as an index, but sometimes this is not permitted. Discuss.

20. What functions can be done using a DO that cannot also be done using various combinations of other statements?

EXERCISES

Consider the program segments in the first three exercises, which contain IF THEN-ELSE structures, and indicate the errors, if any, in each case.

1.
```
        IF(KOUNT-40) THEN KOUNT=KOUNT+1
        END IF
```

2.
```
        IF(I.LT.J) THEN
        ELSE
            KOUNT=KOUNT+J
        ELSE IF(J.LT.K)
            KOUNT=KOUNT+K
```

3.
```
        IF(A.EQ.B-C) THEN
            KOUNT1=KOUNT1+1
        ELSE
            A=A-1.0
    400     KOUNT2=KOUNT2+1
            IF(C.GT.B) THEN
            C=C-1.0
            GO TO 500
        END IF
    500 A=A+1.0
        IF(A.LT.C) THEN
            GO TO 400
        END IF
```

4. Consider the following error-free program segment.
```
        IF(X.GT.Y) THEN
            KOUNT1=KOUNT1+1
            IF(Y.GT.Z) THEN
                KOUNT2=KOUNT2+1
            END IF
        END IF
```

Does the following program segment have the same effect as the above program segment? Explain.

```
IF(X.GT.Y) THEN
    KOUNT1=KOUNT1+1
END IF
IF(Y.GT.Z) THEN
    KOUNT2=KOUNT2+1
END IF
```

5. Does the following program segment have the same effect as the error-free program segment given in Exercise 4 above? Explain.

```
IF(X.GT.Y) THEN
    KOUNT1=KOUNT1+1
END IF
IF((X.GT.Y).AND.(Y.GT.Z)) THEN
    KOUNT2=KOUNT2+1
END IF
```

6. Indicate the number of times the loops, controlled by the following DOs, will be executed prior to a normal exit.

```
DO 1 J=1,10,1
DO 2 K=1,10
DO 3 L=2,10
DO 4 M=1,10,2
DO 5 N=2,10,2
DO 6 JJ=10,10,10
DO 7 KK=10,2
DO 8 LL=8,40,8
DO 9 MM=2,24,3
DO 10 NN=5,100,5
```

7. Examine the following labeled DOs. If invalid, indicate why.

```
1 DO 5 H=17,27,9
2 DO 4 I=A,B,C
3 DO 3 J=K,L
4 DO 2 K=K,L
5 DO 1 L=K,K
```

8. Examine the following partial program. What kind of table does it write?

```
       N=1
       DO 50 K=2,10,1
           N=N*(K-1)
           WRITE(3,60)N
50     CONTINUE
```

7 / IF-THEN-ELSE and DO Loop Structures

PROBLEMS

The first five problems are designed to review IF-THEN-ELSE structures. The remainder require loop control by means of one or more DO statements.

For Problems 1 through 5, design each program so that it has the appropriate loop control that assumes an unknown number of records to be processed. The record is derived from a personnel file and has the following layout:

Record position	Field name
1-8	Employee's first name
9-17	Employee's last name
18	Sex code (1 for female; 2 for male)
19	Income type code (1 for hourly wage; 2 for weekly salary)
20-22	Seniority (in weeks of continuous employment)

The data for running the first five programs are as follows:

1-8	9-17	18	19	20-22
FUCHSIA	FIDGET	1	1	3
GEORGE	GERSHWIN	2	2	568
HOWARD	HUGHES	2	2	650
IRA	IRATE	2	1	2
JESSE	JAMES	2	1	85
KING	KOENIG	2	2	190
LUCY	LUCIOUS	1	2	249
MINNY	MOOSE	1	1	51
NICK	NAPLES	2	1	331
OREN	ORATORIO	2	1	26
PENNY	PINCHER	1	2	447
QUINCY	QUENCHER	2	1	14

1. The firm has a trial period of four weeks for employees that are newly hired. After this time, they attain "seniority status." Write a program to calculate the average seniority of only employees who have five or more weeks continuous employment with the firm.

The decision control is to be done with an IF THEN. Use the GO TO only to loop back to the statement that reads in the personnel record.

The required input is given in the description preceding this problem. The required output is one line in the following format.

Line position	
1-2	Number of senior employees (integer)
21-25	Sum of weeks for all senior employees (integer)
41-45	Average weeks for the senior employee (1 decimal place)

Assume that there is at least one employee who has more than four weeks seniority.

2. Write a program to calculate the average number of weeks employed for employees who have four or less weeks' seniority *and* the average number of weeks employed for employees who have five or more weeks' seniority.

The decision control is to be done with an IF THEN and an ELSE. Use the GO TO only to loop back to the statement that reads in the personnel record.

The required input is given in the description preceding the problems. The required output is as follows:

First   Output this message starting in position 1:
EMPLOYED FOUR WEEKS OR LESS
Second   Skip down two lines and for employees with four or less weeks output the same type of data in the same format as shown in Problem 1.
Third   Skip down four lines and output this message starting in position 1:
EMPLOYED FIVE WEEKS OR MORE
Fourth   Skip down two lines and for employees with five or more weeks output the same type of data in the same format as shown in Problem 1.

Assume that there is at least one employee with four or less weeks seniority and at least one employee with more than four weeks seniority.

3. The personnel department of the firm requires a breakdown of employees' seniorities. Averages are required for the following categories.

a. Employees with four or less weeks' seniority.
b. Employees with more than 4 but less than 53 weeks' seniority.
c. Employees with more than 52 but less than 261 weeks' seniority.

Do not process any records with more than 260 weeks' seniority. Write a program that will accomplish these requirements.

The decision control is to be done by an IF THEN with associated ELSE IFs. Use the GO TO only to loop back to the statement that reads in the personnel record.

The required input is given in the description preceding the problems. The required output is to be similar to the output described in Problem 2.

Assume that there is at least one employee in each of the three categories given above.

4. Write a program that determines if the employee earns an hourly wage and, *if so*, that calculates (*a*) the average weeks for hourly employees with 260 weeks or less seniority and (*b*) the average weeks for hourly employees with more than 260 weeks seniority.

The decision control is to be done with one IF-block that contains a nested IF-THEN-ELSE structure. Use the GO TO only to loop back to the statement that reads in the personnel record.

The required input is given in the description preceding the problems. The required output is to be similar to the output described in Problem 2.

Assume that there is at least one hourly employee with 260 or less weeks' seniority and at least one hourly employee with more than 260 weeks' seniority.

7/IF-THEN-ELSE and DO Loop Structures

5. This problem has two parts. Part *b* is a continuation of Part *a*.

    a. The management of the firm desires a report that analyzes employee seniority by income type (hourly and salary) and by sex (female and male).

    The decision control is to be done by one IF-THEN-ELSE structure that contains other nested IF-THEN-ELSE structures. Use the GO TO only to loop back to the statement that reads in the personnel record.

    The required input is given in the description preceding the problems. The required output is a two-part report that is described below.

    The first part of the report is an "Employee Listing" that gives the contents of the personnel records. However, when the sex code is 1, output the word *FEMALE*; when 2, output the word *MALE*. When the income type code is 1, output the word *HOURLY*; when 2, output the word *SALARY*. Do these sex and income type code conversions by means of appropriate alphanumeric assignment statements. The "Employee Listing" is formatted as follows:

```
                    SENIORITY REPORT
                   * EMPLOYEE LISTING *

FIRST NAME   LAST NAME    SEX     PAY TYPE   SENIORITY (WEEKS)
XXXXXXX      XXXXXXXXX    XXXXXX  XXXXXX            XXX
```

The second part of the report is a "Categorical Analysis" that provides an analysis of seniority by various categories. This is formatted as follows:

```
                 SENIORITY REPORT
              ** CATEGORICAL ANALYSIS **

                       NUMBER      WEEKS (AVERAGE)
      FEMALE
           HOURLY        XX             XXX.X
           SALARY        XX             XXX.X
      MALE
           HOURLY        XX             XXX.X
           SALARY        XX             XXX.X
```

The column heading NUMBER indicates that underneath appears the count for each category; e.g., the count for the FEMALE salary category. The column heading WEEKS (AVERAGE) indicates that underneath appears the average weeks' seniority (to one decimal place) for each category.

This program *cannot* assume that there will be at least one employee in each category. Therefore the program is to check whether there is or there is not a count within each category. This check is to be done by means of IF-THEN-ELSE structures. If it is determined that a category does not have a count of one or more employees, then output the message NO EMPLOYEES IN THIS CATEGORY. This message is to start at the same position under the heading NUMBER as the count. For example, if there were no hourly female employees, then the message would appear as follows:

```
                                  .
                                  .
                                  .
                     NUMBER    WEEKS (AVERAGE)
       FEMALE
          HOURLY   NO EMPLOYEES IN THIS CATEGORY
          SALARY         xx            xxx.x
                                  .
                                  .
                                  .
```

    b. The CATEGORICAL ANALYSIS report is to give the counts and averages for the same sex and pay type categories, as in Part *a* above, *but only for those employees who have more than 52 weeks' seniority*.

    6. Write the program described in Problem 11 in the preceding chapter with the following change only: use a DO statement for loop control. For your convenience, the problem is repeated below.

    Assume you take a job at a pencil factory for 31 days. The factory has a large inventory but is short of cash, so you agree to be paid in pencils. You are to receive one pencil the first day. Each succeeding day you are to receive twice as many pencils as the day before. Thus, you will receive two the second day, four the third, eight the fourth, etc.

    Write a program to compute the number of pencils you will earn each day and a running total of your "earnings." No input record is to be used. Output is to be on a printer, indicating on 31 successive lines the line number, your pay for each day, and the accumulated amount of your "earnings" to date. Output is to be in FORMAT(I3,2I14).

    7. Few specific problems have been solved by as many generations of programming students as the classic "Indian Problem," which follows. Peter Minuit purchased a 31-acre island from the Manhattan Indians in 1626 for about $24 worth of beads, cloth, and trinkets. How much would the $24 be worth today if it had been deposited in a savings account with interest compounded annually? Write a program to solve the problem for three different interest rates (3, 5 and 7 percent) assuming a time period of 350 years. Do not read any input records. Output is to be three double-spaced printed lines, one for each interest rate. Each line should include an appropriate descriptive message and the computed amount written in an F20.2 field. *Caution:* do not attempt to write 350 lines of output for each rate; locate the WRITE statement so it can be executed only three times. (One of the illustrative examples in the last section of this chapter may be useful as a general coding guide.)

    8. This problem is identical to Problem 13 in the preceding chapter except that a DO should be used for loop control. The revised problem follows.

    Prepare a program to compute the social security deduction and net pay for each employee and to compute the total social security deduction and total net pay for all employees. Time and a half is paid for all hours in excess of 40. Assume that the social security rate is 6.7 percent and that all employees are subject to this deduction.

    The input data deck contains one card for each of the 10 employees in the following format:

Employee number (cols. 1-4)	Date of birth (5-10)	Hours worked (11-15)	Rate per hour (16-19)	Dept. number (20)	Employee name (61-80)
1001	100948	39.00	6.50	1	PATRICIA B. ANDERSON
1002	111249	35.00	7.80	2	WASHINGTON H. BROWN
1003	111249	39.25	5.65	3	JANE ANN COOPER
1004	111249	41.75	7.00	4	RAYMOND D. DOOLITTLE
1005	111249	60.00	6.00	5	SAMUEL R. ENGERS
1006	111249	38.50	6.20	6	PATRICIA FITZGERALD
1007	111249	80.00	7.00	7	MARTIN S. GERSZEWSKI
1008	111249	45.00	5.00	8	CARL J. HILL
1009	111249	18.00	6.42	9	RAYMOND P. INOMOTO
1010	111249	50.00	9.00	1	MARK A JOHNSON

Use a DO statement for loop control. Read only the input data fields required to solve the problem.

Required output for each employee is one line containing the following data fields from left to right:

Field name
Employee name
Employee number
Rate per hour
Hours worked
Social security deduction
Net pay

"Dress up" output with reasonable spacings between fields and with a heading indicating the contents of each field. (The net pay field, for example, may be headed up with the words *NETPAY*.)

Required output for the final line (total social security and net pay for all employees) should be positioned so it appears directly below the fields totaled with the decimal points aligned.

9. Write a program to compute and write an interplanetary weight chart indicating how much a person would weigh on various planets based on the following facts:

Planet	Percentage of earth weight
Moon	16
Mars	38
Venus	85
Jupiter	264

No input data records are to be used. Use a DO statement to control the computation and writing of Earth weights from 90 through 220 pounds in increments of 5 pounds. Corresponding weights for the other planets are also to be computed and written under control of the DO statement.

The first header line (in the output) should contain the word *INTERPLANETARY* and the second the words *WEIGHT CHART*. The third line should be blank, and the fourth should contain the names of the planets in the following sequence from left to right:

EARTH MOON MARS VENUS JUPITER

Use only one WRITE statement to write the header lines. The output data should be single-spaced following the header lines. Weights are to be carried to one decimal place.

10. Write a program to compute for each employee: (1) current gross pay; (2) current social security deduction; (3) current net pay (gross pay less social security deduction); (4) new year-to-date cumulative gross earnings; and (5) new year-to-date cumulative social security deductions.

Input data are the weekly payroll records for 10 employees in the following format:

Old year-to-date earnings (cols. 1-8)	Old year-to-date soc. sec. ded'ns (9-15)	Rate per hour (16-20)	Hours for current week (21-25)	Employee name (26-45)	Employee number (46-48)
29900.50	2003.33	15.00	10.00	Eric Anderson	110
40652.00	2659.90	14.50	40.00	Manuel Fernandez	160
40652.00	2659.90	24.50	40.00	Kim Fong	170
39575.00	2651.53	22.50	50.00	Lena Jackson	200
39699.95	2659.90	26.15	40.00	Bruce McLeod	230
05815.00	0389.61	31.01		Sandy Puccinelli	270
39600.00	2653.20	31.00	38.00	Alice Romero	300
01000.00	0067.00	20.00	40.00	Nancy Smith	320
29700.00	1989.90	18.50	51.00	George Takemoto	330
38700.00	2592.90	27.50	45.00	Kenneth Williamstead	450

Note that the hours field is blank on one record; this intentionally simulates a "missing data field" error.

Use a DO statement for loop control. Do not compute overtime in this program.

Assume the social security deduction rate is 6.7 percent for the first $39,700 of earnings during the year. Thus, some employees may have no social security deduction for the week, some may have a deduction on only a portion of their current weekly earnings, and others on all of their weekly earnings.

Output is to be single-spaced on a printer with one line for each employee with fields in the following sequence from left to right:

Field name
Employee name
Current gross pay
Current social security deduction
Current net pay
New year-to-date gross pay
New year-to-date social security deduction

7/IF-THEN-ELSE and DO Loop Structures

Allow reasonable spacing between output fields. "Dress up" the output with descriptive headings.

11. Write the program described in Problem 5 in this chapter, but expand it to include the following minor modification. Management has decided that all employees who have worked for the company more than 20 years are to receive a taxable $25 bonus each pay period. Assume that employee number 160 is the only person currently eligible for this bonus. Further assume that the exact location of this particular input record is unknown, so all input records must be tested for employee number 160; when the record is detected, the appropriate pay adjustment should be made.

12. Write the program described in Problem 5 in this chapter, but expand it to include four or more defensive programming tests to assure that input and output are reasonable. Assume that (1) the pay rate should not be less than $15 or more than $31; (2) the hours should be more than zero but should not exceed 50; (3) the old year-to-date earnings should not exceed $56,000 and (4) gross pay should not exceed $1,200. More tests may be included, if desired, and more input records may be included to assure that all tests are properly working. For each test that the input or output does not pass, print a brief descriptive error message, and avoid normal processing of that record.

13. Write a program to compute and print the speed chart illustrated below. It indicates the time required to travel one mile for all speeds evenly divisible by 10 from 10 m.p.h. through 250 m.p.h. No input data cards may be used—this must be a "self-operational program." A DO loop is required.

Speed	Time to travel one mile
10	6 MINS 0.0 SECS
20	3 MINS 0.0 SECS
30	2 MINS 0.0 SECS
40	1 MINS 30.0 SECS
50	1 MINS 12.0 SECS
60	1 MINS 0.0 SECS
70	0 MINS 51.4 SECS
80	0 MINS 45.0 SECS
90	0 MINS 40.0 SECS
	etc. through:
250	0 MINS 14.4 SECS

14. Write a program to calculate and print an installment note payment schedule. The program should read one input card with the following data in appropriate format:

Amount borrowed	$5,000
Annual interest rate	5%
Number of monthly payments	25

The following formula can be used to calculate equal monthly payments that include principal and interest:

$$(R*((1.+R)**T)/(((1.+R)**T)-1.))*A$$

where R is the interest rate per month, T is the time in months, and A is the amount borrowed.

Output should indicate the annual interest rate, the amount borrowed, and five columns with the following information:

> Month (1 through 25 in this case)
> Total payment (interest and principal) for month
> Interest payment for month
> Remaining balance due (after monthly payment)

"Dress up" output with descriptive headings. Design the program so that the final payment will be adjusted as necessary (because of rounding errors) to reach a final balance of zero.

8

One-dimensional arrays

Some programs must be designed to store large quantities of related data. Each data item must always be assigned a unique variable name because it is impossible to store two or more different data items in the same place at the same time. In previous chapters in this book, the programmer has been responsible for assigning all variable names. This chapter covers various methods of directing the compiler to assign a unique variable name to each item in a related group. The programmer is required to assign a variable name to the group, but the compiler will assign a different subscript to this name for each item with the group. The subscript, which makes the variable name unique, also identifies the position of the item within the group. Data stored in this manner are called an *array*. It is difficult to appreciate the real power of a computer until the use of arrays has been mastered. When a program includes an array, the variable name assigned to the group must be specified, and the compiler must always be given descriptive information regarding the array size and type.

DEFINITION OF ARRAYS

An array is a list, or table, of related data items stored internally in a reserved area. Each item in an array is called an *array element*. All elements in a given array must be in the same mode. A *one-dimensional array* is simply a list of either integer, floating point, or alphanumeric data values. To illustrate a one-dimensional array, assume that a list of integers consists of the following values in the order indicated:

7, 6, 4, 3, and 2

The programmer might assign the variable name LIST for convenience in referring to this integer array. The mode of the variable name assigned to the array must agree with the mode of the data values; if the above array consisted of floating point instead of integer values, a floating point variable name would be required.

Use of subscripts to reference array elements

A customary way of referring to individual items within a list is by *subscript*. "LIST sub one" refers to the first item in a list, "List sub two" refers to the second item, etc. Thus, in ordinary mathematical notation, the elements in the preceding integer array called LIST would be:

$$LIST_1 \text{ is } 7$$
$$LIST_2 \text{ is } 6$$
$$LIST_3 \text{ is } 4$$
$$LIST_4 \text{ is } 3$$
$$LIST_5 \text{ is } 2$$

Previous chapters have indicated that FORTRAN does not permit the use of *superscripts* in the usual method, because input and output media have no provision for such indication. Instead of indicating "R raised to the power of two" as R^2, for example, the superscript is indicated by two preceding asterisks (R**2). Likewise, *subscripts* cannot be indicated in the usual method. In FORTRAN, subscripts are enclosed in parentheses that follow the variable name. To illustrate, the individual elements in the previous LIST array example, subscripted as required in FORTRAN, would be:

$$LIST(1) \text{ is } 7$$
$$LIST(2) \text{ is } 6$$
$$LIST(3) \text{ is } 4$$
$$LIST(4) \text{ is } 3$$
$$LIST(5) \text{ is } 2$$

Subscripts are not permitted on independent variable names that are not associated with an array. Subscripted variable names are required, however, if the source program contains an array and must be used to address symbolically an element within an array. The variable name for each array element is always the array variable name followed by a unique subscript. Rules for independent variable names, previously covered, also apply to array variable names. It should be noted that the length and composition of the subscript is not considered when composing the array variable name. In effect, it is something "extra" that is added to the end of a valid variable name.

A subscript may be any *integer* expression, i.e., a constant, a variable name, or any combination of constants and/or variable names separated by arithmetic operators.

Following are some examples of proper subscript form:

NAME(3)
AMOUNT(N)
UNITS(K+2)
ID(J−1)

More-complex subscript expressions may be used, but the above examples are the most commonly used forms.

8 / One-Dimensional Arrays

A subscript identifies the position of an element within an array that has a finite number of elements. Do not use an expression with a value that is less than one or a value that is greater than the number of elements in the array.

Use of a DIMENSION statement to define arrays

No array can appear in a source program unless it is described by a specification statement. A DIMENSION statement is one type of specification statement that can be used to direct the compiler to assign reserved sequential fields for storing an array. A DIMENSION statement specifies the array variable name, the type of data, and the number of elements in an array. One DIMENSION statement may be used to specify any number of arrays. A DIMENSION statement must always precede any other statement that references the array.

An array may be "overdimensioned," but it should not be "underdimensioned." If a DIMENSION statement specifies that any array contains 100 elements, the compiler will reserve storage accordingly; any number of elements up to a maximum of 100 can be stored in this array—but not more. When an array is "overdimensioned," it not only wastes storage but can also increase execution time. Whenever possible, an array should be dimensioned exactly; but if the size of an array is unknown, it must be scaled to allow for the maximum number of elements that may be produced by the program.

General form The general form of a DIMENSION statement used to describe a one-dimensional array is:

| 1 2 3 4 5 | 6 | 7 |
nnnnn   DIMENSION vn(ne)$_1$, vn(ne)$_2$, . . . vn(ne)$_m$

Legend:

nnnnn	Any unique one- to five-digit integer that specifies the statement *number*. It may be used at the programmer's option, but it is never required because this statement should not be referenced by another statement in the source program.
DIMENSION	A keyword specifying the type of statement.
vn	A *variable name* assigned to an array. It must be followed by (ne) and be consistent in mode to the type of data contained in the array.
(ne)	An unsigned integer, greater than zero, that specifies the *number of elements* in the array identified by the variable name immediately preceding. This information is used by the compiler to reserve storage area for the described array.
vn(ne)$_1$, . . . vn(ne)$_m$	A list of one or more array specifications that must be separated by commas.

Illustrative examples Suppose that a program contains three different one-dimensional arrays. The first two arrays have been assigned the variable names A and DIFF, which each contain a maximum of six elements; the third array, ITEMS, contain a maximum of 100 elements.

Any one of the following statements can be used to describe these arrays:

```
|12345|6|7
   820    DIMENSION A(6),DIFF(6),ITEMS(100)
          DIMENSION DIFF(6),A(6),ITEMS(100)
          DIMENSION ITEMS(100),A(6),DIFF(6)
```

As illustrated in the above statements, the array specifications may appear in any sequence or be in any mode. As previously indicated, a separate DIMENSION statement can be used for each array, but it is usually less convenient.

The form of an array specification raises several interesting questions that will be covered next.

How does the compiler know, when it encounters A(6) in a statement, for example, if it specifies an array containing a maximum of six elements or if it refers to the sixth element in an array called A? The compiler makes this decision based on the type of statement in which A(6) appears. A DIMENSION statement does not contain subscripted variable names; READ, WRITE, and assignment statements are not used to describe arrays.

If A(6) appears in a DIMENSION statement, how does the compiler know if it describes a numeric or an alphanumeric array? This decision is based on other statements in the source program. If the A array is initialized by an arithmetic statement, for example, it is obviously numeric; if initialized by a READ statement, the referenced format code specifies if the array is numeric or alphanumeric.

If A(6) describes a numeric field, what determines if the elements are in integer or floating point mode? The first letter of the variable name implies the mode. (It is possible to override this *implicit defition of mode* as described in Chapter 4 and briefly reviewed in the following section of this chapter.) The mode of an array name must always agree with the mode of the data contained in the array. If the array is initialized by a READ statement, the mode of the variable name must agree with the format code specification. If an array is initialized by an arithmetic statement, the programmer must be cautious in assigning an array name because the rules of hierarchy, previously discussed, determine the mode of evaluation of an arithmetic expression; if the expression contains only integer data, the evaluation will be in integer mode; but if a mixed-mode expression is used, the evaluation will be in floating point mode.

When data are in floating point mode, what determines if they are single-precision or double-precision? If an array established by a READ statement is referenced to a D format code field, the data are in double-precision exponential form; if an array is referenced to an E format code field, it is in single-precision exponential form unless an implicit specification statement is used to override the implicit definition of mode. An array established by a READ statement referenced to

8 / One-Dimensional Arrays

an F format code field is single-precision unless an implicit specification statement overrides the implied mode. If an array is established by an arithmetic statement, the rules of hierarchy apply; an arithmetic expression including one or more double-precision floating point constants or variable names will always be evaluated as double-precision. Even though an arithmetic expression is evaluated in single-precision mode, it may be stored in double-precision if the variable name to the left of the equal sign is specified as a double-precision variable name. Implicit specification of mode is covered in the next section.

Use of other specification statements to define arrays

Numeric data fields are implied to contain integer or floating point data according to the first letter of the assigned variable name as previously explained. This is a convention of FORTRAN called *implicit definition of mode*. The purpose of implicit specification statements is to allow the programmer the option to override implicit definition of mode. Three types of implicit specification statements are described and illustrated in the following sections.

Implicit specification statements should be located near the beginning of the program before any executable statements.

The INTEGER statement This specification statement overrides the implicit definition of mode and allows the programmer the option of starting an integer variable name with a letter other than *I* through *N*. It can be used with array variable names as well as with independent variable names.

The INTEGER statement can also be used to replace the DIMENSION statement. To illustrate, the following statement specifies a one-dimensional integer array with 100 elements:

```
|12345|6|7
         INTEGER APPLES(100)
```

The REAL statement This specification statement can be used to convert one or more independent and/or array integer variable names to single-precision floating point (*real*) mode. The REAL statement may also be used to dimension one or more arrays:

```
|12345|6|7
         REAL MONEY(100), NETPAY, PLUMS(100)
```

The DOUBLE PRECISION statement This specification statement can be used to convert one or more integer or real variable names (independent and/or array) to double precision floating point mode.

The DOUBLE PRECISION statement can also be used to replace the DIMENSION statement:

```
|12345|6|7
         DOUBLE PRECISION NAME(100)
```

The EQUIVALENCE statement Ordinarily, the compiler assigns each variable name a unique storage location, and this location is not used for anything else. The EQUIVALENCE statement tells the compiler to assign two or more specified variable names to the *same* location. It is a specification statement, which, when used, must follow any DIMENSION or explicit specification statement but must precede all executable statements. The general form is:

```
|12345|6|7
 nnnnn    EQUIVALENCE(vn_a1,vn_a2, . . . vn_am),(vn_b1,vn_b2, . . . vn_bm)
```

Legend:

nnnnn	Any unique one- to five-digit integer that specifies the statement *number*. It may be used at the programmer's option, but it is never required because this statement should not be referenced in the program.
EQUIVALENCE	A keyword specifying the type of statement.
$vn_{a1}, \ldots vn_{am}$	Two or more variable names, enclosed in parentheses and separated by commas, that will share the same internal storage location. The variable names may be subscripted.
$vn_{b1}, \ldots vn_{bm}$	Two or more *optional* variable names, enclosed in parentheses and separated by commas, that will share the same internal storage location. The variable names may be subscripted.

To illustrate, the following statement reserves only one storage location, and the independent variable names PEARS, DATES, PRUNES, and FIGS all refer to it:

```
|12345|6|7
         EQUIVALENCE (PEARS,DATES,PRUNES,FIGS)
```

The programmer must be particularly cautious that these independent variable names do not interfere with each other. They all share the same storage location, so they will always have the same current value. If the value of any one is changed, the values of all are changed.

To illustrate further, the following statement will cause PEARS and DATES to share one location and PRUNES and FIGS to share another:

```
|12345|6|7
         EQUIVALENCE (PEARS,DATES),(PRUNES,FIGS)
```

Some programs, particularly if they include arrays, are so long that they threaten to exceed the storage capacity of the computer. Since the EQUIVALENCE statement conserves storage space, it can be used to advantage in long programs that include relatively independent sections. If A is used in one section, for example, and B in another in such a way that they do not interefere with each other, one storage location can be saved by making both share the same location. Saving one storage location, of course, is not significant. But if A and B are *array* names, major savings are possible. Thus the statements:

8/One-Dimensional Arrays

|1|2|3|4|5|6|7
```
DIMENSION A(10000),B(10000)
EQUIVALENCE(A,B)
```

declare that arrays A and B both share the same 10,000 storage locations. Unfortunately, all computer systems do not use the same techniques for declaring *arrays* to be equivalent, so programmers are cautioned to check local requirements. A common programming error is to specify two variables to be equivalent when they are, in fact, different. It is improper to specify an array with 100 elements, for example, to be equivalent to one independent variable; likewise, integers should not be declared equivalent to floating point values.

A programmer might find the EQUIVALENCE statement particularly useful at debugging time if he has not been consistent in spelling one or more variable names. Suppose, for example, a variable name is indicated as PRINC in some statements and as PRIN in others. Rather than search through the program and change one of the variable names each time it appears, one EQUIVALENCE statement can be used to cause both to refer to the same thing. This statement can also be used to advantage when several programmers work on a program together and, by mistake, each uses a different variable name to refer to the same thing. However, it should be recognized that correcting bad code with "patches" may be an expedient way to get a program operational but it does not improve readability. It is usually better to rewrite bad code than to patch it.

Order of statements

As previously indicated, some specification statements must precede others. An acceptable order for the statements presented thus far in this book is as follows:

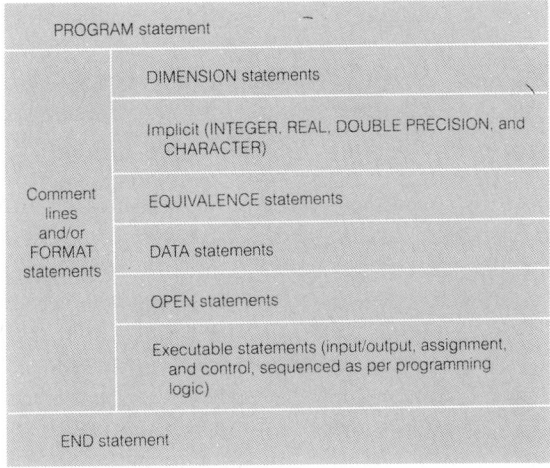

USE OF ARRAYS IN PROGRAMMING

A program may contain as many arrays as is required for the problem to be solved and is permitted by the capacity of the computer. To demonstrate the use and convenience of arrays in general, and one-dimensional arrays in particular, various alternative methods of solution of the following illustrative problem will be presented throughout a major portion of this chapter.

Illustrative problem

An input file consists of three data records, in identical format, each containing one unsigned positive floating point data field. All input data are to be totaled and divided by three to compute the average; the difference between the value contained in each input data field and the average of all input values is to be computed. Output is to consist of three records in identical format, each containing two floating point data fields; one data field is to contain the input value, the other the difference between the input value and the average of all input values. It should be noted that all input data values must be stored in different internal locations so that they will be available for computing the average, for computing the difference between each input value and the average, and also for output after all computations are finished.

The input records contain the following data:

	Record columns	*Actual data*
Record 1	1–4	1.15
Record 2	1–4	1.75
Record 3	1–4	1.60

One method of solving this problem would be to use only one variable name, such as DATA, in the READ statement. Each time a record is read in, however, the current value of DATA would change. The program would have to be designed to save each input value at three unique variable names such as SAVE1, SAVE2, and SAVE3, because each input value is required for further processing after the average of all input values has been computed. One way to do this would be to use three identical READ statements, each followed by an arithmetic statement. The first arithmetic statement could store the current value of DATA at SAVE1, the next at SAVE2, and the last at SAVE3. This would be an inconvenient method of solving the problem.

Another method of solution would be to prepare two identical sets of input records. The first set of three records would be read individually, the total accumulated, and the average computed. Next, each record in the second set of records would be read, the difference between the average and the input value would be computed, and then the input value and difference would be written. This also would be an inconvenient method of solving the problem.

The most convenient method would be to assign a unique variable name to each input value when the READ statement is executed. This unique variable name may be assigned by the programmer or by the compiler. Variations of each method will be discussed next.

8/One-Dimensional Arrays

As covered in preceding chapters, the following partial program could be used to read the input data:

|12345|6|7
  81   FORMAT(F4.2)
        READ(1,81)A1
        READ(1,81)A2
        READ(1,81)A3

This partial program would assign a unique unsubscripted variable name to each input value; these stored values would then be available for further processing.

When the READ list exceeds the number of available format codes, the FORMAT statement is automatically reused until the list is satisfied. Thus, the programmer could also use the following partial program to read the input data:

|12345|6|7
  82   FORMAT(F4.2)
        READ(1,82)A1,A2,A3

Fundamental array techniques

The illustrative problem requires only three input cards—but what if it contained 500? Using either of the preceding two techniques, the programmer would be required to prepare either 500 READ statements or one READ statement with 500 unique variable names. In this case, it would be more convenient to use an array, as illustrated next.

Array input through DO and READ statements If the programmer uses a DO statement to read in an array, the partial program might appear as follows:

|12345|6|7
  83   FORMAT(F4.2)
        DO 8 LOOP=1,3
           READ(1,83)A(LOOP)
   8   CONTINUE

The DO index (LOOP) will have a current value of one on the first pass through the DO range, two on the second, and three on the third. The above partial program will thus cause the computer to assign automatically the subscripted variable names A(1) to the value from the first card, A(2) to the second, and A(3) to the third.

It should be noted that the preceding partial program will direct the computer to read 500 values into the array if the DO statement test value is simply changed from 3 to 500. Consider the difficulty of writing a program to stored 500 different data items if an array, combined with the powerful DO statement, was not used. Instead of a relatively short program, a long, repetitious one would be required. This should indicate clearly one convenience of an array.

Addressing elements in an array Each element, or data value, within an array must have a unique subscripted variable name; if a variable name is not associated with an array, it cannot be subscripted. If an element in any array is required in a source program statement, it must be called for, or addressed, by its unique subscripted variable name. Execution of the first of the following two arithmetic statements, for example, will double the current value of the third element in an array called "X" and store the product at the symbolic address DOUBLE; execution of the second statement will double the first element and store the product at the second element in the same array.

|12345|6|7
```
      DOUBLE=X(3)*2.
      X(2)=X(1)*2.
```

Of course, following execution of the two preceding statements, the current values of X(3) and X(1) will remain unchanged, but the current value of the second element in the X array will be double the current value of the first element.

Going back to the illustrative problem, if the input data had been read in as an array, as indicated, they would be stored as follows:

Subscripted variable name	Stored data
A(1)	1.15
A(2)	1.75
A(3)	1.60

The next step in the solution to the problem is to compute the total and average of the three values stored in the array. There are several ways this can be done. The average, for example, can be computed by one statement:

|12345|6|7
```
      AVE=(A(1)+A(2)+A(3))/3.00
```

It can also be computed by two statements:

|12345|6|7
```
      SUM=A(1)+A(2)+A(3)
      AVE=SUM/3.00
```

It can also be computed by four statements:

|12345|6|7
```
      SUM=0.00
      DO 7 N=1,3
    7 SUM=SUM+A(N)
      AVE=SUM/3.00
```

The first of the three preceding illustrations would be the most convenient for computing the total and average because the illustrative problem has only three elements in the array. If the array had 500 elements instead of only three, however, the first two methods would require the programmer to list 500 subscripted variable names separated by plus signs. The last of the three preceding illustrations obviously would be the most convenient in this case because only the test value of the DO statement would have to be changed from three to 500. It should be pointed out that if the data had not been read in as an array, the programmer could not use the third method illustrated; the compiler can make a variable name unique only by assignment of different subscripts, and only elements in an array may have subscripted variable names. This should illustrate another convenience of an array.

Initializing arrays thorugh DO and assignment statements As previously covered in this chapter, a DO and a READ statement can be used to set up initial values in an array at input time. Arrays can also be initialized via a DO statement and an arithmetic assignment statement.

Suppose it is decided to initialize another one-dimensional array in the illustrative problem. The following statements will initialize an array named DIFF, with each element containing the difference between the average and each element of the A array:

```
|12345|6|7
      DO 5 L=1,3
    5    DIFF(L)=A(L)-AVE
         .
         .
         .
     process
```

The three values in the A array are 1.15, 1.75, and 1.60, so 1.50 is the average. The DIFF array would thus be as follows:

Subscripted variable name	Stored data
DIFF(1)	−0.35
DIFF(2)	0.25
DIFF(3)	0.10

A DO can be used in combination with either an alphanumeric assignment statement or with an arithmetic assignment statement.

It may be necessary, for example, to initialize all elements in an alphanumeric array to blanks, and all elements in an integer array to zero. Assuming the appropriate declarations have been made (e.g., CHARACTER and DIMENSION statements), the following routine will do the job for the two arrays, each containing N elements:

```
|12345|6|7
      DO 6 K=1,N
         ALFANU(K)=' '
         NUMBER(K)=0
    6 CONTINUE
```

Initializing arrays through DATA statements The DATA statement is particularly convenient for initializing all elements in an array:

```
|12345|6|7
       DIMENSION A(500),I(100)
       DATA A/500*0.0/,I/100*1/
```

The 55 official United States Postal Service abbreviations can be included in a program with these statements:

```
|12345|6|7
       DIMENSION STATE(55)
       DATA STATE/'AL','AK','AZ','AR','CA', . . . 'WY'/
```

Array output through DO and WRITE statements If the DIFF array, previously discussed, is *not* used, the following partial program can be used to write the output for the illustrative problem:

```
|12345|6|7
  800  FORMAT(F4.2,2X,F5.2)
       DO 9 K=1,3
           DIFF=A(K)—AVE
           WRITE(2,810)A(K),DIFF
    9  CONTINUE
```

If the DIFF array *is* used, the following partial program can be used to write the output:

```
|12345|6|7
  811  FORMAT(F4.2,2X,F5.2)
       DO 9 K=1,3
           WRITE(2,811)A(K),DIFF(K)
    9  CONTINUE
```

Illustrative array routines

The number of routines and combinations of routines that can be used to create and manipulate array elements is almost infinite. This section illustrates and briefly describes some selected array routines. Each can be used as illustrated or modified and/or combined with other routines to solve many types of programming problems.

These routines are designed to demonstrate various techniques and to show the treatment of array elements as clearly as possible rather than to illustrate the optimum solution to the problem. Many of the illustrations are self-explanatory; complex routines are discussed in more detail. It is assumed that all arrays are properly dimensioned.

In all cases, the variable N is used to indicate the number of array elements.

Creating duplicate arrays Some programs must include two or more duplicate arrays. The original array may have to be retained for output, but various manipulations of the elements in the duplicate array(s) may be required. The following statements cause two duplicates of an existing array to be created:

8 / One-Dimensional Arrays

```
|12345|6|7
     DO 7 I=1,N
         COPY1(I)=ARRAY(I)
         COPY2(I)=ARRAY(I)
   7 CONTINUE
```

Duplicating an array in inverse order Sometimes it is necessary to reverse the order of elements in an array. An array in ascending sequence, for example, may have to be changed to descending sequence. The following statements will not change the original array but will create a new array in reversed sequence (N is the number of elements in the array):

```
|12345|6|7
     K=N
     DO 7 I=1,N
         CHANGE(I)=ARRAY(K)
         K=K-1
   7 CONTINUE
```

Creating an array by merging existing arrays Some problems require creation of an array that contains all or selected elements from two or more existing arrays. The illustrated routine will result in creation of a new array called MERGE. It will contain elements of the two existing arrays combined or "merged" in the following sequence:

New array	
MERGE(1)	J(1)
MERGE(2)	K(1)
MERGE(3)	J(2)
MERGE(4)	K(2)
MERGE(5)	J(3)
Etc.	Etc.

Note that an increment value of two is used in the DO statement in this routine:

```
|12345|6|7
     L=1
     DO 7 I=1,N,2
         MERGE(I)=J(L)
         MERGE(I+1)=K(L)
         L=L+1
   7 CONTINUE
```

In the above case, the value of N must be equal to the number of elements in the MERGE array.

Selecting the largest value from any array The following statements select the largest value from an array with N elements and store the value at BIGNUM:

```
|12345|6|7
      BIGNUM=ARRAY(1)
      DO 7 I=2,N
         IF(ARRAY(I).GT.BIGNUM)BIGNUM=ARRAY(I)
    7 CONTINUE
```

Note that the index is initialized at two to avoid comparing the value of the first element to itself. This routine initializes BIGNUM to the current value of the first element in the array. All other elements in the array are compared with the current value of BIGNUM; the current value of BIGNUM is replaced by the current value of any array element that contains a higher current value. This routine does not change the current value of any array element.

Counting how many times a specific value appears in an array The following statements will count the number of times the value 88 appears in an integer array, called NARRAY, with N elements:

```
|12345|6|7
      LOOK4=88
      KOUNT=0
    1 DO 3 I=1,N
         IF(NARRAY(I).EQ.LOOK4)KOUNT=KOUNT+1
    3 CONTINUE
```

The variable name KOUNT is incremented by one each time the current value 88 is encountered in the array.

Searching an array for a specific value This illustrative routine demonstrates an exit from the DO range before iteration is complete if the current value 88 is found in any array element. The DO index is used to indicate, at the variable name LOCATN, the specific element in the array where the first 88 was encountered:

```
|12345|6|7
      LOOK4=88
      DO 2 I=1,N
         IF(NARRAY(I).EQ.LOOK4) THEN
            LOCATN=I
            GO TO 4
         END IF
    2 CONTINUE
    4 ...
```

Searching two arrays for matching values Some problems require that two arrays be searched for the first set of matching current values. The following statements solve this problem. LOCAT1 and LOCAT2 indicate the specific location in each array where the first set of matching values is encountered, and KURVAL indicates the current value of the first match:

8 / One-Dimensional Arrays

```
|12345|6|7
         DO 2 I=1,N
            DO 1 K=1,N
               IF(NARRAY(I).NE.KARRAY(K))GO TO 1
                 LOCAT1=I
                 LOCAT2=K
                 KURVAL=NARRAY(I)
                 GO TO 4
      1     CONTINUE
      2  CONTINUE
      3  FORMAT('NO MATCH FOUND')
         WRITE(3,3)
      4  ...
```

Note that this routine, as designed, requires a CONTINUE statement as the last statement in *both* DO ranges. On each pass through the outer loop, the inner loop will cycle N times or until a match is found. The DO loop is designed to exit from the side, but provision is made for a message to be written if it exits from the bottom.

Sorting values of array elements into algebraic order Arranging data values in an ordered sequence is a process called *sorting*. A routine to sort array element values into algebraic sequence is more complex and not as self-explanatory as the other routines presented in this chapter.

To begin with an elementary example, assume that a *two-element array* is to be sorted into *ascending* numeric sequence. The following routine compares the values at the two storage locations and interchanges the contents if these values are *not* in ascending sequence:

```
|12345|6|7
         IF(ARRAY(1).GT.ARRAY(2)) THEN
            SAVE=ARRAY(1)            ⎫
            ARRAY(1)=ARRAY(2)        ⎬  "switch routine"
            ARRAY(2)=SAVE            ⎭
         END IF
```

Note that the IF statement compares the value of the two elements. If the value of the first is less than or equal to the second, the statements that interchange the contents of the two locations are ignored. If the value of the first element is greater than the second, however, the statements that cause the interchange are executed. Note also that this interchange process requires a third storage location (SAVE), as is shown in Figure 8-1.

Now, assume that a *four-element array* is to be sorted into *ascending* sequence. The following routine will compare the value of the first element to each of the other three in turn. The elements will be interchanged whenever the value of the first is greater than the value of the other element in a given comparison. After completion of the routine, the largest value will be located in the last (fourth) position in the array.

Figure 8-1
Interchanging the location of two values

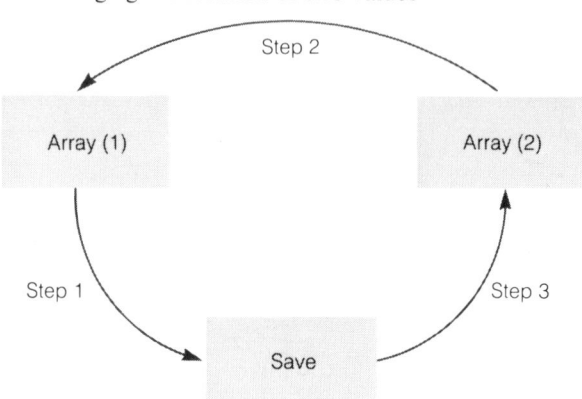

```
|12345|6|7
      N=4
      NESTED=N-1
      DO 10 I=1,NESTED
         IF(ARRAY(I).GT.ARRAY(I+1)) THEN
            SAVE=ARRAY(I)           ⎫
            ARRAY(I)=ARRAY(I+1)     ⎬   "switch routine"
            ARRAY(I+1)=SAVE         ⎭
         END IF
   10 CONTINUE
```

Note that the DO statement will cause *three* passes through the loop. The effect of the preceding routine is illustrated with assumed values in Figure 8-2.

It should be particularly noted that the preceding routine is designed to sort only one array element; that is, the highest value is transferred to the last (fourth) position, but the sequence of the other array elements, as to each other, is not changed. To sort the next highest value it is necessary to repeat the same routine, except that one less pass is required because the last element is already sorted; therefore, it is unnecessary to compare its value to that of any other element. To decrease the number of passes through the routine, it is necessary to change the test value (NESTED) of the DO statement. Assuming that the test value is changed from 3 to 2, the effect of repeating the routine is shown in Figure 8-3.

Note that after the second execution of the sorting routine, the values of only two elements are properly ordered. The routine must be repeated again to order properly the remaining two elements; but, again, one less pass is required. Assuming that the test value (NESTED) of the DO statement is changed to one, the effect of executing the routine a third time is illustrated in Figure 8-4.

Figure 8-2
Appearance of a specific array during various stages of the sorting process

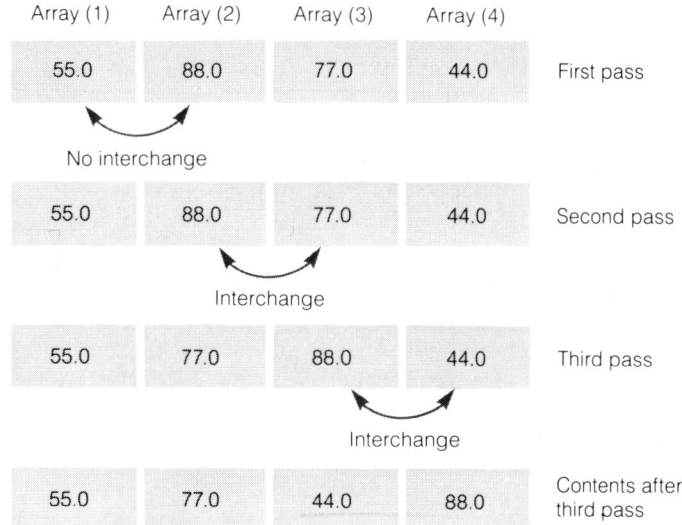

Figure 8-3
Appearance of a specific array during various stages of the sorting process

Figure 8-4
Appearance of a specific array during various stages of the sorting process

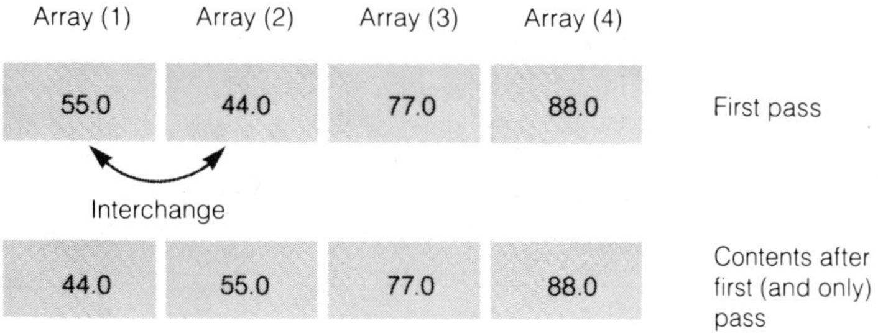

Following the third execution of the sort routine, all four array elements are properly ordered. Obviously, to sort a five-element array, the routine must be executed four times; and likewise, to sort a 100-element array, it must be executed 99 times. But note again that each time the routine is repeated, the test value (NESTED) of the DO statement can be decreased because there is one less value to sort on each succeeding pass through the loop.

As pointed out in Chapter 7, the rules of FORTRAN do not permit the test value of a DO statement to be changed *within* the DO range. Thus, it is required that it be changed after a normal exit from the DO range and that the loop then be reentered at the DO statement. One method of doing this is to nest the sorting routine within an outer DO loop that is designed to control the index value of the nested DO. This method is illustrated in the following routine, which will sort an array containing N elements into *ascending* algebraic sequence:

```
|12345|6|7
      N=4
      *** SORT ROUTINE ***
      L=N-1
      NESTED=N
      DO 11 M=1,L
         NESTED=NESTED-1
         DO 10 I=1,NESTED
            IF(ARRAY(I).GT.ARRAY(I+1)) THEN
               SAVE=ARRAY(I)           ⎫
               ARRAY(I)=ARRAY(I+1)     ⎬  "switch routine"
               ARRAY(I+1)=SAVE         ⎭
            END IF
 10      CONTINUE
 11   CONTINUE
```

The routine illustrated above uses an outer DO to control execution of a nested DO that does the actual sorting. It demonstrates how an outer DO can be used to initialize and change the test value of a nested DO; each time control passes to the nested DO, it has a different test value. To illustrate the effect of this routine, assume the same array values as previously shown in Figure 8-2. After all values are compared and the first normal exit is made from the nested DO, the second (largest) value is located at ARRAY(4); but all other values are moved up to the first three array positions and remain in the same sequence in relation to each other. Control then returns to the outer DO, which subtracts one from the test value of the nested DO. The nested DO is then executed a second time, but because the test value is changed, it compares only the first three unsorted values. This time it moves the next highest value to ARRAY(3). Control then returns to the outer DO and back again to the nested DO, which reverses the locations of the remaining two values during its final execution.

Each routine illustrated in this section was designed to sort an array into ascending sequence. (If the array contains some identical values, technically the ordered array will not be in ascending sequence but will be "nondescending.") What would be the effect of changing the logical IF operator from ".GT." to ".LT."? With this minor modification, the previously illustrated routines will sort an array into descending (or "nonascending") sequence.

The preceding discussion was restricted to sorting one array only, but the programmer is often required to sort two or more related arrays based on the sequence of one of the arrays. Suppose, for example, an input data file consists of four records, one for each type of inventory stocked by a company. The records include the following information in the fields indicated:

Record number	Identification number	Number of units	Price per unit
1	257	100	2.00
2	864	400	3.00
3	396	300	1.00
4	432	200	4.00

Assume further that the information included in the identification number, number of units, and price per unit fields has been read into three arrays named ID, NUNITS, and PRICE respectively. The problem requires that all three arrays be sorted in ascending sequence based on the PRICE array so that the following output can be printed:

Line number	Identification number	Number of units	Price per unit
1	396	300	1.00
2	257	100	2.00
3	864	400	3.00
4	432	200	4.00

To solve this problem, the "switch routine" illustrated previously can be expanded so that each time elements in the PRICE array are interchanged the corresponding elements in the ID and NUNITS array are also interchanged. This "tagalong" method is illustrated below:

```
|12345|6|7
      IF(PRICE(I).GT.PRICE(I+1)) THEN
C
         SAVEP=PRICE(I)       ⎫
         IDSAVE=ID(I)         ⎪
         NUSAVE=NUNITS(I)     ⎪
C                             ⎪
         PRICE(I)=PRICE(I+1)  ⎪
         ID(I)=ID(I+1)        ⎬  "switch routine"
         NUNITS(I)=NUNITS(I+1)⎪
C                             ⎪
         PRICE(I+1)=SAVEP     ⎪
         ID(I+1)=IDSAVE       ⎪
         NUNITS(I+1)=NUSAVE   ⎭
      END IF
```

Other array input/output techniques

Previous sections covered basic input, manipulation, and output of arrays. This section includes descriptions and examples of alternative and sometimes more convenient techniques.

Array input through a READ statement with an "implied DO" FORTRAN provides an even more efficient method of reading data into an array than illustrated in previous sections. Whenever possible, the programmer should use a READ statement with an "implied DO" to read an array instead of using a DO statement and a READ statement. This method reduces execution time as well as programming time. An "implied DO" can be used *only* with READ and WRITE statements. (An "implied DO" in a WRITE statement is illustrated later in this chapter.)

When an "implied DO" is used, it appears in the READ list and includes all information of a regular DO statement except the first two elements: "DO sn." The keyword DO is omitted to distinguish it from a regular DO statement; a statement number is not referenced because, unlike a regular DO, which can be used to control a series of statements, an "implied DO" controls only the number of variables in the READ statement in which it appears. For this reason, this type of READ statement is sometimes called *self-indexing*.

To distinguish it from variable names, which normally appear in a READ list, an "implied DO" specification must be enclosed in parentheses. Within the parentheses are one or more subscripted variable names separated by commas and followed by the "implied DO," which must be preceded by a comma. If the increment value is omitted, one is assumed as in a regular DO statement.

The following partial program uses a READ statement with an "implied DO" to read in the entire array in the illustrative problem:

|12345|6|7
```
      84  FORMAT(F4.2)
          READ(1,84)(A(LOOP),LOOP=1,3)
           .
           .
           .
           process
```

An implied DO is a shortcut method for listing a string of variable names in one READ. The above statements have the same effect as the following:

|12345|6|7
```
      84  FORMAT(F4.2)
          READ(1,84)A(1),A(2),A(3)
```

Interrelationship of DIMENSION, READ, and FORMAT Now, array input will be reviewed by using a series of partial programs that demonstrate a variety of techniques. In the following illustration, the array is overdimensioned, the FORMAT indicates one available field (I5) per record, and the DO loop causes the READ statement to be executed 10 times. Ten records will be read, one variable per record.

|12345|6|7
```
          DIMENSION N(100)
       8  FORMAT(I5)
          DO 5 I=1,10
          READ(1,8)N(I)
       5  CONTINUE
```

In the next illustration, the FORMAT indicates 10 available fields (10I3), but each time the READ statement is executed, 1 field only will be read because the READ includes only one variable name. Thus, 10 records will be read, one variable per record.

|12345|6|7
```
          DIMENSION N(100)
       8  FORMAT(10I5)
          DO 5 I=1,10
          READ(1,8)N(I)
       5  CONTINUE
```

In the following illustration, the DO loop is incremented by two, so the READ statement will be executed five times. Five records will be read, two variables per record:

|12345|6|7
```
          DIMENSION N(100)
       8  FORMAT(10I5)
          DO 5 I=1,10,2
          READ(1,8)N(I),N(I+1)
       5  CONTINUE
```

The next partial program will read 10 records, one variable per record:

```
|12345|6|7
      DIMENSION N(100)
  8   FORMAT(I5)
      DO 5 I=1,10,2
         READ(1,8)N(I),N(I=1)
  5   CONTINUE
```

The following example has an implied DO. The READ statement will be executed once only but includes 10 variable names [N(1) through N(10)]. Ten records, one variable per record will be read:

```
|12345|6|7
      DIMENSION N(100)
  8   FORMAT(I5)
      READ(1,8)(N(I),I=1,10)
```

If the preceding FORMAT had indicated 10I5 fields, the ten variables would have been read from one record.

The next example includes a nested DO—an implied DO within a regular DO. The input list includes 10 variables, and the READ will be executed 10 times. One hundred variables will be read, 10 per record, from 10 cards but the first 90 data elements will be lost; extreme caution must be exercised when working with arrays.

```
|12345|6|7
      DIMENSION N(100)
  8   FORMAT(10I5)
      DO 5 I=1,10
         READ(1,8)(N(J),J=1,10)
  5   CONTINUE
```

If the preceding FORMAT statement had indicated 1 available field (instead of 10), 100 records would have been read.

The next example includes a *multiple implied* DO loop. The READ statement, which includes 20 variable names [N(1) through N(10) followed by M(1) through M(10)], will be executed once only. Twenty records, one variable per record, will be read:

```
|12345|6|7
      DIMENSION N(100),M(100)
  8   FORMAT(I5)
      READ(1,8)(NJ(J),J=1,10),(M(K),K=1,10)
```

If the preceding FORMAT statement had indicated 10I5 fields, the 20 variables would have been read from two records.

In the following example, the input list includes 1 independent variable followed by 10 subscripted variables. The 11 variables will be read from one record:

8/One-Dimensional Arrays

```
|12345|6|7
      DIMENSION N(100)
   8  FORMAT(F5.2,10I5)
      READ(1,8) A,(N(K),K=1,10)
```

The input list, in the following example, includes 1 independent variable followed by 20 subscripted variables. The FORMAT must be reused to satisfy the list because it includes only 11 available fields. When the computer returns to reuse the FORMAT, it will return only to the point at which it encounters the open parenthesis that precedes the 10I5 notation, because the last 10 fields are indicated parenthetically. In effect, it sort of locks in to the set of inner parentheses. (When the FORMAT includes more than one set of inner parentheses, it locks in to the *last* set.) Two records will be read—1 independent variable and 10 subscripted variables from the first record, and 10 subscripted variables from the second record:

```
|12345|6|7
      DIMENSION N(100)
   8  FORMAT(I3,(10I5))
      READ(1,8)K,(N(J),J=1,20)
```

The next partial program, which includes a slash in the FORMAT statement, will read three records—1 independent variable from the first record and 10 subscripted variables from each of the following two records:

```
|12345|6|7
      DIMENSION N(100)
   8  FORMAT(I3/(10I5))
      READ(1,8)K,(N(J),J=1,20)
```

Array output through a WRITE statement with an "implied DO" An "implied DO" can be used in a WRITE statement in the same manner as in a READ statement. If the DIFF array is used, the following partial program can be used to write the output for the illustrative problem:

```
|12345|6|7
   812 FORMAT(F4.2,2X,F5.2)
       WRITE(2,812)(A(K),DIFF(K),K=1,3)
```

A WRITE statement with an "implied DO" should always be used whenever possible because it reduces execution time as well as programming time. It should be noted again that an "implied DO" simply specifies the number of variables in the associated I/O statement. Unlike a regular DO statement, an implied DO cannot control a series of statements.

A "self-indexing" WRITE statement may include both independent and array variable names. For example, assume that the output for the illustrative problem was to include, in order, the following fields: Average, Card Number, Input Value, and Difference. The following partial program could be used to write the output:

```
|12345|6|7
   813   FORMAT(F4.2,I1,F4.2,F5.2)
         WRITE(2,813)AVE,(K,A(K),DIFF(K),K=1,3)
```

Note how the "implied DO" is enclosed in parentheses to distinguish it from the independent variable name AVE appearing in the WRITE list. Also note that K (card number) must be within the parentheses containing the "implied DO", or it will be undefined.

Reading and writing arrays without using subscripts Before concluding the discussion of one-dimensional arrays, one more programming shortcut will be covered. It should be noted that this technique cannot be used when it is necessary to READ or WRITE only selected elements in an array; it can be used only to READ or WRITE an entire array.

When an array is used in program, the general rule is that the variable name of the array cannot appear in any statement unless it is subscripted. There is one exception to this rule: an unsubscripted array name may be used in I/O statements; that is, READ and WRITE statements. This method is preferred but can be used only if an entire array is to be read or written and if a specification statement indicates the exact number of elements in the array. (Specification statements were covered earlier in this chapter; the illustrations in this section, as in previous sections, assume that all arrays are properly described in the program.)

Reading arrays without subscripts The following statement will read in the entire A array in the illustrative problem that had one three-element array:

```
|12345|6|7
   814   FORMAT(F4.2)
         READ(1,814)A
```

The above statements will produce the same results as the DO and READ or the "self-indexing" READ, previously illustrated. The computer will assign automatically the unique subscripted variable name A(1) to the first element read in, A(2) to the second, and A(3) to the third.

In the illustrative problem, each array element was entered in a separate input record. If all three elements had been punched in the first 12 columns of one record, the following statements could be used to read in the array:

```
|12345|6|7
   815   FORMAT(3F4.2)
         READ(1,815)A
```

A(1) would be read from the first four columns, followed by A(2) and A(3).

There is an advantage to have more than one array element in a record. A card reader, for example, is an extremely slow mechanical device compared to the electronic speed of a computer. Thus, if a large array is to be read from a card reader, it requires less input time, and is therefore more efficient, if each card contains as many array elements as possible. If a 4,000-element integer array, for example, is punched one element per card in I2 format code, 4,000 cards will have to be read from the card reader; but only 100 cards can contain the entire array if each card contains 40 elements in 40I2 format code.

A READ statement may include any combination of unsubscripted array variable names, subscripted array variable names, and independent (nonarray) variable names; but the programmer must be extremely cautious when using such combinations. A thorough knowledge of the operation of the READ statement is required, and the input data file must be properly formatted and sequenced to obtain the desired results.

The FORMAT statement specifies the type, location, and length of data fields in an input record. The order of the variable names in a READ list (from left to right), however, specifies the order in which data will be read into internal storage. When an unsubscripted array variable name is encountered in the list, the entire array is always read before continuing on to the next variable name. To illustrate the effect of a combination of different types of variable names in a READ list, consider the following statement:

|12345|6|7
  816   READ(1,8)A,B,C(1),D

Assume that A is an independent variable name, B and D are unsubscripted array variable names, and C(1) is the first element of the C array. The above statement will store in order: A, the entire B array, C(1), and finally the entire D array.

Writing arrays without subscripts The following statements will write out the A array only in the illustrative problem:

|12345|6|7
  817   FORMAT(1X,F4.2)
         WRITE(2,817)A

The above statements will cause A(1) to be recorded in the first output record, A(2) in the second, and the final element in the array, A(3), in the third. If the format code is changed to 3F4.2, the A array will be recorded in the first 12 columns of one record in the following sequence: A(1), A(2), and A(3).

The current values of the variable names in a WRITE statement are always written in the sequence in which they appear in the list, from left to right. Whenever an unsubscripted array variable name is encountered in the list, the entire array is written, as indicated in the preceding illustration. To illustrate, the following statements would cause the entire A array to be written, followed by the entire DIFF array:

```
           |12345|6|7
      818  FORMAT(1X,F4.2,2X,F5.2)
           WRITE(2,818)A,DIFF
```

The current values of the elements in the two arrays are:

Array element	Current value
A(1)	1.15
A(2)	1.75
A(3)	1.60
DIFF(1)	−0.35
DIFF(2)	0.25
DIFF(3)	0.10

Thus, the preceding statements will result in the following output:

		123456789
Record 1	1.15 1.75
Record 2	1.60 −0.35
Record 3	0.25 0.10

The above output, of course, does not meet the requirements of the illustrative problem, and it demonstrates that the programmer cannot always take advantage of all shortcuts available in FORTRAN.

It would be possible to use this shortcut technique to solve the problem if another array, called AMERGE, for example, was created. The AMERGE array should contain the combined, or *merged*, elements of the A and DIFF arrays in the following sequence:

AMERGE elements	A and DIFF elements
(1)	A(1)
(2)	DIFF(1)
(3)	A(2)
(4)	DIFF(2)
(5)	A(3)
(6)	DIFF(3)

The required output could then be obtained by the following statements:

|12345|6|7
819 FORMAT(1X,F4.2,2X,F5.2)
     WRITE(2,819)AMERGE

Various routines for manipulating arrays, including a method of creating the AMERGE array, were covered earlier in this chapter.

Solution to illustrative problem The illustrative problem used throughout the preceding sections of this chapter has been discussed and illustrated step by step. Now a complete program providing a solution to the problem will be illustrated, but the program contains two minor changes. To provide a more complete illustration of output possibilities, six input cards are used instead of three; to provide printed instead of punched output, a printer is specified as the output device. The statement numbers used in the listed program correspond to those used in the text to provide a reference to the description of each program step. This program and the resulting printed output are illustrated in Figure 8-5.

DEBUGGING TECHNIQUES

Basic debugging techniques are covered in Appendix A. This section is restricted to a few observations and suggestions regarding the more advanced topics covered in this chapter.

Programs that include arrays, because they are more powerful and

Figure 8-5
Solution to illustrative problem

```
        PROGRAM CHAP8
        DIMENSION A(6),DIFF(6)
C
        OPEN(1,FILE='INPUT')
        OPEN(3,FILE='OUTPUT')
C
C   *** ILLUSTRATIVE PROBLEM, CHAPTER 8 ***
C
    814 FORMAT(F4.2)
        READ(1,814)A
C
     88 SUM=0.00
        DO 7 N=1,6
           SUM=SUM+A(N)
      7 CONTINUE
        AVE=SUM/6.00
C
        DO 5 L=1,6
           DIFF(L)=A(L)-AVE
      5 CONTINUE
C
    813 FORMAT(' INPUT CARD',I2,2X,F4.2,2X,F5.2)
        WRITE(3,813)(K,A(K),DIFF(K),K=1,6)
C
        STOP
        END
        INPUT CARD 1   1.15   -.35
        INPUT CARD 2   1.75    .25
        INPUT CARD 3   1.60    .10
        INPUT CARD 4   1.50   0.00
        INPUT CARD 5    .01  -1.49
        INPUT CARD 6   2.99   1.49
```

A program providing a printed solution to the illustration program used throughout the preceding sections of this chapter—with one minor change: six input records are used instead of three. Resulting output follows the program listing.

complex, will probably be infested with more programming bugs. Perhaps the most common errors are (1) omitting or improperly positioning DIMENSION statements, (2) including invalid subscript forms, and (3) exceeding the declared size of an array. The first two of these error types should be detected from diagnostic messages generated during the first compilation attempt. However, when array boundaries are exceeded the results are unpredictable; some compilers generate diagnostic messages at execution time, but others do not. Programmers should attempt to protect against array boundary violations by using defensive programming techniques. It should be remembered that a subscript value should never be less than one nor greater than the number of specified array elements; a good program will include appropriate tests to detect violations and, if they are found, will write descriptive error messages.

Debugging complex programs may be made easier by temporarily including extra statements that will help trace the flow of control and report the critical values in loops. The values of variables to be tested in control statements (such as IFs and DOs) should be printed immediately prior to execution of such statements. The values of subscripts and of other critical variables may be printed as deemed appropriate. These extra output values should then be compared to their expected values. In addition to printed variable values, short messages such as ENTERING READ LOOP may also be useful. A few such "flow tracer" statements can sometimes result in a significant decrease in debugging time and effort. Of course, these temporary extra statements should be removed after they have served their purpose.

Finally, it is suggested that any complex programming problem be solved with a divide-and-conquer approach. Big problems should be divided into small, manageable pieces. It is easier to write, read, and debug a program that is divided into a number of relatively short subsections (preferably as independent as possible). Programmers should avoid writing long strings of code with complex loops and with branches around branches. If a program is well structured with independent sections, a divide-and-conquer approach can also be used in debugging. It is often possible to skip over several sections and test a reduced portion of the program. An easy way to do this is to insert two statements: a GO TO that targets a CONTINUE. For example, the following two statements could be added to any program that does not already have any statements numbered 9999:

```
|12345|6|7
        GO TO 9999
        .
        .
        .
 9999   CONTINUE
```

This approach can be an efficient time-saver but must be used with caution. Other illustrations of the divide-and-conquer approach are included in a later chapter that covers subprograms.

REVIEW QUESTIONS

1. What is an array?

2. Why is it invalid to reference an array element by a zero subscript?

3. Describe the function of the DIMENSION statement.

4. An *integer constant* must be used to describe the array size in a DIMENSION statement. Why is it invalid to use variable names or floating point constants?

5. What are the advantages, if any, in having a choice of specification statements for defining an array?

6. Which of the following specification statements can be used to reserve space for an array?

   DATA   EQUIVALENCE
   DIMENSION   INTEGER
   DOUBLE PRECISION REAL

7. "Some of the specification statements (see Number 6 above) can be particularly helpful at debugging time." Discuss.

8. Describe the function of the EQUIVALENCE statement.

9. What is meant by implied mode of an array name? Can it be changed?

10. Which of the following statements is preferable for initializing KOUNT?

   READ . . . KOUNT
   KOUNT=0
   DATA KOUNT/0/

EXERCISES

1. Identify the errors, if any, in each of the following statements, or series of statements.

   a. DIMENTION T(50)
   b. EQUIVALENCE (K)
   c. DOUBLE PRECISION M(50),R,M(30)
   d. N=100
      DIMENSION W(N)
   e. DIMENSION J(100),L(10)
      INTEGER A,B,C,D,J(100)
      EQUIVALENCE (J,A),(B,C,D,I)
      DATA X10/10*0.0/

2. Code *two different* DATA statements, either of which will do the required job, for each instruction below.

    a. Assign the integer values one through four to the independent variables N, M, L, and K respectively.

    b. Assign the real values 1.00 through 4.00 to the independent variables W, X, Y, and Z respectively.

    c. Assign a zero to each of the independent variables F, G, H, and I.

    d. Assign a zero to each of the four elements in a real array identified by the variable name TABLE.

    e. Assign BLUE, GRAY, GOLD, and PINK to the four-element alphanumeric array identified as COLOR.

3. For each independent series of statements below, indicate (1) how many variables will be read and (2) how many records will be read.

a.
```
      DIMENSION X(100)
      DO 40 K=1,10
          READ(1,30)X(K)
   30 FORMAT(F4.2)
   40 CONTINUE
```

b.
```
      DIMENSION X(100)
      DO 40 K=1,10
          READ(1,30)X(K)
   30     FORMAT(2F4.2)
   40 CONTINUE
```

c.
```
      DIMENSION X (100)
      DO 40 K=1,10,2
          READ(1,30)X(K),X(K+1)
   30     FORMAT(2F4.2)
   40 CONTINUE
```

d.
```
      DIMENSION X(100)
      READ(1,30)(X(K),K=1,10)
   30 FORMAT(F4.2)
```

e.
```
      DIMENSION X(100)
      READ(1,30)(X(K),K=1,10)
   30 FORMAT(2F4.2)
```

f.
```
      DIMENSION X(100)
      READ(1,30)(X(K),X(K+1),K=1,10,2)
   30 FORMAT(2F4.2)
```

g.
```
      DIMENSION X(100)
      READ(1,30)X
   30 FORMAT(F4.2)
```

h.
```
      DIMENSION X(100)
      READ(1,30)X
   30 FORMAT(2F4.2)
```

8 / One-Dimensional Arrays

      i.   DIMENSION X(100)
            DO 40 J=1,10
               READ(1,30)(X(K),K=1,10,1)
   30   FORMAT(F4.2)
   40   CONTINUE

      j.   DIMENSION X(100),Y(100)
            DO 40 J=1,10
               READ(1,30)X(J),(Y(K),K=1,10,1)
   30   FORMAT(12F4.2)
   40   CONTINUE

PROBLEMS

1. A one-dimensional integer array called N and a one-dimensional integer array called M are to be read from input data records. Each array should contain 10 elements within the rage of −999 through +999. All elements of the N array should be entered in one data record, but each element in the M array should be entered in a separate record.

After reading the two arrays, square each element and store the results in two additional arrays called NSQ and MSQ.

Finally, write out the four arrays with appropriate descriptive information to identify the output.

2. Write a program that will print a four-column table indicating the following information about a group of 20 students: name, age, sex code, and marital status code. An asterisk is to precede the names of all single females who are 19 or 20 years of age.

Input consists of a deck of 20 records, 1 for each student, with the following fields in A8,I2,2I1 format: name, age, sex code (1= male, 2=female), and marital status code (1=single, 2=married, 3=divorced, 4=widowed). Design your own input deck using care to select values that will properly test your program. Select first names only so that they can be entered in the eight-position field. Use four arrays, one for each input field.

Output should include descriptive columnar headings.

3. Write a program that will generate a two-column table showing, in the first column, all metric values from 0 through 100 in increments of 5 (i.e., 0, 5, 10, 15, 20, etc.), and in the second column all corresponding inch values carried to two decimal places. One meter equals 39.37 inches. Set up the metric values in an integer array called METERS and the inch values in a floating point array called INCHES. Output should include appropriate descriptive columnar headings.

4. Write a program that will (1) read into an array as many as 999 input records, each with a person's age entered in the first three columns; (2) count the number of persons in each 10-year category and store this information in another array; and (3) write a bar graph indicating the age frequency distribution in the following general form:

Age frequency distribution

```
           0      5     10     15     20     25     30     35     40     45     50
           +....+....+....+....+....+....+....+....+....+....+....+
Age
    0   I X
   10   I XX
   20   I XXX
   30   I XXXX X
   40   I XXXX X XXX
   50   I XXXX X XXXX
   60   I XXXX X
   70   I XXX
   80   I XX
   90   I X
  100   I X
  110   I
```

Prepare an input file of about 40 or 50 data records with any values you desire, but be sure to omit age values in at least one category. Use appropriate control to indicate the number of data records to be read. Initialize another array with Xs and write out as many elements as required to indicate the frequency distribution.

5. Write a program to (1) calculate the average (arithmetic mean) monthly sales in uints for each salesperson; (2) sort the averages from smallest to largest; and (3) write one average per line on sequentially numbered lines. The program should be designed so it will solve the problem for a variable number (maximum 100) of salespersons and a variable number (maximum 12) of monthly sales values (maximum 999 units). A header record should be used to indicate the number of input records (one for each salesperson) and the number of sales data fields (one per month) to be read from each record. Assume each input record has the same number of sales data fields; thus, the average for each salesperson will be calculated based on the same number of months (indicated on the header record).

Label the output with brief descriptive headings such as LINE NUMBER and AVERAGE FOR XX MONTHS, where XX indicates the appropriate number indicated on the header record. Numeric averages should be in terms of the nearest whole unit (zero decimal positions).

Design appropriate input records that include all the data indicated below:

Employee		Units sold during month			
ID	Name	1	2	3	4
1	Tom	70	60	38	56
2	Dave	92	98	100	97
3	Sara	68	78	73	73
4	Mary	75	74	73	74
5	Lee	75	65	88	76
6	Sue	60	70	65	65
7	Jo	92	85	88	88
8	Ken	65	76	88	76
9	Jose	84	86	85	85
10	Kay	86	68	77	77

8 / One-Dimensional Arrays

Also design appropriate controls to process sales data for the *first three months* only.

For your convenience, the fourth-month values are the averages of the first three months so they may be used as check figures for your program output.

6. Write the program described in Problem 5 in this chapter, but modify it as indicated below.

   a. Add the necessary statements so the program will begin by reading alphanumeric data into an *array* from an 80-column input record and then write this data before writing any other descriptive output headings. In this case the alphanumeric data read and written should be: FIRST QUARTER SALES, 19XX, where XX is the current year.
   b. Add and/or modify appropriate statements as required so that the output includes two more columns, one for the ID numbers and one for the names. They must be printed in the same order as the corresponding sorted averages; that is, the ID number and name of the salesperson with the lowest average should be printed on the first line, the second lowest on the second line, etc. Include brief descriptive headings for the extra two output columns.
   c. This program requires 10 data records (following the 2 header records). Change the sequence of these 10 records to simulate random order. If the program is properly designed, this should not affect output.

7. Long programs are often written in sections, or *modules*. After the first module is debugged and tested, other modules are added to the basic program, debugged, and tested in turn until the entire program is completed. This modular method isolates errors and can reduce programming time. A program to determine grades for students enrolled in a computer programming class is used to demonstrate this method. The program requires:

   a. Computation of the average (arithmetic mean) numeric grade of each student.
   b. Computation of the average (arithmetic mean) numeric grade of the class.
   c. Computation of the adjusted numeric grade of each student.
   d. Assignment of letter grades based on the adjusted numeric grades of each student.
   e. Sorting the adjusted average grades into algebraic sequence.
   f. Reversing the order of the sorted array.
   g. Computation of the standard deviation.

The input file contains 20 records in the following sequence and format:

Student number (cols. 1-2)	Student name (cols. 5-12)	Test score (15-17)	Test number (20)
1	A. DOAKS	87	1
2	B. DOAKS	79	1
3	C. DOAKS	70	1
4	D. DOAKS	70	1
5	E. DOAKS	79	1
6	F. DOAKS	74	1
7	G. DOAKS	93	1
8	H. DOAKS	70	1
9	I. DOAKS	68	1
10	J. DOAKS	100	1
1	A. DOAKS	89	2
2	B. DOAKS	95	2
3	C. DOAKS	66	2
4	D. DOAKS	62	2
5	E. DOAKS	77	2
6	F. DOAKS	86	2
7	G. DOAKS	83	2
8	H. DOAKS	64	2
9	I. DOAKS	48	2
10	J. DOAKS	100	2

Examine the input data carefully. Note that 10 students are enrolled in the class and have been assigned identification numbers 1 through 10. Each student has two records in the input data file, one for each test taken during the term. The first 10 records in the input file are sorted by student number, 1 through 10 and contain the test scores for the first test. The last ten records in the input file are also sorted by student number, 1 through 10, and contain the test scores for the second test.

Output is to be printed and dressed up with descriptive headings. Following the headings, there should be one output line for each student, each line including the following fields in order from left to right:

> Student number
> Student name
> First test score
> Second test score
> Average test score
> Adjusted test score
> Letter grade

To simplify the programming logic, the student number may be ignored on input and the program designed to indicate automatically the student numbers from 1 through 10 in the output.

Output for the class average should be printed directly below the first, second, and average test score fields with the decimal points properly aligned.

Output is to include also the sorted adjusted averages, which may be printed in any location below the previous described output.

Write a program in a series of modules, as indicated below, to solve this problem. The requirements for all modules should be carefully examined to reduce the number of changes required as each succeeding module is added to the program. The first module sets up the basic framework for the program. Following modules are to be added, one at a time, to the existing program.

Module 1
    a. Write all headings.
    b. Compute and print the following output for each student:
        i. Student number.
        ii. First test score.
        iii. Second test score.
        iv. Average test score (arithmetic mean).

Module 2
Compute and print the following output:
    i. Class average for first test.
    ii. Class average for second test.
    iii. Class average for all tests.

Module 3
The instructor believes the average for all tests should be 80; if it is more, the tests were too easy; if less, the tests were too hard. Each student, therefore, is to have his or her actual test average adjusted accordingly. Add 5 points to each student's actual average, for example, to determine his or her adjusted average if the class average is 75; deduct 4 if it is 84; and make no adjustment if it is 80.

Compute and print the adjusted average for each student.

Module 4
Include the students' names in the output.

Module 5
Letter grades are assigned on the basis of the adjusted average of each student as follows:

Adjusted average	Letter grade
90 or more	A
70–89	C
Less than 70	F

Compute and write the letter grade for each student.

Module 6
Sort and write the adjusted average test scores in ascending algebraic order.

Module 7
Reverse the order of the elements in the sorted array (or create another array in inverse order) and write the results.

Module 8
Compute the standard deviation of the average student test scores (see Part B-4, Module 1) and write the result. Standard deviation may be computed by the formula:

$$\text{STDDEV} = \sqrt{\frac{\Sigma(X_i^2) - \left(\frac{(\Sigma X_i)^2}{N}\right)}{N}}$$

9

Two-Dimensional and Three-Dimensional Arrays

A two-dimensional array is simply a list of integer, floating point, or alphameric data elements arranged in rows and columns. It is also called a *matrix*. A three-dimensional array is two or more related two-dimensional arrays. Specific elements in these types of arrays are referenced by a unique subscript; the rules for selecting array variable names and subscripts are the same as those described in the preceding chapter. Because the form is different, however, these types of arrays must be described and subscripted accordingly. The specification statement must indicate multiple dimensions, and the variable name of each element must include multiple subscripts.

TWO-DIMENSIONAL ARRAYS

A two-dimensional array consists of horizontal lists of elements called *rows* and vertical lists called *columns*. Following is an illustration of this type of array:

	Column 1	Column 2	Column 3	Column 4	Column 5	Column 6
Row 1	4.00	3.75	2.25	3.00	2.00	3.00
Row 2	3.25	2.25	0.50	0.25	2.00	3.75
Row 3	2.00	2.00	2.00	2.00	1.50	2.50
Row 4	2.25	1.75	1.00	1.25	1.75	1.00
Row 5	3.50	3.25	2.25	2.00	3.25	3.75

Assume that the illustrated array corresponds to the physical arrangement of a parking lot. The lot has 30 parking spaces arranged in five rows and six columns as indicated. The floating point data, contained in the array elements, represent the receipts for each parking space for one day. These data can be stored as one or more one-dimensional arrays. They can be read, for example, as one array with 30 elements, as five arrays with six elements each, or as six arrays with five elements each. Suppose, however, that the problem requires computation of the average receipts for only the interior parking spaces in the lot. It is more convenient to solve this problem with a single two-dimensional array than with a series of one-dimensional arrays. To demonstrate how to manipulate data elements in a two-dimensional array, the illustrated parking lot array is assigned the variable name SPACES and is used as an example throughout this chapter.

Multiple subscripting

A single element in a two-dimensional array must be referenced by an array variable name followed by *two* subscripts separated by commas and enclosed in one set of parentheses. The first subscript refers to the row, the second to the column.

To refer to the element (with a current value of 1.00) located in row 4, column 3 in the SPACES array, for example, the specification is:

SPACES(4,3)

If the independent variable names K and L have current values of 4 and 3 respectively, the same element can be referred to as:

SPACES(K,L)

The rules for subscript composition, previously covered in Chapter 8, also apply to each subscript when multiple subscripts are used. Thus, if J and K have current values of 2 and 4 respectively, the array element in row 2, column 6 can be referenced by any of the following unique subscripted variable names:

SPACES(2,6)
SPACES(J,3*J)
SPACES(K-2,K+2)
SPACES(2*K-6,2*J+2)

Multiple dimensioning

The specification statement used to describe a two-dimensional array must specify the maximum number of rows and columns. The following statement specifies the exact dimensions of the SPACES array:

|12345|6|7
DIMENSION SPACES(5,6)

The dimensions are separated by a comma, and the number of rows precedes the number of columns as in the case of a subscript. One DIMENSION statement may be used to describe as many one-dimensional and/or two-dimensional arrays as is required by the program and allowed by the capacity of the computer. It should be noted that 30 storage spaces are reserved for the two-dimensional array SPACES (5 times 6).

Reading and writing two-dimensional arrays

Two-dimensional arrays may be read and written the same ways as one-dimensional arrays. The programmer, however, must be concerned with an extra subscript.

To illustrate, assume there are 30 input data records with one SPACES element each in the following sequence:

|12345|6|7

Record 1	4.00
2	3.75
3	2.25
4	3.00
5	2.00
6	3.00
7	3.25
8	2.25
etc. through	
Record 30	3.75

A comparison of the above data with the parking lot data on the first page of this chapter will indicate the proper input sequence. The first six elements should be read into row 1, the next six into row 2, and so forth until all five rows have been read into the "5-by-6" array named SPACES.

```
|12345|6|7
      DIMENSION SPACES(5,6)
   20 FORMAT(F4.0)
      DO 100 NUMROW=1,5
         READ(1,20)SPACES(NUMROW,1)
         READ(1,20)SPACES(NUMROW,2)
         READ(1,20)SPACES(NUMROW,3)
         READ(1,20)SPACES(NUMROW,4)
         READ(1,20)SPACES(NUMROW,5)
         READ(1,20)SPACES(NUMROW,6)
  100 CONTINUE
```

Note that the preceding routine will read the array *rowwise*; that is, it will read all row 1 elements first, then all row 2 elements, etc. Six READ statements were used, one for each row, to make it easier for the reader to follow the logic. A more practical approach would be to use two DO statements, as illustrated next.

```
|12345|6|7
      DIMENSION SPACES(5,6)
   20 FORMAT(F4.0)
      DO 70 NUMROW=1,5
         DO 60 NUMCOL=1,6
            READ(1,20)SPACES(NUMROW,NUMCOL)
   60    CONTINUE
   70 CONTINUE
```

Again, the above routine will read the array rowwise; that is, it will read the elements in the following sequence: SPACES(1,1), SPACES(1,2), SPACES(1,3), and so forth through SPACES(1,6); then it will continue with SPACES(2,1), SPACES(2,2), etc. The last element read will be SPACES(5,6).

A more efficient routine to do the same job is illustrated next.

|12345|6|7
```
      DIMENSION(5,6)
  20  FORMAT(F4.0)
      DO 50 NUMROW=1,5
          READ(1,20)(SPACES(NUMROW,NUMCOL),
  $         NUMCOL=1,6)
  50  CONTINUE
```

Again, the above routine will read the elements rowwise.

Now, assume there are 30 input data records with one element per record but that the sequence is changed to:

Record	Value
1	4.00
2	3.25
3	2.00
4	2.25
5	3.50
6	3.75
7	2.75
etc. through	
30	3.75

In this case, the input elements are ordered *columnwise* instead of rowwise; that is, the first element, as before, is row 1, column 1, but the second element is row 2, column 1 instead of row 1 column 2. Because the input data elements are ordered in this sequence, they must be read accordingly. The following series of statements will read the elements columnwise:

|12345|6|7
```
      DIMENSION SPACES(5,6)
  20  FORMAT(F4.0)
      DO 50 NUMCOL=1,6
          READ(1,20)(SPACES(NUMROW,NUMCOL),
  $         NUMROW=1,5)
  50  CONTINUE
```

The order in which the elements will be read by the above statements is:

1. SPACES(1,1)
2. SPACES(2,1)
3. SPACES(3,1)
4. SPACES(4,1)
5. SPACES(5,1)
6. SPACES(1,2)
7. SPACES(2,2)
8. SPACES(3,2)
9. SPACES(4,2)
10. SPACES(5,2)
11. SPACES(1,3)

etc. through SPACES(5,6)

Note that the programmer may elect to read rowwise or columnwise; the method used must agree with the sequence of the input data elements. The program may be written to agree with the order of the data elements, or the data elements may be ordered to agree with the program; the point is that there must be agreement. If an array is specified to have five rows and six columns, any attempt to input data into six rows will fail because space has not been reserved for a sixth row. Even in the case of square arrays (such as "6-by-6"), the program and input order must agree so it will be obvious whether a particular element is stored at, say row 2, column 1 or row 1, column 2. Programmers must be sure that they know what is located where, or disasters may occur at electronic speed. It is not difficult to work with two-dimensional arrays, but extreme care must be taken.

Array elements are not actually stored in the computer in rows and columns; they are stored consecutively. The sequence in which elements in a "3-by-2" array are stored is:

```
1,1
2,1
3,1
1,2
2,2
3,2
```

Thus, two-dimensional arrays are, in effect, stored columnwise. The first subscript (indicating the row) changes faster and assumes all possible values for each value of the second subscript (indicating the column). This columnwise storage sequence is automatic and always the same regardless of the sequence in which data elements are read.

The importance of internal storage sequence is illustrated in the next three paragraphs, which include a repetition of several key concepts for the purpose of emphasis.

When a READ or WRITE statement contains an *unsubscripted* variable name, the entire array, as dimensioned in the specification statement, is always written. In the case of a 30-element, one-dimensional array, the order in which the array is read or written is element numbers 1 through 30. If a 30-element, two-dimensional array is specified, the order of transfer into or out of memory is more complex.

The value of the first subscript, representing the row, is increased more rapidly; the value of the last subscript, representing the column, is increased less rapidly. Assume, for example, that the following statements are used to describe, READ, and WRITE the parking lot array called SPACES:

```
|12345|6|7
      DIMENSION SPACES(5,6)
    8 FORMAT(F.40)
      READ(1,8)SPACES
      WRITE(2,8)SPACES
```

9 / Two-Dimensional and Three-Dimensional Arrays

The order in which the elements will be read, stored, and written is:

1. SPACES(1,1)   7. SPACES(2,2)
2. SPACES(2,1)   8. SPACES(3,2)
3. SPACES(3,1)   9. SPACES(4,2)
4. SPACES(4,1)   10. SPACES(5,2)
5. SPACES(5,1)   11. SPACES(1,3)
6. SPACES(1,2)   Etc. through SPACES(5,6)

Regardless of the method of input, two-dimensional array elements are always stored in the order indicated. Thus, the shortcut method of using an unsubscripted variable name in the READ statement requires extreme care in the preparation of the FORMAT statement and in the arrangement of array elements in the input data file. This shortcut method can be used for output only if the array elements are stored in a sequence corresponding to the desired output format.

Assume that the elements of the SPACES array are recorded in five input records as follows:

```
         |123456789
Record 1  4.00 3.75 2.25 3.00 2.00 3.00
Record 2  3.25 2.25 0.50 0.25 2.00 3.75
Record 3  2.00 2.00 2.00 2.00 1.50 2.50
Record 4  2.25 1.75 1.00 1.25 1.75 1.00
Record 5  3.50 3.25 2.25 2.00 3.25 3.75
```

The following partial program can be used to describe, read, and write the above data using a two-dimensional array:

```
|12345|6|7
      DIMENSION SPACES(5,6)
    7 FORMAT(6F5.2)
      DO 8 NUMROW=1,5
         READ(1,7)(SPACES(NUMROW,NUMCOL),NUMCOL=1,6)
    8 CONTINUE
      DO 9 NUMROW=1,5
         WRITE(3,7)(SPACES(NUMROW,NUMCOL),
    $       NUMCOL=1,6)
    9 CONTINUE
```

This partial program will write the output in identical format to the input, but all data will be shifted left one position because a printer is specified as the output device. Note that two DOs are used for reading and for writing in this partial program (one DO statement and one "implied DO").

Illustrative routines   Each element in a two-dimensional array can be individually addressed; thus, any routine used for one-dimensional arrays can be applied if adjustment is made for the multiple subscripts. Only three routines are illustrated in this section; it is assumed that the SPACES array is dimensioned and read as indicated in the preceding section.

The following routine will compute the average of the six elements in row 3 only:

```
|12345|6|7
      NUMROW=3
      SUM=0.0
      DO 7 NUMCOL=1,6
          SUM=SUM+SPACES(NUMROW,NUMCOL)
    7 CONTINUE
      AVE=SUM/6.0
```

To compute the average of the five elements in column 6 only, the following routine can be used:

```
|12345|6|7
      NUMCOL=6
      SUM=0.0
      DO 7 NUMROW=1,5
          SUM=SUM+SPACES(NUMROW,NUMCOL)
    7 CONTINUE
      AVE=SUM/5.0
```

The next routine illustrates a problem that is much easier to solve with a two-dimensional array than with a series of one-dimensional arrays. It will compute the average receipts from the 12 *interior* parking spaces only.

```
|12345|6|7
      SUM=0.0
      DO 7 NUMROW=2,4
          DO 6 NUMCOL=2,5
              SUM=SUM+SPACES(NUMROW,NUMCOL)
    6     CONTINUE
    7 CONTINUE
      AVE=SUM/12.0
```

Note how the initialization and test values cause columns 1 and 6 as well as rows 1 and 5 to be ignored; only the values of the interior elements are totaled and averaged. If the initialization and test values are changed to 1 and 5 in the outer DO, and to 1 and 6 in the nested DO, the sum of *all* elements in the array will be computed. In this case, the last statement must be changed to calculate the average for 30 rather than 12 elements.

The next two routines are not directly related to the parking lot problem. They are designed to emphasize the relationship between the READ statement and the sequence of the input data cards.

The following partial program assumes the first record in the data file is a header record that indicates the number of rows and columns to be read. The remaining records in the data file contain one element per record.

9 / Two-Dimensional and Three-Dimensional Arrays

```
|12345|6|7
         DIMENSION X(100,100)
    8    FORMAT(2I3)
         READ(1,8)NUMROW, NUMCOL
    9    FORMAT(F5.2)
         DO 30 I=1,NUMROW
            DO 20 J=NUMCOL
               READ(1,9)X(NUMROW,NUMCOL)
   20       CONTINUE
   30    CONTINUE
```

Assuming the header record indicated there were two rows and three columns, the above routine will cause the first data record element to be stored at X(1,1), the second at X(1,2), the third at X(1,3), the fourth at X(2,1) the fifth at X(2,2) and the last at X(2,3). Note that if all six elements were entered on one record, and the FORMAT statement were changed accordingly, the program would fail because each time the second READ was executed, one element only would be read.

The next partial program produces the same results but uses a *nested implied DO* to replace the two DO statements in the preceding illustration.

```
|12345|6|7
         DIMENSION X(100,100)
    8    FORMAT(2I3)
         READ(1,8)NR,NC
    9    FORMAT(F5.2)
         READ(1,9)((X(I,J),J=1,NC),I=1,NR)
```

Note that the self-indexing READ is executed once only. Thus, all six elements could be read from one record if the FORMAT statement were changed accordingly. Note also that if NC and NR were interchanged in the self-indexing READ, the array would be stored sequentially at X(1,1) , X(2,1) , X(1,2) , X(2,2) , X(1,3) and X(2,3) , instead of X(1,1), X(1,2) , X(1,3) , X(2,1) , X(2,2) and X(2,3). Stated another way, the array would be read column by column instead of row by row. Of course, the data records must be sequenced accordingly if the desired results are to be obtained.

The following routine will merge two one-dimensional arrays into one two-dimensional array:

```
|12345|6|7
         DIMENSION ONEA(3),ONEB(3),TWO(2,3)
         DO 8 K=1,3
            TWO(1,K)=ONEA(K)
            TWO(2,K)=ONEB(K)
    8    CONTINUE
```

The following routine will store the elements of a two-dimensional array in two one-dimensional arrays:

```
      |12345|6|7
            DIMENSION ONEA(3),ONEB(3),TWO(2,3)
            DO 8 K=1,3
                ONEA(K)=TWO(1,K)
                ONEB(K)=TWO(2,K)
          8 CONTINUE
```

THREE-DIMENSIONAL ARRAYS

A one-dimensional array is simply a series of data elements of a defined length. A two-dimensional array is a series of data elements of defined length and width. A three-dimensional array is a series of related two-dimensional arrays; in addition to the surface dimensions of length and width, it also has depth. It consists of rows, columns, and *ranks*.

To illustrate a three-dimensional array, assume that there are two parking lots, instead of only one. For identification purposes, the lots are numbered 1 and 2. Each contains 30 parking spaces arranged in five rows and six columns as previously described.

Multiple subscripting

A single element must be referenced by an array variable name followed by *three* subscripts because a three-dimensional array is arranged in rows, columns, and ranks. The subscripts are separated by commas and enclosed in one set of parentheses. The first subscript refers to the row, the second to the column, and the third to the rank. In the example, the rank identifies the parking lot number.

To illustrate, the element located in row 4, column 3, rank (lot number) 2 is specified as:

$$SPACES(4,3,2)$$

As previously indicated, any valid integer expression may be used for any or all of the multiple subscripts.

Multiple dimensioning

The specification statement used to describe a three-dimensional array must indicate, in order, the maximum numbers of rows, columns, and ranks. The following statement specifies the exact dimensions of the SPACES array for both parking lots:

```
      |12345|6|7
            DIMENSION SPACES(5,6,2)
```

This statement reserves 60 storage spaces for the SPACES array (5 times 6 times 2). One DIMENSION statement may be used to describe as many arrays are is required by the program and allowed by the

9 / Two-Dimensional and Three-Dimensional Arrays

capacity of the computer; the arrays described may be one, two, and/or three-dimensional and may appear in any sequence.

Reading and writing three-dimensional arrays

Three-dimensional arrays are not actually stored in rows, columns, and ranks. Like all arrays, they are stored consecutively. The general rule for storage of any multiple-dimensional array is that the first subscript varies fastest and the last varies slowest.

Programmers cannot control the pattern in which array elements are stored, but they can control the sequence in which array elements are read and written. The elements in a three-dimensional array may be read or written in any sequence by using regular DOs or implied DOs. When subscripted variable names are used, the programmer has complete control of the input and output sequence. This general concept was explained and illustrated in the section on two-dimensional arrays and needs no further elaboration. If the extreme shortcut technique is used for input and/or output, the programmer must be thoroughly familiar with the automatic storage sequence which is reviewed in the following two paragraphs.

An *unsubscripted* variable name can also be used to read or write an entire three-dimensional array. As with a two-dimensional array, however, extreme caution must be exercised because three-dimensional arrays are always stored internally as follows:

The first storage space is reserved for the element whose subscripts are all 1s. The value of the first subscript, representing the row, increases most rapidly; and the value of the last subscript, representing the rank, increases least rapidly. Thus, the 60-element array SPACES will be stored internally as follows:

1. SPACES(1,1,1)
2. SPACES(2,1,1)
3. SPACES(3,1,1)
4. SPACES(4,1,1)
5. SPACES(5,1,1)
6. SPACES(1,2,1)
   Etc. through:
7. SPACES(5,6,1)
   Then:
8. SPACES(1,1,2)
9. SPACES(2,1,2)
10. SPACES(3,1,2)
    Etc. through:
    SPACES(5,6,2)

Assume that the elements of the SPACES array are entered in 10 records. The first five records contain six elements each, as illustrated in the section on two-dimensional arrays, and indicate the receipts from parking lot number one. The last five records are in identical format but indicate the receipts from parking lot number two.

The following partial program can be used to describe, read, and write two tables. The first table written will indicate the receipts for each column and row for rank 1, and the second for rank 2.

```
|12345|6|7
      DIMENSION SPACES(5,6,2)
    2 FORMAT(6F5.2)
      DO 4 NUMRNK=1,2
        DO 3 NUMROW=1,5
          READ(1,2)(SPACES(NUMROW,NUMCOL,NUMRNK),
     $      NUMCOL=1,6)
    3   CONTINUE
    4 CONTINUE
      DO 6 NUMRNK=1,2
        DO 5 NUMROW=1,5
          WRITE(3,2)(SPACES(NUMROW,NUMCOL,NUMRNK),
     $      NUMCOL=1,6)
    5   CONTINUE
    6 CONTINUE
```

Note that three DOs are used for reading and for writing in this routine (two DO statements and an "implied DO"). In this case the READ and WRITE referenced the same FORMAT statement; in many cases output requirements would differ from input.

Illustrative routines

Any routine used for one- or two-dimensional arrays can also be used for three-dimensional arrays if adjustment is made for the multiple subscripts. Variations of the routines used to illustrate two-dimensional arrays are used in this section to illustrate three-dimensional arrays; it is assumed that the SPACES array is dimensioned and read as indicated in the preceding section.

The following routine will compute the average of the six elements in row 3, rank (lot number) 1:

```
|12345|6|7
      NUMRNK=1
      NUMROW=3
      SUM=0.0
      DO 7 NUMCOL=1,6
        SUM=SUM+SPACES(NUMROW,NUMCOL,NUMRNK)
    7 CONTINUE
      AVE=SUM/6.0
```

The following routine will compute the average of the 10 elements in column 6, rank 1 and 2:

```
|12345|6|7
      NUMCOL=6
      SUM=0.0
      DO 7 NUMRNK=1,2
        DO 6 NUMROW=1,5
          SUM=SUM+SPACES(NUMROW,NUMCOL,
     $      NUMRNK)
    6   CONTINUE
    7 CONTINUE
      AVE=SUM/10.0
```

The next routine will compute the combined average receipts of only the *interior* parking spaces for both lots:

```
|12345|6|7
         SUM=0.00
         DO 7 NUMRNK=1,2
            DO 6 NUMROW=2,4
               DO 5 NUMCOL=2,5
                  SUM=SUM+SPACES(NUMROW,NUMCOL,
     $                  NUMRNK)
    5          CONTINUE
    6       CONTINUE
    7    CONTINUE
         AVE=SUM/24.0
```

Before concluding the discussion on three-dimensional arrays, it should be emphasized that they are very powerful and have many applications. The SPACES array, for example, can be changed so that the rank indicates the receipts for each day of the week, month, or year. Furthermore, arrays may exceed three dimensions. The logic is more complex with, say, seven dimensions, but the general concepts are the same with all multiple-dimension arrays.

The examples in this chapter were designed to illustrate what two- and three-dimensional arrays are, how they work, and when they might be used. The programming logic can be quite complex when these types of arrays are used. Before attempting to work with them, a programmer should have considerable experience and a thorough familiarity with arrays of one dimension.

REVIEW QUESTIONS

1. What statements may be used to declare two- or three-dimensional arrays?

2. How does the computer "know" whether a DIMENSION statement is describing a one-dimensional or a two-dimensional array?

3. If a DIMENSION statement includes a variable name followed by two constants within parentheses, what does the first constant represent? What does the second represent?

4. Assume a two-dimensional array has been properly declared. The first subscript in the variable name represents what? The second subscript represents what?

5. Assume a three-dimensional array has been properly declared. In referring to elements by a variable name, what does the first subscript represent? What does the second represent? The third?

6. Are two-dimensional arrays read and written rowwise or columnwise? Discuss.

254   Standard FORTRAN Programming: A Structured Style

   7. Are two-dimensional arrays stored internally rowwise or columnwise? Discuss.

   8. In what order are three-dimensional arrays stored internally? Discuss.

   9. Describe the difference, if any, between the valid subscript forms for one-dimensional arrays and two- or three-dimensional arrays.

   10. The statement:

   $$READ(1,20)(((X(I,J,K),I=1,4),J=1,3),K=1,2)$$

   is designed to read an array with how many dimensions? How many elements?

EXERCISES

   For each independent series of statements below, indicate (1) how many records will be written and (2) how many variables will be written on each line. Stated another way, describe the printed output in terms of rows and columns.

   1.
   ```
               DIMENSION X(100)
               DO 40 K=1,10
                  WRITE(3,30)(X(J),J=1,10)
         30       FORMAT(10(1X,F5.2,2X))
         40    CONTINUE
   ```

   2.
   ```
               DIMENSION X(10,10)
               DO 70 K=1,10
                  DO 60 J=1,10
                     WRITE(3,50)X(K,J)
         50          FORMAT(10(1X,F5.2,2X))
         60       CONTINUE
         70    CONTINUE
   ```

   3.
   ```
               DIMENSION X(10,10)
               DO 50 K=1,10
                  WRITE(3,40)(X(K,J),J=1,10)
         40       FORMAT(10(1X,F5.2X))
         50    CONTINUE
   ```

   4.
   ```
               DIMENSION X(10,10)
               DO 50 K=1,10
                  WRITE(3,40)(X(J,K),J=1,10)
         40       FORMAT(10(1X,F5.2,2X))
         50    CONTINUE
   ```

   5.
   ```
               DIMENSION X(10,10)
               WRITE(3,30)((X(J,K),J=1,10),K=1,10)
         30    FORMAT(10(1X,F5.2,2X))
   ```

   6.
   ```
               DIMENSION X(10,10)
   ```

```
                    WRITE(3,30)X
             30     FORMAT(10(1X,F5.2,2X))
  7.                DIMENSION X(10,10)
                    WRITE(3,30)X
             30     FORMAT(5(1X,F5.2,2X))

  8.                DIMENSION X(5,10,2)
                    WRITE(3,30)X
             30     FORMAT(5(1X,F5.2,2X))

  9.                DIMENSION X(5,10,2)
                    WRITE(3,30)X
                    FORMAT(10(1X,5.2,2X))

 10.                DIMENSION X(5,10,2)
                    DO 70 K=1,2
                       DO 60 J=1,5
                          WRITE(3,60)(X(J,N,K),N=1,10)
             50           FORMAT(10(1X,F5.2,2X))
             60        CONTINUE
                    WRITE(3,80)
             80     FORMAT(/ /1X)
             90     CONTINUE

 11.                DIMENSION X(10,10)
                    NROW=10
                    NCOL=10
                    DO 70 K=1,NROW
                       WRITE(3,60)(X(K,L),L=1,NCOL)
             60        FORMAT(1X,10F7.2)
             70     CONTINUE

 12.                DIMENSION X(10,10,10)
                    NROW=10
                    NCOL=10
                    NRANK=10
                    DO 70 J=1,NRANK
                       DO 60 K=1,NROW
                          WRITE(3,50)(X(K,L,J),L=1,NCOL)
             50           FORMAT(1X,10F7.2)
             60        CONTINUE
             70     CONTINUE

 13.                DIMENSION X(10,10,10)
                    NROW=10
                    NCOL=10
                    NRANK=10
                    WRITE (3,30)(((X(J,K,L),K=1,NCOL),J=1,NROW),
                  $    L=1,NRANK)
             30     FORMAT(1X,10F7.2)
```

PROBLEMS

1. Write a program to compute the sum and arithmetic average (mean) of the columns and rows in a two-dimensional array. Set up a "5-by-5" array and read the values one through nine into the first *three* columns and rows. Compute the row and column sums and store these values in the fourth row and column. Compute the row and column means and store in the fifth row and column. Output should be in the following general form:

```
 1.0    2.0    3.0     6.0    2.0
 4.0    5.0    6.0    15.0    5.0
 7.0    8.0    9.0    24.0    8.0
12.0   15.0   18.0
 4.0    5.0    6.0
```

Note that four array elements are excluded in the output.

2. Write a program that will turn the elements, in a two-dimensional array, 180 degrees. Initialize a "7-by-7" alphameric array using seven input data records with the following data:

Record	Column
	1 2 3 4 5 6 7
1	EEEEEEE
2	E
3	E
4	EEEEE
5	E
6	E
7	EEEEEEE

Set up another seven-by-seven array with the identical elements but with the columnar data in reversed sequence. Output from the two arrays should appear as follows:

```
EEEEEEE      EEEEEEE
E                  E
E                  E
EEEEE          EEEEE
E                  E
E                  E
EEEEEEE      EEEEEEE
```

3. Expand the program described in Problem 2 in this chapter so that it includes a third array with the elements turned 90 degrees. Output from the three arrays should appear as follows:

9 / Two-Dimensional and Three-Dimensional Arrays

```
EEEEEEE      EEEEEEE      EEEEEEE
E                  E      E   E   E
E                  E      E   E   E
EEEEE        EEEEE        E   E   E
E                  E      E   E   E
E                  E      E       E
EEEEEEE      EEEEEEE      E       E
```

4. Legislative bills, amendments, resolutions, etc., are often distributed to committee members in 80-column format with the lines numbered in multiples of 10. Write a program that will handle this task using a two-dimensional array. Process at least five input data records to test the program.

5. Assume that a six-question opinion survey asks the respondent to check one of five various responses for each question. Assume further that one data record had been prepared for each respondent with each response coded one through five and entered in the column corresponding to the question number. If the respondent failed to answer a question, the appropriate column has been left blank.

Write a program to compute the number of one, two, three, four, and five responses to each of the six questions. Prepare your own data file of at least 10 records, to test the program. Two arrays (both two-dimensional) should be used—one for the data and the other to accumulate the number of various responses to each question.

Write out both arrays with descriptive array, columnar, and row identifications. WRITE statements should include nested implied DOs.

6. International Sales Corporation calculates each salesperson's gross pay on the basis of a salary plus commission as indicated in the two tables below.

Domestic sales		
Sales revenue	Commission rate	Salary
zero to $ 10,000	.010	$ 0
$10,0001 to 30,000	.015	250
30,001 to 60,000	.020	300
60,001 to 100,000	.025	400
more than 100,000	.030	500

Foreign sales		
Sales revenue	Commission rate	Salary
zero to $ 10,000	.000	$ 0
$10,001 to 30,000	.015	200
30,001 to 75,000	.020	300
75,001 to 150,000	.035	500
more than 150,000	.040	800

The commission rate is based on the sales revenue level attained. For example, if a salesperson has $20,000 domestic sales revenue, the commission should be 1½ percent of $20,000 (not 1 percent of the first $10,000 and 1½ percent of the excess); the commission should be added to the $250 salary, in this case, to determine the salesperson's gross pay.

Write a program to store the information, from the above tables, in a three-dimensional array. Use information from the stored tables to calculate the gross pay for each of the following salespersons:

Salesperson number	Sales revenue	Class of sale
1	$100,000	Foreign
2	40,000	Domestic
3	5,000	Domestic
4	5,000	Foreign
7	15,000	Foreign
8	200,000	Foreign
10	200,000	Domestic

Output should include salesperson number and gross pay. Omit output for any salesperson whose gross pay is zero. Identify the output with brief descriptive headers.

10

Subprograms

The first five chapters in this book covered the basic statements required to write complete source programs and explained how the computer can be used to translate these programs into the unique language it is designed to understand and obey. Chapters 6 and 7 covered progressively more sophisticated programming techniques and various shortcuts available to the programmer. Chapters 8 and 9 illustrated and explained how to tell the computer to assign a unique variable name to each element in an array or, in effect, to write portions of statements. This powerful concept of causing the computer to help write the program will now be developed further. This chapter illustrates and explains how the computer can be used to write a minor or even a major portion of a program.

Many programs include various mathematical functions (such as the trigonometric sine of an angle) that can require an arithmetic statement with a long and/or complex expression when written with the five arithmetic operators (+, −, *, /, and **). This type of arithmetic statement must sometimes be repeated in several places in one or more programs. Furthermore, many programs include various routines that require a rather long series of statements (such as a routine for sorting, computing compound interest, or generating random numbers). These routines must sometimes be repeated several times in one program and are frequently required in many different programs.

To avoid writing or rewriting long and/or complex program segments, a *subprogram* can be used. A subprogram is defined as a set of instructions that performs a specific task under the control of another program. It is usually used for frequently repeated tasks and must be written only once. The computer can be told to include an available subprogram at almost any point in any program. Subprograms provide an obvious convenience to the programmer and many of them are relatively easy to use.

It should be noted that a subprogram is designed to solve only part of a problem. One or more of these parts are combined with other parts to form a larger and whole program designed to solve the problem. The various parts are "called for" and joined in proper order by a *calling program*. The calling program that controls the whole program is sometimes called the *main-line program*. Subprograms can also be used as calling programs, but there must always be one main line. Long programs are typically written as a series of subprograms which are individually tested and debugged, then joined to form a complete system of coordinated programs designed to solve the whole complex problem. This technique, called *modular programming*, makes it possible to assign several programmers to one problem and thus reduce the time required to complete the job. In this case, the main-line program may be a sort of "skeleton" program which calls for many subprograms of considerable size, which, in turn, may call for other subprograms.

In terms of length, when should a program be divided into parts, and when should parts be subdivided? This is a question that the programmer, or programming supervisor, must decide. As a general rule, whenever a program, subprogram, or parts thereof become too long to be printed on one page or to be displayed on a cathode ray tube (CRT), the programmer should consider subdivision. This is simply a matter of good programming structure and follows the divide-and-conquer technique previously recommended.

A subprogram is usually written only once, as previously indicated. Fortunately, the individual programmer is not required to write most subprograms because they have already been written by someone else. FORTRAN provides many subprograms, some of which are illustrated in this chapter. Most computer centers have a library of subprograms that have been written by their staff or obtained from other computer centers. Before attempting to write a long, complex program, programmers should always check with their computer center to determine which subprograms are available locally or can be obtained from various sources. Unless the program to be solved is very unusual, someone has probably already written, tested, and debugged the various routines required. In fact, complete programs may be available that require few, if any, changes to solve the problem. Many computer centers belong to one or more organizations that may have hundreds of complete programs and subprograms available for a wide variety of applications. Take advantage of the work of others instead of "reinventing the wheel."

The four types of FORTRAN subprograms are covered in the first four main sections of this chapter. Each type is fully discussed in a different section. Consequently, a few topics are appropriately included in more than one section. This slight redundancy is intentional, so that each section will "stand alone" for the convenience of the reader.

10/Subprograms

LIBRARY FUNCTION SUBPROGRAMS

Standard FORTRAN provides many "built-in" subprograms. Many of these are of interest only to experienced programmers or to those who must solve complex mathematical problems. Selected examples of mathematical function subprograms are included in this section to illustrate a few of the many available; a lengthy list is given in Appendix D. No attempt will be made to enter into a full discussion of mathematical functions. Such a discussion is reserved for a course in mathematics. This section does, however, explain and illustrate how a mathematical function subprogram is used in FORTRAN. A FORTRAN-supplied built-in mathematical function subprogram is commonly called a *library function*. This is the only type of subprogram included in this section, so, for convenience, it usually will be referred to simply as a subprogram.

General description

Subprograms are already compiled and ready to go. Each has been assigned a unique variable name that follows the regular rules of variable names previously covered in this book. To "call for" a subprogram, the programmer uses the appropriate variable name in a statement. The effects of such a call depend upon the job the subprogram is designed to do and upon the subprogram type. There are two types.

One is called *intrinsic*, or *in-line*. It is designed to perform a relatively simple task such as changing a value from negative to positive or from integer to real. Thus, it is composed of relatively few machine-language instructions. When a FORTRAN program is compiled, the appropriate set of machine-language instructions is inserted into the object program in each place where this type of subprogram is called. If the same subprogram is called four times in a source program, the same subprogram will appear four times in the compiled object program.

The second type is called *external*, or *out-of-line*. It is designed to perform a more complex task, such as calculating a hyperbolic tangent in radians or calculating square root the best way in terms of computer efficiency. Thus, it is composed of a relatively long set of machine-language instructions. When a FORTRAN program is compiled, the appropriate set of machine-language instructions is inserted into the object program in a special place (usually at the beginning or end) *once only* to minimize program storage space. Stated another way, this type of subprogram is stored with, but not within, the main line. Appropriate machine-language instructions are provided so that each time this type of subprogram is called, control passes to the right place and then returns.

Object program structure will obviously differ according to the type of subprogram called. However, the general concept is the same. Programmers should understand this general concept. Control passes from the main line to the subprogram and then returns to the main line. Assuming two calls to the same subprogram, this control flow concept can be illustrated schematically as follows:

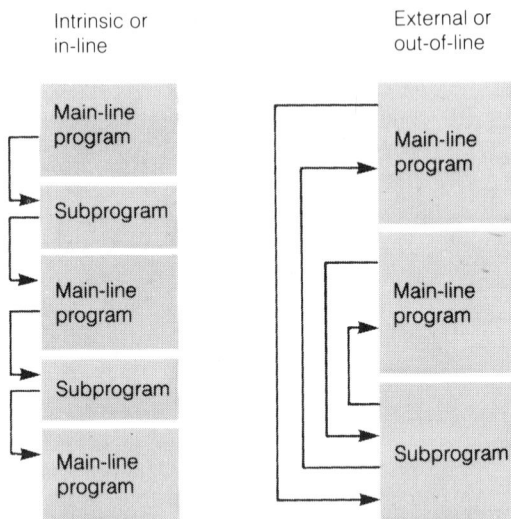

A variable name that refers to a subprogram is sometimes called an *arithmetic function,* a *function variable name,* or simply a *function.* The last term will be used throughout the remainder of this section.

Most functions require a set number of *arguments,* usually either one or two. An *argument* is defined as an arithmetic expression, the current value of which is used by the subprogram to compute the result.

Using subprograms

To use a subprogram, the programmer simply writes the function followed by one or more arguments enclosed in parentheses and separated by commas. For instance, one subprogram is designed to extract square root; the function is SQRT, and one argument is required. The use of this subprogram is illustrated by the following arithmetic statement:

```
|12345|6|7
          ANSWER=SQRT(144.0)
```

When a function is included in an arithmetic expression, the computer executes the subprogram, using the argument(s) supplied by the programmer; and the result of the computation becomes the current value of the function. The computer then returns to the "calling program" and continues on, using the current value of the function in the same manner as if it had been written in the expression as a constant. In the preceding illustrated statement, the current value of the function will replace, or initialize, the current value of ANSWER. In the following statement, the current value of the function will be added to the current value of ALPHA; and the resulting sum will replace, or initialize, the current value of ANSWER:

|12345|6|7
ANSWER=SQRT(BETA)+ALPHA

In the following paragraph, the above statement is used to illustrate the difference between functions, other types of variable names, and programmer-supplied constants.

Functions are variable names, but they are not handled by the computer in the same manner as other types of variable names appearing in expressions. To illustrate, the current values of ALPHA and BETA remain unchanged and are available for later use in the program. The current value of the function SQRT is not available for later use, however, because it refers to a subprogram rather than to a symbolic address where the current value of a variable name is stored. The current value of the function SQRT is handled by the computer in the same manner as if it had been written in the expression as a constant; but a function is not identical to a programmer-supplied constant, which always has the same current value each time a statement is executed. The current value of the function can change because the current value of BETA can change each time the subprogram is executed. Thus a subprogram may yield a different result each time it is executed.

The first letter of a function, like any other variable name, always implies the mode. Thus, SQRT implies that the current value of the function will be established in floating point rather than in integer mode.

Because the current value of SQRT will be handled by the computer like a programmer-supplied constant, an obvious question is whether the computer will yield a single-precision (real) or double-precision constant. The programmer who writes a constant can specify it to be double-precision. If, however, a subprogram yields a constant, the function used by the programmer determines the type. All subprograms are designed to establish the current value of a function in only one specific mode (integer, real, or double-precision). The subprogram "called for" by the function SQRT is specifically designed to yield a single-precision (real) constant. If a double-precision current value is desired, the programmer may use a DOUBLE PRECISION specification statement or, more conveniently, use a different function. (In this case, the programmer would use DSQRT on some computers.)

An argument is an arithmetic expression, so it may be a constant, a variable name, or various combinations of constants and/or variable names separated by operational signs. There are restrictions, however, as to the mode of arithmetic expressions used as arguments. Each subprogram requires a specific mode of argument (integer, real, or double-precision). If an argument is in mixed mode, the rules of hierarchy determine the specific mode as in the case of any other arithmetic expression. (Programmers must always be cautious when using mixed mode expressions.)

Also, each subprogram has specific requirements as to the number of arguments that can be used with a function; most must have either one or two; but some must have two or more.

Subprograms are easy to use, but they must be selected with care because each has special requirements.

Illustrative examples

Following are a few examples of FORTRAN/Supplied Subprograms. Each requires one single-precision argument and establishes a single-precision current value to the function. Each example has a double-precision counterpart on many computers.

Function	Calls subprogram to compute:
SIN	Trigonometric sine
COS	Trigonometric cosine
ATAN	Arctangent
TANH	Hyperbolic tangent
ALOG	Natural logarithm
ALOG10	Common logarithm
ABS	Absolute value
SQRT	Square root

Functions can be used in any arithmetic expression; they are not limited to arithmetic statements. An arithmetic expression may contain one or more functions; the same function may appear more than once in the same expression; and an expression may contain one or more nested functions. The following statements illustrate some valid expressions containing one or more functions:

```
|12345|6|7
       IF(SQRT(A+B))7,8,8
       B=SIN(A)/COS(A)
       C=SQRT(A*2.0)+SQRT(B)
       D=SIN(SQRT(A))
       E=SIN(SQRT(ALOG(A*A)))
```

Note that a nested function is actually an argument of another function. In any arithmetic expression, parentheses can be used to control the sequence of evaluation. Thus, with nested functions, the innermost function is evaluated first.

It might be questioned why a subprogram is provided to extract square root, because either of the following statements will apparently produce the same results, but the second requires a longer expression.

```
|12345|6|7
       ROOT=A**.5
       ROOT=SQRT(A)
```

The reason for providing a square root function is simply that it is faster than the exponential function. It is recommended that the subprogram be used to calculate square root.

Consider the following three statements:

|12345|6|7
```
     UNITS=NUNITS
     AMOUNT=UNITS*PRICE
     AMOUNT=FLOAT(NUNITS)*PRICE
```

The third statement above does the job of the first two; the function FLOAT changes the integer to floating point to avoid an inconsistent mode expression.

Now consider the following three statements:

|12345|6|7
```
     XABSLU=X
     IF(X.LT.0.0)XABSLU=-X
     XABSLU=ABS(X)
```

The last statement above uses the function ABS to set a variable to the absolute value of X. It does the job better and faster than the preceding two statements.

All subprograms presented previously in this section required only one argument, and all but one also required that the function and argument be in the same mode. FORTRAN also provides some subprograms that require two or more arguments and several different combinations of function and argument modes. (It should be noted that when more than one argument is required for a particular subprogram, all arguments must be in the same mode.) To demonstrate this type, five very useful subprograms for determining the largest value in a series of arguments are presented next.

Function	Mode of current value established for function	Required mode of argument
MAX0	Integer	Integer
AMAX1	Real	Real
DMAX1	Double precision	Double precision
MAX1	Integer	Real
AMAX0	Real	Integer

The following statements demonstrate how these functions can be used in expressions:

|12345|6|7
```
     NUMBIG=MAX0(I,J,K,L,M,N)
     BIGNUM=AMAX1(A,B)
     HUGE=DMAX1(U,V,W,X)
     M=(MAX1(A,B,C))+(N*7)
     A=(AMAX0(J,K,L))+(B*7.0)
```

It should be noted that the last two statements illustrated above do *not* contain mixed mode expressions. The computer handled the arguments in the mode indicated when selecting the largest value, which is then converted to a different mode before establishing the current value of the function. The expression is not in mixed mode because the function is consistent in mode to other elements in the expression.

It is emphasized again that relatively few selected examples of library functions are included in this section. Many more are available (see Appendix D) that handle a wide variety of tasks. Use library functions whenever possible; they save time and improve programs.

SUBROUTINE SUBPROGRAMS

The type of subprogram covered in this section is not a part of the calling program. It is a separate and distinct program unit. The computer must be told that it is a subprogram rather than an independent program. The statement used to make this declaration is the SUBROUTINE statement.

There is only *one* type of subroutine subprogram. To distinguish it from the three types of function subprograms (covered in other sections of this chapter) and as a matter of convenience, it will simply be called a *subroutine*.

General description

When a subroutine is used, the calling program sends values by way of arguments. An *argument* is defined as an arithmetic (or alphanumeric) expression, the current value of which is used by the subprogram to perform its task.

Values are also returned by way of arguments, so a subroutine may return as many values as there are arguments. It is not limited to returning one value per argument, however. Since array names are permitted as arguments, the subroutine may send back perhaps hundreds or thousands of values for each argument (one for each array element). On the other hand, if a value is not changed by the subroutine, the subroutine will return the same value it received. Thus, in effect, it may return no values. Arguments are required only when values must be transferred back and forth between the calling program and the subroutine.

A subroutine is identified by a unique name, composed by the programmer, which must follow the same rules of length and composition as a regular variable name. No values are ever associated with this name, so there is no implied mode and there are no restrictions on the first letter. This name performs no function other than to identify a subroutine, so it will be called simply a subroutine *name*.

The SUBROUTINE statement

Only one SUBROUTINE statement is permitted in a subroutine, and it must be the first. The general form is:

```
|12345|6|7
nnnnn    SUBROUTINE name(darg₁,darg₂, . . . dargₘ)
```

10/Subprograms

> **Legend:**
>
> nnnnn — Any unique one- to five-digit integer that specifies the statement *number*. It is never required, but it may be used at the programmer's option.
>
> SUBROUTINE — A keyword that specifies a SUBROUTINE subprogram. It must follow the general rules of composition for variable names.
>
> name — The programmer-supplied subroutine name.
>
> $(darg_1, \ldots darg_m)$ — One or more optional nonsubscripted variable names enclosed in parentheses and separated by commas. They are selected by the programmer to serve as dummy arguments. They may be omitted in some types of subroutines.

The CALL statement

This statement is required in a calling program to "call for" a subroutine. The general form is:

> ```
> |12345|6|7
>  nnnnn   CALL name(arg₁,arg₂ . . . argₘ)
> ```
>
> **Legend:**
>
> nnnnn — Any unique one- to five-digit integer that specifies the statement *number*. It is required only if referenced by another statement in the calling program. It may always be used at the programmer's option.
>
> CALL — A keyword specifying the type of statement.
>
> name — The subroutine name.
>
> $(arg_1, \ldots arg_m)$ — One or more optional arguments enclosed in parentheses and separated by commas. Arguments may be any type of arithmetic or alphanumeric expression, but only independent and array variable names are illustrated in this section.

The RETURN Statement

A RETURN statement is used in a subroutine. It terminates execution of the subroutine and returns control to the calling program, which may be another subprogram or the main line. When control is returned to the calling program, values are also returned if the subroutine includes dummy arguments. The calling program then continues executing. The RETURN statement indicates the logical end of the subroutine; if it is omitted, no value can be returned.

The general form of a RETURN statement is:

> ```
> |12345|6|7
>  nnnnn   RETURN
> ```
>
> **Legend:**
>
> nnnnn — Any unique one- to five-digit integer that specifies the statement *number*. It is required only if referenced by another statement in the subroutine. It may always be used at the programmer's option.
>
> RETURN — A keyword specifying the type of statement.

Illustrative examples

A RETURN in a subroutine may be considered the counterpart of a STOP in a main-line program. However, a RETURN stops execution of the subroutine *only*—it does not stop the main line. Whenever a STOP is executed, in the main line or in any type of subprogram including a subroutine, the effect is the same—execution of the main line and all its related subparts is terminated.

To start with an elementary but practical example, suppose a company has several programs that require the same message or header line to be printed. Instead of including the same FORMAT and WRITE statements in several programs, one subroutine can be written to do the job. The following subroutine will write a header line:

```
|12345|6|7
      SUBROUTINE HEADER
    7 FORMAT(10X,'NAME',13X,'AMOUNT')
      WRITE(3,7)
      RETURN
      END
```

All programs requiring this subroutine could include the following statement:

```
|12345|6|7
      CALL HEADER
```

When the CALL statement is executed, the subroutine will write the header line, then return control to the calling program. Notice that no arguments are used and that no values are exchanged in this example.

Most subroutines have dummy arguments. They receive values from actual arguments when called and return values to actual arguments when the subroutine has finished its job. Values follow control. When control passes to the subroutine, values are sent; when control returns to the calling program, values are returned. This general concept of arguments serving as a sort of "two-way street" is illustrated schematically below where two different calls are made to the same subroutine.

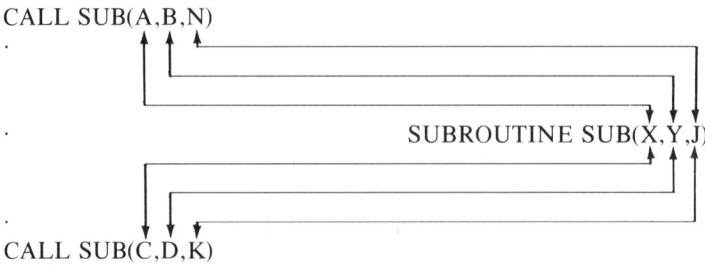

Array routines included in Chapter 8 will be used as subroutines in the next two illustrative examples.

The following subroutine exchanges values with the calling program. It is designed to initialize all elements in the calling program array to zero.

```
|12345|6|7
      SUBROUTINE ZERO(ARRAY,N)
      DIMENSION ARRAY(100)
      DO 7 I=1,N
         ARRAY(I)=0.0
    7 CONTINUE
      RETURN
      END
```

The name of the subroutine is ZERO. The subroutine is designed to work with floating point values, but it may start with any letter because the name assumes no value. Thus, the name could be MIKE, but a more descriptive term is preferred. The current values of the dummy arguments ARRAY and N are established by the calling program. Note that this subroutine will change each nonzero element in ARRAY, but it will not change the current value of N, which is used as a test value for the DO statement.

Suppose a calling program has a 100-element array, properly dimensioned, called GRAPES. It contains single-precision floating point data that the computer has completed processing, so the values of the individual elements need not be saved. It is desired to use the previously illustrated subroutine to replace the data with zeros. The following two statements in the calling program will perform the desired task:

```
|12345|6|7
      NUMELM=100
      CALL ZERO(GRAPES,NUMELM)
```

When the CALL statement is executed, 101 current values will be transferred from the two actual arguments to the two dummy arguments. GRAPES is the name of a 100-element array, so this one argument will transfer 100 current values to the subroutine. On the other hand, NUMELM is an independent variable name, so it will transfer only one current value. When the subroutine RETURN statement is executed, the current value of each element in the dummy array (ZERO) will be transferred back to the actual array (GRAPES) in the calling program. The current value of the other dummy argument will also be transferred back, but in this case it is unchanged, so, in effect, only the array values are exchanged. Notice again how the arguments are a sort of two-way street—they transfer values back and forth to each other.

Assume now that a calling program has a DIMENSION statement that specifies three arrays named ARRAY1, ARRAY2, and ARRAY3; the lengths are 300, 200, and 100 respectively. Single-precision (real) data have been read into all elements in ARRAY3, but no data have been placed in the elements of the other two arrays. A DIMENSION statement reserves space for an array, but it does not initialize the elements within the array to any specific value. Thus, ARRAY1, and ARRAY2 contain garbage. Suppose it is necessary to create two duplicates of ARRAY3, and the other two arrays are to be used to store the duplicate data.

The following subroutine is designed to create two duplicates of an array:

```
|12345|6|7
      SUBROUTINE DUPTWO(ARRAY,COPY1,COPY2,N)
      DIMENSION ARRAY(1),COPY1(1),COPY2(1)
      DO 7 I=1,N
         COPY1(I)=ARRAY(I)
         COPY2(I)=ARRAY(I)
    7 CONTINUE
      RETURN
      END
```

The following two statements in the calling program will solve the problem:

```
|12345|6|7
      N=100
      CALL DUPTWO(ARRAY3,ARRAY1,ARRAY2,N)
```

This problem is designed to illustrate several points:

1. There is no conflict caused by the use of the same variable name (N) to specify the number of elements in the dummy and actual arrays because the calling program and the subroutine operate independently of each other.

2. Two of the arrays in the calling program contain garbage, but the first 100 elements in each will be duplicates of ARRAY3 when the subroutine has finished its job.

3. The dummy arrays are specified to contain only one element, but they work with three arrays containing 100 elements each. Actual arrays must have a dimension large enough to accommodate all elements in an array, but this is not required for one-dimensional dummy arrays. The purpose of a DIMENSION statement in a subroutine, or other type of subprogram, is only to specify that the variable names are array names. Thus, dummy arrays may be specified as minimum size. It is beyond the scope of this book to explain the details of what happens within the computer, but essentially the calling program passes the beginning address and length of the actual arrays to the subprogram, which then works with the actual arrays. In other words, instead of actually transferring values, the calling program tells the subroutine where these values are located. Thus, less processing time and less storage space are required because less data are transferred and the values of the actual and dummy arrays share the same storage locations.

10/Subprograms

Many computers require that multiple-dimensioned arrays be described as the same size in the calling program and in the subroutine. To make subroutines more flexible, standard FORTRAN permits "adjustable dimensions." It was previously stated that a DIMENSION, or other array-defining statement, must use integer constants to specify array sizes. This general rule applies to main lines but not to subprograms, which may use integer variables for sizing arrays. To illustrate, the first two statements in a subroutine might appear as follows:

```
|12345|6|7
      SUBROUTINE SUB(X,J,K,L, . . .)
      DIMENSION X(J,K,L)
```

Whenever the above subroutine is called, the name of the actual array and its exact dimensions would be included in the CALL statement. Different CALLS could specify different arrays of different sizes. Thus, the subroutine array has "adjustable dimensions."

To conclude, an illustration is given that presents a complete mainline calling program, called MAIN, and a called SUBROUTINE subprogram called SORT (which is based on the sort routine given in Chapter 8). MAIN and SORT, shown in Figure 10-1, perform the following tasks:

1. MAIN reads three floating point arrays, called X, Y, and Z, each with a variable number of elements. Preceding the data for each array is an integer *header control* record that gives the count of elements in that array. The data used to produce the output for this illustration were:

X	Y	Z
12345	12345	12345
7	3	5
41.23	02.97	80.00
27.60	00.75	63.00
30.71	01.58	55.15
99.44		79.49
72.31		24.99
15.01		
10.88		

2. MAIN produces a report that shows the three sorted arrays in columnar fashion. (The output is included in Figure 10-1.)

Note that the library subprogram MAXO is used to determine the number of output lines. Also observe that even though all array elements were initialized to zero in the DATA statement, unwanted zeros were avoided in the output. This was done by suppressing the printing of any array elements beyond the range of the corresponding element count. Finally, notice that the subroutine returns an array, which includes many values. Other types of subprograms can return only one value, as discussed in following sections.

Figure 10-1
Illustration of main-line calling program and subroutine

```fortran
      PROGRAM MAIN
      DIMENSION X(9),Y(9),Z(9)
      DATA X/9*0.00/Y/9*0.00/Z/9*0.00/
C
      OPEN(1,FILE='INPUT')
      OPEN(3,FILE='OUTPUT')
C
      WRITE(3,10)
   10 FORMAT('1',T6,'X',T21,'Y',T36,'Z'///)
C
C INPUT K1 (RECORD COUNT OF ARRAY X) FROM HEADER RECORD
C
      READ(1,5)K1
      DO 100 I=1, K1
         READ(1,7)X(I)
  100 CONTINUE
      CALL SORT(K1,X)
C
C INPUT K2 (RECORD COUNT OF ARRAY Y) FROM HEADER RECORD
C
      READ(1,5)K2
      DO 200 I=1, K2
         READ(1,7)Y(I)
  200 CONTINUE
      CALL SORT(K2,Y)
C
C INPUT K3 (RECORD COUNT OF ARRAY Z) FROM HEADER RECORD
C
      READ(1,5)K3
      DO 300 I=1, K3
         READ(1,7)Z(I)
  300 CONTINUE
      CALL SORT(K3,Z)
C
C OUTPUT ALL 3 ARRAYS WITH NO MORE LINES THAN THERE ARE
C NUMBER OF ELEMENTS IN THE LARGEST ARRAY
C
      MAXMUM = MAX0(K1,K2,K3)
C
C TNE LOOP BELOW IS DESIGNED TO SHOW BLANKS INSTEAD OF
C ZEROS IN ANY UNUSED ARRAY ELEMENTS IN OUTPUT LINES
C
      DO 400 LINE=1, MAXMUM
         IF (LINE .LE. K1) WRITE(3,15) X(LINE)
   15    FORMAT('+',T5,F5.2)
         IF (LINE .LE. K2) WRITE(3,17) Y(LINE)
   17    FORMAT('+',T20,F5.2)
         IF (LINE .LE. K3) WRITE(3,19) Z(LINE)
   19    FORMAT('+',T35,F5.2)
         WRITE(3,21)
   21    FORMAT(1X)
  400 CONTINUE
C
    5 FORMAT(I1)
    7 FORMAT(F5.2)
      STOP
      END
      SUBROUTINE SORT(N,ARRAY)
C
C THIS SUBPROGRAM IS BASED ON THE SORT ROUTINE
C GIVEN PREVIOUSLY IN THE ILLUSTRATIVE ARRAY ROUTINES
C IN THIS BOOK
C
      DIMENSION ARRAY(9)
      L=N-1
      NESTED=N
      DO 11 M=1, L
         NESTED=NESTED-1
         DO 10 I=1, NESTED
            IF(ARRAY(I) .GT. ARRAY(I+1)) THEN
               SAVE=ARRAY(I)
               ARRAY(I)=ARRAY(I+1)
               ARRAY(I+1)=SAVE
            END IF
   10    CONTINUE
   11 CONTINUE
      RETURN
      END
```

```
       X                Y                Z

     10.88             .75            24.99
     15.01            1.58            55.15
     27.60            2.97            63.00
     30.71                            79.49
     41.23                            80.00
     72.31
     99.44
```

10/Subprograms

ONE-STATEMENT MATHEMATICAL FUNCTION SUBPROGRAMS

This section covers one type of subprogram that can be written in FORTRAN by the programmer for his or her own special applications. A one-statement mathematical function subprogram is a part of a main-line or other calling program. It is written in FORTRAN and is included in, and compiled with, the calling program. After compilation, it is stored in a special place and does its job only when "called for" by a statement in a calling program.

When programmers write this type of subprogram, they must compose their own variable name (called a *function*) and also decide how many arguments will be required. An *argument* is defined as an arithmetic expression, the current value of which is used by the subprogram to compute a result. Before this type of subprogram can be used, it must be explicitly described to the computer. The statement used for this purpose is a special type of arithmetic statement commonly called a *function defining statement*, or *arithmetic statement function*, or simply a *statement function*. This statement begins with the programmer-supplied function name by which it is referenced in a calling program. It must follow any specification statements but must precede all executable statements in the calling program.

General description

The general form of a function-defining statement is:

```
|12345|6|7
nnnnn    function(darg₁,darg₂, . . . dargₘ)=ae
```

Legend:

nnnnn	Any unique one- to five-digit integer that species the statement *number*. It is never required but may be used at the programmer's option.
function	A variable name selected by the programmer as the unique name of his or her subprogram.
$(darg_1, \ldots darg_m)$	One or more nonsubscripted variable names enclosed in parentheses and separated by commas. They are selected by the programmer to serve as *dummy arguments*.
=	A required separator.
ae	Any *arithmetic expression*, which must include each independent variable name that serves as a dummy argument (subscripted variable names are not permitted). It specifies the operation to be performed when the function is referenced in the calling program.

Dummy arguments

The arguments in a function-defining statement are called *dummy arguments*. They are used to indicate how many arguments are required when the subprogram is "called for" by the main program. Each dummy argument must be unique in the statement in which it appears but may be used as a dummy argument in more than one function-defining statement or even as a variable name outside the function-defining statement. When a subprogram is "called for," actual arguments are substituted for the dummy arguments. The actual and dummy arguments must correspond in number, mode, and sequence.

The calling program and subprogram transfer values to each other. The current value of an actual argument in the calling program is transferred to the subprogram where it becomes the current value of a dummy argument. After the subprogram has completed its job, the current value of the function is transferred back to the calling program.

Illustrative examples

To illustrate, assume that Mary and John Smith are writing a long program that requires three very similar IF statements. Each must appear many times in different places in the program. The arithmetic expressions required for the three IF statements, identical except for the first variable, are:

$$(A+Q+R+S+T+U+V+W)$$
$$(B+Q+R+S+T+U+V+W)$$
$$(C+Q+R+S+T+U+V+W)$$

Assume further that each time the IF statements appear in the program, the variable names have different values. Rather than prepare many long IF statements, they could prepare their own subprogram with the following statement:

|12345|6|7
```
    SMITH(X)=X+Q+R+S+T+U+V+W
```

The function (programmer-supplied name) of the subprogram is SMITH. The dummy argument is X, and it appears first in the series of variable names instead of A, B, or C. The function, followed by an actual argument substituted for the dummy argument, is used to "call for" the subprogram. For example:

|12345|6|7
```
    IF(SMITH(A)) . . .
    IF(SMITH(B)) . . .
    IF(SMITH(C)) . . .
```

In the first IF statement, the current value of the actual argument (A) will be substituted for the current value of the dummy argument (X) in the subprogram expression. Thus, the current value of the function SMITH will be evaluated as follows:

$$A+Q+R+S+T+U+V+W$$

Similarly, B and C will be substituted for the dummy argument in the other examples.

A function-defining statement may include one or more other functions. A partial program, which includes three dummy arguments in one FORTRAN-supplied function, is illustrated below:

|12345|6|7
```
       SMITH(X,Y,Z)=Y+R*SQRT(X**4.0)*(Y/(6.0+Z))
     2 ZAP=X+SMITH(A,B,C)
```

When statement number 2 is executed, the current values of the actual arguments A, B, and C will be substituted for the current values of the dummy arguments X, Y, and Z respectively. Thus, ZAP will be computed by evaluating the following arithmetic expression:

$$X+B+R*SQRT(A**4.0)*(B/(6.0+C))$$

The dummy argument X may appear in statement number 2 because it may be used as a variable name *outside* the function-defining statement. Note, however, that A is substituted for X only where it appears in the subprogram expression.

A program may include as many "arithmetic functions" as the programmer desires (within the capacity of the computer). These subprograms may be included in any main-line program or in any FUNCTION or SUBROUTINE subprogram (described in this chapter). Arithmetic functions are useful for a limited number of applications, but for those applications they can be a very useful tool for getting the job done. They should be used whenever appropriate.

FUNCTION SUBPROGRAMS

The type of subprogram covered in this section is a separate subprogram rather than a part of the calling program. It may contain many statements and is similar in appearance to a complete independent program, so the computer must be told that it is a subprogram rather than a main line. The statement used to make this declaration is the FUNCTION statement. A subprogram that includes this statement is technically termed a *FUNCTION Subprogram*. To distinguish it from a one-statement function subprogram, which is *implied* to be a subprogram, a more descriptive term might be *Declared-FUNCTION Subprogram*. Like other types of subprograms previously described, it is "called for" by a unique variable name (function). It is designed to return one value to the calling program.

General description

A general description of a FUNCTION Subprogram follows.

1. It is written in FORTRAN. The programmer must select a unique variable name to serve as the function. The function must appear in the subprogram as well as in the calling program which references it. The programmer must also specify one or more dummy arguments. Actual and dummy arguments must agree in number, mode, and sequence. An *argument* is defined as an arithmetic expression, the current value of which is used by the subprogram to compute the result.

2. It may include a whole series of statements designed to compute one result, which becomes the current value of the function in the calling program. In fact, it may be almost the same as a complete and independent program.
3. The first statement must be a FUNCTION statement. The keyword declares it to be a function subprogram.
4. When control passes to a subprogram, it executes independently of the calling program. Thus, the variable names and statement numbers may be the same as those in the calling program. (They must, of course, be unique within the subprogram.)
5. It may include subscripted variable names and dummy arrays. The dummy arrays must be defined and dimensioned because the subprogram operates independently of the calling program. DIMENSION statements should appear at the beginning of the program following the FUNCTION statement, which must always be first.
6. It must include a statement that sets the current value of the function to the desired result before control is returned to the calling program.
7. The mode of the current value returned to the function in the calling program can be specified in two ways: (1) implicitly by the first letter of the variable name that serves as the function, or (2) by preceding the keyword FUNCTION in the first statement of the subprogram with the specification INTEGER, REAL, or DOUBLE PRECISION.
8. The computer must be told when to terminate execution of the subprogram and return the result to the calling program because the number of statements is not set and can vary. The STOP statement is the last statement executed in a complete independent program. Instead of a STOP, a counterpart called a RETURN statement is used in this type of subprogram (one RETURN statement is required, but more than one may be included). The RETURN statement terminates execution of the subprogram and returns control to the calling program. One or more STOP statements may also be included in a subprogram. In fact, they are sometimes required by the program logic. Execution of a STOP statement will, of course, terminate execution of the main line as well as all related subprograms.
9. The subprogram does not have a set number of statements and is compiled independently of the calling program. The terminal point, therefore, must be indicated by an END statement.

Two special types of statements are required for this type of subprogram. A general description of each type follows.

The FUNCTION statement

A FUNCTION subprogram must begin with a FUNCTION statement. The general form is:

```
|12345|6|7
nnnnn    type FUNCTION function(darg₁,darg₂, . . . dargₘ)
```

Legend:	
nnnnn	Any unique one- to five-digit integer that specifies the statement *number*. It is never required, but it may be used at the programmer's option.
type	May be used at the programmer's option to specify the mode of the current value returned to the function of the calling program. It is omitted if the mode is implied by the first letter of the function. The type may be either INTEGER, REAL, or DOUBLE PRECISION. If the mode is not implied, it must also be indicated in the calling program by a specification statement. The calling program and subprogram operate independently, but both use the same function name; thus, the mode must be implied or specified in both.
FUNCTION	A keyword that specifies a FUNCTION subprogram.
function	A variable name selected by the programmer to serve as the unique name of his or her subprogram. It must also be included in some other statement in the subprogram that sets the current value of the function to the desired result before control is returned to the calling program. Like any other unique variable name, it may appear more than once in the subprogram.
$(darg_1, \ldots darg_m)$	One or more subscripted variable names enclosed in parentheses and separated by commas. They are selected by the programmer to serve as *dummy arguments*.

The RETURN statement

A RETURN statement terminates execution of the subprogram and returns control to the calling program, which may be another subprogram or the main line. When control is returned to the calling program, one value is also returned. The calling program then continues executing. The RETURN statement indicates the logical terminal point in the subprogram; and if it is omitted, no value can be returned. A STOP statement can also be included in a subprogram, but the execution of a STOP statement terminates the execution of the main line as well as all related subprograms. The FUNCTION subprogram ordinarily does not contain a STOP statement because its usual purpose is to perform some type of calculation and then return the result to the calling program.

The general form of a RETURN statement is:

```
|12345|6|7
 nnnnn   RETURN
```

Legend:	
nnnnn	Any unique one- to five-digit integer that specifies the statement *number*. It is required only if referenced by another statement in the subprogram. It may always be used at the programmer's option.
RETURN	A key word specifying the type of statement.

Illustrative examples

To start with an elementary example, a subprogram to multiply pi (3.14159) times a variable name that appears in the calling program is used to demonstrate the general structure of a FUNCTION Subprogram:

```
|12345|6|7
      FUNCTION SMITH(X)
      SMITH=X*3.14159
      RETURN
      END
```

The function (programmer-supplied variable name) of the subprogram is SMITH. The dummy argument is X, which is also included in the arithmetic statement that establishes the current value of the function before control is returned to the calling program. Note particularly that the dummy argument must appear in the arithmetic statement to the right but not to the left of the equal sign.

The function, followed by an actual argument, is used to "call for" the subprogram. The following example illustrates two "calls" to the previously illustrated subprogram, which is repeated here for clarity:

```
          Main line                        Subprogram
|12345|6|7                          | 12345|6|7
      .                                   FUNCTION SMITH(X)
      .                                   SMITH=X*3.14159
      A=1000.00                           RETURN
      ANS=SMITH(A)                        END
      .
      .
      IF(SMITH(A).NE.1.)STOP
```

The current value of A (the *actual* argument) in the calling program will be substituted for the current value of X (the *dummy* argument) in the subprogram. Thus, the current value of the function SMITH will be evaluated as follows:

$$A*3.14159$$

After the evaluation is completed, the result will be stored at the function SMITH in the subprogram. Next, the RETURN statement will cause this result to be transferred back to the calling program where it will become the current value of the function SMITH. The calling program then will continue executing statements in the normal manner. Note that the calling program and the subprogram transfers values to each other. First the calling program sends 1000.00 to the subprogram, which, in turn, sends 3141.59 back. On the first call, this returned value is stored at ANS; on the next call, this returned value stops the program. The calling program is a main line, but it could be another subprogram. FUNCTION subprograms and SUBROUTINE subprograms (discussed in an earlier section) may call each other. There must, however, always be one main line with overall control.

The preceding example is not very practical because it is easier to solve the problem by including the constant 3.14159 directly in the calling program. It is presented to illustrate the general form and function of a FUNCTION subprogram. A more practical illustration is presented next.

The following subprogram (named TOTAL) will compute the sum of all values stored in an array. Because the subprogram operates independently of the calling program, the dummy array must have its own DIMENSION statement. (If two- or three-dimensional arrays are used, some computers require that the actual and dummy arrays be described as the same size.)

```
|12345|6|7
      FUNCTION TOTAL(ARRAY,NUMELM)
      DIMENSION ARRAY(500)
      TOTAL=0.0
      DO 7 INDEX=1,NUMELM
          TOTAL=TOTAL+ARRAY (INDEX)
    7 CONTINUE
      RETURN
      END
```

Now suppose the calling program has several actual one-dimensional arrays, all properly dimensioned and established. It is desired to compute the sum of an array named ZEBRA, which contains 100 elements, and to compute the average (arithmetic mean) of any array called CAMEL, which contains 300 elements. The following partial calling program can be used:

```
|12345|6|7
      . . .
      KOUNT=100
      NUMBER=300
      SUM=TOTAL(ZEBRA,KOUNT)
      AVE=TOTAL(CAMEL,NUMBER)/300.0
```

How does the subprogram dummy array (ARRAY) get the current values of the elements in the two actual arrays (ZEBRA and CAMEL)? They are supplied automatically by the calling program. Remember, the current value of an argument is always sent to a subprogram; if the argument is an array variable name, the entire array is sent. Note that this type of subprogram can receive many values, but it can return only one.

The FUNCTION subprogram has only two minor restrictions. It cannot contain a SUBROUTINE statement (covered in another section), and it cannot have more than one FUNCTION statement. Thus, it can be used for almost any purpose including reading and writing.

It is emphasized again that it may not be necessary for the programmer to write his or her own subprograms. The computer center may have many that have already been written by someone else and that might be used to the programmer's advantage. It has been stated before but is worth repeating: "Don't reinvent the wheel."

SUMMARY

A brief summary of each type of subprogram follows:

Type	Supplied by programmer	Basic features	Name composition
Library functions	No	Provided by FORTRAN; one value returned	Provided by FORTRAN
One-statement mathematical functions	Yes	Limited to one arithmetic statement; one value returned	Same rules as other variable names; mode of name determines mode of value returned
FUNCTION	Yes	Generally four or more statements (including END); one value returned	Same rules as other variable names; mode of name determines mode of value returned
SUBROUTINE	Yes	Generally, four or more statements (including END); may return more than one value	Same rules as other variable names; mode of name has no significance

THE COMMON STATEMENT

In previous sections of this chapter, arguments were used to transfer values to and receive values from subprograms. As stated, the purpose of an argument is to make data available to a called subprogram by indicating explicitly an independent or array variable name that specifies the location of the data the subprogram is to work with. When arguments are used to pass values back and forth, the actual transfer takes place at *execution* time.

If a program includes several programmer-supplied subprograms, each of which requires the transfer of many values, long strings of arguments repeatedly listed can be tedious and subject to error. To eliminate the necessity of listing arguments each time a subprogram is called, FORTRAN provides another shortcut. A COMMON statement can be used to tell the subprogram at *compilation* time where the data will be located when the subprogram is called. Arguments to provide this information are neither required *nor allowed* because the subprogram already "knows" the location of data at execution time. In effect, the arguments are *implied*. When a COMMON statement is used, a program will execute faster because argument data are not passed back and forth at execution time.

The COMMON statement is a specification statement that is nonexecutable. It must precede any executable statements in the program or subprogram in which it appears. Its general form is:

```
|12345|6|7
nnnnn    COMMON vn₁(ne₁ₐ,ne₁ᵦ,ne₁c), . . . vnₘ(neₘₑ,neₘᵦ,neₘc)
```

Legend:

nnnnn	Any unique one- to five-digit integer that specifies the statement number. It is never required, but it may be used at the programmer's option.
COMMON	A keyword that identifies the type of statement.
$vn_1, \ldots vn_m$	One or more independent or array variable names that this statement will assign to a special common block of storage in the order in which they are listed.
$(ne_{1a}, \ldots ne_{1c})$	One, two, or three unsigned integer numbers representing the *number of elements* in a one-, two-, or three-dimensional array. These numbers are omitted when an independent variable name is used. They are also omitted when an array variable name is used if the array has been assigned dimensions by a preceding DIMENSION or an explicit specification statement.

As previously stated, the same variable name, such as DEMO, may be used in two or more different subprograms without conflict because the compiler will assign a different *actual* storage location to DEMO for each subprogram in which it appears. The programmer can tell the compiler that DEMO has a common meaning and should be assigned the same actual storage location by including the following statement in *each* subprogram in which DEMO appears:

```
|12345|6|7
         COMMON DEMO
```

Like the EQUIVALENCE statement, the COMMON statement causes storage to be shared; however, these two statements are used for different situations. EQUIVALENCE is used when two or more different variable names in the *same* program or subprogram are to share the same storage location; COMMON is used when two or more variable names in *different* subprograms (or in the main line and one or more different subprograms) are to share the same storage location. The special storage area reserved by the COMMON statement is sometimes called the *COMMON block*.

More than one variable name may be listed in a COMMON statement. For example, if the following statement is included in *each* of two different subprograms:

```
|12345|6|7
         COMMON ABLE,BAKER
```

ABLE in one subprogram will be assigned the same area in the COMMON block as ABLE in the other subprogram; likewise, BAKER in one will share storage with BAKER in the other. The same results will be obtained if the sequence of the variable names is reversed:

|12345|6|7
          COMMON BAKER,ABLE

In this case, the sequence of the variable names in the COMMON statement must be the same in both subprograms because the compiler associates the first variable name in one subprogram to the first variable name in the other subprogram and, likewise, the second to the second.

The preceding examples illustrate cases in which storage space was to be shared by the *same* variable names. The COMMON statement can also be used to cause storage to be shared by *different* variable names. Assume, for example, that the first subprogram includes this statement:

|12345|6|7
          COMMON A,B,C

and the second subprogram this one:

|12345|6|7
          COMMON X,Y,Z

The preceding two statements specify that the variable names A, B, and C in the first subprogram are to share storage with X, Y, and Z in the second; A will share with X, B with Y, and C with Z. It should be noted that the first subprogram may include the variable names X, Y, and Z in other statements without conflict. Because these variable names are not specified in the COMMON statement of the first subprogram, they will *not* share storage with X, Y, and Z in the second. They can be made to share storage with X, Y, and Z in the second as well as A, B, and C in the first, by including an appropriate EQUIVALENCE statement in the first subprogram.

A COMMON statement may include independent and/or array variable names. If an array name is included, it must be assigned dimension in either this statement or in a preceding DIMENSION or implicit specification statement. (As a general rule, an array must be assigned dimension in the first statement in which its name appears. The only exception to this rule is that the name of a dummy array must appear in a FUNCTION or SUBROUTINE statement before it is assigned dimension.) The following two statements:

|12345|6|7
          DIMENSION ARRAY(100)
          COMMON ARRAY

can be replaced by this single statement:

```
|1|2|3|4|5|6|7
        COMMON ARRAY(100)
```

The programmer may elect to use different statements to assign dimensions to different arrays as illustrated below:

```
|1|2|3|4|5|6|7
        DIMENSION X(50)
        REAL N(100)
        COMMON A(200),N,X
```

Now, the effects of the COMMON statement will be illustrated by an elementary example. Assume the following partial main-line program:

```
|1|2|3|4|5|6|7
        COMMON A,B,C
        B=1.0
        C=2.0
        CALL SUB
        Z=C*2.0
        WRITE(3,99)Z
     99 FORMAT(F4.1)
        STOP
        END
```

and the following subprogram:

```
|1|2|3|4|5|6|7
        SUBROUTINE SUB
        COMMON A,Y,Z
        A=3.0
        Z=A+Y
        RETURN
        END
```

If the COMMON statements were omitted in the preceding illustration, it would be necessary to include the arguments A, B, and C in the CALL statement and A, Y, and Z in the SUBROUTINE statement. Note that B and C in the main line as well as Y and Z in the subprogram are initialized by arithmetic statements in the main line. A in the main line and A in the subprogram, however, are both initialized in the subprogram. Execution of the second arithmetic statement in the subprogram (Z=A+Y) will cause the current value of Z in the subprogram and C in the main line to be changed to 4.0, but Z in the main line is not affected because it does not share storage with any other variable name. Likewise, execution of the final arithmetic statement in the main line (Z=C*2.0) will initialize Z in the main line to 8.0 but will not change the current value of Z in the subprogram.

The preceding illustration included only one CALL statement, so the programming convenience of using COMMON statements (instead of arguments) to pass information back and forth was not clearly demonstrated. It should be obvious, however, that the COMMON statement can provide quite a shortcut when many calls are made.

In all previous illustrations in this section, an equal number of variable names was always listed in the corresponding COMMON statements; that is, if three variable names were specified as COMMON in the main line, for example, three were also specified as COMMON in the subprogram. This practice was followed because it was assumed that the data sharing storage were always the same type. It is possible to store different types of data in the same place (but not at the same time), in which case the number of variable names in the corresponding COMMON statements will not necessarily be equal. Before illustrating this point, the manner in which data are stored will be briefly reviewed.

The COMMON statement reserves a special area of storage called a *COMMON block*. Data are stored in this COMMON block in the sequence in which the independent variable names appear in the COMMON statement. Suppose a double-precision floating point value may be represented by 64 contiguous bits, but a single-precision (real) or integer value may be represented by 32. Internal storage is divided into groups of *bits*; each group of, say, eight bits is called a *byte*; and each byte is considered to be one storage location because it is the smallest addressable unit of storage. So, stated another way, a double-precision value may be stored in eight contiguous locations, but a single-precision or integer value may be stored in only four.

To illustrate how integer data are stored in a COMMON block, assume that I and J are independent variable names and K is a four-element array. The following statement:

```
|12345|6|7
      COMMON I,J,K(4)
```

may reserve 24 storage locations in the COMMON block. I will be assigned the first four locations, J the next four, the first element of the K array the next four, the second element the next four, etc.

Now that the necessary background has been developed, a more complex application will be illustrated. Assume that a COMMON block is reserved by a calling program and its three subprograms. The following statements appear in the calling program:

```
|12345|6|7
      DOUBLE PRECISION X,Y
      COMMON X,Y
```

The next statement appears in the first subprogram:

```
|12345|6|7
      DOUBLE PRECISION Z
      COMMON Z,A,B
```

the following in the second subprogram:

|12345|6|7
     REAL I,J
     COMMON C,D,I,J

and the following in the third subprogram:

|12345|6|7
     COMMON K(3),L

Figure 10-2 illustrates the manner in which the COMMON block will be shared.

Figure 10-2
Illustrative COMMON block shared by a calling program and its three subprograms

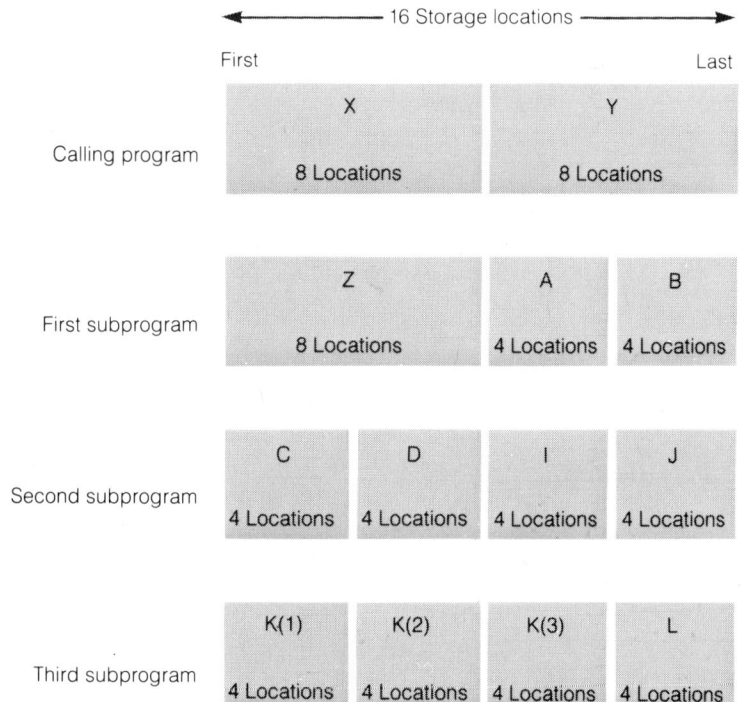

Note that X in the calling program shares storage with Z in the first subprogram, with C and D in the second, and with K(1) and K(2) in the third. The calling program may validly reference X or Z, but even though C and D, as well as K(1) and K(2), share the same storage, they cannot be referenced by the calling program. Variable names sharing the same storage can be validly referenced only by a program or subprogram that uses corresponding locations to store the *same types of data*. Thus, in these preceding illustrations, the calling program can reference X, Y, and Z, the first subprogram can reference A and B, as well as I and J (which were included in a REAL statement), etc.

As illustrated, the COMMON statement is very powerful, but it must be used with caution. When a change is made in a COMMON statement, either directly or indirectly (such as a change in a DIMENSION, explicit specification, or EQUIVALENCE statement), extreme care must be taken to see that all corresponding COMMON statements are changed accordingly.

THE POWER OF SUBPROGRAMS

The first section of this chapter covered the "built-in" subprograms provided by FORTRAN. As indicated, these subprograms are already compiled and ready to go. They are usually stored on a high-speed external device such as a magnetic disk drive where they are almost instantaneously available to a calling program. It is emphasized that other types of subprograms can also be stored on magnetic disk, for example, where they are available to any calling program similar to the "built-in" subprograms provided by FORTRAN. This makes it possible for a very short "skeleton-type" main program to call a subprogram that will solve a complete problem.

For instance, a program to compute the weekly payroll can be written as a subprogram that performs the complete job, then compiled and stored so it is available to a short calling program. Subprograms can also be used as calling programs. To carry this almost to the extreme, each Friday a short calling program can call a subprogram named FRIDAY which, in turn, can call other subprograms which will execute several or all jobs required for that day. This is not as simple as it may appear, but it demonstrates the power of subprograms.

Subroutines can be particularly useful when long and/or complex programs are written. The problem may be segmented into several distinct logical parts, and different programmers assigned to each part. After developing, debugging, and testing the program in segments, the various parts may then be joined together by a calling program to solve the complete problem. Advanced techniques are also available that permit long programs to be segmented into subroutines, which, in turn, may be written in languages other than FORTRAN but which may be called by a FORTRAN calling program. This technique permits various programming specialists to combine their efforts to solve complex problems.

Finally, this book is designed to serve as both a text and reference manual for beginning FORTRAN programmers. No attempt has been made to include all there is to be known about the language. It is recommended that the appropriate ANSI publications and manufacturers' manuals be referred to for more advanced applications.

REVIEW QUESTIONS

1. Distinguish between a main-line program and a subprogram.

2. In general, what advantages do subprograms offer?

3. In general, what types of problems are library functions designed to solve?

4. Distinguish between (*a*) intrinsic or in-line, and (*b*) external or out-of-line library functions.

5. In what ways do library functions and arithmetic statement functions differ? In what ways are they similar?

6. Which is probably more commonly used, library functions or arithmetic statement functions? Discuss.

7. Distinguish between the RETURN and END statements. Also, distinguish between the RETURN and STOP statements.

8. Why is an END statement required for FUNCTION and SUBROUTINE subprograms but not required for arithmetic function subprograms?

9. What types of subprograms can FUNCTION subprograms call? What types can SUBROUTINE subprograms call?

10. Which is probably more commonly used, FUNCTION or SUBROUTINE subprograms? Discuss.

11. Compare and contrast COMMON and EQUIVALENCE statements.

12. Four general types of subprograms are covered in this chapter. Describe how each is "called."

EXERCISES

1. One of the library functions is MOD, which requires two integer arguments. The first is divided by the second; the value returned is not the quotient but the *remainder* from the integer division. Study the following series of statements:

LEAPYR=0
IF(MOD(NYEAR,4).EQ.0)LEAPYR=1

Describe the effects of these statements and a practical use.

2. Study the following series of statements:

```
    DIMENSION ID(100),MF(100)
    DO 40 K=1,100
        MF(K)=MOD(ID(K),2)
40  CONTINUE
```

Describe the effects of these statements and a practical use.

3. A straightforward sort routine, which is a slight variation of an illustration in Chapter 8, is given below. Assume that the routine works (it does, but don't be distracted by the logic). Examine the routine carefully. Code the exact statements that will convert it into a subprogram and indicate their location in the subprogram. Also, write a statement that will "call" your subprogram from an assumed main-line program.

```
        DO 100 J=2,N
            DO 90 K=1,J
                IF(ARRAY(J).GE.ARRAY(K))GO TO 90
                SAVE=ARRAY(J)
                ARRAY(J)=ARRAY(K)
                ARRAY(K)=SAVE
90          CONTINUE
100     CONTINUE
```

4. Consider the following main line and subroutine carefully. Describe the main-line output.

```
    A=2.0                       SUBROUTINE SUB(A,X,J)
    B=3.0                       A=X+FLOAT(J)
    K=4                         J=J+1
    CALL SUB(A,B,4)             RETURN
    X=A*B                       END
    L=K+4
    WRITE(3,80)A,B,X,K,L
80  FORMAT(1X,3F5.1,2I3)
    STOP
    END
```

PROBLEMS

1. Select any complete FORTRAN program that you have previously written and convert it into a SUBROUTINE subprogram. Write a mainline program that will call in and execute your subprogram. Leave a STOP statement in your subprogram so that control cannot return to the main line. Test for this condition by including a statement in the main line which will write a brief message if control does return.

2. This simple problem requires a main line and three subprograms. Write the main line so it will (a) write the literal 1ST MESSAGE; (b) call a subprogram that will (i) read an input card containing the value 144, (ii) extract the square root of this value by using another subprogram, and (iii) write the result, (c) write the literal 2ND MESSAGE; (d) call a subprogram which will write the literal SUB MESSAGE; and (e) write the literal 3RD MESSAGE.

3. Write a main line program that will allow for as many as 1,000 input cards, but use a header card to indicate that only 10 input cards are to be processed. Design your own input test deck; each card should contain a four-position student number field and a three-position test score field. Use two different subprograms to return a value to the main line; one must calculate the mean (arithmetic average) of the test scores, and the other must count the number of scores that exceed the mean. Also use one subprogram that may perform any task you might choose. Output should be identified and should include each student number, each test score, the mean, the number of scores greater than the mean, and some value or literal to indicate that a subprogram was used.

4. Select an available "canned program" at your computer center that is of interest to you. Use it to process a set of data records you are to prepare.

Appendix A
Debugging techniques

Detecting and correcting programming errors is a process called *debugging*. Fortunately, the programmer can get substantial help from both the compiler and the computer system in locating any errors encountered during compilation or execution. A program may have to be rerun several times before it is completely "checked out." Reruns may save hours of debugging, but it is the programmer's responsibility that each run will be helpful. The purpose of this appendix is to discuss the debugging process in general and to explain and illustrate various debugging techniques. A few more advanced techniques are discussed in the final section of Chapter 8.

THE DEBUGGING PROCESS

If the appropriate system control records (see Appendix C) are used, the source program will be listed (printed) by the high-speed printer. Any violation of the rules of FORTRAN will cause compilation to terminate, but the compiler will cause diagnostic messages and error summaries to be listed also. These messages and summaries should be used by the programmer to detect the type of error and its exact or general location within each listed statement. After any and all errors encountered during compilation are debugged, the source program can be compiled into an object program and storage maps listed on the printer. The compiler's job is now complete, and control will pass from the compiler to the computer system. If the program is to be compiled and executed in the same run, it will be *linkage edited* and ready for the next processing step, which is execution of the object program.

An object program can be terminated during esecution in several ways. It may be terminated, for example, by power failure, machine malfunction, operator intervention, or by an automatic timing device. It can also be terminated automatically as a result of a programming error that makes it impossible for the computer to execute the object program. When this latter type of error is encountered, the computer system (and the compiler) will generate and list an error code indicating

Appendix A/Debugging Techniques

the reason for the termination. This error code should be used to detect both the type of error and the type of statement being executed at the time the program failed. After any and all errors encountered during execution of the object program are debugged, the program can be executed.

After the program has been executed, the programmer must carefully examine the output to determine if it provides the correct solution to the problem to be solved. Even though the program has been compiled and executed, it may require more debugging. The programmer may not have allowed for all possibilities or may have committed other logic errors. Errors in programming logic can cause a variety of results. The output, for example, may be from the wrong device or it may contain incorrect data; it is also possible that no output can be produced by the program. Correcting logic errors can be the most difficult step in the debugging process.

To summarize, the debugging process requires locating and correcting, in order, any:

1. Errors terminating compilation.
2. Errors terminating execution.
3. Errors in programming logic.

Each of these three types of programming errors is discussed and illustrated in turn in the pages that follow.

ERRORS TERMINATING COMPILATION

If the programmer violates the rules of FORTRAN, the compiler will flag all incorrect statements and cause diagnostic messages to be included in the program listing. The messages are brief but self-explanatory. They vary according to the compiler used but are illustrated here to indicate what to look for. Two types of messages can be generated—statement error messages and summary messages.

Statement error messages

If a statement violates a rule of FORTRAN, both the type and general location of the violation are indicated within the program listing.

On the line below a violation, the compiler used for most illustrations in this appendix causes a dollar sign to be printed, which acts as a pointer to indicate where the violation was encountered by the compiler. The actual error of omission or commission will usually be found in the exact location or immediately preceding or following the location indicated by the dollar sign. (Some computers substitute arrows for dollar signs.)

On the line below the dollar sign pointing to the general location of the violation, a diagnostic message may be printed indicating the type of error encountered by the compiler.

The compiler scans the statements from left to right searching for violations of the rules of FORTRAN. It should be noted that it will always detect and indicate the first violation in a statement but may not indicate any or all additional violations. It should also be noted that detection of the first *violation* does not necessarily mean detection of the first *error*. For example, suppose the statement:

|12345|6|7
      READ(1,7)A,B,C,D,E,F,G

was incorrectly written with five of the six required commas omitted:

|12345|6|7
      READ(1,7)A B C D E F,G

Embedded blanks are permitted in variable names, so no violation has occurred; thus no error would be indicated. But if the sixth comma were also omitted, there would be a violation; the compiler would cause a dollar sign and a statement error message such as NAME LENGTH to be listed.

Because the compiler may indicate only the *first* violation, any statements with error indications should be carefully checked for additional violations and errors.

Summary messages

All summary messages appear at the end of the program listing. They identify errors the compiler cannot associate with any particular statement. A valid statement, for example, may reference another statement such as statement number 17. If no statement in the program is numbered (labeled) 17, the compiler cannot determine the statement the programmer intended to reference. In this case, a diagnostic summary message such as UNDEFINED LABELS will appear at the end of the program listing. This message is followed by a list of all undefined labels referenced in the program.

Debugging illustration program—first run

The program that follows (Figure A-1) contains a variety of errors that might be encountered by the programmer (explained in the table following it). This same program, after debugging, is illustrated again (Figures A-4 and A-5) in the last section of this appendix. The illustrative program is supposedly designed to:

1. Compute the regular, bonus, and total pay for 10 employees.
2. Compute the total pay for all employees.
3. Print the output complete with descriptive colunar headings.

The input file contains 11 records. The first 10 contain the integer code 1, 2, or 3 to indicate the amount of bonus for the individual employee.

Code	Amount of bonus
1	Double the regular pay
2	Equal to the regular pay
3	One-half the regular pay

Figure A-1
Illustrative debugging program containing error messages*

```
              C     DEBUGGING ILLUSTRATION PROGRAM
              C         *** 1ST RUN ***
              C
              C     THIS  1ST RUN  ILLUSTRATES
              C     SOME OF THE MANY DIAGNOSTIC
              C     ERROR MESSAGES WHICH CAN BE
              C     GENERATED BY THE COMPILER.
              C     BECAUSE THIS PROGRAM CONTAINS
              C     ERRORS,IT CAN NOT COMPILE AND
              C     THUS CAN NOT EXECUTE OR
                    PRODUCE ANY OUTPUT.
                  $
01) SYNTAX
              C
                  1 FORMAT(//4X,'EMP',T29,'REGULAR',
                   1T47,'TOTAL')
                  2 FORMAT(7H    NO.,T10,'HOURS',T17,
                   1'RATE',T23,'CODE',T30,'PAY',T38,
                                                   $
01) SYNTAX
                    'BONUS',T48,'PAY'/)
                                    $
01) SYNTAX
                  3 FORMAT(I5,2F6.2,I2)
                  4 FORMAT(I6,T9,F6.2,T15,F6.2,T24,I2
                   1,T28,F7.2,T37,F7.2,T46,F7.2)
                  5 FORMAT(T33,'GRAND TOTAL',T45,F8.2)
                  6 WRITE(3,1)
                  7 WRITE(3,2)
                  8 FINALTOT=0.00
                                $
01) NAME LENGTH
                  9 KOUNT=0
                 10 READ(1,333),NUMEMP,HOURS,RATE,KODE
                                $
01) SYNTAX
                 11 REGPAY=HOURS*RATE.
                                    $
01) SYNTAX
                 12 GO TO(13,15,17,22)KODE
                                       $
01) COMMA

                 13 BONUS=REGPAY*2.00
               A14 GO TO 18
                $
01) SYNTAX
                 15 BONUS=REGPAY
                 21 GO TO 18 NOW
                              $
01) SYNTAX
                    BONUS=REGPAY/2.00
                $
01) LABEL
                 18 TOTPAY=REGPAY+BONUS
                 19 WRITE(3,444)NOEMP HOURS,RATE,KODE
                                     $
01) NAME LENGTH
                   1REGPAY,BONUS
                              $
01) NAME LENGTH
                 20 FINTOT+TOTPAY=FINTOT
                                       $
01) SYNTAX
                 21 GO TO 10
                   $
```

Figure A-1 *(continued)*

```
01) DUP. LABEL
          22 WRITE(3,5)FINTOT
         111 FORMAT(F7.1
                         $
01) SYNTAX
         112 FORMAT(F7.1 F9.0)
                         $
01) SYNTAX
         113 FORMAT(I5,F6.2,E6.2,D7.5,1234E+04))
                         $
01) SYNTAX
         114 UP=DOWN
         115 GO TO 1
                         $
01) ILLEGAL LABEL
          12 STOP
                $$
01) DUP. LABEL          02) NO END CARD


                             UNDEFINED LABELS
      00333        00017        00444
```

* Error messages the illustrative debugging program (Figure A-1) contains, in sequence of these statement errors, are explained in the table below.

Statement number	Cause of error indication
None	Column 1 does not contain the letter C to indicate that this is a *comment* rather than a statement.
2, Continuation 1	Close (rightmost) parenthesis is missing.
2, Continuation 2	No continuation character in Column 6. This also caused the preceding error indication.
8	FINALTOT exceeds six characters in length.
10	Comma not allowed preceding first variable name.
11	Period (or decimal point) not allowed.
12	Comma omitted preceding KODE. The compiler flagged this as an error but ANSI Standards allow this optional omission.
A14	Alphabetic letter not permitted in statement number.
21	Variable name not permitted following a completed statement.
None	Any statement following an unconditional GO TO, IF, RETURN, or STOP statement must have a number (label) or it cannot be referenced or executed. *LABEL is a statement error message that does not terminate compilation.* It serves as a warning that the program contains a statement that cannot be executed.
19	Comma omitted between variable names. The computer assumes only one name that exceeds six characters in length because embedded blanks are permitted in variable names.
19, Continuation 1	Comma omitted following KODE on first line of statement number 19. Computer assumes REGPAY is a continuation of KODE, thus the variable name exceeds six characters in length.
20	Arithmetic statement in improper form (reversed).
21	This statement number (label) has appeared earlier in the program.
111	Close (rightmost) parenthesis omitted.
112	Comma omitted between format codes.

Appendix A / Debugging Techniques 295

113	This is a tricky error to detect. The first format code begins with the number "one" instead of the letter "I." This statement contains additional violations that were not indicated by the compiler.
114	No error is indicated because the statement is correctly written. It is included here to indicate that a meaningless statement, if it is in proper form, is not detected.
115	Statement number (label) 1, references a FORMAT statement instead of an executable statement.
12	Two errors are indicated: (1) statement number (label) 12 has appeared in a previous statement in the program, and (2) the program does not contain an END statement.

The last record in the input file contains the integer code 4. This record is used to cause a branch to statement number 22, which will WRITE the total pay for all 10 employees.

Statements numbered 111, 112, 113, 114, and 115 are not related to the problem. They are included only for the purpose of illustrating additional errors in the program. An explanation of each error message immediately follows Figure A-1.

Following the program listing, one summary message appears. It indicates that statement numbers 333, 17, and 444 were referenced in the program, but no statements are numbered as such.

Figure A-1 illustrates the type of error messages generated by IBM "F-level" compilers. As previously indicated, the manner in which errors are indicated, as well as the wording of explanatory messages, differs according to the compiler used. More powerful compilers generate more useful messages and may also correct some types of minor programming errors. For an example of output from more powerful compilers, refer to Figure A-2, which was processed by an IBM "G-level" compiler, and to Figure A-3, which was processed by a WATFIV compiler.

ERRORS TERMINATING EXECUTION

Errors causing termination of a program at the time of *compilation* were covered in the preceding section. This section is limited to errors causing termination at the time of *execution*.

If a program is terminated automatically because of an error occurring during execution of a FORTRAN program, the compiler will cause a message to be written on SYSLST (printer). The purpose of the message is to indicate the reason for termination. The form and content of this "diagnostic" varies from compiler to compiler; the message may be self-explanatory, but more typically it is limited to a concise code.

Error Codes

A complete written list of execution error codes with explanations should be available at any computer center using FORTRAN language.

Figure A-2
Illustrative debugging program processed by an IBM "G-level" compiler

```
              C     DEBUGGING ILLUSTRATION PROGRAM
              C         *** 1ST RUN ***
              C
              C     THIS  1ST RUN  ILLUSTRATES
              C     SOME OF THE MANY DIAGNOSTIC
              C     ERROR MESSAGES WHICH CAN BE
              C     GENERATED BY THE COMPILER.
              C     BECAUSE THIS PROGRAM CONTAINS
              C     ERRORS,IT CAN NOT COMPILE AND
              C     THUS CAN NOT EXECUTE OR
     0001           PRODUCE ANY OUTPUT.
                $
***********01)  IEY013I SYNTAX**********************************************
     0002         1 FORMAT(//4X,'EMP',T25,'REGULAR',
                 1T47,'TOTAL')
     0003         2 FORMAT(7H    NO.,T10,'HOURS',T17,
                 1'RATE',T23,'CODE',T30,'PAY',T38,
                                                                          $
***********01)  IEY013I SYNTAX**********************************************
     0004         'BONUS',T48,'PAY'/)
                $
***********01)  IEY013I SYNTAX**********************************************
     0005         3 FORMAT(I5,2F6.2,I2)
     0006         4 FORMAT(I6,T9,F6.2,T15,F6.2,T24,I2
                 1,T28,F7.2,T37,F7.2,T46,F7.2)
     0007         5 FORMAT(T33,'GRAND TOTAL',T45,F8.2)
     0008         6 WRITE(3,1)
     0009         7 WRITE(3,2)
     0010         8 FINALTOT=0.00
                $
***********01)  IEY003I NAME LENGTH*****************************************
     0011         9 KOUNT=0
     0012        10 READ(1,333),NUMEMP,HOURS,RATE,KODE
                $
***********01)  IEY013I SYNTAX**********************************************
     0013        11 REGPAY=HOURS*RATE.
                                                                          $
***********01)  IEY013I SYNTAX**********************************************
     0014        12 GO TO(13,15,17,22)KODE
                $
***********01)  IEY004I COMMA***********************************************
     0015        13 BONUS=REGPAY*2.00


     0015        A14 GO TO 18                                       1ST ONLY
                $
***********01)  IEY013I SYNTAX**********************************************
     0016        15 BONUS=REGPAY
     0017        21 GO TO 18 NOW
                $
***********01)  IEY013I SYNTAX**********************************************
     0018           BONUS=REGPAY/2.00
     0019        18 TOTPAY=REGPAY+BONUS
     0020        19 WRITE(3,444)NOEMP HOURS,RATE,KODE
                $
***********01)  IEY003I NAME LENGTH*****************************************
                 1REGPAY,BONUS
                $
***********01)  IEY003I NAME LENGTH*****************************************
     0021        20 FINTOT+TOTPAY=FINTOT
                $
***********01)  IEY013I SYNTAX**********************************************
     0022        21 GO TO 10
                $
***********01)  IEY006I DUPLICATELABEL**************************************
     0023        22 WRITE(3,5)FINTOT
     0024       111 FORMAT(F7.1
                                                                          $
***********01)  IEY013I SYNTAX**********************************************
     0025       112 FORMAT(F7.1 F9.0)
                $
***********01)  IEY013I SYNTAX**********************************************
     0026       113 FORMAT(I5,F6.2,E6.2,D7.5,1234E+04))
                $
***********01)  IEY013I SYNTAX**********************************************
     0027       114 UP=DOWN
     0028       115 GO TO 1
                $
***********01)  IEY005I ILLEGAL LABEL***************************************
     0029        12 STOP
                $   $
***********01)  IEY006I DUPLICATELABEL*********02)  IEY015I NO END CARD*****

                            IEY022I   UNDEFINED LABEL
       333                     17                 444
```

Appendix A / Debugging Techniques   297

Figure A-3
Illustrative debugging program processed by a WATFIV compiler

```
            C      DEBUGGING ILLUSTRATION PROGRAM
            C           *** 1ST RUN ***
            C
            C      THIS 1ST RUN ILLUSTRATES
            C      SOME OF THE MANY DIAGNOSTIC
            C      ERROR MESSAGES WHICH CAN BE
            C      GENERATED BY THE COMPILER.
            C      BECAUSE THIS PROGRAM CONTAINS
            C      ERRORS,IT CAN NOT COMPILE AND
            C      THUS CAN NOT EXECUTE OR
     1             PRODUCE ANY OUTPUT.
            C
***ERROR***  UNDECODEABLE STATEMENT
     2        1 FORMAT(//4X,'EMP',T29,'REGULAR',
                1T47,'TOTAL')
     3        2 FORMAT(7H    NO.,T10,'HOURS',T17,
                1'RATE',T23,'CODE',T30,'PAY',T38,
***ERROR***  NO CLOSING RIGHT PARENTHESIS
     4           'BONUS',T48,'PAY'/)
***ERROR***  UNDECODEABLE STATEMENT
***ERROR***  FIRST CHARACTER OF THE STATEMENT WAS NOT ALPHABETIC
***ERROR***  NO CLOSING QUOTE OR NEXT CARD NOT CONTINUATION CARD
     5        3 FORMAT(I5,2F6.2,I2)
     6        4 FORMAT(I6,T9,F6.2,T15,F6.2,T24,I2
                1,T28,F7.2,T37,F7.2,T46,F7.2)
     7        5 FORMAT(T33,'GRAND TOTAL',T45,F8.2)
     8        6 WRITE(3,1)
     9        7 WRITE(3,2)
    10        8 FINALTOT=0.00
**WARNING**  NAME FINALTOT IS TOO LONG TRUNCATED TO SIX CHARACTERS
    11        9 KOUNT=0
    12       10 READ(1,333),NUMEMP,HOURS,RATE,KODE
***ERROR***  EXPECTING OPERATOR BUT ) BEFORE , WAS FOUND
    13       11 REGPAY=HOURS*RATE.
***ERROR***  ILLEGAL USE OF DECIMAL POINT.UNEXPECTED . BEFORE END-OF-STATEMENT
    14       12 GO TO(13,15,17,22)KODE
***ERROR***  MISSING OPERATOR.UNEXPECTED KODE
***ERROR***  EXPECTING OPERATOR BUT END-OF-STATEMENT WAS FOUND
    15       13 BONUS=REGPAY*2.00
    16      A14 GO TO 18
***ERROR***  INVALID CHARACTERS IN COL 1-5. STATEMENT NUMBER IGNORED.PROBABLE CAUSE
             STATEMENT PUNCHED TO LEFT OF COLUMN 7
    17       15 BONUS=REGPAY
    18       21 GO TO 18 NOW
***ERROR***  EXPECTING OPERATOR BUT NOW    WAS FOUND
    19          BONUS=REGPAY/2.00
**WARNING**  UNNUMBERED EXECUTABLE STATEMENT FOLLOWS A TRANSFER
    20       18 TOTPAY=REGPAY+BONUS
    21       19 WRITE(3,444)NOEMP,HOURS,RATE,KODE
                1REGPAY,BONUS
**WARNING**  NAME NOEMPHOURS   IS TOO LONG TRUNCATED TO SIX CHARACTERS
**WARNING**  NAME KODEREGPAY   IS TOO LONG TRUNCATED TO SIX CHARACTERS
    22       20 FINTOT+TOTPAY=FINTOT
***ERROR***  ILLEGAL QUANTITY ON LEFT OF EQUALS SIGN
    23       21 GO TO 10
***ERROR***  STATEMENT NUMBER     21 HAS ALREADY BEEN DEFINED
    24       22 WRITE(3,5)FINTOT
    25      111 FORMAT(F7.1
***ERROR***  NO CLOSING RIGHT PARENTHESIS
    26      112 FORMAT(F7.1 F9.0)
    27      113 FORMAT(I5,F6.2,E6.2,D7.5,1234E+04))
***ERROR***  INVALID USE OF COMMA.  5,F6.  IS INVALID
    28      114 UP=DOWN
    29      115 GO TO 1
***ERROR***  THIS STATEMENT TRANSFERS TO     1,WHICH IS NON-EXECUTABLE
    30       12 STOP
***ERROR***  STATEMENT NUMBER     12 HAS ALREADY BEEN DEFINED
**WARNING**  MISSING END STATEMENT END STATEMENT GENERATED
**WARNING**  FORMAT STATEMENT    3 IS UNREFERENCED
**WARNING**  FORMAT STATEMENT    4 IS UNREFERENCED
***ERROR***  MISSING FORMAT STATEMENT   333 USED IN LINE    12
***ERROR***  MISSING STATEMENT NUMBER    17 USED IN LINE    14
***ERROR***  MISSING FORMAT STATEMENT   444 USED IN LINE    21
**WARNING**  FORMAT STATEMENT  111 IS UNREFERENCED
**WARNING**  FORMAT STATEMENT  112 IS UNREFERENCED
**WARNING**  FORMAT STATEMENT  113 IS UNREFERENCED
             $ENTRY

CORE USAGE     OBJECT CODE=   1160 BYTES,ARRAY AREA=    0 BYTES,
               TOTAL AREA AVAILABLE=  131536  BYTES

DIAGNOSTICS    NUMBER OF ERRORS=      20, NUMBER OF WARNINGS=   10,
               NUMBER OF EXTENSIONS=       0

COMPILE TIME=  0.92 SEC,EXECUTION TIME=   0.00 SEC,
               WATFIV - VERSION 1 LEVEL 3 MARCH 1971
```

The error codes probably most often encountered by beginning programmers who use IBM "F-Level" compilers are:

Code number	Type of error	Explanation
212	Data	The computer has been instructed to read more characters from a record than it actually contains. If cards are used for data input, the FORMAT statement specifies more than 80 positions. This error often occurs as a result of miscounting when X instead of T format codes are used to ignore input fields.
216	Program	The computer has been instructed to read from a device that can be used for output only. Check READ statements. The device number specified is assigned to a printer, punch, or other output-only device.
217	Program	The computer has been instructed to write on a device that can be used for input only. Check WRITE statements. The device number specified is assigned to a card reader or other input-only device.
218	Program	The specified device number of a FORTRAN logical unit is not between 1 and 15 inclusive. Check READ and WRITE statements. Possibly device number and FORMAT number are reversed.
219	Data	An end-of-file condition has occurred on an I/O device. The computer has been instructed to read or write a record but has found no record in proper format in the device specified. Check programming logic for loop control. Computer may have returned to a READ command after all records have been read. If program specifies the number of times to return to the READ, perhaps some data cards are missing. If header card or trailer card technique is used, perhaps header or trailer card contains incorrect data or the data are not contained in the fields indicated by the FORMAT statement.
223	Data	An input or output record contains an invalid character according to the FORMAT specification. Perhaps the error is in the FORMAT statement specification rather than in the data.
225	Data	An interruption has occurred during execution of an arithmetic statement. Check arithmetic statements. Perhaps a variable name has been misspelled or has been improperly initialized. Maybe mode of input data does not agree with input format codes.
214	Data	The computer has been instructed to perform an exponentiation and has found the base equal to zero or has found the exponent to be negative or zero. Examine arithmetic expressions containing an integer base raised to an integer power.
242	Data	The computer has been instructed to perform an exponentiation and has found the base equal to zero or has found the exponent to be negative or zero. Examine arithmetic expressions containing a single-precision (real) base raised to an integer power.
243	Data	The computer has been instructed to perform an exponentiation and has found the base equal to zero or has found the exponent to be negative or zero. Examine arithmetic expressions containing a double-precision base raised to an integer power.

| 244 | Data | The computer has been instructed to perform an exponentiation and has found the base equal to zero or has found the exponent to be negative or zero. Examine arithmetic expressions containing a floating point (real) base raised to a real power. |
| 245 | Data | The computer has been instructed to perform an exponentiation and has found the base equal to zero or has found the exponent to be negative or zero. Examine arithmetic expressions containing a double-precision base raised to a floating point (real) power. |

ERRORS IN PROGRAMMING LOGIC

After a program has been debugged of all errors indicated by the compiler, it can be compiled; after it has been debugged of all errors indicated by the computer system, it can be executed. After it is executed, however, the output may not provide a proper solution to the problem to be solved. The program may require more debugging to correct and eliminate logic errors committed by the programmer. This can be the most difficult step in the debugging process. The problem to be solved, the source program, and the output produced (if any) must be analyzed carefully to determine the cause of the invalid output. This requires an understanding of the effect of each statement in the source program as well as some sound reasoning by the programmer.

Detecting logic errors

If an executed program produces no output, the first step should be to examine the source program to determine why a WRITE statement was not executed. Whenever a WRITE statement containing a list of variable names that references a valid FORMAT statement is executed, there will always be some output even though it may be garbage.

If invalid output is produced, the first step should be to check the input data file, if any, to determine if it contains complete and correct data (as the saying goes: "garbage in, garbage out"). Next, the input data file should be compared to the appropriate READ and FORMAT statements to determine if they agree. After the programmer is assured that valid input was properly read in, the next step should be to examine the program logic.

The variety of reasons why an executed program can produce invalid results is almost infinite. In general, the program may (1) include incorrect, incomplete, or improper statements, (2) include improperly sequenced statements, and (3) omit required statements. Perhaps the best approach to use in detecting logic errors is first to examine carefully the output and then to determine why it was produced by examining the source program.

If the output is supposed to contain several fields, it is usually preferable to debug one field at a time. Assume, for example, that the output statement was WRITE (3,100)A,B,C,D,E and that all output fields contained invalid data. One of the fields, for example A, should be selected to be debugged first. The programmer should use the source program to follow the sequence of execution of all statements containing the variable name A. Some programmers prefer to work backward through the program, starting with the WRITE statement. All nonexecutable statements describing the A field should also be examined. After debugging the A field error, the other fields should be selected one at a time and similarly debugged. Quite often, the correction of one source of error will correct several or all additional errors, but occasionally it can create other problems.

The reason for some output errors can be quite obvious. If the output was written by the wrong device, for example, the WRITE statement referenced the incorrect device number; if a series of output fields are in improper sequence, the FORMAT and/or WRITE statements are incorrect; if printed output drops the first character and/or line spacing is incorrect, the FORMAT statement does not provide proper line spacing control.

The computer system can help the programmer detect some types of logic errors. One or more asterisks may appear in an output field if the format code does not provide sufficient field length for the output or if the WRITE statement contains an undefined variable name.

Most logic errors are not easy to detect, particularly those occurring in arithmetic and control statements. Typical arithmetic statement errors include improper operational signs, improper sequence of operations, and an incorrect or incomplete formula for the problem to be solved. Typical control statement errors include not allowing for all possibilities, improper branching and improper loop control. If a bug is particularly difficult to find, someone should be asked for help. Quite often a programmer becomes so involved with a problem that he or she overlooks an obvious cause of the trouble.

To summarize, the compiler can be used to detect all violations of the rules of FORTRAN; the computer system will detect all errors occurring during execution; but the programmer must detect logic errors. Good programming comes from experience, and experience— well, that comes from poor programming!

Debugging illustration program— second run

To illustrate the effect of logic errors, the same program used to illustrate compiler-generated error messages in the first section of this appendix (Figure A-1) is used again. The second run of this program (Figure A-4) has been debugged of all violations of the rules of FORTRAN, and all unnecessary statements have been removed. The program has been compiled and executed, but it contains invalid output.

Correcting logic errors The following step-by-step explanation illustrates one method of locating and correcting the logic errors that caused the invalid output in Figure A-4:

1. All 10 lines of the "Emp. no." output field contain an asterisk in each of the five columns of the field.
    a. An examination of the input data reveals they are complete and correct. The employees are numbered consecutively 1 through 10, and the input data were properly read in.

Appendix A/Debugging Techniques

Figure A-4
Illustrative debugging program containing logic errors

```
C    DEBUGGING ILLUSTRATION PROGRAM
C        *** 2ND RUN ***
C
C    THIS  2ND RUN  HAS BEEN
C    DEBUGGED OF ALL  1ST RUN
C    ERRORS INDICATED BY THE
C    COMPILER AND UNECESSARY
C    STATEMENTS REMOVED. IT WILL
C    COMPILE AND EXECUTE BUT
C    OUTPUT WILL BE INVALID
C    BECAUSE OF PROGRAMMING
C    LOGIC ERRORS.
C
     1 FORMAT(//4X,'EMP',T29,'REGULAR',
      1T47,'TOTAL')
     2 FORMAT(7H       NO.,T10,'HOURS',T17,
      1'RATE',T23,'CODE',T30,'PAY',T38,
      2'BONUS',T48,'PAY'/)
     3 FORMAT(I5,2F6.2,I2)
     4 FORMAT(I6,T9,F6.2,T15,F6.2,T24,I2
      1,T28,F7.2,T39,F5.2,T46,F7.2)
     5 FORMAT(T33,'GRAND TOTAL',T45,F8.2)
     6 WRITE(3,1)
     7 WRITE(3,2)
     8 FINTOT=0.00
     9 KOUNT=0
    10 READ(1,3)NUMEMP,HOURS,RATE,KODE
    11 REGPAY=HOURS*RATE
    12 GO TO(13,15,17,22),KODE
    13 BONUS=REGPAY*2.00
    14 GO TO 18
    15 BONUS=REGPAY
    16 GO TO 18
    17 BONUS=REGPAY/2.00
    18 TOTPAY=REGPAY+BONUS
    19 WRITE(3,4)NOEMP,HOURS,RATE,KODE,
      1REGPAY,BONUS
    21 GO TO 10
    20 FINTOT=FINTOT+TOTPAY
    22 WRITE(3,5)FINTOT
    23 STOP
       END
```

Output from above program

EMP NO.	HOURS	RATE	CODE	REGULAR PAY	BONUS	TOTAL PAY
*****	40.00	2.00	1	80.00	*****	
*****	40.00	2.00	2	80.00	80.00	
*****	40.00	2.00	3	80.00	40.00	
*****	38.50	4.74	2	182.49	*****	
*****	41.25	6.00	2	247.50	*****	
*****	36.00	2.00	1	72.00	*****	
*****	18.50	1.30	1	24.05	48.10	
*****	40.50	2.00	3	81.00	40.50	
*****	32.00	3.50	3	112.00	56.00	
*****	20.00	1.00	1	20.00	40.00	
				GRAND	TOTAL	0.0

  b. The output format code (I6) indicates a field length of five columns because the first character of the first field is dropped when a printer is used for output. This field length is more than adequate for the output data.

  c. The WRITE statement uses NOEMP as the variable name. The only other statement in the program using the employee number is the READ statement where the variable name is spelled differently (NUMEMP). Thus, the output is invalid because the WRITE statement includes an undefined variable name. Stated another way, the computer does not know the current value of NOEMP because it has not been told by the program. This error can be corrected by changing the variable name to NUMEMP in the WRITE statement, by changing the variable name to NOEMP in the READ statement, or by changing both the READ and WRITE statements to include the same, but differently spelled, valid integer variable name such as NUMBER. As a matter of practicality, it is easier to change one statement than two; in this case, it is easier to change the WRITE statement because, as indicated below, it requires another change as the result of another error.

2. The "Bonus" field also contains an asterisk in each of the five columns of the output field (F5.2) but only in 4 of the 10 printed lines.

  a. An examination of the output reveals that the amount of BONUS is correct for 6 of the 10 printed lines. The next step is to determine why four lines contain invalid output.

  b. An analysis of the problem and the source program indicates that any employee with a bonus code of 1 should earn a $100 bonus if his or her regular pay is $50. The output reveals that the four lines containing invalid data each correspond to an employee who earned in excess of $100 in bonus. Thus, the error is in the format code (I5) because it does not provide adequate space for output that exceeds 99.99 (five positions).

This error can be corrected by changing the format code. (It should be noted that changing one format code may require several others to be changed, including the format codes for the column headings. In this case, only one format code requires a change.)

3. The "Total pay" field contains no output data for any of the 10 employees. An examination of the WRITE statement immediately reveals the reason; the last name in the WRITE list is BONUS. This error can be corrected by adding the variable name TOTPAY to the end of the WRITE list.

4. The "Grand total" is also invalid.

  a. An examination of the output indicates that the WRITE statement was executed because the literal GRAND TOTAL and the value 0.0 were printed.

  b. A careful examination of the source program reveals that

FINTOT was initialized to zero but was not incremented as each employee's card was processed. This error was caused by an unconditional GO TO statement preceding the arithmetic statement that was to do the incrementing. This error can be corrected simply by changing the sequence of two statements; statement number 20 should precede rather than follow statement number 21. The programmer should be very cautious when the sequence of a statement in the source deck is changed, because one such change may necessitate many more changes in other statements. In some cases, a whole series of statements may have to be renumbered, and control statements may have to be changed to reference different statements.

Debugging illustration program— final run

Figure A-5 illustrates the same program used throughout this appendix after all logic errors have been debugged. The resulting output provides the correct solution to the problem to be solved.

Figure A-5
Illustrative debugging program after final debugging

```
C     DEBUGGING ILLUSTRATION PROGRAM
C           *** FINAL RUN ***
C
C     THIS  FINAL RUN HAS BEEN
C     DEBUGGED OF ALL LOGIC ERRORS
C     CONTAINED IN THE  2ND RUN.
C     THE OUTPUT WILL BE CORRECT.
C
    1 FORMAT(//4X,'EMP',T29,'REGULAR',
     1T47,'TOTAL')
    2 FORMAT(7H    NO.,T10,'HOURS',T17,
     1'RATE',T23,'CODE',T30,'PAY',T38,
     2'BONUS',T48,'PAY'/)
    3 FORMAT(I5,2F6.2,I2)
    4 FORMAT(I6,T9,F6.2,T15,F6.2,T24,I2
     1,T28,F7.2,T37,F7.2,T46,F7.2)
    5 FORMAT(T33,'GRAND TOTAL',T45,F8.2)
    6 WRITE(3,1)
    7 WRITE(3,2)
    8 FINTOT=0.00
    9 KOUNT=0
   10 READ(1,3)NUMEMP,HOURS,RATE,KODE
   11 REGPAY=HOURS*RATE
   12 GO TO(13,15,17,22),KODE
   13 BONUS=REGPAY*2.00
   14 GO TO 18
   15 BONUS=REGPAY
   16 GO TO 18
   17 BONUS=REGPAY/2.00
   18 TOTPAY=REGPAY+BONUS
   19 WRITE(3,4)NUMEMP,HOURS,RATE,KODE,
     1REGPAY,BONUS,TOTPAY
   20 FINTOT=FINTOT+TOTPAY
   21 GO TO 10
   22 WRITE(3,5)FINTOT
   23 STOP
      END
```

Figure A-5 *(continued)*
Output from preceding program

EMP NO.	HOURS	RATE	CODE	REGULAR PAY	BONUS	TOTAL PAY
1	40.00	2.00	1	80.00	160.00	240.00
2	40.00	2.00	2	80.00	80.00	160.00
3	40.00	2.00	3	80.00	40.00	120.00
4	38.50	4.74	2	182.49	182.49	364.98
5	41.25	6.00	2	247.50	247.50	495.00
6	36.00	2.00	1	72.00	144.00	216.00
7	18.50	1.30	1	24.05	48.10	72.15
8	40.50	2.00	3	81.00	40.50	121.50
9	32.00	3.50	3	112.00	56.00	168.00
10	20.00	1.00	1	20.00	40.00	60.00
					GRAND TOTAL	2017.63

Appendix B
Interactive terminal operation for FORTRAN programming

There are many different terminal configurations that can be used for time-sharing access to a central computer system or as input/output to a microprocessor. Each of these configurations has a keyboard by which programs or data may be entered. Most also have a cathode ray tube (CRT) scope for visual display. Display can also be obtained from a printing device. However, because of the higher cost of printers, terminals often consist only of a CRT and a keyboard, or several such terminals may share one printer. The terminal configuration that is assumed for this appendix is a keyboard and a CRT.

In spite of the diversity of terminals and of the computer-operating software with which they are used, there are basic operations that are common to all terminals. The following sections present these basic operations used for on-line FORTRAN programming.

SIGNING ON

1. Be sure that the power to the terminal is on and that the various device switches are appropriately set.
2. Depress the appropriate keyboard key to send an initiating signal to the computer's operating software. This tells the system that you are ready to start.
3. Note that the operating software will start sending you messages and questions displayed on the CRT. This starts the interaction between the computer and you.
4. Respond to the messages and questions when the prompt symbol (e.g., question mark, carat, slash) appears on the CRT. The operating software will ask you for information such as account number, password, and system desired.
5. Depress the RETURN key to transmit a line of information to your allotted computer working storage area.

Courtesy IBM Corporation.

CREATING A PROGRAM FILE OR A DATA FILE

1. Prepare and "desk check" your new program and data *before* signing on the terminal. It is a costly waste of terminal time to compose programs and data on-line.
2. Tell the operating software that you are going to input a program or a data file and give the file a name.
3. Set the tabs. A recommended tab setting for *program* lines is position 7 for the start of a FORTRAN line and positions 10, 13, 16, etc., for indentation of nested DOs and IF-THEN-ELSE structures.
4. Key in the program or data lines. If you detect an error as you are keying a line, depress the BACKSPACE key. The information stored in every position over which you backspace is deleted. If the entire line is to be removed, depress the DELETE key.
5. Depress the RETURN key to enter the line into your working storage area.
6. Key in the command that saves the program (or data) by taking it from your working storage and placing it permanently into a disk storage area. The program (or data) is now stored as a disk file and can be referenced by its name. Note that you can store permanent disk files for three practical purposes:
   a. You can, when you are keying in a lengthy program or set of

data, periodically store the lines permanently so that if there is a computer system malfunction, you will not have to restart from the beginning.
  b. You may enter part of the program (or data) into permanent storage and complete the rest later.
  c. You can store the entire program (or data) for later compilation and execution.

MODIFYING A PROGRAM FILE OR A DATA FILE

1. Tell the system to get your stored program (or data) disk file. If the file is currently in working storage, skip this step.
2. Call the edit (i.e., text editor) system.
3. Locate the line in the file you want to modify. You can locate a line by knowing:
   a. Its line number within the file.
   b. Its relative position from the file's starting line.
   c. Its relative position from the file's ending line.
   d. Its relative position from the "current" line. The current line is the last line displayed on the CRT.
4. Display one or more lines that you want to examine for possible error and modification. There are commands that can stop and resume the display at any time.
5. Modify the lines in error. Depending on the type of edit command given, the modification can be made to the current line, to a group of lines, or to the entire file. Some of the general modification commands are as follows: (Note that the term *character group* denotes a string of *one or more* contiguous characters.)
   a. Add a character group into one or more lines.
   b. Add one or more new lines before or after the current line.
   c. Replace a character group with a different character group in one or more lines.
   d. Replace one or more lines, with the same number of lines, before or after the current line.
   e. Delete a character group from one or more lines.
   f. Delete one or more lines before or after the current line.
6. Make sure that the modifications were done correctly. Then replace the old, permanent disk file with the newly modified file.

DELETING A PROGRAM FILE OR A DATA FILE

1. Delete the content (but not the name) of a permanent disk file and replace the content with a working storage file.
2. Delete the old permanent file name by assigning it a new file name. Although the file content is the same under the new file name, the old file name no longer exists for retrieval.
3. Purge the name and content of a program (or data) file from permanent disk storage. Be careful not to purge a file that you may need later.

4. Purge the program (or data) file in working storage either by giving a specific command to do this, or by not saving it (in a permanent disk file) before signing off.

COMPILING A PROGRAM
1. Retrieve the program file from disk if it is not already in working storage.
2. Compile the program, carefully examine the results, and correct any errors before you attempt execution. You can stop and restart compilation at any time with the appropriate commands.

EXECUTING A PROGRAM
1. Retrieve the program and data files from disk if they are not already in computer working storage.
2. Execute your compiled FORTRAN program. You may print the source listing and execution results by giving the appropriate commands. You can stop and restart the program execution at any time with the appropriate commands.
3. Modify the program and data files, as appropriate, if errors exist.

SIGNING OFF
1. Release the terminal by issuing the proper termination command. Before you do this, make sure that any newly created or modified file (that you wish to retain) has been permanently stored on disk.
2. Follow any shutdown procedures that are required for your terminal.

Appendix C
System control commands

System control commands direct the overall operations of the computer. They serve as a sort of operations manager in the sense that they tell the computer what to do and when to do it. For example, they may specify the beginning of a job and identify the program and/or programmer. They might next call for a specific compiler that will use the source program written in FORTRAN (or some other computer language) to generate an object program. They may then direct the computer to execute this object program. They may, of course, be used to specify numerous other tasks that are beyond the scope of this appendix. Beginning programmers need not be concerned with all the details of system control commands but should know their general purpose. As previously stated, they tell the computer what to do and when to do it.

Computer systems operate on a *job* basis. A job consists of all system control commands, all FORTRAN statements and comments, and all input data records (if any) needed by the computer to perform a given task. System control are written in a special language commonly called *job control language* or, more simply, JCL. Unlike FORTRAN, which is device independent, JCL varies according to the computer. Furthermore, the specific required commands (commonly called JCLs) are determined by the specific installation and may be changed according to local needs and desires; that is, installations with identical computers may require different JCLs. The reader is therefore cautioned to determine local requirements before submitting jobs for processing.

One purpose of this brief appendix is to describe the purpose of JCLs. Another is to distinguish between and to illustrate the interrelationship of JCLs, FORTRAN programs, and input data records. The general concept is the same, regardless of the computer used. This is demonstrated in the following section where four different job control languages are illustrated.

JOB COMPOSITION

Here is the job composition required at one particular type of installation:

```
// JOB PAYROLL   735-3100 DONALD H. FORD
// OPTION LIST,LINKNODUMP,LOG
// EXEC FORTRAN
             .
             .
             .
       FORTRAN source program
             .
             .
             .
/*
// EXEC LNKEDT
// EXEC
             .
             .
             .
     Input data records (if any)
             .
             .
             .
/*
/&
```

Another installation requires the following job composition:

```
// PAYROLL   JOB 7653100,FORD.D.H.
// STEPNAME EXEC FORTGCG
// FORT.SYSIN DD *
             .
             .
             .
       FORTRAN souce program
             .
             .
             .
// GO.SYSIN DD *
             .
             .
             .
     Input data records (if any)
             .
             .
             .
//
```

Another installation has the following requirements:

```
JOBNAME.
USER(usernum,password)
BANNER.    BIN=NN   (where NN is a bin number from 1 to 30)
BANNER.    Student Name
FTN5(GO)
```

Appendix C / System Control Commands

    7/8/9   (7 8 9 multipunched in column 1)

                            FORTRAN source program

    7/8/9   (7 8 9 multipunched in column 1)

                          Input data records (if any)

    7/8/9   (7 8 9 multipunched in column 1)
    6/7/8/9   (6 7 8 9 multipunched in column 1)

Note that the three previous illustrations have different JCLs, but their general concepts are the same. Each illustration starts with a JOB statement that indicates the beginning of a job and identifies the programmer. A subsequent JCL identifies the compiler being called; e.g., FORTRAN, FORTGCG, and FTN5 (each an acronym for a specific FORTRAN compiler). The same JCL, e.g., FTN5(GO), or a later JCL, e.g., EXEC and GO, declares that the program should be executed. The source program, of course, precedes the input data records. A final JCL indicates the job end.

The number of JCLs in the foregoing illustrations varied from five to nine. Some installations and applications require more, others less. Sometimes the first JCL will indicate the beginning of a job and, at the same time, imply the end of the preceding job as well as imply the specific compiler to be called. Perhaps the only other JCL required will direct the computer to execute the program. For example, installations using a WATFIV compiler may require a job composition similar to this final illustration:

    $JOB PAYROLL   765311 FORD.D.H.

            FORTRAN source program

    $ENTRY

            Input data records (if any)

Appendix D
Library functions

There are two types of built-in mathematical function subprograms. *Intrinsic* functions are part of the FORTRAN compiler. Those listed in this appendix are common to *all* standard installations. *External* functions are not part of the compiler but, for programming purposes, are treated as if they were. They are stored in a computer system library and are common to *most* installations. Specific installations may remove from their library some of those in the basic list. They may also expand their library to include a variety of additional functions to meet their specific needs.

As indicated above, for programming purposes both types are used in the same way. Either type is called for by using its unique variable name as explained in Chapter 10. The complete collection of built-in mathematical function subprograms is commonly called *library functions*. Local computer center reference manuals will provide a complete list of their library functions. Some common standard library functions are included in Table D-1.

Table D-1
Intrinsic mathematical functions

Name of function	Explanation	Number of arguments	Type of argument	Type of value returned
IABS	Absolute value of argument	1	Integer	Integer
ABS		1	Real	Real
DABS		1	Double-precision	Double-precision
FLOAT	Convert integer to real	1	Integer	Real
IFIX	Convert real to integer	1	Real	Integer
ISIGN	Transfers sign of second argument to absolute value of first	2	Integer	Integer
SIGN		2	Real	Real
DSIGN		2	Double-precision	Double-precision

Table D-1 *(continued)*

Name of function	Explanation	Number of arguments	Type of argument	Type of value returned
IDIM DIM	Difference of arguments made possible	2 2	Integer Real	Integer Real
SNGL}	Most significant part of double-precision argument made real	1	Double-precision	Real
MOD AMOD DMOD	Modular arithmetic —value of first argument modulus the second (remaindering)	2 2 2	Integer Real Double-precision	Integer Real Double-precision
AINT DINT	Sine of argument times absolute value of largest argument (truncation)	1 1	Real Double-precision	Real Double-precision
MAX0 MAX1 AMAX0 AMAX1 DMAX1	Largest value of the arguments	2 or more 2 or more 2 or more 2 or more 2 or more	Integer Real Integer Real Double-precision	Integer Integer Real Real Double-precision
MIN0 MIN1 AMIN0 AMIN1 DMIN1	Smallest value of the arguments	2 or more 2 or more 2 or more 2 or more 2 or more	Integer Real Integer Real Double-precision	Integer Integer Real Real Double-precision
EXP DEXP	Natural anti-logarithm of argument (e raised to the argument power)	1 1	Real Double-precision	Real Double-precision
ALOG DLOG	Natural logarithm of argument	1 1	Real Double-precision	Real Double-precision
ALOG10 DLOG10	Common logarithm of argument	1 1	Real Double-precision	Real Double-precision
TAN DTAN	Arctangent of argument in radians	1 1	Real Double-precision	Real Double-precision
SIN DSIN	Trigonometric sine of argument in radians	1 1	Real Double-precision	Real Double-precision
COS DCOS	Trigonometric cosine of argument in radians	1 1	Real Double-precision	Real Double-precision
SQRT DSQRT	Square root of argument	1 1	Real Double-precision	Real Double-precision
TANH DTANH	Hyperbolic tangent of argument in radians	1 1	Real Double-precision	Real Double-precision

Index

A

A format code, 88
ABS, 43, 312
AINT, 313
Algorithm, 23
ALOG, 313
ALOG10, 313
Alphanumeric, 51, 53
AMAX0, 313
AMAX1, 313
American National Standards Institute, Inc., 5
AMIN0, 313
AMIN1, 313
AMOD, 313
AND, 144-45
Annotation symbol, 27
Apostrophes, literal within, 109-10
Arguments
  actual, 262, 266, 274-75
  dummy, 268, 273, 275
Arithmetic expressions, 60-64, 141
  evaluation of, 61
  mode, 63
  rules for writing, 60-64
Arithmetic IF statement, 133-41
Arithmetic operation, hierarchy of, 61
Arithmetic operators, 54
Arithmetic statements, 58-66
  equals sign in, 59
  general form, 58-59
  mixed mode, 64
Array variable name, 208, 243, 250
Arrays
  arrangement in storage, 231, 246, 251
  dimensioning, 209-11, 243, 250
  dummy, 270, 276
  elements, 207
  illustrative routines, 218-26, 247-50, 252-53
  subscripting, 208, 243, 250
Assignment statements, 58, 74

B

BACKSPACE, 43
Batched mode processing, 15-16
Binary digit, 12
Bit, 12
Blank
  character, 41
  format code; see X format code in statements, 51, 71, 89, 99, 106
Branching, 121
Bugs; see Errors
Built-in arithmetic functions, 261-66, 312-13

C

CALL, 43, 267
CALL statement, 267
Calling program, 261, 266-67, 273, 275
Card
  code, 17-18
  column, 16
  data, 82-83
  description, 16-17
  field, 18-19
  file, 19
  FORTRAN program, 44-47
  punch device, 8
  reader device, 8
  record, 19, 82-83
  row, 16
Carriage control, 99
CHARACTER, 43, 73
CHARACTER statement, 73-74
Characters
  alphabetic, 41
  carriage control, 99
  numeric, 41
  special, 41
  valid FORTRAN, 41
Codes
  alphabetic characters, 17-18
  carriage control, 99
  device, 91, 94
  format, A, 88
  format, D, 89
  format, E, 89
  format, F, 86
  format, H, 108
  format, I, 84
  format, / (slash), 102, 106-7
  format, T, 90
  format, X, 89
  Hollerith, 17-18
  numeric characters, 17
  special characters, 18
Coding form, 30
Columns
  array, 242
  card, 16
Comments, 31, 33, 46
COMMON, 43, 281

COMMON—*cont.*
  block, 284-85
  statement, 280-87
Compilation and debugging, 35-36, 290-304
Compilers, 4
Computed GO TO statement, 122-32
Computer languages, 2-4
Computer system, 6-13
Connector symbol, 27
Console, 7
Constants
  double-precision decimal form, 48
  double-precision exponential form, 50
  integer, 47
  real, 48-49
  single-precision decimal form, 48-49
  single-precision exponential form, 49-50
Continuation
  character, 46, 72
  field, 46-47
CONTINUE, 43, 180
CONTINUE statement, 180
Control statements
  CALL, 267
  computed GO TO, 123
  CONTINUE, 180
  DO, 183
  ELSE, 170
  ELSE IF, 173
  END, 118
  END IF, 166
  GO TO, 122
  IF, arithmetic, 134
  IF, logical, 142
  IF THEN, 165
  OPEN, 31
  RETURN, 267, 277
  STOP, 118
  structured programming, 119-21
Controlled loops, 147-51
Core, 10-11
COS, 313
Counting numbers, 44

D

D exponent, 51
D format code, 88
DABS, 43, 312
Data card, 82-83
DATA statement, 70
DBLE, 43
DCOS, 313
Debugging, 35-290-304
Decision symbol, 27
Defensive programming, 151-52
DEFINE, 43
Delimiters, 54-55
Device codes, 91, 94
DEXP, 313
DFLOAT, 43

Diagnostics, 234, 291
DIM, 43, 313
DIMENSION, 43, 209
DINT, 313
Disk drive, 8-10
Disk pack, 8-10
Division, floating point, 48, 65-66, 141
Division, integer, 48, 65-66
DLOG, 313
DLOG10, 313
DMAX1, 313
DMIN1, 313
DMOD, 313
DO, 43, 183
DO loops, 191, 193, 227, 229
DO range, 181, 191-92
DO statement, 183
Documentation, 46
DOUBLE PRECISION, 43, 211
DSIN, 312
DSQRT, 313
DTAN, 313
DTANH, 313
Dummy argument, 268, 273, 275

E

E exponent, 49-50
E format code, 87-88
Elements of an array, 207
Elements of FORTRAN statements, 43-44
ELSE, 43, 170
ELSE IF, 43, 173
END, 35, 43, 118
END IF, 43, 166
END statement, 118-19
ENDFILE, 43
Equal sign meaning, 59
EQUIVALENCE, 43, 211
EQUIVALENCE statement, 211-13
Errors
  coding, 213
  diagnostic messages, 234, 291
  logic, 299-300
  statement messages, 291
  summary messages, 292
  terminating compilation, 291-95
  terminating execution, 295-99
  truncation, 48, 65-66, 141
Executable statements, 41-42
EXIT, 43
Exit, from DO loop, 192
EXP, 313
Exponents, D and E, 49-51
Expression
  arithmetic, 60-64, 141
  in IF statement, 141
  logical, 143-45
EXTERNAL, 43

F

F format code, 86
Field, 18-19

Index

File, 19
FIND, 43
FLOAT, 43, 312
Floating point
  arithmetic, 48, 61-64
  numbers, 48-49
  variable names, 52-53
Flowchart, 25-29
Flowchart symbols, 27
FORMAT, 43
Format codes
  A, 88
  D, 89
  E, 89
  F, 86
  H, 108
  I, 84
  / (slash), 102, 106-7
  T, 90
  X, 89
FORMAT statement, 84
  parentheses in, 84-85, 102, 195
  slashes in, 102-7
FORTRAN, 4-5
  character set, 41
  coding form, 30
  keywords, 43
  supplied subprograms, 261-66, 312-13
FUNCTION, 43
FUNCTION statement, 276
Function subprograms
  declared, 275-80
  FORTRAN-supplied, 261-66, 312-13
  one-statement, 273-75

G

Garbage, 17
GO TO, 43
GO TO statement
  computed, 122-32
  unconditional, 122

H

H format code, 108
Hierarchy of operations, 61
Hollerith (H) code, 108
Hollerith message, 105-9
Horizontal spacing, 99
  overformatting, 112
  T format code, 111
  X format code, 111-12

I

I format code, 84
IABS, 43, 312
IBM card, 16-17
Identification field, 47
IDIM, 43, 313
IF, 43, 134, 142
  arithmetic, 134
  logical, 142
IF block, 165-68
IF-THEN-ELSE, 165-80

IFIX, 43, 312
Implicit definition of mode, 66
Implicit specification statements, 66-68, 211
Index value, 123, 183
Initialization of variable names, 69-70
Input/output
  output image, 98
  statements
    READ, 90, 151, 227, 229-30, 245
    WRITE, 94, 229, 231, 246
  symbol, 27
INTEGER, 43, 211
  arithmetic, 48, 65-66
  constants, 47
  division truncation, 66
  statement, 211
  variable names, 52-53
Intrinsic subprograms, 312
I/O device codes, 90, 94
ISIGN, 43, 312

J-K

Job composition, 309
Key words, 43

L

Label, 44
Library functions, 261-66, 312-13
Line spacing control, 99, 102, 106-7
Literal
  within apostrophes, 109-11
  Hollerith, 108-9
Logic errors, 299-300
Logical IF, 142
Loop control, by
  header card variable, 148
  program constant, 148
  special feature, 150-51
  trailer card variable, 149
Looping, 121, 145-51, 180-82

M

Magnitude, 47-48
Main-line program, 260
Mathematical function subprograms, 261-66, 312-13
MAX0, 313
MAX1, 313
Measuring numbers, 44
MIN0, 313
MIN1, 313
Mixed mode expressions, 63
Mixed mode statements, 64
MOD, 313
Multiple dimensioning, 243, 250
Multiple DO statements, 188
Multiple subscripting, 243, 250

N

Names; see Variable names
Nested DO loops, 188
Nested parenthetical expressions, 63

Nonexecutable statements, 42
NOT, 144-45
Numbers
  counting, 44
  double-precision floating point, 51
  Hollerith code for, 17
  integer, 47
  magnitude, 47-48
  measuring, 44
  real; *see* single-precision floating point, *below*
  single-precision floating point, 48
  statement, 44-45
Numeric characters, 41

O

Object program, 2
One-dimensional arrays, 207-35
OPEN, 31, 43
Operators
  arithmetic, 54
  hierarchy of, 61
  logical, 144
  relational, 143
OR, 144-45
Order, of
  computation, 61
  program statements; *see inside cover*
  storage of array elements, 231, 246, 251
Output; *see* Input/output
Overformatting, 112

P

Paper feed control character, 99, 102, 106-7
Parentheses, in
  arithmetic expressions, 61-62
  FORMAT statement, 84-85, 102, 195
PAUSE, 43
Predefined process symbol, 27
Printer carriage control, 99, 102, 106-7
Problem analysis and definition, 22-25
Processing symbol, 27
PROGRAM, 31, 43
  object, 2
  source, 3
  statement sequence, 76; *see also inside cover*
Punched cards, 16-17

R

Range, DO, 181, 191-92
Rank, array, 250
READ, 43, 90
READ statement, 90, 151, 227, 229-30, 245
REAL, 43, 211
Real (F) format code, 86
REAL statement, 67, 211
Record, 19
RETURN, 43, 267, 277
RETURN statement, 267, 277

REWIND, 43
Rows
  array, 242
  card, 16

S

Scaling, 96
Sequence of statements, 76; *see also inside cover*
SIGN, 43, 312
SIN, 313
Skip (X) format code, 89
Slash
  in FORMAT statement, 102-7
  in letter O, 29
SNGL, 43, 313
Sorting, routine for, 224, 226
Source program order, 96; *see also inside cover*
Special characters, 18
Specification statements, 66-68, 70, 73, 209, 211-12
SQRT, 313
Statements, 26, 41
STOP, 35, 43, 118
STOP statement, 35, 118
Structured programming, 119-21
Subprograms
  FUNCTION, 275-80
  library functions, 261-66, 312-13
  one-statement, 273-75
  SUBROUTINE, 266-72
SUBROUTINE, 43, 266
SUBROUTINE statement, 266-67
Subscripted variable names, 208, 243, 250
Symbols, flow chart, 27
System control commands, 309-11

T

T format code, 90
TAN, 313
TANH, 313
Terminal symbol, 27
Terminating a program, 118, 268, 277
Testing and executing programs, 37
Three-dimensional arrays, 250-52
Truncation
  carriage control character, 98
  decimal fractions, 48, 65-66, 141
  integer division, 48, 65-66
  minus sign, 97
Turn-around, 15
Two-dimensional arrays, 242-50
Types of statements, 41-42

U-V

Unconditional GO TO statement, 122
Uncontrolled loops, 146
Variable names, 51, 208, 243, 250
  alphanumeric, 53
  array, 208, 243, 250
  composition of, 51-52

Variable names—*Cont.*
  floating point, 52
  implicit definition of mode, 52, 66
  integer, 52
  real, 52
  subprogram, 261, 266-67, 273, 275, 280, 312-13
  subscripted, 208, 243, 250

W-Z

WRITE, 43, 94
WRITE statement, 94, 229, 231, 246
X format code, 89
Zone punch, 18

This book has been set VIP in 10 and 9 point Times Roman, leaded 2 points. Chapter numbers are 56 point and chapter titles are 24 point Serif Gothic. The size of text area is 26 by 49 picas.

001.6424 F699s
Ford, Donald H.
Standard FORTRAN programming
143363

JOINT EDUCATIONAL CONSORTIUM

3 1864 00403 5061
OBU 001.6424 F699s
Ford, Donald H.
Standard FORTRAN programming :
R.D. Irwin, 1982.